PIERS PLOWMAN

The C-Text and Its Poet

BY

E. TALBOT DONALDSON

WITH A NEW PREFACE BY THE AUTHOR

ARCHON BOOKS
1966

[*Yale Studies in English, Volume 113*]

LIBRARY OF CONGRESS CATALOG CARD NUMBER: 66–20230
PRINTED IN THE UNITED STATES OF AMERICA

To

FRANCIS DONALDSON

PREFACE TO THE 1966 EDITION

IN the eighteen years that have passed since the original publication of this book, the direction of *Piers Plowman* studies has entirely altered, so that the question of authorship seems no longer to be of primary interest to scholars of Middle English literature—indeed, it may already have ceased to be so at the time of the book's publication, for the controversy I thought I might reawaken was never forthcoming. This is not to say that all or even the majority of scholars now believe in single authorship: the problem seems merely to have lost its importance as Middle English studies have turned away from the biographical and historical to the literary and textual. The poem in its three versions exists as a literary fact that is of the greatest interest to readers whether it is the work of one author or of many. Those who are still most acutely interested in the question of authorship are perhaps the editors of the B- and C-texts, for the oft-stated opinion (referred to below on page 232) that consideration of all problems presented by the poem must await the appearance of better texts than Skeat's has turned out to be the direct opposite of the truth: in trying to edit the B-text, Professor George Kane and I found that we were unable to proceed intelligently or honestly until we had come to a firm decision whether or not B and C were the work of the A-poet. It was this fact that induced Professor Kane to reexamine the bases upon which theories of authorship must depend, especially the historical and literary-historical evidence that was supposed to point to multiple authorship. The results of this reexamination, which strongly confirms the theory of single authorship to which we were, admittedly, predisposed, have recently been published in clear, concise, and powerfully logical form.[1]

If the purpose of my book on the C-text was primarily to consider a question that now seems to be of no general interest, one may well wonder why I sanction its reprinting. I do so because I believe that the examination of the process of poetic revision that my work entailed may still be of value to readers of *Piers Plowman.* I am happy that I did not confine myself exclusively to trying to "prove" that Langland wrote the C-text. Though I still think he did, I am more sceptical than ever whether any such proof is possible through literary analysis. Yet the analysis itself may help lead to a better understanding not only of the C-text but of the other texts as well; and I hope that my attempt to demonstrate that the C-reviser, whoever he was, was an intelligent poet, who understood the B-text as well as any one ever has done, is still relevant.

Apart from correcting several errors, I have made no changes in the main

1. *Piers Plowman: The Evidence for Authorship* (London, 1965).

body of the text. There are, to be sure, many things that I would now say differently—so many, indeed, that if I started to revise I should probably end up like the C-poet, writing an entirely new book that would say much the same as the earlier one said. I should warn the reader not to put much faith in my statistical sections, either those having to do with alliteration or those having to do with the nature of the successive revisions. If Professor Kane and I had completed our edition of the B-text, and if Professor George Russell had completed his of the C-text, then it would be possible to provide accurate statistics, but as it is, the only firmly established text in print is that of A in Professor Kane's edition.[2] Comparison of this with our provisional text of B shows that both the earlier versions of the poem were far more regular in their alliteration than Skeat's editions suggest, and that they have about the same proportion—a very small one—of irregular lines; it also shows that many of what seem in Skeat to be small revisions of A by B are in fact only scribal corruptions that had got into the B-archetype, so that my table in Appendix C much exaggerates, as I feared it might, the amount of petty revision made by B. As far as C is concerned, comparison of our B-text with Professor Russell's provisional C-text shows that, while the venerable statement that C often revised to improve the alliteration or to correct the sense of lines in his copy of B is not without validity, the paradoxical fact that C also wrote a great many new irregularly alliterating lines and often failed to correct lines that were patently corrupt in his copy of B is even more striking than appears from my remarks on pages 39–40. If this is evidence that he was not the same man as B, it is also evidence that directly contradicts the theory of Manly and other proponents of multiple authorship that C was a pedantically careful technician whose chief motive in revising was to correct the text of a poem he admired but could not have written.

I am least happy about Appendix B, insofar as it actually is what it purports to be, an attempt to establish the "authenticity" of the C-text. If by authenticity one means the existence of the C-version of the poem as an historical fact, then it is unnecessary to do more than point out that the many MSS representing with more or less fidelity a common archetype distinct from A and B prove that C did indeed exist. If, on the other hand, by authenticity one means the fidelity with which the common archetype of C reproduces the author's original, then one will have to examine all the MSS and throughout the whole poem, not just two passus, and one will have to have at one's command far more sophisticated techniques than I possessed when I wrote the appendix. Specifically, of the carefully numbered "assertions" on page 235, only (1) and (3) are valid. As for (2), it is not correct to say that exact agreement of readings between the archetypal texts

---

2. *Piers Plowman: The A Version* (London, 1960). The far less exhaustively edited text of Thomas A. Knott and David C. Fowler, *Piers the Plowman: A Critical Edition of the A-Version* (Baltimore, 1952), in general agrees with Kane's readings.

of B and C in the last two passus of the poem insures that the readings are original; for if, despite what I say in (a), these passus were not revised by C, then the B- and C-MSS ultimately represent the same, possibly corrupt MS tradition, not different ones capable of supporting each other. This fact, in turn, renders assertions (b) and (c) irrelevant, though as a matter of fact, as well as being irrelevant they are incorrect. Cross-contamination between two different MS traditions may not be ruled out simply because it is invisible—indeed, contamination becomes least visible when it is most pervasive. As for accidental—or better coincidental—agreement of separate traditions in unoriginal variation, far from being rare, this is very common indeed. Finally, both (4) and (5) represent statements of hope, not reason, for no text or MS may be assumed to be correct in any reading which is not demonstrably correct, and the fact that a text or MS is demonstrably correct in a great many readings has no bearing on other readings where its correctness cannot be demonstrated. Yes despite my rueful awareness that my main purpose and most of my specific assumptions were mistaken, I have let the appendix stand because by far the larger part of it is concerned with the pragmatic business of determining original readings in a large number of lines where B and C vary from one another, and I am relieved to observe that my adherence to assertion (3) kept me on the right path. In all but a few of the lines I discuss subsequent investigation has confirmed my choice of the original reading. Therefore I offer the appendix not as an attempt to prove the authenticity of the C-text, but in order to demonstrate how the editorial process operates—an accidental effect that now seems far more valuable than the one I had originally intended.

Over the years, I have found that the part of my book I have consulted most often was Appendix A, the listing of the MSS of *Piers Plowman,* and the wear-and-tear apparent in pages 227ff. of copies belonging to libraries and other scholars suggests that this appendix is the one unequivocally useful portion of the book. Therefore I have entirely revised the list in order to bring it up to date.

E. TALBOT DONALDSON

Beaconsfield
April, 1966

PREFACE

THE C-text of *Piers Plowman* has, in recent years, been generally neglected by students of the poem. On the whole, the reasons for this neglect have been good: the difficulties inherent in A and B, the earlier and, as most persons agree, the better versions, are so great that it has seemed only sensible to simplify the problem of the *Piers Plowman* group by ignoring its least attractive—and in some ways most suspect—member. But a complex problem can never be adequately solved in simple or partial terms and neglect of the C-text could not, without grave distortion of the general problem, be indefinitely continued. The valuable work that has been performed on the A- and B-versions by a number of scholars—led by the late R. W. Chambers—has now so far advanced the problem that the complicating factor of the C-text must now be brought into consideration. Just as the editors of the projected critical text of *Piers Plowman* discovered that textually the three versions could not be treated separately, so, I suggest, scholars will find the event to be with matters other than textual. It is for this reason that the present study was undertaken.

The purpose of these chapters is chiefly to demonstrate the probability that the author of C was the same as the author of B, and much of the book is devoted to adducing evidence in support of this probability. I recognize, however, that despite my conviction of unity of authorship it remains only a probability, and that the problem of authorship is itself only part of the larger problem of what *Piers Plowman,* taken as a single poem with three manifestations, is all about. Hence I have not hesitated to discuss matters that concern only indirectly the question of authorship, so long as these seem likely to contribute something to our general knowledge and understanding of *Piers Plowman.* In doing this, I have become persuaded of the correctness of the principle that the C-poet, whoever he was, thoroughly understood and, despite minor differences of opinion, heartily sympathized with the poem in its B-form, and that the C-text, as Skeat long ago said, is "the best possible commentary" upon B. This means that while C may be an additional complicating factor in the problem of *Piers Plowman,* it may also contain invaluable aids to its solution. Continued neglect of C tends, therefore, not only to distort the problem but actually to postpone our arriving at any solution to it. I hope that this study will succeed, if in nothing else, in reinstating the C-text to its important position in *Piers Plowman* studies.

I had originally intended to make a detailed comparison of the whole of B with the whole of C, but I soon came to realize that the result would be unprintable, or, if printed, unreadable. I therefore limited my study to a half-dozen aspects of the problem, selecting those which have figured most largely in previous discussions, in addition to several which seemed to offer fruitful rewards to research. The study originally took the form of a dissertation submitted to the Faculty of the Yale Graduate School in 1943 in candidacy for the degree of Doctor of Philosophy. Of the present book, the first three chapters, some of the fifth, and the second appendix formed a part of the dissertation. The revision of old material and the addition of new was performed during the academic year 1946–47, when I held the position of research instructor of English at Yale. Since September of 1947, when the manuscript reached its present form, there have appeared a number of studies of *Piers Plowman,* some of which are of the greatest interest. I should like to have referred to these, but considerations of time made further revision impossible.

My thanks are due to Mrs. John Archer Gee for her assistance in typing the manuscript; to my wife for countless useful suggestions throughout the composition of the book, for help in reading proof, and, above all, for her constant cheerfulness while living at close quarters with *Piers Plowman* for so extended a period; to Professor Frederick A. Pottle for reading the manuscript and for saving me from several serious errors; to Professor Benjamin C. Nangle, editor of Yale Studies in English, for his advice and for his patience in handling the technical problems involved in getting the book into publication; to the members of the appropriate committees of the American Council of Learned Societies and of Yale Studies in English for granting subventions in aid of publication; and to my father, whose generosity, combined with that of scholarly organizations just named, made publication possible. But my largest debt is to Professor Robert J. Menner, in whose course in Middle English Literature this study originated. To have had, at every step along the road, the benefit of his inexhaustible enthusiasm and great wisdom is surely one of the richest experiences, both in pleasure and in profit, that a scholar could have. To him is chiefly owing whatever is substantial in the following pages.

E. Talbot Donaldson

Saybrook College
June, 1948

CONTENTS

LIST OF CUE TITLES AND ABBREVIATIONS

Editions

William Langland. *The Vision of William concerning Piers (the) Plowman, together with Vita de Dowel, Dobet, et Dobest, secundum Wit et Resoun*. W. W. Skeat, ed. EETS, 28, 38, 54, 67, 81. London, 1867–84. 4 vols., 5 parts.

EETS, I	I (1867) : *The "Vernon" Text, or Text A.*
EETS, II	II (1869) : *The "Crowley" Text, or Text B.*
EETS, III	III (1873) : *The "Whitaker" Text, or Text C.*
EETS, IV	IV (1877–84) : *General Preface, Notes, and Indexes.*
CP, I, II	William Langland. *The Vision of William concerning Piers the Plowman in Three Parallel Texts, together with Richard the Redeless*. W. W. Skeat, ed. Oxford, 1886. 2 vols.

Secondary Sources

Ackermann	Konrad Burdach. *Der Dichter des Ackermann aus Böhmen und seine Zeit*. Berlin, 1926–32.
CHEL, II	J. M. Manly. " 'Piers the Plowman' and Its Sequence," *The Cambridge History of English Literature*, II. New York and Cambridge, England, 1908, pp. 1–48.
DNB	*Dictionary of National Biography*. London, 1885–1901.
DuCange	C. D. DuCange. *Glossarium Mediae et Infimae Latinitatis*. L. Favre, ed. Niort, 1883–87.
EETS	Early English Text Society. Arabic numerals indicate old series, roman numerals indicate extra series.
Mind	R. W. Chambers. *Man's Unconquerable Mind*. London, 1939.
Migne	J.-P. Migne. *Patrologiae Cursus Completus. . . . Series Latina*. Paris, 1844–65.
Mysticism	J. J. Jusserand. *Piers Plowman: a Contribution to the History of English Mysticism*. M. E. R., tr. Revised and enlarged by the author. London, 1894.
OED	*A New English Dictionary on Historical Principles*. Oxford, 1888–1933.

Periodicals

Anglia	*Anglia: Zeitschrift für englische Philologie*
HLB	*The Huntington Library Bulletin*
JEGPh	*The Journal of English and Germanic Philology*
JGPh	*The Journal of Germanic Philology*
LMS	*London Mediaeval Studies*
MedAev	*Medium Aevum*
MLN	*Modern Language Notes*
MLQ	*Modern Language Quarterly*
MLR	*The Modern Language Review*
MPh	*Modern Philology*
PMLA	*Publications of the Modern Language Association of America*
RES	*The Review of English Studies*
Scrutiny	*Scrutiny: A Quarterly Review*
Speculum	*Speculum: a Journal of Mediaeval Studies*
StPh	*Studies in Philology*
ZVgL	*Zeitschrift für vergleichende Litteraturgeschichte*

NOTE TO THE READER

All quotations from *Piers Plowman* are from Skeat's EETS edition. Skeat's brackets and his italics indicating expansions have not been reproduced. Brackets appearing in quotations in this book surround readings differing from those of Skeat. Such readings are explained in the notes.

For a full list of authorities cited consult the Index, which is limited to bibliographical matter.

PIERS PLOWMAN

I

The C-Text and Its Critics: Authorship and Literary Value

SOME years ago the late Samuel Moore attempted to show that the earlier tradition concerning *Piers Plowman* supported the theory of multiple authorship, and that the burden of the proof therefore rests upon those who believe that all three versions of the poem were written by one man.[1] Moore did not, I think, succeed in his aim,[2] but he did succeed incidentally in demonstrating that tradition exerts a powerful influence upon those who study the poem. Furthermore, although despite Moore's arguments the dominant tradition before the appearance of Skeat's great editions[3] seems to have favored unity of authorship, the elaborate theory put forth by Manly at the beginning of this century,[4] and the authoritative publication in which it was first fully presented, have succeeded in establishing another, perhaps even stronger, tradition for multiple authorship. This has occurred rather paradoxically in spite of the fact that the weight of the evidence adduced since Manly's time has been largely on the opposite side. Tradition is a notorious laggard, and in this instance it has been lent inertia by the fact that for every reader who follows the arguments on authorship as they appear there are ten or twenty who begin and end with the *Cambridge History of English Literature*. For this reason those who argue for single author ship—and they seem, willy-nilly, to have accepted the burden of the proof since Manly's time—are at something of a disadvantage. R. W. Cham-

1. "Studies in *Piers the Plowman*. 1. The Burden of Proof: Antecedent Probability and Tradition," *MPh*, XI (1913–14), 177–93. Moore actually left it to the reader to place the burden of the proof, but carefully arrayed his evidence to favor the multiple-authorship theory.
2. See p. 6, n. 4, below.
3. William Langland, *The Vision of William concerning Piers (the) Plowman, together with Vita de Dowel, Dobet, et Dobest, secundum Wit et Resoun*, W. W. Skeat, ed., EETS, 28, 38, 54, 67, 81 (London, 1867–84, 5 parts, 4 vols.) : I (1867), the "Vernon" Text, or Text A; II (1869), the "Crowley" Text, or Text B; III (1873), the "Whitaker" Text, or Text C; IV (1877–84), General Preface, Notes, and Indexes. Later Skeat edited the poem for the Clarendon Press, with the three texts printed in parallel form: *The Vision of William concerning Piers the Plowman in Three Parallel Texts, together with Richard the Redeless* (Oxford, 1886, 2 vols.). The notes to the later edition are sometimes important as containing Skeat's second thoughts. All quotations from the poem in this book are from the EETS volumes.
4. J. M. Manly, " 'Piers the Plowman' and Its Sequence," in *The Cambridge History of English Literature* (New York and Cambridge, England, 1907–33, 15 vols.), II (1908), 1–48. Manly's opening gun was his brief note, "The Lost Leaf of 'Piers the Plowman,' " *MPh*, III (1905–6), 359–66.

bers once remarked that it had been insufficiently realized that the multiple-authorship argument "begins by taking for granted the very thesis which it claims to prove."[5] Conversely, the defense of the single-authorship theory often proceeds as if the thesis it wants to disprove were the commonly accepted one, and those of us who believe in a single author tend to modify and weaken our own *modus operandi* in order to conform to rules arbitrarily laid down by the opposition. Thus in the course of writing these chapters I have more than once found myself hesitating to explain some passage in B by means of its elaboration in C merely because to do so would violate the assumption, to which I in no way adhere, that C was capable of misunderstanding B.

Because of the importance of tradition, regardless of the side upon which it rests its weight, and because of the complexity of the tradition concerning *Piers Plowman,* I have thought it necessary in this chapter to review briefly the treatment given the C-text by scholars and critics, particularly in the period that has passed since Manly first presented his thesis.[6] In my title I have yoked the subject of authorship with that of literary value. A priori there is no reason for such an association, but in historical fact the two subjects have been frequently treated as one, since the reason most often advanced for believing in multiple authorship is the supposed inferiority of one version to another. For example, a catalogue of Manly's four poets, A1, A2, B, and C, reads virtually in descending order of excellence,[7] and it was necessary for Chambers and others to clear A2 and B of the charge of acute and all-pervading incoherence before they could establish (as, despite the persistence of the Manlian tradition to the contrary, I believe they have) that A1, A2, and B were all written by the same author.[8] The undoubted, if exaggerated, inferiority of C to B remains as a great stumbling block to acceptance of the theory that C was B. Moreover, as we shall see in this review, this inferiority, which starts out by being relative, tends to become with certain critics an absolute, so that the C-text becomes not only not so good as B but actually a poor thing in its own right. It is with this sort of judgment of the C-text's literary value that the student of C is faced. And it is apt to be this sort of judgment, unless it can be shown to be

5. *Man's Unconquerable Mind* (London, 1939), p. 171.

6. A full review of *Piers Plowman* scholarship has been made by Moore, *MPh,* xi, 177–93, and by M. W. Bloomfield, "Present State of *Piers Plowman* Studies," *Speculum,* xiv (1939), 215–32.

7. Cf. Manly's successive characterizations of A1, A2, B, and C in *CHEL,* ii, 5, 19–20, 26–7, 34–6.

8. See particularly the articles by Chambers, "Long Will, Dante, and the Righteous Heathen," *Essays and Studies by Members of the English Association,* ix (Oxford, 1924), 50–69; "Incoherencies in the A- and B-Texts of *Piers Plowman* and Their Bearing on the Authorship," *LMS,* i (1937), 27–39; and "*Piers Plowman:* a Comparative Study," *Mind,* pp. 88–171.

wrong, that will, in the end, prevent acceptance of any theory identifying C with B.

We have no way of knowing which of the three texts of *Piers Plowman* was the most popular with the poet's contemporaries. Of the fifty-one MSS of the poem still in existence,[9] seventeen contain the A-version complete or very nearly complete; fifteen contain the B-version, or a large part of it;[1] and nineteen contain the C-version. There are, however, six MSS of the A-text which, at its conclusion, continue with C down to the end; and three predominantly B-MSS begin with two and a half passus of C.[2] If MSS were preserved in exact proportion to their popularity we might say that C was, by a small margin, the most popular of the versions, but inasmuch as survival does not operate with such precision, it is probably safe to say only that C was no less popular with the poet's contemporaries and their immediate descendants than A and B.

In 1550 Robert Crowley made the first printing of *Piers Plowman*[3] and by choosing a B-MS rather than the C-MS he had also consulted[4] he insured the popularity of the B-version for the succeeding two and a half centuries. Whether his choice was motivated by literary considerations, or whether his B-MS was merely easier to work with than his C-MS, is not known. But in publishing the poem at all Crowley showed good business judgment. The ecclesiastical satire, which is the first thing —and, unhappily, sometimes the last thing—that any one notices about *Piers Plowman,* made it popular reading in an England still in the throes of the Reformation. Crowley was able to print two more editions the same year and eleven years later Owen Rogers ventured a reprint.[5] As a result, the form of *Piers Plowman* that was known to Drayton, Spenser, Milton, Dryden, and others[6] down through the time of Thomas

9. See Appendix A for a list of MSS. In arriving at the total of fifty-one I have excluded the following: A-MS Pembroke College, Cambridge; B-MSS Crl-2-3, Hm2, Caius College, Cambridge, 201, and Bodleian, James 2; C-MS Caius College, Cambridge, 669. Cr denotes the lost MSS from which Crowley printed, and the others are but fragments

1. For purposes of textual analysis Crowley's edition of 1550 is considered as a sixteenth B-MS and is so listed in Appendix A.

2. See Appendix A for information on these.

3. *The Vision of Pierce Plowman, now fyrste imprynted by Roberte Crowley, dwellyng in Ely rentes in Holburne. Anno Domini. 1505* [for 1550]. See *EETS,* II, xxxi and n. There is some variation in title pages that was not known to Skeat.

4. See *EETS,* II, xxxiii–xxxiv, and xxxiv, n. 4. Evidence exists that Crowley also consulted an A-MS. *Idem,* p. xxxv, n. 2.

5. For Crowley's later printings and for Owen Rogers' edition, see *EETS,* II, xxxiv–xxxvi.

6. See *EETS,* IV, 863–71; also Kitty Marx, *Das Nachleben von Piers Plowman* (Quakenbrück, 1931). Actually, it is difficult to tell from references by later authors which text of *Piers Plowman* they were familiar with, but after 1550 the presumption is in favor of the printed editions. It is possible that Milton's "Engins and thir Balls of missive ruin," *Paradise Lost,* VI, 518–19, may have derived from the *gonnes* of C, XXI,

Warton[7] was that of the B-text. MSS of A and C reposed, apparently unread, in the libraries of England.

Recognition of the existence of the two unprinted versions came only gradually. In 1775 Tyrwhitt, in a note to his edition of the *Canterbury Tales*,[8] mentioned that the MSS of *Piers Plowman* he had consulted differed widely from the version printed by Crowley. He could not, he said, "help observing, that these Visions have been printed from so faulty and imperfect a Ms. that the Author, whoever he was, would find it difficult to recognize his own work."[9] Apparently Tyrwhitt had seen a C-MS, but he did not realize that he had to deal with another version, as distinct from another MS, of the poem, and his preference for the MS-form he had seen did not involve a literary judgment, but a textual one, resulting probably from the fact that when B and C are compared C seems the fuller version.[1] The distinction between MSS and versions was first made by Joseph Ritson, who, in his bibliography of English literature published in 1802, printed the first eleven lines of the poem as they appeared in Crowley and as they appeared in one of the several C-MSS Ritson had consulted. He went on to observe that the "subsequent variations, throughout the poem, are stil more considerable; so that it appears highly probable that the author had revised his original work, and given, as it were, a new edition."[2] With surprising modesty Ritson refused to commit himself on the chronology of the two versions he had discovered, nor did he express any preference between them, merely noting that none of the C-MSS he had seen was superior to that from which Crowley had printed "either for accuracy or antiquity."[3]

293, although, as Skeat points out, *EETS*, iv, 869, Milton's mention of the poem in *Smectymnuus* suggests by its wording that he was familiar with Rogers' edition of the B-text.

7. Thomas Warton, *The History of English Poetry* (London, 1775–81, 3 vols.), i (2d ed.), 266–86, reproduced several long passages from Crowley's edition, but did not make use of any of the MSS to which he had access. Among these was a MS of the C-class, Bodleian, Digby 102. See Warton, *Observations on the Fairy Queen of Spenser* (2d ed., London, 1762, 2 vols.), ii, 216.

8. *The Canterbury Tales of Chaucer* [Thomas Tyrwhitt, ed.] (London, T. Payne, 1775–78, 5 vols.).

9. *Idem*, iv, 74, n. 57.

1. I do not know for certain that Tyrwhitt's MS was of the C-class, but if it had been an A-MS he could scarcely have judged Crowley's version to show more imperfections. Tyrwhitt may, however, have seen a mixed A-C MS such as T: see Appendix A.

2. [Joseph Ritson,] *Bibliographia Poetica: a Catalogue of Engleish Poets, of the Twelfth, Thirteenth, Fourteenth, Fifteenth, and Sixteenth, Centurys, with a Short Account of Their Works* (London, 1802), p. 30, n.

3. *Ibid.* There is evidence for supposing that Ritson had at one time distinguished three forms of the poem. In a MS notebook of his in the British Museum (Addl. 10285), thought to have been composed between 1780 and 1800, is the following statement about the poem: "The differences as well between the printed copies on the one hand and most if not all the MSS. on the other, as between the MSS. themselves is very remarkable. Of the latter indeed there appears to be two sets, of which the one has scarcely 5 lines

The C-text was first printed in 1813, from the beautiful MS belonging to Heber, by the amateur antiquary Thomas Whitaker.[4] Like Ritson, Whitaker clearly distinguished between two distinct versions of the poem and like Ritson he considered them the work of one poet, observing that they both "bear marks, not of the same spirit and genius only, but of the same peculiar and original manner, so that it is scarcely to be conceived that they are interpolations of successive transcribers."[5] Whitaker went a step farther than Ritson by claiming his own as the earlier version, bearing "every mark of being the first but vigorous effort of a young poet."[6] Though he is clear upon this point, Whitaker is far from making clear his idea, if he had any, of the exact relation between his own and Crowley's text, which he condemns as having been printed "from a MS. of late date and little authority."[7] It is difficult to tell whether Whitaker preferred the C-text because of literary merit, or because he thought his single C-MS was more reliable than anything Crowley had access to, but from the general tenor of his remarks, as well as from the fact of his edition, we are, I suppose, to understand that he had a genuine appreciation of C as a work of literature. If so, he is the first of C's champions.

It was Richard Price who, while preparing an edition of Warton's *History* in 1824,[8] first became aware of the existence of the A-version of *Piers Plowman*. Having made this discovery, Price was in a position to take issue with Whitaker's notion of the chronology of B and C, something that he did with extreme circumspection, merely warning that Whitaker's thesis on the priority of C was "not to be admitted without considerable hesitation."[9] He agreed with Whitaker, however, on the impossibility of attributing to scribal interference the various versions of *Piers Plowman* and, presumably, on the unity of authorship of the versions.[1] Price made no judgment on the relative literary worth of the three texts, though he defended the textual excellence of Crowley's printing against the disparagements of Whitaker and Tyrwhitt.

---

togr. in common with the other." See Bertrand H. Bronson, *Joseph Ritson: Scholar-at-Arms* (Berkeley, 1938, 2 vols.), I, 325–6.

4. Robert Langland, *Visio Willi de Petro Plouhman, Item Visiones ejusdem de Dowel, Dobet, et Dobest*, T. D. Whitaker, ed. (London, 1813).

5. *Idem*, p. xxxiii.

6. *Idem*, p. xxxi. It is remarkable how closely this comment resembles later characterizations of the A-text. Cf. J. J. Jusserand, "*Piers Plowman*: the Work of One or of Five," *MPh*, VI (1908–9), 309, who says that A appears to have been written "with all the vigor and vivacity of younger manhood."

7. Whitaker, *op. cit.*, p. xix.

8. Thomas Warton, *The History of English Poetry* [Richard Price, ed.] (London, 1824, 4 vols.).

9. *Idem*, II, 482.

1. "That one man was the author of the three versions is implicit in his [Price's] discussion of them, though he does not categorically say so." Elsie Blackman, "Notes on the B-Text MSS. of *Piers Plowman*," *JEGPh*, XVII (1918), 489.

With Thomas Wright's editions of the B-text in 1842 and 1856,[2] *Piers Plowman* criticism became considerably less tenuous and took on, indeed, a more modern tone. Wright had early become interested in the poem, subjecting Whitaker's edition to a thorough, and on the whole unfavorable, examination as early as 1824.[3] Although Wright did not commit himself on the A-version, about the status if not the existence of which he was remarkably vague,[4] on the subject of the two later versions he was specific in every respect, and first phrased the statement of their dual authorship in words that have since then been echoed on numerous occasions. Wright, unlike Whitaker, recognized B as the earlier of the two versions and considered that the C-text was inferior to it. "In general the first text [B] is the best, whether we look at the mode in which the sentiments are stated, or at the poetry and language."[5] Furthermore, he felt that the variations between the two were such that they precluded the possibility of one author's having revised his own work:

It would not be easy to account for the existence of two texts differing so much; but it is my impression that the first [B] was the one published by the author, and that the variations were made by some other person, who was perhaps induced by his own political sentiments to modify passages, and was gradually led on to publish a revision of the whole. It is certain that in some parts of Text II. [C] the strong sentiments or expressions of the first text are softened down.[6]

Thus Wright laid the groundwork for future attacks upon the authorship of C, at the same time pointing out how those attacks might be made through C's political "caution," if not through C's general inferiority to B. In passing one might, however, observe that Wright's attack itself consists in very little more than the mild sentences quoted

2. *The Vision and the Creed of Piers Ploughman,* Thomas Wright, ed. (London, 1842, 2 vols.); *The Vision and Creed of Piers Ploughman* (2d revised ed., London, 1856, 2 vols.). It is to the second edition that I refer.

3. "The Visions of Piers Plowman," *The Gentleman's Magazine* (April 1834), pp. 385–91. The article is unsigned, but see *EETS,* iv, 872.

4. It is curious that Wright, who had long acquaintance with MS T of the A-class, quoting it frequently in his notes, and who was also acquainted with Price's edition of Warton's *History,* which he also quotes, never seems to have realized that there was an A-text and that it was a distinct form of the poem. Doubtless his failure was in part caused by the fact that T is a mixed MS, continuing with the C-text at the conclusion of A, xi. In any case, his failure seems to me to impair the value of any judgments of his either on the authorship or on the chronology—the last of which he conceived correctly. In his survey of the tradition Moore, *MPh,* xi, 185–7, accords Wright's opinions the fullest authority, at the same time condemning Whitaker's as worthless, at least partly because Whitaker was unaware of the existence of the A-text. Strictures applied to one must, however, be applied to the other. Moore's presentation has some of the earmarks of a Balkan election, where the polls are controlled by the party in power. Since the tradition for multiple authorship before Skeat begins and ends with Wright, Moore's inference that the tradition favored multiple authorship hardly seems fair.

5. Wright, *op. cit.,* i, xxxv.   6. *Idem,* i, xxxiv.

and that he cited only one instance of C's political caution;[7] and he never, indeed, bothered to point out any considerable number of passages which would demonstrate B's superiority to C.[8]

With Skeat's edition of *Piers Plowman* the poem was made available in all three of its forms. It is now sixty-three years since the last of his five volumes was published, and eighty since the first,[9] and though textually his edition leaves much to be desired in the light of work that has been done and MSS that have been discovered since his time, on the whole it stands up remarkably well today. It was Skeat who first settled the chronology of the texts—so satisfactorily, indeed, that his arrangement has been called into question but once since.[1] It was he who formulated the theory of single authorship for all three versions. And his judgments on their literary value still seem as sane as any that have been made. Concerning the text with which we are dealing, Skeat spoke as follows: "The C-text is inferior to the B-text in general vigour and compactness. On the other hand, it is the fullest of the three texts, and the most carefully finished. It contains the author's last corrections after a most careful revision, and is evidently intended as a final form, requiring no further touches."[2] Though it may be necessary to take issue with some of the details of this statement, its purport seems wholly satisfactory.

That the C-text might be the work of a different author from B Skeat never, apparently, seriously considered.[3] Nor did he comment directly upon Wright's suggestion, contenting himself with a rather oblique re-

7. See B, Pro., 112–22, C, I, 139–46. I discuss C's politics at length in Chapter IV. In his earlier article Wright had expressed the belief that "there would be no difficulty in showing that there are many passages in the text thus chosen [by Whitaker], which it is improbable ever came from the author of Piers Plowman." *The Gentleman's Magazine* (April 1834), p. 386. But the lack of difficulty appears to have been a will-o'-the-wisp, for Wright never really attempted proof of his assertion.

8. In his article Wright had, by printing a few selections from his own MS beside the parallel passages of Whitaker's text, thought to show "the great superiority" of the B-text. See *The Gentleman's Magazine* (April 1834), p. 391. The passages include, besides the one cited in the note above, only B, Pro., 1–37, C, I, 1–38, and B, Pro., 46–55, C, I, 47–53. They are incorporated into the notes of Wright's edition, in which, however, appears little additional critical comment on C.

9. The A-text was published in 1867; the final volume of the notes in 1884.

1. By Gertrud Görnemann, *Zur Verfasserschaft und Entstehungsgeschichte von "Piers the Plowman"* (Heidelberg, 1916). Miss Görnemann's thesis, that all three versions of the poem are but scribal recastings of one original MS, is interesting but untenable. Her individual arguments have been answered by Fritz Krog, *Studien zu Chaucer und Langland* (Heidelberg, 1928).

2. *EETS*, III, lxviii.

3. I have found only two places in which Skeat directly considers the possibility of divided authorship. One is in connection with C's long insertion in Passus IV, the distinction between *mede* and *mercede*, which Skeat believed unquestionably genuine, though he mentioned the alternative. The other is C's passage on false priests, which Skeat thought bore some marks of being the work of some one other than the poet. See *EETS*, III, lxxxvi and 450.

ply. In describing a group of the poet's insertions in C, Skeat notes:

It is quite clear on what principle the poet made them; and, if they be carefully examined, they will be found to be *so skilfully adjusted as quite to exclude the supposition that any one but himself could have done it*. This is a very important matter, as it assures us that the double revision of the poem is *all his own work;* and, although this might have been inferred from the style and character of the writing, it is most satisfactory to have the proof of it brought home to us in a way that cannot well be mistaken. It is also the more necessary, because there certainly are indications that the poet inclined, at the last, to the softening down and modification of some of his sentiments. Mr Wright has drawn attention to this in one instance, where he prints two short passages side by side, and draws the inference that "in this instance the doctrine is stated far more distinctly and far more boldly in the first text than in the second." . . . That is to say, the poet grew more conservative in his ideas and more careful in his expressions as he grew older; a result so common and natural that it is not to be wondered at, but may be accepted as the fact.[4]

This is virtually the sum of Skeat's recorded opinions on the authorship of the C-text. Whether it is to be considered an adequate answer to Wright's suggestion of multiple authorship will depend on the bias and temperament of the reader.[5] It is to be observed that Skeat goes part of the way with Wright in conceding C's political caution. Other passages that Skeat believed to illustrate this, as well as passages that seemed to him to betray C's increasing age, are discussed in his notes. Yet on the whole Skeat regarded the C-text with great respect, pointing out a number of minor improvements, as well as one passage that proved that C had not "in any way lost his vigour of expression when he chose to exert it."[6] "If we prefer the B-text as a whole," Skeat concludes, "we must never forget that the C-text is the best possible commentary upon it, and is often, indeed, much more, as it contains some additional passages which it would be a pity to have lost."[7]

As this last quotation indicates, Skeat considered B the best form of the poem and the B-text became the conventional text for study. In 1908 Manly remarked that "the C-text, on account of the larger mass of material in it, has received the almost exclusive attention of

4. *EETS,* III, lxxix. Skeat avoids direct mention of Wright's theory of authorship. The passage is that mentioned on p. 7, n. 7, above. See Wright, *op. cit.,* I, xxxv.

5. Moore, *MPh,* XI, 190–3, criticizes Skeat for failing to reply directly to Wright's argument on divided authorship. But it is possible that Skeat, like Moore, believed that the problem of authorship could be solved only in the light of all three texts, not just two of them, and that Wright's failure to recognize the individuality of A invalidated his comments. Skeat had the highest admiration for Wright (see *EETS,* II, xxxvi, n. 2) and perhaps did not wish to emphasize the older scholar's failure to recognize what Price had already made clear. See *EETS,* I, xiii; IV, ix.

6. *EETS,* III, lxxix. The passage is C, x, 71–161. Two other passages cited in defense of the aging poet are from *Richard the Redeless.*

7. *EETS,* III, lxviii.

scholars,"[8] but this scarcely seems to have been the case, as a survey of histories of literature published before 1908 will show.[9] Indeed, the complaint might quite legitimately be reversed, "B-text" being substituted for Manly's "C-text." Until the appearance of Skeat's edition of C in 1873 one could only have read the last version of the poem in Whitaker's expensive and inaccurate printing. In 1869 Skeat had already published his shortened B-text for the Clarendon Press—the often-reprinted student's edition[1] in which probably nine out of ten persons have read such portions of *Piers Plowman* as they have read. The tradition which regarded B as the most satisfactory version of *Piers Plowman*, started by Crowley and continued by Wright, was perpetuated by Skeat.[2]

But the tradition in favor of B never became a tradition in disfavor of C until Manly launched his devastating criticism. The author of the latest version was also the least of the four poets believed by Manly to have done extensive work on the poem:

Of the changes and additions made by C we can here say very little, mainly for the reason that they are numerous, and small, and not in pursuance of any well-defined plan. There are multitudinous alterations of single words or phrases, sometimes to secure better alliteration, sometimes to get rid of an archaic word, sometimes to modify an opinion, but often for no discoverable reason, and, occasionally, resulting in positive injury to the style or the thought. Certain passages of greater or less length are entirely or largely rewritten, rarely for any important modification of view; never, perhaps, with any betterment of style. At times, one is tempted to think they were rewritten for the mere sake of rewriting, but many whole passages are left practically untouched. Transpositions occur, sometimes resulting in improvement, sometimes in confusion. Excisions or omissions may be noted which seem to have been made because C did not approve of the sentiments of the omitted passages; but there are other omissions which cannot be accounted for on this ground or on that of artistic intention. . . .[3]

On the whole, it may be said that the author of the C-text seems to have been a man of much learning, of true piety and of genuine interest in the welfare of the nation, but unimaginative, cautious, and a very pronounced pedant.[4]

This is indeed the damnation of faint praise.

Manly's characterization of C is of great importance to the student

---

8. *CHEL*, II, 4.

9. See, for example, W. J. Courthope, *A History of English Poetry* (London, 1895–1910, 6 vols.), I, 200–46 (B-text); Henry Morley, *English Writers* (2d ed., London, 1887–95, II vols.), IV, 285–354 (B-text with a few additions from C); Bernhard ten Brink, *Geschichte der englischen Litteratur*, A. Brandl, ed. (2d ed., Strassburg, 1899–1912, 2 vols.), I, 410–28 (B-text).

1. *The Vision of William concerning Piers the Plowman*, W. W. Skeat, ed. (Oxford, 1869). There had been ten impressions by 1932.

2. B's popularity was undoubtedly increased because Skeat thought that the MS of B which he was editing was the author's autograph. See *EETS*, II, ix, and *CP*, II, lxviii.

3. *CHEL*, II, 34–5.   4. *Idem*, p. 36.

of the C-text, so much truth does it mix with so much error. It is in Manly that the easy transition is made from "inferiority to B" to "inferiority" and this occurs despite the fact that Manly's remarks are largely impressionistic. He never tried to give them anything like adequate substantiation but was, seemingly, content to have catalogued all C's literary defects and none of his virtues. Such concrete illustrations of C's weakness as he did offer are of varying persuasiveness and sometimes seem, indeed, to have been drawn from an impoverished store.[5] Many of them have been ably opposed by Jusserand[6] and others. Nevertheless, the general tenor of Manly's description of the C-text has been permitted to stand for the most part unquestioned. The point he most emphasizes is the purposelessness of C's revisions and, by way of complement, the trivial quality of the mind that made them. Thus after reading Manly we are able to picture clearly to ourselves a petty, crotchety old man engaged in butchering some one else's work. In his accomplishment in regard to the C-poet, Manly seems to have derived something from Theophrastus: he succeeded in summarizing a personality so plausibly and so concisely that the reader tends to accept it as true solely on the basis of its verisimilitude. Manly's is the portrait of C that still hangs in the halls of literature, the portrait that whoever goes to the *Cambridge History* will see.

At the same time that Manly was preparing for the press his hypothesis of multiple authorship, T. D. Hall published an article in which he applied principles of criticism very like Manly's to the problem of C.[7] Hall's judgment took the now familiar form. He hoped to show that "not only is the C-text a debasement of the author's own work, but that the nature of many of the changes precludes the supposition of their being from the hand which penned either the original (A) or the enlarged (B) *Vision.*"[8] The C-poet, he finds, was "essentially a schoolman and a moralist, with little imaginative sensibility," but, unlike Manly, Hall does not find C altogether without virtues, even though these are insufficient to counteract his deficiencies. "The author of C has here and there a good thing of his own, but the value of his work as a whole is antiquarian rather than literary."[9] Hall thought that the uninhibited fashion in which C rearranged the B-text was an indication of multiple

5. A number of Manly's specific criticisms of C are discussed in this book. The originals will be found, not in Manly's chapter in the *Cambridge History*, but in his reply to Jusserand's reply to his chapter. See Manly, "The Authorship of *Piers Plowman*," *MPh,* VII (1909–10), 116-23, 130-1. 136. In the *Cambridge History* he gave but two examples of C's poor work, both "misapprehensions" of B by C, seen at C, I, 9–18 and 177–81. See *CHEL,* II, 38–9.

6. See J. J. Jusserand, *"Piers Plowman,* the Work of One or of Five: a Reply," *MPh,* VII (1909–10), 289–326, *passim.*

7. Theophilus D. Hall, "Was 'Langland' the Author of the C-Text of 'The Vision of Piers Plowman'?" *MLR,* IV (1908–9), 1–13.

8. *Idem,* p. 4.   9. *Idem,* p. 13.

authorship, for he did not believe "that the author could have dealt so destructively with his own workmanship—the fruit, be it remembered, not of his unripe youth, but of his mature age."[1] The value of Hall's criticism lies in his illustrations, which are fuller than those given by Manly. Hence his conclusions are both weightier and easier to deal with, since their bases are carefully explained. But because his bomb burst at nearly the same time as Manly's, and was therefore lost in the smoke of the larger explosion, Hall's article has never received the consideration it deserves. It lends Manly some of the support his own theory in regard to C lacks.[2]

In warfare it is good strategy to meet a heavy attack by yielding relatively unimportant ground in order to retain ground that is absolutely essential for the safety of one's position. Faced by an attack upon the whole traditional conception of the three versions of *Piers Plowman,* those who held to single authorship felt it well to yield something to their opponents. The C-text, which is not likely to attract fanatical devotees, offered itself as a handy sacrifice. Furthermore, the nature of the attack almost inevitably made C the logical front on which to give ground, for the success of the opposing party depended upon the inference that no author would spoil his own work. Since on the basis of historical fact this inference is exceedingly dubious, a good many examples were produced—the best of which was Wordsworth—to show that authors could and frequently did spoil their own work.[3] But this answer involves an important concession in that it assents to the assumption that the C-text *is* an example of spoiled work, so that the defenders of single authorship were either forced to wash their hands of C, as Chambers did,[4] or else to talk of it in disparaging terms dictated by the opposition. Thus one can read all of Jusserand's fascinating book on *Piers Plowman*—[5] published long before the controversy—without once being given the impression that he felt that the C-text was in any sense a debasement of B. Yet in the exigencies of the controversy Jusserand gives at least oblique sanction to Manly's characterization of C, remarking that it "amounts to saying, as everybody will agree, that C is the work of an older man than A and B. . . . Increasing piety, more care for politics, more cautiousness, less imagination, a greater show of learning . . . are so many characteristics of age."[6] To Manly's charge that C often revised "for no

---

1. *Idem,* p. 12.

2. I refrain from listing here Hall's specific criticisms, since most of them are discussed in later chapters.

3. See Jusserand, *MPh,* VI, 319–22; also R. W. Chambers and J. H. G. Grattan. "The Text of 'Piers Plowman,'" *MLR,* XXVI (1931), 42–3.

4. See pp. 15 ff., below.

5. Originally published as *L'Épopée mystique de William Langland* (Paris, 1893). The edition cited here is *Piers Plowman: a Contribution to the History of English Mysticism,* M. E. R., tr., revised and enlarged by the author (London, 1894).

6. *MPh,* VI, 317. For certain revisions Jusserand defended C vigorously, notably for

discoverable reason" and sometimes with "positive injury to the style or the thought," Jusserand replies, "Precisely; and this is what an author, in the evening of life, would do for his own work and what no one else would."[7] In a sense, this is like giving the affirmative answer to the loaded question about beating one's wife.

Among recent scholars, the unflattering reputation of C has been chiefly maintained by Miss Mabel Day, who, in several spirited attacks on the theory of unified authorship,[8] has made extensive use of the proposition—similar to Manly's and Hall's, though more drastically stated—that C's revisions are of such a sort as to preclude the possibility that he was B. Miss Day does, indeed, grant that C has a vividness of style "when he is writing on a theme about which he feels strongly."[9] But that he was often so writing she does not concede. On the whole she finds him an unusually dull-witted sort of person who, when he was not misunderstanding his original outright, was at least flattening it—almost maliciously, it would seem—by pointless paraphrase and the substitution of generalities for graphic details.[1]

Zwei Seelen wohnen, ach! in meiner Brust,

but if we are to agree with Miss Day, it was the pettifogger in C that maintained the ascendancy. The charge of misunderstanding his original is perhaps the ultimate degradation that has been visited upon the C-poet.[2]

Aside from Miss Day, recent scholars concerned directly with *Piers Plowman* have, on the whole, followed Chambers' example and steered clear of the C-text,[3] while concentrating their energies upon the problems

---

his changes in the Rat's speech at C, I, 177–9; his addition of C, I, 10; his omission of B, II, 176; and his omission of Piers's tearing of the pardon. See *MPh*, VI, 306, 315–17. Mention should be made here of the interesting work of Otto Mensendieck, who contributed to the controversy two articles adducing evidence for the theory of single authorship: "Die Verfasserschaft der drei Texte des Piers the Plowman," *ZVgL*, XVIII (1910), 10–31; and "The Authorship of Piers Plowman," *JEGPh*, IX (1910), 404–20. See also his book, *Charakterentwickelung und ethisch-theologischen Anschauungen des Verfassers von Piers the Plowman* (London, 1900). Mensendieck sensibly observed that there were many passages "wo C den Gedanken viel schärfer fasst und ausdrückt als A oder B"— a fact that the controversialists tended to overlook. See *ZVgL*, XVIII, 31.

7. *MPh*, VI, 318.

8. Mabel Day, "Alliteration of the Versions of 'Piers Plowman' in Its Bearing on Their Authorship," *MLR*, XVII (1922), 403–09; "Duns Scotus and 'Piers Plowman,'" *RES*, III (1927), 333–4; "The Revisions of 'Piers Plowman,'" *MLR*, XXIII (1928), 1–27; " 'Din' and 'Doom' in 'Piers Plowman,' A, II, 183," *MLR*, XXVI (1931), 336–8.

9. *MLR*, XXIII, 6.   1. *Ibid.*

2. I discuss a number of Miss Day's criticisms in the following pages. Despite the fact that Chambers and Grattan, *MLR*, XXVI, 1–51, have overthrown the main lines of Miss Day's argument as it affects A and B, her judgments on C have, for the most part, not been answered.

3. See p. 15, below.

of A and B.[4] C itself has been regarded with a sort of respectful diffidence. Thus F. A. R. Carnegy, in the introduction to a study of B, observes:

One might choose C as the basis of one's examination—as I confess, I did—as being the longest and completest of the three texts, but it soon becomes plain that such a course of action cannot fail to lead one hopelessly astray. Certain striking alterations which C has made in his B original convinced me of this.[5]

Similarly, Nevill Coghill remarks that "for the development of the character of Piers . . . the C Text offers some complications of rearrangement which might cloud the immediate issue"[6] and confines his study to B. There is, perhaps, somewhat more diffidence in these attitudes than respect. Wells, however, in his modern rendering of *Piers Plowman*,[7] introduces into what is basically a B-text a number of passages from C which either do not occur in B or which he feels are better expressed in C than in B, even though by so doing he produces an amorphous version of the poem. The reverse of the respectful attitude toward C is exemplified by Miss Greta Hort, who states flatly, "The C-text . . . is negligible; it changes and enlarges the earlier passus of the B-text, but the changes are not of such a kind as to indicate more than the work of an 'intelligent'—and meddlesome—scribe."[8] To this one can only oppose Konrad Burdach's comment on a similar sort of judgment expressed by Miss Gertrud Görnemann, "Whoever attributes such variations to scribes has extraordinary notions about the intellectual capacity and the freedom of action of medieval copyists."[9] In Miss Hort's statement we

4. See Bibliographical Index under Carnegy, R. W. Chambers, Coghill, Dunning, Hort, and H. W. Wells.

5. F. A. R. Carnegy, *The Relations between the Social and Divine Order in William Langland's "Vision of William concerning Piers the Plowman"* (Breslau, 1934), p. 2. Carnegy's textual study, *An Attempt to Approach the C-Text of Piers the Plowman* (London, 1934) is extremely useful.

6. Nevill Coghill, "The Character of Piers Plowman Considered from the B Text," *MedAev,* II (1933), 109.

7. Henry W. Wells, *The Vision of Piers Plowman, Newly Rendered into Modern English* (New York, 1935: republished 1945). Wells's two articles, "The Construction of *Piers Plowman,*" *PMLA,* XLIV (1929), 123–40, and "The Philosophy of Piers Plowman," *PMLA,* LIII (1938), 339–49, are of the greatest importance to an understanding of the poem, particularly in its B-form.

8. Greta Hort, *Piers Plowman and Contemporary Religious Thought* (London, no date), p. 3, n. 1. Miss Hort later (p. 22) remarks that the poet tells us that "his work was to sing the Psalms and say the Offices for the Dead." The Offices for the Dead (Placebo and Dirige) are not mentioned in connection with the author in B, but at C, VI, 46.

9. Burdach, *Der Dichter des Ackermann aus Böhmen und seine Zeit* (Berlin, 1926–32), p. 229, n. 1: "Wer . . . derlei Abweichungen auf das Walten des 'Schreibers' zurückführt, hat wunderliche Vorstellungen über die geistigen Fähigkeiten und die Bewegungsfreiheit mittelalterlicher Kopisten!"

have, I think, an example of the power of tradition, for it scarcely seems possible that a scholar of Miss Hort's acuteness and erudition could have given such a judgment after a study of the C-text.

It was Burdach himself, perhaps the most accomplished medievalist to turn his attention to the poem—though, unhappily, his work seems to have been largely ignored by others in the field—who began what one may hope will prove to be a new era in the history of the C-text. Burdach's study of *Piers Plowman* was only incidental to his study of *Der Acker-mann aus Böhmen*. Thus he embarked upon the subject possibly without the bias that one is apt to get from reading the literature of the controversy and with a freshness of appreciation that comes most readily from a frontal attack. He was careful to avoid becoming embroiled in the question of authorship. He did, however, consider the three versions of *Piers Plowman* a unity, in intention and in effect, if not in authorship[1] and, although he adopted B as the basis for his commentary, his many references to C display a considerable respect for that text. Fairly frequently he pauses over one of C's alterations to consider some new and important idea that he finds there and even, sometimes, to admire the artistic expression.[2] If one had confined one's reading of *Piers Plowman* to Burdach, as, I fear, a good many have confined their reading of the poem to the *Cambridge History,* one would come away with the impression that the C-text, while it might offer certain difficulties to twentieth-century powers of understanding, was nevertheless the work of a man of large intellectual and imaginative scope. One would certainly receive no suggestion of the dull and tepid soul that the literature of the controversy has sketched for us. In reading Burdach, one feels that C, the problem child, has grown into one of the most interesting, dignified, and even attractive members of the *Piers Plowman* family.

Appreciation for the C-text comes from another quarter. A critic of repute, D. A. Traversi, uses C as the basis of a short reconsideration of the poetic technique of *Piers Plowman* and finds the poet extremely effective in attaining his artistic ends.[3] That this text should figure alone—even in a noncomparative study—in a discussion of the art of poetry would probably come as something of a surprise to those steeped in the literature of the controversy. As a matter of fact, one of the passages Traversi uses as an illustration of the poet's artistry was given a good deal of prominence—all of it to C's disadvantage—in the controversy itself.[4] But Traversi is not concerned with the controversy, with the result that he has a freshness of approach in considering the esthetics of C that complements Burdach's treatment of the text as a vehicle of

---

1. *Idem,* p. 314.
2. See, for example, *idem,* pp. 225; 228; 229, n. 1; 240, n. 1; 266, n. 2; 310; 312, n. 3, etc.
3. "The Vision of Piers Plowman," *Scrutiny,* v (1936–37), 276–91. Traversi does not mention A or B.
4. *Idem,* pp. 282–3. The passage is C, I, 1–13, discussed at length in Chapter III, below.

medieval religious and social ideas. It is possible that in our reading of C we are sometimes infected with a jaundice of both esthetic and intellectual faculties.

I have hitherto refrained from discussing the opinions of R. W. Chambers because I wished to conclude this review with that scholar whom every one must continue to associate most closely with any topic relating to *Piers Plowman*. Chambers' fully deserved reputation as a scholar of the first rank, combined with the thirty years that he devoted largely to the poem, makes anything he had to say about it of the greatest importance to the student, and one can only proceed with trepidation when one is forced, as I am at times in the following pages, to take issue with any of his conclusions. I venture to do so because he himself was not primarily concerned with the C-text. Whether rightly or wrongly, he did not believe that the problem of C was germane to the problem of the essential unity of *Piers Plowman*.[5] From the beginning of his study of the poem until his death, his interest lay in demonstrating, as I think he succeeded in doing, the unity of A and B.[6] As a result of his concentration on the earlier texts there are, perhaps, some aspects of C that Chambers did not take into full account, and despite the fact that in his own work he cut C adrift, he would, I am sure, have welcomed any honest effort to show that C also has a share in the unity of *Piers Plowman*.

From the time of his first article on the poem[7] Chambers kept his mind open on the subject of the authorship of the C-text, even though he was willing to acknowledge, sometimes emphatically, the inferiority of C to B. As one who had respect for tradition, he was at pains to point out that this inferiority need not inevitably indicate independent authorship, since critics of Skeat's ability, as well as others less erudite, had "noticed some tendency towards a weakening in C,"[8] without therefore being impelled to suspect the work of an editor. Although he was not altogether persuaded that C was the same as B, when Miss Day attacked the unity of A and B largely through the medium of the C-text,[9] Chambers, while vindicating A and B, also defended with great effect the possibility of common authorship for C.[1] He was content, however, to regard Miss Day's conclusions regarding C as not proved, rather than positively wrong, and he spontaneously echoed one of the most damaging of the charges to be made against the C-text, "The amazing thing about C is the reckless way in which he paraphrases and alters the B-text, changing a fine line or passage into something altogether worse, not here or there,

5. See p. 17, below.
6. See the articles cited on p. 2, n. 8, above.
7. "The Text of 'Piers Plowman,'" *MLR,* IV (1908–9), 357–89, written in collaboration with J. H. G. Grattan.
8. "The Authorship of 'Piers Plowman,'" *MLR,* V (1910), 29.
9. In *MLR,* XXIII, 1–27.   1. In *MLR,* XXVI, 1–51.

but constantly."[2] Elsewhere he repeated the old accusation that some of the C-revisions "seem to be made simply for the sake of alteration."[3] But so far as the authorship is concerned, Chambers insisted that it is impossible to say "how far it is inconceivable for an author, in revision, to spoil his own work."[4]

In one of his last published studies of *Piers Plowman* Chambers proposed—with I do not know how much conviction—a compromise theory, scarcely capable of scientific proof, but still rather satisfying in human terms. The poet, a poor man, may have been asked for a copy of his poem and, since he had none to spare, he may have sat down himself to make one; and "as he wrote he made alterations, sometimes for the better, sometimes otherwise. He had probably no idea of superseding his earlier work; he was just letting his fancy play on the copy he was writing."[5] But before

> . . . þis werk was wrouȝt, ere wille myȝte a-spie,
> Deþ delt him a dent and drof him to þe erþe,

and some nameless John But went on with the copying. "I have sometimes thought that the poet may have died, leaving his work of addition unfinished, and that some friend may have taken great liberties in issuing the C-text."[6] In at least one of the C-additions—the one that begins the sixth passus—Chambers detected "the authentic voice of the aged scholar."[7] Chambers' theory regarding the C-text is perhaps best summarized in a remark made some years ago, ". . . No evidence for multiple authorship that will endure scrutiny has yet been produced, although C is probably much interpolated."[8] Unfortunately, Chambers never published any list of the supposed interpolations.

This review has demonstrated that in the critical tradition the problem of the authorship of the C-text has, from the very beginning, been closely connected with the not necessarily relevant problem of its literary value. Indeed, one might justly summarize the material examined by saying that whether or not any given scholar has believed in single authorship has depended, to a rather large extent, on how bad—to put it baldly—he considered the C-text. Skeat did not think it bad at all and Skeat believed in single authorship. Manly thought it very bad and Manly believed in multiple authorship. Chambers thought it fairly bad and Chambers (though he may have had independent reasons, based on his study of the MSS) believed it to have been interpolated. Since, as I have tried to emphasize, the majority of scholars and critics have devoted themselves to A and B, and since, as seems obvious, they have, with but two exceptions, more often than not read C in order to find out

2. *Idem,* p. 27.   3. *Mind,* p. 167.   4. *MLR,* XXVI, 11.
5. *Mind,* p. 167.   6. *Ibid.*   7. *Idem,* p. 168.
8. Preface to Allan H. Bright, *New Light on "Piers Plowman"* (London, 1928), p. 23.

what he did to B rather than what he was trying to do in his own right, I suggest that the lesson to be learned is that we read the C-text as a thing in itself in order to determine just how bad or how good it really is. We shall, of course, have to refer constantly to B. But perhaps something is to be gained if we reverse the usual process and make C the basis of our study and B merely the reference. With a work so vast and, frequently, so difficult as *Piers Plowman,* our minds are apt to become as stiff as our muscles do when we overexercise them. If, after long struggle, we think we have mastered the meaning of a passage in B, only to find that the corresponding lines in C seem to mean something different, we are apt to cater to our weariness by simply assuming that C is not worth our further exertion: C's grapes, indeed, look sour. Thus when we announce, as sooner or later we are all tempted to do, that C mistook change for improvement, we may ourselves be mistaking change for deterioration.

Despite my own affection for the C-text I shall, in the following pages, do nothing so rash as to try to overturn the generally held opinion that the C-text is inferior to B. To this opinion, in general and with reservations, I subscribe. Nevertheless, I do resist any tendency to exaggerate C's inferiority—to construe the adjective *inferior* as a positive rather than as a comparative. I should not wish to waste my own time or the reader's on a study of an inferior piece of literature. But C is a good deal more than just a casual recension of B, despite the many opinions to the contrary. In its own right the C-text is, I am convinced, a magnificent poem, intellectually profound, artistically effective. The primary purpose of this book is, indeed, to adduce evidence for the unity of authorship of *Piers Plowman* but, as I have said before, if while doing this I can help to restore to the C-text some of its lost dignity, I shall consider my time well spent, no matter how far short of fulfillment my primary purpose falls. I should like in any case to make evident the utter injustice of such a statement concerning C as that of Miss Hort which is quoted above. If the poet of C was a different man from the poet of B, then the fourteenth century is the richer by one poet of the first rank.

But one cannot bring into being first-rate poets where they did not exist before. Nor do I think it necessary to try to do so. Chambers once remarked that "we might agree that the C-text was the work of another hand, without the essential unity of *Piers Plowman* being impaired."[9] Yet it is difficult to see why this is not a sort of antitrinitarian heresy. Tradition is firm enough on the three manifestations of *Piers Plowman* and one may wonder why it is possible to exclude any one of the members. If we believe that the C-text is a great poem, then we have almost no choice but to attribute it to the great poet who wrote two other great poems, the A- and B-texts.

9. *LMS,* I, 27.

A NOTE ON THE DATE OF THE C-TEXT

Skeat assigned the C-text to the year 1393, thirty-one years after the composition of A, and sixteen years after the revision by B.[1] Skeat admitted that his dating of C was "conjectural,"[2] saying that he would "not object to the opinion that the true date is later still."[3] His chief reason for choosing 1393 was provided by the passage C, IV, 203–10, in which Conscience tells the King, presumably Richard II, that Meed and her sister, Unseemly Tolerance, have brought it about

Þat no lond loueþ the, and ȝut leest þyn owene.

Skeat saw in these lines a reference to the events of 1392, when Richard's quarrel with the Londoners deprived him of his long-enjoyed popularity.[4] In the mention of Lombards in connection with the King at C, v, 194 Skeat saw an allusion to the maltreatment of a certain unfortunate metic who was willing to lend the Crown money after the citizens of London had emphatically refused such a loan.[5] The long disquisition on *mede* and *mercede*, with its emphasis on bribery, Skeat believed pointed to the later, rather than the earlier, years of Richard's reign.[6]

Although his dates for A and B have been frequently questioned—and changes suggested which would put the A-text as late as 1377 and the B-text as early as 1370[7]—on the whole very little criticism has been made of Skeat's date for C, despite, or possibly on account of, the lack of any substantial body of corroborative evidence. Jusserand, believing that the first passage referred to above reflected conditions following the Parliament of Shrewsbury in 1398, favored 1398–99[8] but no one has come strongly to his support.[9] Coghill, because of C's omitting the mention of the Abbot of Abingdon, who in 1393–94 showed himself a prelate of great and savage power, believes that C "cannot have been earlier than 1394,"[9a] but C might have had other reasons for the change.[9b] Sister Mary Aquinas Devlin, in a

1. For Skeat's dating of C, see *EETS*, III, xi–xix; of A, *EETS*, I, xxxi–xxxiv; of B, *EETS*, II, ii–vi.

2. *EETS*, III, xviii. 3. *Idem*, p. xvii. 4. *Idem*, pp. xvi–xvii.

5. *Idem*, p. xvii. 6. *Idem*, pp. xvii–xviii. See C, IV, 287–415.

7. For attempts to change the date of the A-text, see Oscar Cargill, "The Date of the A-text of Piers Ploughman," *PMLA*, XLVII (1932), 354–62; Bernard Huppé, "The A-Text of *Piers Plowman* and the Norman Wars," *PMLA*, LIV (1939), 37–64; J. A. W. Bennett, "The Date of the A-Text of *Piers Plowman*," *PMLA*, LVIII (1943), 566–72. For the B-text, see Huppé, "The Date of the B-Text of *Piers Plowman*," *StPh*, XXXVIII (1941), 34–44; A. Gwynn, same title *RES*, XIX (1943), 1–24; Bennett, same title, *MedAev*, XII (1943), 55–64.

8. *Mysticism*, pp. 56–8.

9. Manly, *CHEL*, II, 34, holds Jusserand's date "more probable" than Skeat's, but cites Knighton to show that relations between the King and the people were strained as early as 1386.

9a. Introduction to Wells's translation, p. xxvii. See also Coghill, "Two Notes on *Piers Plowman*," *MedAev*, IV (1935), 83–94.

9b. C altered to make the Abbot of Abingdon the Abbot of England. This may have been in keeping with his policy of generalization. See Chapter III.

dissertation that I have seen only in summary,[3] has studied the possibilities for a date earlier than Skeat's. The most important single piece of evidence she has adduced is the fact that in the *Testament of Love* by Thomas Usk, who was put to death in 1387, appear unmistakable traces of the influence of the C-text[4]—traces that were, curiously enough, first pointed out by Skeat himself in 1897.[5] It seems certain that Usk was familiar with the C-text and equally certain that his death occurred in 1387. Hence we seem to have a definite *terminus ad quem* for the C-text—or for a considerable portion of it. Sister Mary Aquinas suggests that the allusions in C to royal unpopularity might conceivably have reference to the last years of Edward III, so that it might be possible to date C as early as 1377. She is tempted to choose a date before 1381, thus accounting for C's failure to mention the Peasants' Revolt[6] but, on the evidence, finds that the revision might have been made any time between 1377 and 1387.

My own investigations have done nothing either to corroborate or disprove any date between 1377 and 1399. Following the lead of Bradley,[7] I at one time attempted to do something with the prophetic passages, which C rewrote while retaining all of B's mystification, but although I entertained myself with a fascinating array of possibilities, including the signs of the zodiac, I got nowhere. Furthermore, since the passages are prophetic, it is possible that even if they do contain dates, these are not the dates of the composition of the text. A somewhat less fanciful approach through the medium of topical reference has also led nowhere. It appears that C was greatly preoccupied with the principle that bishops should not dread great lords and I hoped to find a clear example of a bishop who was particularly craven during the eighties and nineties, but the whole era seems full of bishops who might, at one time or another, be said to have compromised with the temporal powers, and I found no one outstanding case. It scarcely seems worthwhile to multiply the already large number of dubious topical references in *Piers Plowman*. For the present, it seems best to accept Sister Aquinas' suggestion, tacitly, if perhaps unconsciously, concurred in by Skeat, for a year before 1387 for the date of the completion of C. The most important fact for our purposes is that no one has successfully challenged the position of the C-text as the latest of the versions of the poem and that only by a rearrangement of the order of the texts would the question of authorship be seriously affected.

3. "The Date of the C Version of *Piers the Plowman*," *Abstracts of Theses, University of Chicago, Humanistic Series*, IV, 1925–26 (Chicago, 1928), pp. 317–20.

4. Cf. *Testament* (edited by Skeat in the Oxford *Chaucer*, Vol. VII, *Chaucerian and Other Pieces* [Oxford, 1897]), I, 5, 117–19: "Wening his owne wit more excellent than other; scorning al maner devyse but his own," with C, VII, 24–5: "Wene þat ich were witty and wyser þan a-noþere; Scorner and vnskilful to hem þat skil shewede"; *Testament*, I, 7, 61: " 'better is it to dey than live false,' " with C, XVIII, 41: "*melius est mori quam male uiuere*," a paraphrase of Tobit 2.21 repeated at C, II, 144 and paraphrased at VIII, 209–10; *Testament*, III, 7, 10: "First, the ground shulde be thy free wil, ful in thyne herte," with C, XIX, 4 ff., where the Tree of Charity, which Usk is imitating, is said to grow in *Cor Hominis*.

5. See *Chaucerian and Other Pieces*, p. 458.

6. A common but probably unnecessary temptation. See Chapter IV.

7. Henry Bradley, "Some Cruces in 'Piers Plowman,' " *MLR*, V (1910), 340–2.

II

The Mechanics of the C-Revision

1. *Introductory*

IT will be well, before we plunge into a study of the actual contents of the C-text, to interpose a descriptive analysis of the revision itself, placing emphasis upon matters that are more extrinsic than intrinsic to the effect the text produces. In this chapter, therefore, I shall discuss several topics that relate to the form of the revision: first, its size and shape, and the probable method by which it was carried on; second, its division into passus; and third, its alliteration. The first two topics may seem, at first glance, altogether mechanical, and hence scarcely worth a detailed study. Nevertheless, knowledge of them is essential to a full understanding of the revision. Concerning the importance of the third topic no one will have any doubt. One might, however, suppose that alliteration would be treated along with style and such a procedure is more usual than the one I propose to follow. The two are kept separate in this book partly because the problem of C's style is large enough without adding alliteration to it, but chiefly because of the fact that, whereas in the study of its style we come close to the heart of the C-revision, in the study of its alliteration we can scarcely do more than scratch its surface. This second reason will, I think, become clear as we progress in our examination of the C-text.

2. *Mathematics and Method of Revision*

The reader has but to consult Skeat's parallel-texts edition of *Piers Plowman* in order to recognize that both the B- and C-revisions were extremely thorough and a brief examination will probably suggest to him that the C-text represents a more thorough recasting of B than the B-text—exclusive of the B-continuation—does of A. Statistically, B's revision represents an expansion of A's twenty-four hundred lines[1] to about thirty-two hundred—an increase of about one-third—plus an addition of over four thousand lines, so that the complete B-text contains

1. Excluding A, XII, which contains, in its fullest form, 117 lines. As printed by Skeat, A (Pro.–XI) contains 2,467 lines; B (Pro.–XX), 7,241; C (I–XXIII), 7,354. In the part paralleling A, the B-text (Pro.–X) contains 3,206; the C-text (I–XII, 303), 3,654. The B-continuation (XI–XX) contains 4,035; its equivalent in C (XII, 304–XXIII), 3,700. For obvious corrections of Skeat's totals for the A-text and its equivalents in B and C, see Appendix C. Skeat introduced thirty-nine spurious lines into his A-version, so that the corrected figure for A is 2,428. For possibly spurious lines in B, see n. 3 below.

over seventy-two hundred. C revised almost the whole of B—he left intact only the last two passus[2]—lengthening the poem by about a hundred lines. Hence C's *revision* was more extensive than B's, if only because he had more material before him to revise. But C's total mathematical addition to B is but a fraction of B's addition to A and constitutes an increase of only about 1½ per cent over the length of the B-text.[3]

More informative than these general figures would be statistics showing the relative frequency of alterations in B and C, passus by passus, but the situation in regard to the preserved MSS of all versions prohibits such a compilation. It has been conclusively demonstrated that all our MSS of B derive from one archetype which was not the author's autograph and which deviated from it fairly frequently.[4] Of the C-MSS we possess two or three fairly distinct families, although the best of these includes only a portion of the C-text. Nevertheless, the C-text as a whole undoubtedly comes closer to being what the C-poet wrote than does the B-text to what the B-poet wrote. For the A-text the numerous MSS give a wide variety of readings, but it is uncertain how closely even a critical A-text will approach the A-poet's original. For these reasons, and because no critical texts of any version are in existence, the statistics we draw up will be descriptive chiefly of the versions printed by Skeat— even if we make certain obvious corrections—and not of the original texts.

It is possible, however, to arrive at a minimum figure, of some interest in itself, for the lines which B and C retain unchanged from the earlier texts. Ruling out the possibility of intertextual contamination,[5] we may

2. See Appendix B. Also Chambers, *Mind*, p. 167, and preface to Bright's *New Light on "Piers Plowman,"* p. 15.

3. Skeat's edition of the B text contains 160 lines from MS R (Bodleian, Rawlinson Poet. 38) which are of doubtful authenticity. See Appendix C, note on MS R; also Blackman, *JEGPh*, xvii, 501–03; Chambers, "The Manuscripts of *Piers Plowman* in the Huntington Library, and Their Value for Fixing the Text of the Poem," *HLB*, viii (1935), 12–13. If these lines are omitted, C's addition will be higher by about 2%. In this book, for reasons set forth in Appendix C, I have treated R's lines as if they formed a genuine part of the B-text, though I have avoided basing any argument on a premise involving them.

4. The situation in regard to the MSS of B and C is discussed in Appendix B. For reasons set forth in detail there, in this book I have assumed that the best MSS of C (the "i"-group, particularly as represented by MS X, and the "t"-group, where available) represent the author's original with a high degree of accuracy, while the B-MSS are less reliable. So far as the A-group is concerned, MS T, corrected by readings from other MSS, gives us a better form of the original A-text than MS V, printed by Skeat. Where the best MSS of A and C agree against B, I have, in making intertextual comparisons, assumed that the AC-reading also represents the original B-reading. See Blackman, *JEGPh*, xvii, 518–21; Chambers and Grattan, *MLR*, xxvi, 1–9.

5. So far as is known, there is no cross-contamination between the reliable MSS of C and the reliable MSS of B. There is, however, a possibility of B-contamination in some of the best A-MSS. See Chambers and Grattan, *MLR*, xxvi, 36–7, where VHU are spoken of as possibly B-contaminated. Because of this possibility, I have exercised caution in regard to A-readings, trusting only MS T, which forms the basis for Knott-Fowler's and Kane's A-texts, except when it is obviously wrong.

assume that such lines as read the same in A and B, in B and C, or in all three versions, represent an uncorrupted reading, since scribal deviation would, except in very rare instances, cause disagreement, rather than agreement, among distinct versions. From an examination of the lines of that part of the poem in which the three texts run parallel one may derive the following statistics—inaccurate, to be sure, but all erring in common by exaggerating the differences between the texts. Of 2,428 lines in A (Prologue–xi), 1,669 appear unaltered in B (Prologue–x). Thus the received B-text preserves 68.7 per cent of A. Some 759 of A's lines are omitted or appear in revised form in B, which makes a net addition of 776. Of 3,204 lines in these passus of B, 1,425, or 44.5 per cent, appear intact in C (i–xii). The C-text omits or revises 2,779 of B's lines and makes a net addition of 269.[6] But while of the total number of lines in the passus of B under consideration the C-text retains 44.5 per cent, of the lines which appear in the same form in A and B the C-text retains 62.3 per cent. On the other hand, of the lines that either are new to B or assume a new form in B, the C-text retains only 25.1 per cent. Considering the matter from another direction, we find that 52.1 per cent of the B-text (Prologue–x) consists of material which has the same form in A. Of the C-text (i–xii), however, only 41 per cent consists of material which has the same form in B: 29.9 per cent is material which has the same form in A, and 11.1 per cent is material received intact from the B-additions and revisions. Of the lines of the long B-addition (Passus xi–xx) only an estimated 37 per cent appear in the same form in the parallel section of C.[7]

From these figures it follows that while B revised a maximum of about three out of every ten lines in the A-text, C revised or omitted a maximum of about eleven out of every twenty in B. The fact that C revised only four out of every ten A-lines preserved in B, while he revised three out of four lines peculiar to B, admits of several different interpretations. Miss Day points out that, if we assume multiple authorship, it is possible to say that "where A and B agreed, C had too much respect for the established version to make large alterations, but that where they diverged, he felt himself free to paraphrase and expand as he wished."[8] This interpretation would be more persuasive if C had showed any great reluctance to tamper with the established version. Actually, he altered it more freely than B—a thorough reviser in his own right—had altered A, and

6. These figures and those following are based upon corrected line-counts, explained in Appendix C.

7. I have not thought it worthwhile to make detailed statistical analysis of the continuation. All percentages relating to it are based on a rough count.

8. *MLR*, xxiii, 5. Miss Görnemann pointed to C's free handling of B as a proof of her theory concerning the scribal origin of the variations between the three texts. See *Zur Verfasserschaft und Entstehungsgeschichte von "Piers the Plowman,"* pp. 99–100.

certainly the fact that C revised four out of every ten AB lines indicates that the phrase "too much respect" is misleading. The matter might be more correctly expressed if we were to say that C had even less respect for lines peculiar to B than he did for those appearing in A and B both. This may be easily explained if we assume single authorship, for many of us find, in re-revising our work, that we concentrate more heavily on our previous revisions than we do on what we have already once allowed to stand—a perfectly reasonable procedure, as Chambers and Grattan have shown from the analogy of Wordsworth.[9] A lingering sense of dissatisfaction, becoming intensified within us as we read our own revisions, is apt to incite us to try for further improvement of what we had originally found inadequate. Furthermore, the process of re-revision is apt to lead us into a general paraphrase, so that, like C, we find ourselves writing almost independently of the basic text. This may account for much that is characteristic of C. We should observe, moreover, that the thoroughness of the C-revision must have required of the reviser almost as great a creative effort as that expended by B in his lengthening of the A-text. To effect a complete rewriting of a poem over 7,200 lines long is no small labor.

Let us examine the C-revision in order to try to discover the plan according to which the reviser was working. In the first place, the *Visio,* as distinct from *Vita,*[1] exhibits four different types of revision. The most obvious of these is a sort of line-by-line, or passage-by-passage, reworking of B—apparent in Passus I–V and IX–X of the C-text. In these portions of the poem the reader can easily follow B and C together for long periods without either losing his place or ruining his eyes. There are, it is true, several thoroughgoing revisions of short passages where the line-by-line correspondence momentarily disappears, such as in the C-version of Lady Meed's speech on the Normandy campaign.[2] But these generally begin or end with a line that has the same form in both texts and thus serves as a catchword. A second type of revision is apparent in C Passus VI through VIII. This part of the poem contains a number of long passages so altered that one hesitates to call them revisions, rather than new material substituted for something omitted. A good example is the confession of Wrath, in which the very structure of a passage in B is altered.[3] Revision of this type also includes transposition from the B-*Vita* of material that is pertinent to the subject C is treating. Thus, part of Clergy's discourse in B, x is added to Reason's sermon in

---

9. *MLR,* XXVI, 42–3.

1. The *Visio* (*visio willelmi de petro plouhman,* as it is called in MS P of the C-group) includes A, Pro.–VIII, B, Pro.–VII, and C, I–X. The *Vita* (*Vita de do-wel, do-bet, & do-best, secundum wyt & resoun,* as it is called in certain A-MSS) includes A, IX–XII, B, VIII–XX, C, XI–XXIII. The short terms are, possibly, more convenient than accurate.

2. C, IV, 232–65, B, III, 185–207.   3. C, VII, 103–63, B, V, 134–81.

C, vi and parts of Hawkin's confession in B, xiii are transferred to the Deadly Sins in C, vii and viii.[4] A third type of revision consists in simple omission without compensation. The disappearance of much of the scene in which, in B, Piers tears the pardon is one of the few examples.[5] Finally, a fourth type of revision consists in the addition of passages of varying length which tend merely to prolong the narrative without in any way altering the framework of the poem. Such are Conscience's diatribe against false priests in Passus i and the autobiographical passage that opens Passus vi.[6]

Despite these various sorts of revision, the basic forms of B and C throughout the *Visio* are altogether similar. The similarity persists even though the C-*Visio* is over six hundred lines longer than the B-*Visio*, which contains only about twenty-four hundred lines to C's three thousand. Only about 170 of the additional lines in C may be accounted for in the transfer of material from the B-*Vita* to the C-*Visio*. That such an expansion was accomplished without disturbing the organic structure of the *Visio* is surprising and is due chiefly to the fact that the bulk of the added material appears in those new passages mentioned above under revision of the fourth type.[7] Now these new passages seem, technically if not artistically, extraneous to the narrative. Furthermore, as I shall try to demonstrate below, some of them are awkwardly fitted into their positions, while some have sources deep in B's *Vita*. These facts suggest that the C-poet added them, not at the time of his first revision, but while he was working on the *Vita*. This means that, so far as the *Visio* is concerned, there were at least two stages in the C-revision. Under such an assumption we may picture C setting to work on the *Visio* with the intention of altering only details everywhere except in the confessions, which he planned to revise completely. Disregarding the inserted passages, we shall find that the first five passus contain chiefly revisions of the first type spoken of above—furbishing of single lines. The real work begins with C, vi, wherein occurs the first of the transpositions from B's *Vita*. As we shall see, the C-poet greatly abridged that portion of the poem (B, x) in which Clergy's harangue appears and it seems highly probable that he already had this reduction in mind at the time that he was working on Passus vi. Therefore with understandable economy he

---

4. The transfers are: B, x, 292–330 to C, vi, 147–80; B, xiii, 278–84 to C, vii, 30–7; B, xiii, 292–313 to C, vii, 41–60; B, xiii, 325–42 to C, vii, 69–85; B, xiii, 344–52 to C, vii, 176–85; B, xiii, 362–8 to C, vii, 260–6; B, xiii, 371–5 to C, vii, 267–71; B, xiii, 384–9 to C, vii, 272–7; B, xiii, 392–9 to C, vii, 278–85; B, xiii, 404 to C, vii, 430; B, xiii, 410–57 to C, viii, 70–117. Many of these passages were partially rewritten as well as transposed. For transpositions within B, v, see p. 25, n. 1, below.

5. B, vii, 116–37 is omitted by C. See Chapter VI for discussion.

6. C, i, 95–124; vi, 1–108.

7. Inserted passages swell C, iv by 152 lines, vi by 104, and x by 151. The rest of the increase, aside from the 170 lines from B, x and xiii, appears in the revision of the confessions.

borrowed a passage from Clergy in order to lengthen and strengthen Reason's sermon, which, despite its brevity in the earlier texts, has the important effect in the narrative of precipitating the confessions of the Deadly Sins. The transposed lines, with their terrifying chiliastic prophecy, serve to increase the motivation behind the confessions.[8]

In the next two passus (C, VII and VIII) occur the most marked examples of the second type of revision mentioned above—reworking of the original material so thoroughly as to affect the very structure. This is accompanied by further transpositions from B's *Vita*, the material being derived from the confession of Hawkin. Here again C had, probably, already formed the plan of shortening the Hawkin incident and economy prompted him to use material that might otherwise go to waste in order to impart a badly needed equality to the disproportionate confessions of the Deadly Sins in B.[9] In the course of his rewriting, C also made several minor shifts in arrangement of the confessions.[1] For the reason that, in this section of the poem, the revised material, the transposed material, and the new material all fit together in perfect harmony, I believe that the reworking was accomplished in the first bloom of the C-revision, when the poet's interest in the interwoven fabric of the *Visio* was still greater than his interest in isolated passages.

Having completed work on the confessions, the C-reviser returned to his earlier manner of line-by-line revision in Passus IX and X. Apart from two long inserted passages, the only considerable change in this part of the poem is the omission of much of the incident concerning Piers, his pardon, and the Priest, which I discuss elsewhere.[2] With the conclusion of the *Visio,* C proceeded, I believe, directly to the *Vita,* the drastic revision of which we shall examine below. It was while he was engaged with the *Vita* that he inserted into the *Visio* those passages which so increase its size. The first of these, the accusation of the false priests by Conscience, has its source in a line or two of B, x, as Skeat pointed out.[3] That it is a later addition is suggested not only by its source but by the fact that, in the best MSS, it is faultily joined into its context and by the further fact that it is obviously an unfinished piece of work, containing the only large number of consecutive nonalliterative lines in

8. Burdach, *Ackermann,* p. 266 and n. 2, considers the prophecy important to the plan of the poem.

9. For an interesting discussion of the confessions as they appear in the earlier versions, see Jusserand, *MPh,* VI, 295–302; *MPh,* VII, 304–05.

1. Lechery, the second of A's and B's sins, is dropped to fourth place in C (C, VII, 170–95, B, V, 72–5, A, V, 54–8). Robert the Robber, the eighth of A's and B's penitents, is moved ahead of Gluttony in C (C, VII, 316–30, B, V, 469–84, A, V, 242–59). Four lines from Sloth's confession in A and B are detached by C and given to Ʒevan Ʒield-Aʒain (C, VII, 309–15, B, V, 463–6, A, V, 236–9). The last lines are of great importance in the theory of the lost leaf. Despite the fact that Chambers, *MLR,* V, 6–9, has shown their pertinence to Sloth's confession, I doubt that any one will argue that C's use of them is not also pertinent.

2. Chapter VI.　　　　　　　3. *CP,* I, 10.

all *Piers Plowman*.[4] The second addition, a shorter diatribe directed chiefly against dishonest tradesmen, has no source that may be readily found within the poem, but it is also exposed at its seams.[5] The third addition, Conscience's long and much-abused distinction between *mede* and *mercede*,[6] is aptly fitted into the fabric of the narrative and has, apparently, no source in another part of the poem. There is, perhaps, no reason to suspect it of being a later addition, except that the style is so similar to that of a passage at the end of Do-Bet, wherein the Samaritan compares the Trinity successively to the operation of a man's hand and to a torch, that I am inclined to think that it was written when the C-author's mind was preoccupied with revising Do-Bet.[7] I should not, however, insist upon the point and perhaps the passage was written during the first stage of the C-revision.

The same can scarcely be said of the autobiographical passage at the beginning of C, vi. Miss Day has already made clear that this passage must have been added after the first C-revision, since the surrounding context, with which it is rather clumsily joined, is peculiar to the C-text.[8] Furthermore, Miss Day has pointed out what is clearly the source of the addition in the conversation between the Dreamer and Imaginative in B, xii, a section of the poem which C subjected to a good deal of abridgement.[9] The evidence for considering the biographical passage an afterthought seems almost conclusive.

This also seems to be true of the two long C-insertions in Passus x.[1] These occur in close conjunction with one another in a passage in which the author is trying to formulate rules to govern the bestowal of alms. The first insertion begins with a description of the sufferings of the poor and then, after a brief exhortation to the rich to let healthy beggars starve, launches into a definition of those curious deserving beggars whom the author calls God's minstrels. The source of the lines on the poor is evidently in B, xiv where Anima, who has been discoursing on the evil effects of wealth on rich men's souls, utters a prayer for God's mercy on the poor[2]—that wonderful prayer for the omission of which C has been so harshly rebuked.[3] The verbal correspondences between the two passages, particularly if one takes into account those lines that C did not omit in his revision of Do-Bet, are unmistakable.[3a] Probably as C read

4. This passage is discussed in greater detail in Appendix B.
5. C, iv, 77–114. The repetition of 77 at 115 is suspicious. Miss Day, *MLR*, xxiii, 8, suggests that C misunderstood the grammatical construction in B, but the assumption is gratuitous.
6. C, iv, 317–409.
7. B, xvii, 137–262, C, xx, 111–228. The similarity of style was observed by Skeat, *EETS*, iii, lxxxvi.
8. *MLR*, xxiii, 1–2.   9. *Idem*, p. 2.
1. C, x, 71–161, 188–281.   2. B, xiv, 160–80, C, xvii, 13–18.
3. See Manly, *CHEL*, ii, 35, and *MPh*, vii, 129–30. The omitted lines are B, xiv, 174–80.
3a. Cf. C, x, 72. *As prisones in puttes and poure folke in Cotes*, with B, xiv, 174, *Ac pore peple, þi prisoneres, lorde, in þe put of myschief;* C, x, 77, *suffren muche hunger*, with B, xiv, 175, *moche care suffren;* C, x, 78, *And wo in winter-tyme*, with B, xiv, 177,

the passage in B, the mention of starving beggars and rich men's alms[5] reminded him of the discussion in his own Passus x which deals with these topics. B's apostrophe on the deserving poor might further have reminded him that in his previous discussion he had, rather characteristically, neglected to identify those persons who did deserve charity, so eager had he been to identify those who did not. He remedied the lack forthwith.

C's mind, like B's, worked in contrasts. Having described, in tender terms, the deserving poor, he added a few lines contrasting them with healthy beggars.[6] Then he remembered that there were some seemingly healthy beggars who were worthy of charitable treatment: God's minstrels. These he had already mentioned briefly in the confession of Sloth,[7] in a passage which, if we can trust the untrustworthy MS R, was originally written by B as a part of Hawkin's confession of sloth.[8] This passage became the starting point for the definition of God's minstrels in C, x, as is evident from the fact that both contain precisely the same logical construction: rich men willingly give hospitality to professional minstrels whose flattery corrupts their hosts; rich men should, therefore, more willingly give hospitality to God's minstrels, who have the opposite effect.[9]

The second insertion in C, Passus x (and the last long insertion in the *Visio*) concerns those false hermits who house themselves by the main highway and, under the cloak of piety, live off the fat of the land. The source for this passage is not far from the source for the first part of the one just discussed and also comes from Anima's monologue. In B, xv, Anima, illustrating the value of patience, considers at some length the lives of the great Christian hermits—Anthony, Egidius, Paul the Hermit.[1] In his revision, C converts these illustrations into a proof of the proposition that some men are able to get through life without begging or borrowing.[2] Apparently as C made the change in emphasis, his mind once more returned to the discussion in C, x and he realized, as he wrote about the good hermits, that he had really not done justice to bad hermits in the rules he had laid down for almsgiving. The second insertion in C, x is the result. It is in the first lines of this, which summarize the passage in B, xv, that the source is clearly indicated by verbal similarities.[3]

Wo in wynter tymes; C, x, 82, *Þat reuthe is to rede,* with B, xiv, 163, *þat reuthe is to here;* C, x, 85, *Boþe a-fyngrede and a-furst,* with B, xiv, 162, *A-fyrst sore and afyngred.* Some, though hardly all, of these similarities might be explained on the ground of common subject and alliterative exigencies.

5. In B, xiv, 160–3, 168.   6. C, x, 98–104.   7. C, viii, 94–117.
8. B, xiii, 434–57 (437–54 are in MS R only).
9. Cf. B, xiii, 437–40, C, viii, 97–100, with C, x, 128–36.
1. B, xv, 263–303.   2. C, xviii, 1–36.
3. Cf. particularly C, x, 200, *And bryddes brouhten to some bred wherby þei lyueden,* with B, xv, 279, *Had a bridde þat brouȝte hym bred þat he by lyued,* where C retains B's alliteration on *by;* also C, x, 198, *And some lyuede by here lettrure and labour of here*

Such I conceive to have been the method of C's revision of the *Visio,* a twofold process, involving on the one hand a line-by-line retouching of seven passus and a thorough rewriting of three, and on the other a later insertion of a number of passages whose presence does not alter the fabric of the original. It almost seems possible that the autograph MS of C, if it should ever come to light, would prove to contain a text of the *Visio* without the later additions. These were probably written on separate sheets and their position in the text indicated by one of those complicated systems of arrows and carets that every reviser finds himself adopting. I am disposed to believe that the author himself never saw a fair copy of his work with all his afterthoughts inserted into the text. If he had, he would have perfected the amalgamation of those passages whose uncovered seams are now obvious to the reader—something that his management of the confessions shows him to have been capable of doing. Furthermore, he would have put into poetic form the passage concerning false priests. As it now stands, this passage seems to have been completed by the C-poet through line 106 of Passus I. The next eighteen lines contain the nonalliterative *exemplum* of Hophni and Phineas, which C apparently summarized in prose, intending to versify it later.[4] The variants that several MSS show for the passage suggest that scribes have had a hand in trying to make up for the author's lapse. What it was that prevented C from completing his work we can only guess: my own suggestion is that he died with the revision unfinished.

We come now to C's revision of the *Vita,* much of which was radically altered. While the C-*Visio,* as I have tried to emphasize, displays a minimum of structural change, the C-*Vita* displays, particularly in its earlier portions, a maximum of the same. The reader, passing from the *Visio* to the *Vita,* will notice the alteration in C's method almost at once. It is true that in rewriting B, VIII, the Prologue to Do-Well, C sticks fairly carefully to the thought and structure of his original.[5] But the fact that he covers the ground in exactly the same number of lines as B—126—is partly set aside by the fact that he indulges in a freer paraphrase than he does in any passage of similar length in the *Visio.* It seems as if he had made up his mind in advance that this was the section of the work with which he was going to deal most vigorously and that though he had really no major improvement to make in these lines, he nevertheless relaxed his fidelity to the original while warming up for the complete revision of the subsequent passus. With B, IX, far-reaching structural revision begins. Line-by-line correspondence now becomes

---

hondes, with B, xv, 286, *And wan with his hondes þat his wombe neded.* C's *lyones* and *beres* (x, 196: compare B, xIV, 293-4) are possibly the result of common subject matter.

4. If one writes out C, I, 107-24 in prose, one gets an even stranger sort of prose than one now has poetry. But probably the original version has been lost through scribal attempts at versification.

5. C, xI, 1-126 parallels B, VIII.

rare. The B-text serves less as a guide for the C-poet than as a taking-off point for original composition. Simultaneously, large sections of B disappear without leaving a trace. In this way some of Wit's monologue in B, IX is omitted and C covers the ground of B's 206 lines in 183 of his own.[6] As we go on through Do-Well, it becomes increasingly difficult to trace the source of C's lines in the B-text, so tenuous are the connections between presumably parallel passages. Lines taken over intact occasionally appear, but so infrequently as to seem like little islands of similarity in a sea of difference. B, Passus X, which contains the monologues of Study and Clergy, C cuts from 472 lines to 302. On the other hand, B, XI, wherein the correspondences between B and C are somewhat easier to detect, C increases, by the addition of a single long speech, from about 430 lines to over five hundred—the only substantial expansion C makes in Do-Well. B, XII, which narrates the encounter with Imaginative, is paraphrased and reduced from 293 lines to 217; while B, XIII, containing the incident of Hawkin, is shortened, by the omission of Hawkin's confession, to the extent of 230 lines. In his revision of B, XIV, which contains the exhortations of Patience and Conscience to Hawkin, C is almost as radical, reducing the passus from 332 lines to about 234 and rewriting the remainder.

It is difficult to tell, in the B-text, precisely where Do-Well concludes and Do-Bet begins.[7] The MSS of C, moreover, give us two different definitions.[8] If, however, we arbitrarily choose C, XVII (B, XV, 1–262) as the last passus of Do-Well, we shall find that C has expended over 500 lines fewer on Do-Well than B has, while effecting a most thorough

6. These and the following line-counts for the *Visio* are corrected. See Appendix C.

7. B, XV in MS W is headed *finit dowel, & incipit dobet.* MSS BC add *primus de* before *dobet.* B, XVI is called by LW *primus de dobet;* by D, *secundus de dobet.* See next note.

8. C, XVIII, which begins opposite B, XV, 262, is headed in MSS of the "p"-group *primus de dobet;* C, XIX, which parallels B, XVI, *secundus de dobet.* In the "i"-group, including MS X, C, XVIII is classed under Do-Well, the colophons adding *& explicit,* and C, XIX is headed *primus de dobet.* MS H2 of the most reliable group "t" heads C, XVIII in much the same fashion as the B-MSS head B, XV (see last note) : *hic finit de do wel. Incipit primus passus de dobetere,* while C, XIX is called *primus de do bet.* It is probable that H2, alone of the C-MSS, preserves a trace of the author's original intention. The "p"-scribe copied only the second sentence in a double colophon, while the "i"-scribe copied only the first sentence, which may originally have omitted the words *primus passus.* The fact that none of the C-MSS mentions Do-Bet until a point opposite B, XV, 262 militates against Coghill's suggestion, *MedAev,* II, 124, that B's Do-Bet begins at B, XV, 144 (paralleling C, XVII, 283), since this point is eighty-nine lines before C's first mention of Do-Bet. It is, of course, possible to argue that the C-text should not govern our attitude toward B, but since the B-poet might have intended Do-Bet to begin anywhere in the 601 lines of Passus XV, it would be reasonable to choose a point that might be paralleled in C's Do-Bet (that is, between C, XVIII, 1 and 322, B, XV, 262 and 601). There is, however, no natural dividing point which conforms so satisfactorily to the sense as that suggested by Coghill. I am disposed to believe that neither B nor C had any very clear idea where Do-Well left off and Do-Bet began. If they had, the division would not have been so ambiguously labeled. For the colophons of C, see Carnegy, *An Attempt to Approach the C-Text of Piers the Plowman,* pp. 24–6.

revision of the remainder. I estimate that in this section C preserves intact somewhat less than a quarter of the lines in the B-text. With Do-Well, therefore, we have an illustration on the grand scale of the principle we have already noticed, that C alters when he alteration finds. It was in Do-Well that B made his most radical changes in the A-text and it is in B's revised Do-Well that C makes his most radical changes— although, of course, C continues his thorough revision beyond the point where the A-text ends. The feeling of inadequacy that originally caused A to break off his poem, and that later caused B entirely to recast A's Do-Well, must have been still latent in C and of sufficient urgency to influence him altogether to rewrite B's Do-Well.

C's thoroughgoing revision continues with the first passus of Do-Bet (B, xvi), although we no longer have the phenomenon of large excisions in the B-text. The preservation in C of B-lines from this passus continues at about 25 per cent. With B, xvii, however, the intensity of the revision begins to abate, C, xx preserving about 53 per cent of B's lines and C, xxi retaining about 63 per cent of B, xviii. It is interesting to notice that as the poem progresses the number of changes in single lines diminishes as if, when more of the reviser's energy was going into complete paraphrase of certain passages, less of it was left for details, so that it seems as if he must have made up his mind in advance either to accept a given passage intact, or to change it altogether. In the last two passus of Do-Bet he seems particularly to have followed this procedure. With the end of B, xviii (C, xxi), the C-revision concludes and the final two passus of the poem, if we had them in their original form, would show no differences between B and C.[9] This means that none of Do-Best was altered. Furthermore, if we accept Coghill's suggestion that Do-Bet does not end until line 176 of B, xix (paralleling C, xxii, 181 as numbered in Skeat's edition),[1] then it appears that C did not revise the end of Do-Bet either. We might observe that, if we assume for Do-Bet the arbitrary boundaries C, xviii, 1 through C, xxii, 181 (B, xv, 263 through B, xix, 176), we shall find that C's version is approximately the same length as B's—1,607 lines in C to 1,576 lines in B.[2] Despite his thorough revision of the first passus of this section, C seems to have been much more nearly content with the length of B's Do-Bet than he was with the length of B's Do-Well. And on the whole he seems to have been more content with the form, too.

In the course of this descriptive analysis of the revision I have not said much concerning the motives underlying C's alterations. An attempt

9. See p. 21, n. 2.

1. *MedAev*, ii, 120–1. The best MSS of both texts head the next-to-last passus (B, xix, C, xxii) *explicit dobet, & incipit dobest.*

2. Counting seven lines lost in B, xix–xx. See Appendix B. It is a curious coincidence that if we accept both of Coghill's boundaries for Do-Bet (see p. 29, n. 8, and also n. 1 above), we find that the C-version contains 1,696 lines to B's 1,695.

to arrive at some of these will be made in the subsequent chapters of this book. Meanwhile I take it to be obvious that the chief motive for C's revision was the desire to improve the B-version of the poem. The frequently repeated statement that C revised for no "discoverable reason,"[3] which is actually just a periphrastic way of saying that we are unable or unwilling to perceive the motive, is, on the face of it, absurd, since improvement is almost the sole reason that any one ever undertakes to revise a piece of work, whether his own or another's.[4] In the *Visio*, for instance, there is apparent a definite and, it seems to me, a successful effort to get rid of the disproportion that characterizes the confessions of the Deadly Sins in B. Furthermore, it is evident that in the addition of his long new passages C thought that he was either clarifying or enhancing by further illustration the points that the poem makes.[5] In the line-by-line polishing, for which most of his critics soundly berate him, the motive, either conscious or unconscious, seems to have been to assimilate his earlier style to that which he later took on. No one has ever denied that there is a distinct difference in style between the *Visio* in A and the *Vita* in B, but it has not been sufficiently emphasized that there is little difference between the style of B's *Vita* and C's style in all his revisions and additions.[6] Therefore I feel it likely that a man who had become accustomed to writing in the manner of the last passus of B would, on revising the earlier passus, tend to rewrite individual lines in his later manner.[7] Such a procedure would account for the fact that it is in the earlier passus of C that detailed revision is more apparent, while in the later passus it becomes increasingly insignificant, almost disappearing entirely in Passus xx and xxi.

The more drastic and, on the whole, more interesting revision of the *Vita* seems to have been motivated by a desire to improve the structure of the narrative itself. What shape this attempted improvement takes in the religious allegory of Do-Well and Do-Bet is the subject of a later chapter.[8] Of C's revision of the incidents involving Wit, Study, and Imaginative I have made no special study.[9] I should, however, hazard the opinion that since in B it is these incidents that are the most difficult to comprehend

3. See Manly, *CHEL*, ii, 35.
4. Revision to obtain modification of political sentiments is a possible motive, suggested by Wright, *The Vision and Creed of Piers Ploughman*, i, xxxiv. But see Chapter IV.
5. Thus the insertions in Passus x, while partially digressive, clarify the rules for almsgiving, and the distinction between *mede* and *mercede* straightens out the meaning of Meed, which A and B left uncertain.
6. If I were to attribute the poem to three authors, I should divide it as follows: the A-*Visio;* the A-*Vita* and the B-revision of both parts of A; the B-continuation and the entire C-revision.
7. For an analysis of C's artistic technique, see Chapter III.
8. Chapter VI.
9. The C-revision of these incidents takes the form for the most part of abridgement, with much of what pertains personally to the poet disappearing.

of the whole poem,[1] mainly because they introduce such a diversity of topics, the C-reviser hoped to provide the reader with a clearer prospect by cutting out some of the undergrowth. To this end he omitted much of the autobiographical material, as well as nearly all those passages in which Chambers was able to read the poet's explanation of why he left the A-text unfinished.[2] Although they are valuable in helping us to understand *Piers Plowman* as a poem issued in several versions, they are less valuable in helping us to understand any one text alone. And we must bear in mind that it was in a single version that the poet, upon three different occasions, placed all his interest. Each of the later texts was, I am sure, expected to replace its predecessor,[3] if not in the public domain, over which the poet had no control, at least in the poet's own heart. The fact that the C-revision bears some marks of being unfinished suggests to me that the poet died short of his final goal. On the other hand it is possible that he never intended to revise Do-Best, which, having been composed most recently, he might have felt to be less imperfect than the earlier parts of the poem, and that the apparently unfinished passages elsewhere are merely the result of impatience.

The evidence produced by this analysis of the revision is capable of being used to support either the single- or the multiple-authorship thesis, since it is conceivable that one who was not B would act in the way I have pictured C as acting. How probable it is that any man would undertake so great a labor with a poem not his own will remain a matter of opinion. It is not, perhaps, unprecedented. But in any case the analysis indicates that the C-reviser, whoever he was, conducted his revision according to a plan that required on his part not only a great love for the poem but a deep understanding of it—deep enough, certainly, so that we should pause before adjudging him guilty of misunderstanding or misusing through stupidity his original. Furthermore, the plan seems both intelligible and intelligent. The most likely person to have made the plan is the poet of B.

3. *Numbering of the Passus*

One of the greatest difficulties encountered in making a comparative study of *Piers Plowman* is the variation among the three texts in the numbering of the passus. Part of the trouble is due to the fact that Skeat printed his C-text from MS P, which, along with all other MSS of the "p"-group, begins the poem with Passus i, while A and B begin

1. With considerable understatement Wells, *PMLA*, xliv, 138, remarks that Do-Well is "the only part of the second half of the poem difficult to follow."

2. See p. 2, n. 8 for the pertinent studies.

3. Because the changes in the religious allegory of Do-Well and Do-Bet in C are so far-reaching, I cannot agree with Chambers' suggestion (*Mind,* p. 167) that the C-poet had "no idea of superseding his earlier work."

it with the Prologue. That this was not the C-poet's intention has been demonstrated by Carnegy,[4] who makes it clear that all MSS of the "i"-group, representing a better MS tradition than "p," agree in heading Skeat's Passus III with the words *Passus Secundus* and that all but one (MS I) call Skeat's second passus *Passus Primus*.[5] It is thus certain that Skeat's Passus I was at one time the Prologue. The confusion in the "p"-group seems to have arisen from the fact that in the earlier MSS of C the first section of the poem was, probably accidentally, left unlabeled. Hence some unwary "p"-scribe, thumbing through to find out what the sections were called and finding them called passus, naturally entitled the first section *Passus Primus* and, being stubborn as well as unwary, he continued with that system of numeration regardless of subsequent developments in his original. The scribe of "i," more honest or more absent-minded than the "p"-scribe, resumed his original's numeration with Skeat's Passus II, though the scribe of MS I does not seem to have caught on until Skeat's Passus III, thereby getting two passus headed *Secundus*. A new edition of C, based on one of the "i"-MSS, would restore a certain amount of harmony that is now lacking by restoring the Prologue.[6]

The remaining changes we must attribute to the reviser himself. The first of these, a reasonable one, takes place in what was originally Passus v of the B-text. In A this passus contains the short sermon of Conscience that precedes the confessions of the Deadly Sins (of which there are six in A), as well as that of Robert the Robber: A, v thus contains 263 lines. In B, Passus v there are included the sermon (now delivered by Reason), somewhat elongated, eight confessions (Wrath's is added), of which Avarice's and Sloth's are greatly expanded, and the action of the whole subsequent passus in A (A, vi), which deals with the preliminaries of the pilgrimage to Truth: B, v thus contains 651 lines. C, vi opens with the long autobiographical passage,[7] proceeds with Reason's sermon expanded by an intrusion from B, x, and breaks off after extending over 250 lines. C's next passus (C, vii) contains the confessions of six of the sins and those of Robert and of the strange Welshman, Ӡevan Ӡield-Aӡain. Having attained 441 lines, the passus rather surprisingly ends, Sloth's confession being postponed until the next. This (C, viii) con-

---

4. *Op. cit.*, pp. 23–5.

5. MS X, which was not known to Carnegy, agrees with the majority of the "i"-group MSS.

6. C has sometimes been blamed for the errors of his scribes. Hall charges that in omitting the title "Prologue" C made "a needless and vexatious alteration of arrangement." *MLR*, IV, 10. Even if it had been made by the C-poet, instead of his scribes, the change is vexatious only if one is reading several texts simultaneously, as one was never intended to do.

7. It is interesting that, as a general rule, both in B and in C the poet talks about himself only at the beginning of a passus. The chief exceptions are C, XII, 163–203, C, XXIII, 183–213, and B, XX, 182–212.

tains in addition the preliminaries of the pilgrimage. In this way C takes three passus to cover the action included by B in one.

Of the three arrangements, A's is by far the best, inasmuch as it divides where the action indicates that division is requisite. B seems to have considered matters more broadly, feeling that not only the confessions but also the pilgrimage, at least in its earlier stages, were dependent on Reason's sermon. Accordingly he grouped all three elements together, thereby achieving the longest passus in any version of the poem. It is possible that C originally intended to divide B's long passus into two. Exclusive of the autobiographical passage, which was probably added later, C's revision of the material in B, v extends to 840 lines. The first 420 of these describe Reason's sermon, the confessions of Pride, Envy, Wrath, Lechery, and Avarice, as well as those of Ʒevan and Robert, and conclude with a nineteen-line speech by Repentance. C's invention of Ʒevan, his transfer of Robert's confession to this place, and his expansion of Repentance's speech[8] suggest that he intended to end a passus here, since the three elements together form a perceptible pause in the action. The following passus would then have gone on with the confessions of Gluttony and Sloth and the initiation of the pilgrimage. But if one adds the autobiographical passage to the first of these hypothetical passus, the result will be an increase making a total of 530 lines—a length that C consistently tries to avoid. Because of this he seems to have compromised by terminating one passus at a logical point of division at the end of Reason's sermon and the other, less suitably, before the seventh Deadly Sin. Sloth's confession was decapitated from the main body of the confessions probably because to include it with them would have had the effect of lengthening C, VII to more than five hundred lines, while reducing C, VIII to less than two hundred. C was apparently more willing than B to interrupt the progress of the narrative in order to allow for the reader's convenience. Only in one passus—C, IV, which contains the speech on *mede* and *mercede* that was probably an afterthought—does he attain the length of five hundred lines. In three others (VII, XXI, and the unrevised XXII) he exceeds four hundred. B, on the other hand, twice goes over six hundred (v and xv) and five times over four hundred (x, xi, xiii, xviii, and xix).[9]

Rejoining one another with the beginning of A, VII (B, VI, C, IX), all three texts remain together during the action of Piers's plowing and the discussion of the pardon. The two short passus that open the *Vita* in A and B (A, IX–X, B, VIII–IX), separated by only the slightest of breaks in the action, are made into one in C, XI, which thus assumes a length

---

8. For the transfers, see p. 25, n. 1, above. C, VI, 331–8 (the spark of fire in the Thames) is mostly new. Cf. B, v, 290–1.

9. The average length of A's passus (excluding XII) is 202 lines; B's, 345; C's 320. C's average deviation from this is 72 lines to B's 111.

normal to C—about three hundred lines. B, x exactly parallels A, xi and C, xii almost exactly parallels them both, though where B increased the length from A's 303 to some 470 lines, C reduced the size to approximately that of A. Passus xii of A—whatever part of it is authentic[1]—was largely ignored by B, who continued the poem in his own way with B, xi. Because of the transfer of material that C makes in order to introduce Recklessness at an earlier point,[2] C is able substantially to improve the division between B, x and xi (C, xii and xiii). C concludes his Passus xii with the Dreamer's abandonment of the search. In B this does not take place until after the first forty lines of Passus xi, so that the abandonment of the search and its resumption occur in such close juxtaposition as to lend little support to the Dreamer's assertion that he followed Fortune for more than forty years.[3] C splits B, xi into two, probably because his considerable addition of material on poverty and patience would have increased its size to nearly five hundred lines. The point of division is a rather curious one. Recklessness, during his long speech on patient poverty, devotes some lines to the perils of wealth, at the conclusion of which the passus ends. C, xiv begins with the exclamation, *Ac wel worth pouerte!* and the speech continues in the direction thus indicated. Although the break seems on the whole to have been one of convenience, C may have had some idea of increasing the emphasis on poverty by means of the opening exclamation—a sort of visual emphasis. C, xiv and B, xi terminate at the same point, immediately after the appearance of Imaginative, a natural point of cleavage.

B's three subsequent passus (xiii–xv) are well bounded. The first treats the banquet at Clergy's house and the confession of Hawkin, the second the conversation between Hawkin, Patience, and Conscience, and the third the Dreamer's conversation with Anima, which takes place after a waking interval. Since he omits Hawkin's confession, C requires only about half as many lines as B for the action of B, xiii. Hence he extends his passus (C, xvi) into the action of B, xiv, suddenly breaking off, after three hundred lines, in the middle of a speech by Patience which is continued in C, xvii. It is interesting, but possibly accidental, that C, xvii begins with a line complementary to the one which opens C, xiv,

---

1. I am disposed to believe the passus genuine through 98 (as numbered in *CP*, I, 326–31, which includes the lines from MS J not printed in *EETS*, I, 137*–41*; see *EETS*, IV, 857–9), at which point the person is changed from first to third. See *CP*, II, 165, n. to 99. For other suggestions, see Manly, *CHEL*, II, 25–6; Edith Rickert, "John But, Messenger and Maker," *MPh*, XI (1913–14), 107–16; Chambers, "The Original Form of the A-Text of 'Piers Plowman,'" *MLR*, VI (1911), 302–23, and *Essays and Studies*, IX, 54. The best survey of the possibilities is contained in Chambers' article in *MLR*, VI, 318–23.

2. B, XI, 1–35 is moved to C, XII, 163–97, a point just before B, X, 336. C, XII concludes with B, XI, 36–42 plus two lines summarizing the abandonment of the search. For the significance of Recklessness, see Chapter VI.

3. B, XI, 46.

Alas! þat richesse shal reue and robbe mannes soule.

This is, perhaps, another instance of eye-emphasis.

C, xvii continues well into the action of B, xv, a procedure that is made possible by C's omission of the Dreamer's waking interval, which provides the boundary between B, xiv and xv. For his next point of division C seizes upon a pause in Liberum Arbitrium's discourse (uttered by Anima in B) and begins Passus xviii with the Dreamer's statement that no man can get along without occasionally begging or borrowing. It is possible that this is still another instance of eye-emphasis, for C is constantly preoccupied with the problem of begging.[4] But if so, it is not a very good one and we may suppose that convenience was the main reason for the break: C had already extended the passus to 370 lines. C, xviii and B, xv terminate at the same point, the conclusion of the discourse of Liberum Arbitrium or Anima. The divisions of the remaining five passus are the same in both texts. Three of them are dictated by the Dreamer's awakening, while the fourth, that between B, xvi and xvii, C, xix and xx, seems to have been made for convenience rather than dictated by logic.

It appears from analysis that A's divisions are the most suitably managed of the three texts and display a nice conformity to the requirements of sense and comfort. B's divisions are in accordance with the natural pauses in the action of the poem but they show little regard for the reader, offering him as much as 650 lines at a sitting. C believed in compromise. He seems to have been more aware than B of the rights of the reader, even though to cater to them involved a violation of the rules of logic. On the whole, C's divisions are most reasonable where they follow the earlier texts. Unless we are willing to accept as legitimate the dubious device of eye-emphasis—a device which has the same general effect as eye-alliteration—C's breaks seem arbitrary and frequently without regard for the movement of the narrative. It will be observed that C departs farthest from B's points of division in those passus of the *Vita* where he is subjecting B to the most strenuous revision. This suggests that C at times lost all track of where B had begun or ended sections and that, after he had completed the labor of composition, he had to go back over his poem in order to mark out the boundaries. In so doing, he favored convenience over logical demands. The result, from the point of view of the literary critic, is something less than happy. But from the point of view of the reader, C's divisions are at least more considerate, not to say merciful, than B's.

C's preoccupation with the process of composition and his consequent neglect of more mechanical matters are in accord with other aspects of his revision, for he fairly often displays an inability to see the woods for

4. See Chapter V.

the trees. At the same time, this fault in C does not necessarily suggest a different mind from B's at work on the poem. The chief difference between B and C here lies in their attitude toward compromise. If C had been as uncompromising as B, the C-text would, like the B-text, have had a series of logically divided but disproportionate passus, ranging in length from one hundred lines to six hundred. Willingness to compromise was engendered in C, I suggest, by the fact that upon the completion of the B-text the poet found himself, probably somewhat to his own surprise, with a great many readers—many more than had been brought to him by the A-text. Hence he became reader-conscious, as the phrase is, and reader-consciousness is something that we shall see is characteristic of C in other respects, particularly manifested in his desire to render the broader implications of his poem unmistakable. So far as his method of composition, which ignored proportion, is concerned, this seems to be a development of a tendency which is apparent in B: a tendency to expand the incidents in various parts of the poem until they attained unruly length and overlaid natural points of cleavage, much as sedimentary deposits gradually obscure a fault in igneous rock—or, to change the simile, much as two snowballs, rolled together, become one snowball.[5] B's and C's common tendency to lose track of dividing lines is as natural in a poet as in nature herself.

4. *Alliteration*

In this section I shall consider briefly the alliteration of *Piers Plowman* from two points of view: first, the alliteration of each version of the poem in its relation to the other versions; second, the alliteration of the poem as a whole compared with that of its contemporaries.

That it is possible to consider the second of these aspects results from the fact that a consideration of the first reveals no important differences among the three texts. As in all Middle English alliterative poetry, the standard pattern for the line in *Piers Plowman* is *aaax,* exemplified in B, Prologue, 14,

I seigh a *t*oure on a *t*oft *t*rielich y*m*aked.

According to Oakden's tabulation[6], 65.2 per cent of A's lines, 70.3 per cent of B's, and 72.1 per cent of C's are of this pattern. This indicates a slightly greater regularity on the part of C than of A and B, though the difference between B and C is hardly impressive. In regard to irregular line-patterns, the figures are even closer, with C showing throughout

5. When the snowball becomes too large, it breaks apart not always at the original point of juncture. Thus after B had made one passus of A, v and vi and C had added to it, C's passus broke into three parts, but not at the point of division in A.

6. J. P. Oakden, *Alliterative Poetry in Middle English* (Manchester, 1930-35, 2 vols.), I, 186.

fewer examples of irregularity than A and B.[7] The greatest discrepancy among the texts in irregular patterns amounts to something less than 3 per cent and in most cases the difference is less than 1 per cent.[8] Furthermore, in every case A and C form the extremes and B the mean in the sequence, so that C is always closer to B than it is to A.[9] It is probable, indeed, that the number of discrepancies is, because of the corruption of the MSS, incorrectly represented for A and B. But while this is so, the error tends toward exaggeration of discrepancies, so that texts more faithful than we now have would display a greater degree of similarity to one another.[1] But in any case, the tendency seems to be toward greater regularity from A to C, a tendency perfectly natural in one poet.

A study of the alliteration of the texts by Miss Deakin reveals the same harmony as Oakden's.[2] Miss Deakin's purpose was to test the validity of Manly's multiple-authorship theory and hence she adopted a system of division like that which Manly had proposed: A1 (Prologue through VIII, 134), A2 (VIII, 135 through XII, 56), B, and C, the last being divided into two parts—the C-text excluding its long additions and the C-text represented by the long additions. This last division gives us, for C, a means of verifying Oakden's figures, for it is possible to argue that his treatment of C as a whole might not give proper importance to the mannerisms introduced by C in the parts where he is not following B's lead. But it appears that C2, writing without a model, acted just as C1 did, revising or retaining old material. On the whole, Miss Deakin's statistics indicate that no irregularities were introduced by the later revisions which were not present in the A-text[3]—or at least in A1. A2 is too short a sample to provide a base for reliable statistics. Moreover, irregularities exist in much the same ratio in the three major divisions,

7. *Idem*, pp. 186–7.

8. *Ibid.* Of the pattern *aaxx* A has 4.5%; B, 3.4%; C, 2.1%. Of complex patterns such as *aabab* A has 2.42%; B, 1.2%; C, .7%. In all other cases the differences are less than 1%.

9. This is true in every one of the thirteen types of line analyzed by Oakden, although there are several types in which B and C or A and B have the same percentage. Oakden's figure for C in nonalliterative lines (the fourteenth type) includes the unfinished passage C, I, 107–24, which gives C the highest percentage of the three texts: .9 to A's .8 and B's .7.

1. Oakden's statistics are, apparently, based upon Skeat's texts with no attempt at correction from variant readings. Because of this, it is important to remember that they cannot be considered even as accurate as it is now possible, by consulting MS T's A-text readings, to make them. Complete accuracy can be attained only when we have discovered a better B-MS than is known to exist, or when we have brought into being a critical B-text. It is likely that Oakden's statistics err in emphasizing discrepancies between the texts, rather than similarities. This is true because the scribe of MS V (Skeat's A-text) spoils good alliteration more often than he improves bad, and because, as may be seen from Appendix B, the scribe of the B-archetype had the same habit as the scribe of V.

2. Mary Deakin, "The Alliteration of 'Piers Plowman,'" *MLR*, IV (1908–9), 478–83.

3. Miss Deakin also relied largely on Skeat's texts, although she made some correction from MS T. She does not give complete statistics for each line-pattern, but the following is typical: *aaaxx*, A1, 8.04%, A2, 8.58%, B, 8.73%, C1, 8.63%, C2, 8.92%. See *MLR*, IV, 479.

A1, B, and C. Miss Deakin justly concluded that there was no evidence in the alliteration to support Manly's theory.

An examination of a different sort led Miss Day to the opposite conclusion,[4] namely, that there were concerned in *Piers Plowman* not only the four poets plus John But that Manly suggested but a total of five poets plus But. Miss Day divided the poem into A1 (Prologue through VIII), A2 (IX through XII, 55), B1 (Prologue through X), B2 (XI–XX), and C, but confined her listing of lines appearing in several texts to the first text in which they appear. Examining the alliteration of unstressed words and syllables such as prepositions, conjunctions, and prefixes, she was able to find a number of discrepancies among the five divisions.[5] Her conclusions, however, as Chambers and Grattan have shown in an amusing *reductio ad absurdum*,[6] are almost altogether vitiated by the fact that the five divisions are of such varying length as to lend themselves to no accurate statistical comparison. Further, by treating the poem in short units of equal length in order to equalize the samples it is possible for one to discover the presence of at least seven hands.[7] The most striking of Miss Day's discrepancies, moreover, exists between the two parts of B, so that if any section is to be attributed to an independent poet, it is B2.[8] Yet there had never been any previous suggestion that the whole B-text was not the work of one man. Actually, it is fair to say that so far as the old divisions A, B, and C are concerned (and even A1 and A2), Miss Day's study bears out what we have already seen in the statistics of Oakden and Miss Deakin. Before we can accept Miss Day's evidence of alliterative variation among the parts of the poem, some one must develop a theory about the dual authorship of B, so that we can make use of the most impressive discrepancy Miss Day has discovered. No one pretends that tests by alliteration are conclusive in themselves.

We have seen from Oakden's statistics that C tends to cling to the regular alliterative pattern *aaax* more firmly than A or B. This regularity was noticed first by Rosenthal,[9] and then by Manly,[1] who at-

---

4. *MLR* XVII, 403–09.

5. I list here some of Miss Day's findings. Alliteration on *and*: A1 (1), B1 (1), B2 (7), C (1), not in A2; *before*: A1 (2), B2 (4), C (5), not in A2, B1; *but*: B1 (2), B2 (7), C (4), not in A1, A2; *for*: A1 (10), B1 (1), B2 (15), C (12), not in A2; *from*: A1 (3), B2 (2), C (5), not in A2, B1; *save*: B2 (4), not in others; *to*: A1 (2), A2 (4), B2 (11), C (5), not in B1; *while*: A1 (3), A2 (1?), not in others; *with*: A1 (7), A2 (1), B1 (12), B2 (19), C (8). This is about what one would expect from samples of such unequal lengths: A1, 1,833 lines; A2, 751; B1, 1,100–1,200; B2, 4,035; C, 2,000.

6. *MLR*, XXVI, 44–9.   7. *Idem*, p. 46.

8. A1, A2, B1, and C resemble each other much more closely than any of them does B2, but then B2 is from two to five and a half times longer than the others.

9. F. Rosenthal, "Die Alliterierende englische Langzeile im 14. Jahrhundert," *Anglia*, I (1878), 447. I have not made greater use of Rosenthal's study because his statistics are rendered invalid by his failure to recognize that the alliteration might fall on unstressed syllables.

1. *CHEL*, II, 35.

tributed some of C's revisions to the desire to attain it. It was likewise noticed by Miss Deakin,[2] and more recently by Miss Day,[3] who makes considerable use of the point in her attack on the single-authorship theory: "C is certainly more particular than is B to have regular alliteration of the form *aaax*, and continually emends for this purpose."[4] In a discussion of some fifty single-line revisions, Miss Day attributes this purpose to C in at least eleven instances, in several of which he is seen "spoiling" the sense of B in order to attain regular alliteration.[5] From this one is apt to get the impression that C was a sort of misguided technician who went through the B-text with an eye blind to everything but irregularities, like an early eighteenth-century scholar reading Chaucer, or like Tottel correcting Wyatt. Since no one has troubled to correct this impression, I should like to devote a paragraph or two to the subject of C as a metrical technician.

First of all, a word about the B-continuation and its parallel in C. Because our B-MSS are at best faulty reproductions of the B-poet's original, this territory becomes a sort of no-man's land of research. There are—particularly in the last five passus—a good many lines where C has correct alliteration and B incorrect.[6] How many of these we can attribute to the corruption of the B-text we do not know—possibly a large number may reasonably be so explained. On the other hand, there are a good many lines that have more regular alliteration in B than they do in C. We have the choice of attributing these to efforts of the scribe of the B-archetype to improve what was originally faulty, to revisions by C in the opposite direction from what we are led to expect, or to corruption in the C-MSS.[7] Despite the uncertainty, we may safely say this: even if we assume that B and C are uncorrupted texts, or corrupted to an equal extent, the discrepancies between them in the matter of *aaax* alliteration will be found not to exceed the less than 2 per cent margin indicated by Oakden's figures; and if we assume, as we have reason to do, that more of the irregularities in B than in C are the result of scribal interference, the margin will become even less.

Let us now turn to that part of the poem where we may certify B's readings by means of the A-text. An examination of the lines which have much the same reading in A and B discloses a total of fifty-two AB-lines with irregular alliteration. C was therefore offered fifty-two opportunities to express his putative interest in achieving regular alliteration of the pattern *aaax*. On exactly twenty occasions he seized the

2. *MLR*, IV, 482; but see p. 41, n. 3, below.
3. *MLR*, XXIII, 7–18, *passim*.   4. *Idem*, p. 7.
5. See her discussion of revisions (1), (3), (5), (11). (25), (32), (35), (36), (43), (48), and (49).
6. See Appendix B for examples from the last two passus.
7. One line which the C-scribes may have altered to improve the alliteration is discussed in Appendix B, pp. 243 f.

opportunity and produced the expected pattern.[8] On thirty-two occasions, however—more than 60 per cent of the total—he neglected to regularize.[9] Sometimes, indeed, he revised without achieving the pattern *aaax* and sometimes he accepted the AB-reading just as it stood. That he was not overwhelmed by respect for the AB-tradition, or for regular alliteration, is indicated by the additional fact that he revised in such a way as to achieve irregular alliteration in eighteen lines that were perfectly regular in A and B.[1] In short, so far as alliteration is concerned, C worked both ways. It follows that his subservience to the regular pattern *aaax* has been seriously exaggerated.[2]

The evidence produced by a comparison of the alliteration of the three texts leads us, then, toward the following conclusion. Since C as a whole shows a slightly larger percentage of regular lines than A or B, he may be said to have been slightly more careful about his alliteration than they. Yet so slight is the improvement in C as compared to B, even on the basis of the texts as they appear in Skeat, that we can hardly say that a picayune interest in regularization of alliteration was one of the compelling motives for the C-revision.[3] Nor can we say that C shows any individualities in his use of alliterative patterns that suggest that he was a different poet from A or B. Rather, the evidence points the other way.

It would be strange, however, if a poem written and rewritten by one man over a long period of years displayed no development whatsoever in poetic technique. Such a development is visible in *Piers Plowman* in the alliteration of unstressed syllables (i.e., C, VIII, 308: *Þat myght folwen ous ech fot for drede of mys-tornynge,* where the stress falls upon the preposition *for*). Miss Deakin observes that this practice is not common at the beginning of A, "but it increases in frequency with remarkable steadiness throughout the whole of A, only pulling up a little now and then at the beginning of a Passus."[4] The phenomenon continues on an increasing scale throughout B and C until, as Miss Deakin says, in the C-additions the relation between alliteration and stress is sometimes so obscured that "one pauses to consider whether a line shall be held to be

8. C, II, 18, 23, 40, 48, 64?; IV, 10–11, 53–4, 286; V, 62, 87; VI, 160; VII, 89, 171–2, 218, 328; VIII, 280; IX, 78; X, 60?, 185; XI, 303. Double lines represent revision of but one line in AB. For the parallel lines in AB, I refer the reader to Skeat's *CP* edition.

9. C, I, 80; II, 196; III, 227; IV, 223, 271, 437?; V, 107; VI, 109, 117; VII, 224, 229, 320, 377; VIII, 188, 200, 218?, 279; IX, 51, 60, 95, 110, 291, 332; X, 23, 289, 320; XI, 35, 70, 72, 129; XII, 105, 110. In the parallels of some of the lines cited here A and B do not agree exactly, but they do agree in not having alliteration *aaax*.

1. C, II, 46?, 55; III, 12; IV, 30, 122, 274; VI, 201; VIII, 222; IX, 167, 209, 221; X, 41, 321; XI, 7; XII, 17, 33, 93, 127.

2. Miss Day, *MLR*, XXIII, 7, suggests that C revised AB, Pro., 34, *And geten gold with here glee (not) synneles, I leue,* because he had "defective alliteration before him." But in five lines cited in the notes above (C, I, 80, II, 55, V, 107, VI, 109, and IX, 332), C has retained, or obtained by revision, the pattern *aaaxx* seen in AB, Pro., 34.

3. Cf. Miss Deakin, *MLR*, IV, 482, "While the poet revised and amended former incorrect lines, he wrote many new lines containing the old errors."

4. *MLR*, IV, 482.

without alliteration, so inconspicuous are the rhyme-letters."[5] The development in C is accompanied by an enlargement of the *senkung* or thesis, "so that there are more words in the line, which, once we grant that the alliteration need not always coincide with the chief stress, makes the task of finding suitable words much easier."[6]

I suppose it is this enlargement of the thesis that every one notices first upon reading the C-text. The reader has but to glance at Skeat's parallel-texts edition to see how much longer the lines are in the C-additions than in A and the first part of B.[7] The development suggests to me an analagous development in Shakespeare's technique—the correct, end-stopped lines of *Love's Labour's Lost* compared with the hypercatalectic, run-on lines of *Antony and Cleopatra*.[8] In the work both of the fourteenth-century poet and of the Elizabethan one can trace a mounting ascendancy of idea over form. It was Miss Deakin who first brought this development to notice and I shall close this part of the discussion with a final quotation from her interesting study:

Never primarily concerned with form, it was most natural that, as the years went by and he [the poet] grew graver and still more concerned with moral ideas, he should care less and less about metrical effect, though long habit and the continual presence of the poem in his mind and before his eyes would prevent technical matters being neglected to any very serious extent.[9]

One might say, both a better and a worse poet.

I shall consider now the alliteration of *Piers Plowman* as a whole in comparison with other poems of the alliterative school. From Oakden's study, as well as from that of Karl Schumacher,[1] it is possible to get a good idea of the position of our poem in relation to its contemporaries. If it could be shown that *Piers Plowman,* in whole or in part, exhibited nothing individual in its technique—that its alliteration represented a sort of norm for the period—then one might reasonably assume that it was the work of a number of poets possessed of a readily obtainable bag of poetic tricks. Yet the fact is that in alliteration *Piers Plowman* resembles closely none of the other poems of the period. Or, to put it

5. *Ibid.*

6. *Idem*, p. 483. This does not altogether accord with Miss Day's statement, *MLR*, XVII, 404, that "the alliteration of prepositions, etc. [unstressed words and syllables] is a much more marked feature of B2, and after it of A1 and C, than of A2 and B1." The difference is probably the result of the different methods of dividing the poem.

7. Cf. A, XI, 209, *A ledere of louedayes and a lond biggere*, with C, XVII, 146 (B, XIV, 308), *He tempreþ hus tonge to-treuthe-ward þat no tresour coueyteþ*. The first line seems to me characteristic of A and the early part of B; the second, of the later part of B and of C.

8. See the comparison of *Julius Caesar,* I, i, 40–55 with *Coriolanus* II, i, 224–40 in Tucker Brooke, *Shakespeare of Stratford* (New Haven, 1926), pp. 124–6.

9. *MLR,* IV, 483.

1. *Studien über den Stabreim in der mittelenglischen Alliterationsdichtung* (Bonn, 1914).

another way, in alliteration the three versions of *Piers Plowman* re-semble closely nothing but each other. A few glances at the studies mentioned will bear this out.

In the first place, let us take for comparison with our poem nineteen of those twenty other poems which form the bulk of the alliterative corpus.[2] The normal pattern for them all is *aaax* and, as we have seen, *Piers Plowman* displays this in 65 to 72 per cent of all its lines. In this it distinguishes itself sharply from seven poems that display a much larger percentage of regularity: the three *Alexander*'s (90.4 per cent for *A*, 96 per cent for *B*, and 86.61 per cent for the *Wars*); the *Parliament of the Three Ages* (84.9 per cent); *Winner and Waster* (90 per cent); the *Destruction of Troy* (99.9 per cent); and the *Siege of Jerusalem* (86.1 per cent).[3] On the other hand, *Piers Plowman* is distinguished from two poems in having a far larger percentage of *aaax* lines than they: *Joseph of Arimathaea* (9 per cent) and *Chevelere Assigne* (12.2 per cent).[4] In *Piers* the use of the same alliterative letter for two or more consecutive lines is rare but in the following six poems it is fairly common: *Morte Arthur* (eighty-six examples in 200 lines); *Patience* (about 15 per cent of the lines are linked); *purity* (about 10 per cent); *Gawain* (about 10 per cent of the long alliterative lines); *Piers Plowman's Creed* (about 10 per cent); and the *Crowned King* (about 24 per cent).[5] We are left with four poems that we may compare with *Piers Plowman: William of Palerne, Death and Life, Scottish Field,* and *St. Erkenwald.* The last of these, however, may perhaps be disqualified from comparison because only 1.43 per cent of its lines show vowel alliteration, while in *Piers Plowman* this occurs in 3.6 to 3.9 per cent of the lines.[6] In *Piers* rather few of the vowel-alliterating lines preserve the same rhyme-letter throughout the line but in *William of Palerne,* on the other hand, 64 per cent of the vowel-alliterating lines keep the same rhyme-letter.[7] Hence we are left with only two short poems that bear a marked resemblance to *Piers Plowman* and they are not long enough to afford a fair sample. We might observe, moreover, that *Piers*'s common habit of rhyming *h* with a vowel is not instanced in *Death and Life* and is doubtful in *Scottish Field.*[8]

2. *Alexander A, Alexander B, Parliament of Three Ages, Winner and Waster, William of Palerne, Joseph of Arimathaea, Chevelere Assigne, Morte Arthur, Destruction of Troy, Siege of Jerusalem, Sir Gawain and the Green Knight, Purity, Patience, St. Erkenwald, Piers Plowman's Creed, Wars of Alexander, Death and Life, Crowned King,* and *Scottish Field.* The twentieth poem, *Mum and the Sothsegger (Richard the Redeless),* is discussed below.

3. Oakden, *op. cit.,* I, 168–9.   4. *Idem,* p. 168.   5. *Idem,* pp. 156–7.

6. *Idem,* p. 159. Schumacher, *op. cit.,* p. 49, credits *Erkenwald* with 1.13%.

7. Schumacher, *op. cit.,* p. 55. No percentage is given for *Piers Plowman,* but the incomplete list of vowel-alliterating lines in the poem made by John Lawrence, *Chapters on Alliterative Verse* (London, 1893), pp. 99–104, indicates that about 4% of them keep the same letter for all the rhyme-words.

8. Schumacher, *op. cit.,* pp. 93–4.

This process of elimination is, I admit, something of a *tour de force,* and I should hesitate to employ it were it not that the impression one receives from reading the other alliterative poems enforces the difference between them and *Piers Plowman.* If, as we have done hitherto, we exclude *Mum and the Sothsegger* (*Richard the Redeless*), we shall find that on the evidence of the various tests *Piers* shares more alliterative practices with *William of Palerne, Morte Arthur,* and the *Gawain* group than with the other long poems. Yet a reading of the pieces most similar to *Piers* shows clearly how distinct their techniques are. The *Morte Arthur,* wherein the tendency to place the rhyme on stout, muscular words produces a sort of dinging effect that contributes materially to the martial spirit of the poem, leaves an impression altogether unlike that of *Piers.* Equally unlike, in the opposite direction, is the technique of *William of Palerne,* whose author frequently went in for repetitive, jingling effects. And the *Gawain* poet seems to have shaped each line with the full measure of his considerable craftsmanship, while in *Piers* one feels that the alliteration of the line was often left to shift for itself by a poet intent solely on the intellectual content of the passage—although, of course, we have but to read the opening lines to realize that he was a master of his form when he wanted to be. Nevertheless, we are apt to feel that the poet of *Patience* was willing to shape his subject to fit the requirements of his form, while the poet of A, B, and C regarded his form merely as a way of getting said something he had to say.

Particularly interesting is the contrast with *Piers* afforded by the alliteration of *Mum and the Sothsegger,* or, as it was formerly called, *Richard the Redeless.*[9] In many respects this is a close imitation of *Piers Plowman* and it succeeded in persuading Skeat that it was the work of the same poet.[1] So far as its alliteration is concerned, Skeat noticed that it shared with *Piers* a disregard for certain of the normal rules and also, contrary to most of the other Middle English alliterative poetry, the practice of rhyming *f* with *v.*[2] Nevertheless, later analyses of the two poems reveal almost irreconcilable discrepancies in alliterative technique. Schumacher shows that in *Richard* (*Mum* was unknown to him) over 44 per cent of the vowel-alliterating lines preserve the same rhyme-letter

9. *Richard the Redeless* was edited by Skeats in EETS, 54 (*EETS,* III, 469–521) with the C-text of *Piers Plowman.* A fragment, apparently another part of the same poem, came to light in 1928 and has been edited, along with a re-edition of *Richard,* under the title *Mum and the Sothsegger* by Mabel Day and Robert Steele, EETS, 199 (London, 1936 for 1934).

1. *EETS,* III, cvii–cxix. There were, of course, more cogent reasons than the alliteration that led to Skeat's opinion. Particularly striking are the similarities in vocabulary. See Day and Steele, eds., *op. cit.,* pp. xiv–xv and notes, *passim.*

2. *EETS,* III, cxiii–cxv. The *f-v* combination is seen in lines where an original Old English initial *f,* having become voiced in certain dialect areas, is rhymed with initial *v* in Romance words: C, II, 23, *The ferst of þo ys fode, and vesture þe secounde.* See p. 46, n. 1, below.

throughout the line, while, as we have seen, this is rare in *Piers*.[3] More-over, Oakden and the editors of *Mum* have counted in the two fragments over a hundred instances of consecutive lines rhyming on the same letter, another device seldom encountered in *Piers*.[4] We are not, of course, interested here in showing that *Piers* and *Mum* had different authors, but it is important to observe that a poem which is an obvious imitation, or derivative, of *Piers Plowman* and sufficiently like it to have fooled a great student of alliterative poetry does not, when examined closely, support the illusion. The poet of *Mum*—if we suppose him to have been making a conscious imitation—has caught many of the peculiarities of his original. But he has caught some which were not in his original and given himself away. *Mum*, like most poems of the period, resembles *Piers* in certain aspects of its alliteration but not in the precise combina-tion of aspects in which A resembles B and B resembles C. The fact remains that the three versions of *Piers Plowman* are, in respect to alliteration, much closer to each other than they are to any other poems of the period.[5]

Assuming for a moment that *Piers Plowman* was the work of several authors, we must wonder at their extraordinary cleverness in catching so justly the alliterative tricks of their original. The artifice is, indeed, such as to put them in the class of very expert literary forgers. Take the matter of *f-v* rhymes, for instance. It can, I believe, be assumed that this device was consciously adopted by the hypothetical revisers from their originals, since, as Chambers has pointed out, it is not likely that there would be four different poets concerned successively in the same poem, all having come naturally by the same provincial dialect peculiarities and all having lived in London long enough for their residence to affect their thought and language.[6] Yet these imitators calculated with great care their use of the *f-v* rhyme, which is a provincial characteristic met with in *Mum* but only sporadically, if at all, in the rest of the alliterative corpus.[7] In A

3. Schumacher, *op. cit.*, p. 55.
4. Day and Steele, *op. cit.*, p. xliii; Oakden, *op. cit.*, I, 156.
5. It might be pointed out that the alliterative discrepancies between A, B, and C are fewer than those between the two fragments of *Mum*, where there is a difference of 8% in the lines of the pattern *aaax*. In *Piers*, the greatest difference is less than 7% (between A and C). Yet there is very good evidence that the two fragments of *Mum* are of the same authorship.
6. Chambers, "The Three Texts of 'Piers Plowman,' and Their Grammatical Forms," *MLR*, XIV (1919), 129–51. Chambers deals especially with the problem of *ben-arn*, *kirk-church*, and *heo-she*, and shows clearly that both forms of such doublets are used in all parts of the poem.
7. Aside from *Piers* and *Mum*, where the *f-v* rhyme is common, the combination occurs, or seems to occur, only in *Winner and Waster* (1), *William of Palerne* (2), *Alexander A* (1), *Joseph of Arimathaea* (2), *Gawain* (2), *Purity* (1), *Patience* (1), *St. Erkenwald* (1), *Siege of Jerusalem* (1), *Morte Arthur* (3), and *Thomas à Becket* (1). Many of these are extremely doubtful; see Schumacher, *op. cit.*, pp. 62–8, who, possibly too skeptically, refuses to allow any but the instances in *William of Palerne*, which he calls "zweifelhaft." *Idem*, p. 212.

I have counted nine uses of it (eight in A1, one in A2) ; in B, thirty-seven uses; and in C, thirty-nine.[8] B is almost three times as long as A : the rhyme occurs slightly over four times as often. C is a little longer than B : the rhyme occurs just twice more than in B.[9] It seems that our revisers must have calculated in advance the number of lines in which they would have to use the *f-v* rhyme in order to preserve the illusion of single authorship. As a calculator, C proves the most accurate, for, while omitting a number of lines in which the rhyme occurred in B, he added an equal number to make up the difference. C was indeed a clever forger.[1]

To sum up : a study of the alliteration of the three versions of *Piers Plowman* furnishes no evidence to support the theory of multiple authorship, while a comparison of the alliteration of *Piers Plowman* with that of contemporary poems suggests that the two later versions could have been written only by the original poet or by very assiduous imitators of him. Lacking, as we do, any examples in the fourteenth century of an imitator's going to an inordinate amount of trouble in order to obtain the dubious reward of anonymity while contributing to his original's reputation, we are led toward the conclusion that the three versions are the work of one poet.

8. The lists of *f-v* rhymes given by Skeat, *EETS*, III, cxiii–cxiv ; Rosenthal, *Anglia,* I, 442–4, 458; and Schumacher, *op. cit.,* pp. 65–6, are incomplete. I append a listing which I hope is more nearly exhaustive, though I have probably missed a few instances : A, Pro., 68, I, 23 (T), II, 155, III, 245, V, 218, 223, 230, VI, 14, IX, 70; B, Pro., 71, 103, 194, I, 23, II, 60, 76, 180, III, 258, V, 388, 404, 412, 416, 443, 450, 457, 530, VIII, 79, XIII, 330, XIV, 37, 79, XV, 60, 314, 367, 455, XVII, 287, XVIII, 94, 120, 152?, 153, 156, 367, XIX, 148, 308, 311 (in its original form), 417, 453, 477 ; C, I, 69, 131, II, 23, III, 61, 191, VI, 49, 58, VII, 35, 74, 433, 438, VIII, 13, 21, 25, 49, 57, 64, 168, X, 93, 232, XI, 77, XIV, 202, XVI, 8, XVII, 222, XVIII, 109, XIX, 89, XX, 269, XXI, 98, 125, 156, 158, 161, 414, XXII, 153, 313, 316, 421, 458, 482.

9. In A there is one instance for every 270 lines ; in B, one for every 196; in C, one for every 189. The slight increase in the later texts is due at least partly to the rhetorical repetition of lines or phrases within a passage. See C, XXI, 156, 158, 161.

1. It is, of course, barely possible that four separate poets might use the rhyme naturally. The area in which initial *f* was voiced covers an extensive territory in the south, and extends to the west. See Richard Jordan, *Handbuch der mittelenglischen Grammatik* (2d ed., Heidelberg, 1934), p. 189, n. ; Oakden, *op. cit.,* I, 29, and map facing p. 38; Samuel Moore, S. B. Meech, and Harold Whitehall, "Middle English Dialect Characteristics and Dialect Boundaries," *Essays and Studies in English and Comparative Literature, University of Michigan Publications, Language and Literature,* XIII (Ann Arbor, 1935), 15–16 and map. A spurious line added in MS E of the A-text rhymes *vicars-fele-fandyn.* See *EETS,* II, vi, n. On the other hand, the area is reduced by the fact that alliterative poetry was normally a product of the people of the west, not of the south. Furthermore, Moore, Meech, and Whitehall note that the voicing was only sporadic within the boundaries outlined—rare, that is, even where it was possible. Hence it is not likely that the revisers formed a little colony of *f*-voicing poets resident in London.

III

The Art of the C-Reviser

WE come now to a subject that lies near the very heart of the dispute about the authorship of the C-text of *Piers Plowman*—the art of the C-reviser. In this chapter the term *art* will be used to apply equally to C's poetic technique and to his narrative technique, for it is upon his sins—the word is convenient, though scarcely accurate—as a poet and storyteller that some of the most persuasive arguments against unity of authorship have been based. These sins are of the two usual sorts, sins of commission and sins of omission, the latter, rather surprisingly, having received the greater emphasis from those who believe that C was a different person from B. Their reasoning runs as follows: it is possible that an aging poet might experience such a diminution of creative power that his later work would suffer by comparison with his earlier, but it is not possible that any poet might experience such a metamorphosis that he would no longer recognize—and hence would be willing to condemn or alter—fine work that he wrought in his younger days. As I have indicated in my first chapter, the attack on the C-poet as a poet has been so telling that the defenders of unity have been driven from their front lines into a secondary position, from which they consider not the literary value of the C-text but the validity of the assertion that poets as good as B are incapable of spoiling their own work. It is my intention, in the present chapter, to return to the front lines.

Between the last and the earliest versions of *Piers Plowman,* differences in poetic and narrative technique do, certainly, exist, but whether these are of such a nature as to cause a general desertion of C is a question that ought to be reopened. In the following pages, therefore, I shall analyze a number of differences.[1] Since some of them may not have been noticed before, I shall at first confine myself to simple exposition, reserving for the end of the chapter my interpretation of the data. Several of C's idiosyncrasies do not, indeed, suggest to me any arguments either for or against unity of authorship, but they are included in the exposition because they are interesting in themselves or because they may, perhaps, contribute to the eventual solution of the problem of *Piers Plowman.* I shall start with illustrations of C's poetic technique and work gradually into the subject of his narrative method.

---

1. In my choice of examples I have tried, where minor points are involved, to adhere as closely as possible to passages where the reading of B may be certified by that of A, but any very close adherence of this sort would limit the discussion too narrowly.

In this discussion it is possible to begin at the beginning of the poem, inasmuch as a large number of the C-poet's mannerisms appear in his revision of the first lines of the Prologue. Moreover, his revision of this passage has received an extraordinarily—if not disproportionately— large share of comment in previous discussions.[2] Indeed, on the first sixteen of C's 7,350 lines have been based some of the most emphatic arguments for multiple authorship. Because of this let us examine the first lines of the poem as they appear in the various versions. A and B agree in opening the Prologue in this way:

> In a somer seson, when soft was the sonne,
> I shope me in shroudes, as I a shepe were,
> In habite as an heremite, vnholy of workes,
> Went wyde in þis world wondres to here.
> 5   Ac on a May mornynge on Maluerne hulles
> Me byfel a ferly, of fairy me thouȝte;
> I was wery forwandred and went me to reste
> Vnder a brode banke bi a bornes side,
> And as I lay and lened and loked in þe wateres,
> 10   I slombred in a slepyng, it sweyued so merye.
> Thanne gan I to meten a merueilouse sweuene,
> That I was in a wildernesse, wist I neuer where.

In his revision, C accepted the first four lines as they stand[3] but inserted after the fourth what has been called the "futile and pithless" line,[4]

> And sawe meny cellis and selcouthe þynges.

He then accepted AB, 5—the May morning on Malvern hills—but continued,

> Me byfel for to slepe for weyrynesse of wandryng;
> And in a launde as ich lay lenede ich and slepte,
> And Merueylously me mette, as ich may ȝow telle,

eliminating almost all the details of AB, 6–12, including bank, bourn, the waters and their merry sound, and the unknown wilderness in which the dream begins. A and B continue as follows (13–17):

> As I bihelde in-to þe est, on hiegh to þe sonne,
> I seigh a toure on a toft trielich ymaked;
> A depe dale binethe, a dongeon þere-Inne,

---

2. See Manly, *CHEL,* II, 38; *MPh,* VII, 131; Jusserand, *MPh,* VI, 316, *MPh,* VII, 293; Hall, *MLR,* IV, 4–5; Chambers and Grattan, *MLR,* XXVI, 10–11.

3. The apparent alterations in C, 1, 2 are scribal: see Appendix B, p. 234, n. 1. In judging C's style, one should not be influenced by the cumulative effect of dialectal differences between Skeat's C and Skeat's B, since in their original forms the two texts probably shared the same dialect, or rather dialect mixture. Note the following doublets, where Skeat's B generally uses the first form and his C the second: *I-ich, his-hus, hire-hure, or-other,* etc. See Chambers, *MLR,* XIV, 129–51.

4. Hall, *MLR,* IV, 7.

With depe dyches & derke and dredful of sight.
A faire felde ful of folke fonde I there bytwene.

C, not content with the simple presentation of the scene, "very unad-
visedly," according to Wright,[5] tells us that Truth was in the tower—
gives us, indeed, not only the scene but its significance (10–19):

> Al þe welþe of þis worlde & þe woo boþe,
> Wynkyng as it were wyterly ich saw hyt,
> Of tryuþe & of tricherye, of tresoun and of gyle,
> Al ich saw slepynge, as ich s하l gow telle.
> Esteward ich byhulde after þe sonne,
> And sawe a toure, as ich trowede, truthe was þer-ynne;
> Westwarde ich waitede in a whyle after,
> And sawe a deep dale; deþ, as ich lyuede,
> Wonede in þo wones, and wyckede spiritus.
> A fair feld, ful of folke, fonde ich þer bytwyne.

By the addition of material C complicates, to some extent, the poetic
approach which in A and B is completely straightforward. Furthermore,
if one is looking for minor discrepancies, one might observe that he gives
the reader information that he himself does not learn until later and then
only after he implores Lady Holy Church to explain the meaning of the
tower and dale. Yet here he distinctly says that he already knew about
these.[6] It was from C's revision of the opening lines that Manly drew
what is probably the most widely known of his arguments against the
unity of authorship. Comparing AB, 11–16 with C, 9–18, he complained
first that C had spoiled the picture, and then added, "The man who wrote
the former might, conceivably, in the decay of his faculties write a passage like the latter; but he could not, conceivably, have spoiled the former,
if he had ever been able to write it."[7]

In these opening lines of the poem the most conspicuous of C's alterations is that of AB, 6–12, the passage that in the earlier versions contains
the charming description of the surroundings among which the Dreamer
lies down to the first of his many naps. Grace is not a common characteristic of *Piers Plowman* in any of its forms, and the gracious, ingenuous
beginning of A and B cannot fail to delight the reader. Yet C's revision
destroys much of the charm. Whether it replaces it with anything as
valuable is a question that will be taken up later. Certainly on the evidence of this passage alone C seems to have had a curious lack of appreciation for a sort of poetry which, as it stood, would have satisfied
almost any other poet. One can scarcely avoid concluding that C, even
if he did not lack creative imagination, did lack that kind of imagination

---

5. *The Vision and Creed of Piers Ploughman*, ii, 505; also *The Gentleman's Magazine*
(April 1834), p. 390.
6. MS X has the present tense *leue* in C, I, 17, but the past *trowed* in 15.
7. *CHEL*, ii, 38.

which, passive in its possessor, is capable of appreciating the beauty of lines already in being. That is, even if it should be possible to find merit in what C substitutes for the omissions he makes, the omissions alone might mark him down as a poor literary critic. If, on the other hand, we agree with Hall that in the C-version of the beginning of the poem "we have exchanged poetry for mere verse,"[8] our condemnation will be so much the more severe.

The effect of this apparent deficiency in C's artistic judgment—"the reckless way," as Chambers and Grattan express it, "in which he para-phrases and alters the B-text, changing a fine line or passage into some-thing altogether worse"[9]—is evidenced in a number of types of revision, all of which are, however, closely related. Sometimes, as in the opening lines, the revision seems, at least at first glance, to be altogether wanton, prompted by no adequate poetic considerations but by sheer impatience to get on with the story. Other examples may readily be found. There is, for instance, the omission of Dame Study's amusing account of the hard and unprofitable sciences—astronomy, geometry, sorcery, alchemy, and the like;[1] the omission of the account of the Dreamer's warm reception by Clergy and Scripture;[2] and the omission of his waking interval, dur-ing which his wit "wex and wanyed," following the Hawkin incident.[3] But probably the best known of these omissions is that of the lines in B, xiv in which Anima prays for God's mercy upon the poor.[4]

At other times C's revision takes the form of a reworking in prosaic terms of an idea imaginatively expressed, as if the poet did not trust the reader to perceive the essential meaning through the veil of figurative language. Sometimes C seems to be intentionally removing naïve ex-pressions, even when these have a highly poetic effect. Rather more frequently, sharply phrased sentiments in B are altered by C into some-thing less biting, so that one is tempted, with Manly, to attribute to C a cautious nature.[5] Most frequently of all we observe C striving to moralize the effect of B's lines, a practice that goes beyond the limits of a dis-cussion of C's poetic technique into his narrative method. Accompanying the moralization is a strongly marked tendency to generalize the sig-nificance of his poem—again, predominantly a narrative technique that has, however, a decided effect on the expression. Elsewhere one may notice C's habit of repeating himself, something that seems at times to indicate negligence in revision and at others to betray a preoccupation, to the point of insistence, with certain favorite ideas. Closely associated with this is his fondness for one or two words or phrases that appear again and again. In the following pages will be given illustrations of the mannerisms mentioned in this paragraph and although each will be

8. *MLR*, iv, 4.
9. *MLR*, xxvi, 27.
1. B, x, 207–15.
2. B, x, 224–7.
3. B, xv, 1–10.
4. B, xiv, 174–80.
5. *CHEL*, ii, 36.

treated separately, the reader will observe that they are all so closely related that often what is true about one is true of the rest. Common to most of them is the replacement of figurative language by flat statement, an alteration that results in the C-text's appearing, at times, more philosophic than poetic.

Let us begin with an example that illustrates one of the most striking— and probably the most damaging—of C's traits. This consists in his reduction of an idea imaginatively expressed to prosaic terms, motivated, apparently, by distrust of the reader's intelligence. Lady Holy Church, speaking to the Dreamer about the comparative values of chastity and charity, says in A and B that a man who lacks charity is spiritually inadequate even though he is

> . . . as chaste as a childe þat in cherche wepeth.[6]

What one might call the unexpected relevance of the figure which symbolizes innocence as a child crying in church is irresistibly appealing to the imagination, particularly in an era, like our own, which sets a high value upon the unexpected. Yet the simile evidently troubled C. Perhaps he felt that the reader might not recognize the poetic relevance of the weeping child. Perhaps he was afraid that some one might feel that a child crying in church was a very naughty child indeed and not at all a fit symbol of chastity. In any case, he revised,

> . . . as chast as a chyld þat noþer chit ne fyghteþ,[7]

substituting an indisputably good child, the pride of his parents and Sunday-school teacher. At the same time, of course, he destroyed the essential poetry of the line, replacing a clear, direct image with one less immediate.

The elimination of vivid visual images is rather characteristic of C. Sometimes it appears in the revision of passages which in B are purely descriptive. Thus the earlier text pictures the gorgeous Lady Meed in some detail:

> Fetislich hir fyngres were fretted with gold wyre,
> And þere-on red rubyes, as red as any glede,
> And diamantz of derrest pris, and double manere safferes,
> Orientales and ewages, enuenymes to destroye.
> Hire robe was ful riche, of red scarlet engreyned,
> With ribanes of red golde and of riche stones;
> Hire arraye me rauysshed, suche ricchesse saw I neuere.[8]

With this description, which might have been that of the heroine of any contemporary romance, C was impatient. He altered:

6. B, I, 178 (A, I, 154).

7. C, II, 177. Miss Day, *MLR*, XXIII, 6, uses this line as an illustration of C's tendency to "flatten his original."

8. B, II, 11–17. A, II, 11–14 gives a shorter, less circumstantial description.

> On alle hure fyue fyngres rycheliche yrynged,
> And þer-on rede rubies and oþer riche stones.
> Hure robe was ryccher þan ich rede couthe,
> For to telle of hure atyre no tyme haue ich nouth.
> Hure a-raye with hure rychesse rauesshede myn herte.[9]

Here it is evident that C is reluctant to linger over the detail of B's description. Adding, perhaps, more sincerity to two conventional excuses than usually accompanies them, he pleads both lack of time and lack of ability in order to hurry on. The main point, Meed's wealth, is emphasized by the four occurrences of the word *rich* (*richly, richer, richness*) and by the summary line, which describes the lady's effect on the Dreamer more succinctly than does B. This impatience with the physical detail appears even in so small a point as the revision of a half-line. Thus B describes the costume of a doctor of medicine as a

> . . . cloke of calabre with alle þe knappes of golde.[1]

But C changes it so that the golden buttons disappear entirely.

Rather more significant is C's impatience with B's description of the appearance of Envy, a passage that has more relevance to the allegory than does the detail of Meed's clothing. The reader will remember B's brilliant portrayal:

> He was pale as a pelet, in þe palsye he semed,
> And clothed in a caurimaury, I couthe it nouȝte discreue;
> In kirtel and kourteby and a knyf bi his syde,
> Of a freres frokke were þe forsleues.
> And as a leke hadde yleye longe in þe sonne,
> So loked he with lene chekes, lourynge foule.[2]

C took literally, applying it to himself, B's modest if conventional disclaimer of descriptive powers and reduced the whole passage to the following line,

> Hus cloþes were of corsement and of kene wordes.[3]

The concrete has become abstract. Envy is no longer wearing real clothing but allegorical cloth—the infection of Hawkin's cloak has come upon Envy's. B's description continues for another seven lines, which C reduces to three. His interest was in the confession, not in the appearance, of the sin.

At other times C's tendency to get away from the concrete and visual into the abstract and ideal betrays itself in his choice, as between two concrete words, of the vaguer one over the more definite. Thus where in B Theology says of Meed that she

9. C, III, 12–16.   1. B, VI, 272 (A, VII, 257). Cf. C, IX, 293.
2. B, V, 78–83.   3. C, VII, 65.

> . . . myȝte kisse þe kynge for cosyn, an she wolde,[4]

C alters it in such a way as to blur the clarity:

> Hue myghte cusse þe kyng as for hus kynswomman.[5]

The same sort of change occurs in Piers's apostrophe to the ladies who have undertaken the pilgrimage to Truth. In B it reads,

> And ȝe, louely ladyes, with ȝoure longe fyngres.[6]

A lovely lady—though the phrase is common—is something that the reader is apt to picture for himself. C revises:

> And ȝe, worþly wommen, with ȝoure longe fyngres.[7]

On Piers's half-acre we might expect to meet more worthy women than lovely ladies. But we can hardly thank C for the change.

Probably the most striking instance of C's marring the imaginative lucidity of the earlier texts appears in his treatment of the lines with which A concludes Passus XI:

> Souteris & seweris, suche lewide iottis
> Percen wiþ a pater noster þe paleis of heuene,
> Wiþoute penaunce, at here partynge, in-to heiȝe blisse![8]

The lines in our B-text have undergone some expansion which weakens the effect:

> Souteres and shepherdes, suche lewed iottes
> Percen with a *pater-noster* þe paleys of heuene,
> And passen purgatorie penaunceles at her hennes partynge,
> In-to þe blisse of paradys, for her pure byleue,
> Þat inparfitly here knewe and eke lyued.[9]

C's version reads as follows:

> And lcwcdc leele laborers and land-tylynge peuple
> Persen with a *pater-noster* paradys oþer heuene,
> Passinge purgatorie penaunceles for here parfit byleyue,
> *Breuis oratio penetrat celum.*[1]

A's lines are undoubtedly the most effective. B's are rather less so, because the expansion of A's third line is clumsy and because his addition, particularly of the fifth line, is prosy. C wisely reduces B's paraphrase to A's length, but through one egregious error loses all the brilliancy of A which is still perceptible in B. He does this, of course, by replacing the fine naïve expression *þe paleys of heuene*—whose walls the Lord's

4. B, II, 132 (A, II, 102).   5. C, III, 146.
6. B, VI, 10 (A, VII, 18).   7. C, IX, 9.
8. A, XI, 301–03. The Latin Skeat prints after 303 belongs to the C-text. See *EETS,* I, 154.
9. B, X, 460–4.   1. C, XII, 294–6.

Prayer pierces—with the needless tautology *paradys oþer heuene*. What-ever the motive for the change—and it is very obscure—the result is disastrous.[2]

At other times C is careful to keep his version free from naïveté, how-ever appealing to the imagination it may be, and perhaps this is what inspired the alteration just discussed. Several passages may be cited in which C removes expressions reminiscent of popular beliefs originating in folklore. Thus the notion that heaven produces precious stones as the earth does vegetation, reflected in the line,

> . . . al þe precious perre þat in paradys wexeth,[3]

is eliminated in the C-revision,

> . . . al þe preciouse perreye þat eny prince weldeþ.[4]

Similarly the popular representation of St. Matthew, *Mathew with mannes face*,[5] gives way in C to the bare mention of the Saint,[6] while the Book of Genesis, called in AB

> . . . Genesis þe gyaunt, þe engendroure of vs alle,[7]

becomes flatly *genesis* in C.[8] Perhaps the most interesting example of this tendency occurs in the course of Piers's instructions to the pil-grims. "When you reach Truth's house," he tells them in B,

> Biddeth amende-ȝow meke him til his maistre ones,
> To wayue vp þe wiket þat þe womman shette,
> Tho Adam and Eue eten apples vnrosted.[9]

Those unroasted apples are not allowed to remain in C, who writes,

> Rydeþ to a-mende-ȝow, mekeþ ȝow to hus mayster grace,
> To openen and vndo þe hye ȝate of heuene,
> That adam and eue aȝens ous alle shutte.[1]

The revision of the second line is as significant as that of the third, since it exhibits another sort of tendency away from the figurative. The gate of heaven, which is, of course, what B is referring to, is explicitly named by C and is not permitted to be represented by just any wicket the reader may have in mind.

2. C's alteration was criticized by Manly, *MPh*, VII, 129. It is interesting that C in-troduced the Latin line from which A was apparently translating. C often makes specific the sources A and B had in their minds. Usually, however, the source is better known. Here the fact that it is obscure advances a slight presumption in favor of C's being the same as A.

3. B, x, 12 (A, xi, 12 in T).　　　4. C, xii, 10.
5. B, vi, 240 (A, vii, 225).　　　6. C, ix, 247.
7. B, vi, 234 (A, vii, 219).　　　8. C, ix, 240.
9. B, v, 610–12. Skeat prints *wayne* in 611, but see corrections to *EETS*, II.
1. C, viii, 248–50.

The examples so far given illustrate what may be termed a negative factor in C's style—his lack of appreciation for or confidence in lines that appeal to the imagination through concrete images. We come now to a positive characteristic of his expression—his caution, or, as I should prefer to put it, his moderation. He appears far more reluctant than A or B to give offense by overstating his case, or to warp truth by exaggeration. For instance, in B Conscience, summarizing his charges against Meed, says of her that she

> . . . of myst that was mute þe mony londes,
> And ouer lordes lawes reuleþ þe rewmes.[2]

This is a specific charge, hitting at certain newcomers among the aristocracy. C alters as follows:

> Muchel yuel is þorw mede meny tyme suffred,
> And letteþ þe lawe þorw here large ȝyftes.[3]

While still specific in intent, the charge is phrased more vaguely and is less likely to prove offensive to any contemporary lords. Again, in regard to the medical profession, Hunger says in B,

> . . . morthereres aren mony leches, lorde hem amende![4]

This bit of plain talk is mitigated in C:

> Ther aren meny luþere leches and leele leches fewe.[5]

Actually, C agrees with B, as his retention of the following line shows:

> Thei don men deye þorgh here drynkes er destyne hit wolde.[6]

But C is careful to make explicit the possibility of there being some good doctors, which in B is scarcely implicit.

Another instance of C's moderation is exhibited in Piers's definition of proper knightly deportment. In a catalogue of prohibitions is included one against accepting gifts from the poor, for, Piers warns the Knight in A and B,

> . . . þow shalt ȝelde it aȝein at one ȝeres ende,
> In a ful perillous place, purgatorie it hatte.[7]

In C, the consequences are less dire:

> For þow shalte ȝulde, so may be, and somdel a-bygge.[8]

Possibly C was troubled by the definite term assigned to the debt by

2. B, III, 295–6. In A, III, 278–9 Meed "of misdoers makeþ hem so riche, þat lawe is lord I-waxen and leute is pore" (so T).
3. C, IV, 453–4.
4. B, VI, 275. A, VII, 260 makes the plurality of doctors liars.
5. C, IX, 296.
6. C, IX, 297 (A, VII, 261, B, VI, 276).
7. B, VI, 44–5 (A, VII, 43–4).
8. C, IX, 41.

Piers. In any case, his revision succeeds in cloaking the threat. In another place, the poet is expressing his confidence that Do-Well is of greater spiritual benefit than pardons. According to A and B, Do-Well

. . . passeþ al þe pardoun of seynt petres cherche.[9]

The bluntness of the sentiment, strongly emphasized by the movement of the line, seems to have made C uneasy, for he softens the impact:

So dowel passeþ pardon and pilgrimages to rome.[1]

The essential sense, of course, is the same and the passage concludes with the poet's emphatic affirmation of the supreme value of Do-Well. But the alteration, with its addition of a second short cut to heaven to accompany the first, succeeds in diverting some of the contempt which in A and B tends to fall upon the Pope himself, as figured in St. Peter.[2]

Deferring for a time further discussion of C's idiosyncrasies as they appear in the poetic technique of his revision, let us turn to the closely related subject of his narrative method. The reader will remember the line C adds in the introduction, telling us that he had a wonderful dream in which he saw

Al þe welþe of þis worlde & þe woo boþe.[3]

We are given in advance an indication of the subject of the dream and the indication is followed up in the succeeding lines, which tell us who dwelt in the tower and who in the deep dale. In A and B we receive no hint of what the poem is about. We understand that it is to be a dream vision, but for all we know it may be another *House of Fame*. In C we are not made to remain in suspense. The dream will concern worldly wealth and worldly woe, Truth and Death. That is, we are about to read a moral and religious poem.

This emphasis that C puts upon the nature of his poem is an instance of a tendency, frequently illustrated, to make the most of moral and theological implications and to make these implications stand out unmistakably. In the line just quoted he gives notice that his purpose is not entertainment and that he is not one of those scurrilous minstrels, tellers of impious tales, whom he is at pains to reprobate a few lines later. So

9. B, vii, 172 (A, viii, 159).   1. C, x, 323.

2. In all three texts the grammar seems to require that the Priest, rather than the poet, is the source of the sentiments expressed. But it is clear that the Priest held directly the opposite point of view. The difficulty can be got around only by assuming that the poet is making a bold use of anacoluthon, and that the subject of the introductory verb (BC *demede*, A *diuinede*) is *I*, carried down from *me* of a few lines before. An investigation of the various meanings of *passen*, which does not necessarily mean "surpass" (see C, xviii, 5), might prove profitable. Manly, *MPh*, vii, 131, tried to make out that only the A-text makes sense and that B and C misunderstood it. But as Jusserand remarked, *MPh*, vii, 322, the lines do not seem "clear, logical or grammatical" in any of the texts.

3. C, i, 10.

throughout the poem he seizes every opportunity to inject the maximum of dogma into the lines of B. To teach, not to amuse, is his constant object. And like a not altogether laudable pedagogue, he seldom stops teaching, always striving to make the poem more didactic. Let us review a few examples. In A and B Lady Holy Church offers the Dreamer the following information about Truth (God) :

> . . . he is fader of feith, fourmed ȝow alle,
> Bothe with fel and with face and ȝaf ȝow fyue wittis
> Forto worschip hym þow with þe while þat ȝe ben here.
> And þerfore he hyȝte þe erthe to help ȝow vchone,
> Of wollen, of lynnen, of lyflode at nede,
> In mesurable manere to make ȝow at ese.[4]

The speech is moral enough as it stands. Yet C moralizes it still further :

> . . . he is fader of faith and formour of alle;
> To be faith-ful to hym he ȝaue ȝow fyue wittes
> For to worshepen hym þer-with while ȝe lyuen here.
> Wherfore he het þe elementes to helpe ȝow alle tymes,
> And brynge forth ȝoure bylyue, boþe lynnen and wollen,
> And in mesure, þouh hit muche were, to make ȝow at ese.[5]

The pious idea that the primary function of man is to worship God is twice stated in C, while A and B considered a single statement enough.[6] At the same time the rather primitive notion of man as consisting of skin and face disappears. The identification of God as the Creator of man gives way to an identification of Him as the Creator of the universe, and C thus tends, in a rather pietistic way, to reduce man's self-importance. But most suggestive is C's definition of measure, to which he adds the fact that God's measure is abundance—an idea that is neatly woven into the fabric of the lines.[7] Here we may see clearly the moralist dominant in the C-reviser.

Another example of C's packing his text with dogma occurs in the same part of the poem, in the lines in which Holy Church explains to the Dreamer who she is. In A and B she tells him,

> I vnderfonge þe firste and þe feyth tauȝte.[8]

The second half-line expresses an obvious fact. C deletes it, replacing it with a weightier idea,

> Ich vnder-feng þe formest and fre man þe made.[9]

---

4. AB, I, 14–19.   5. C, II, 14–19.
6. Notice in C, II, 14–15 the two infinitives of purpose surrounding the clause upon which they depend. This construction is used frequently in all three texts.
7. C, II, 16 is an example of the enlarged thesis. The whole passage provides an excellent illustration of C's manner. Notice the generalizing phrase *alle tymes* in 17.
8. B, I, 76 (A, I, 74).   9. C, II, 73.

The allusion is evidently to that freedom which was bestowed upon man by the Atonement—freedom from an endless term in the prison of hell.[1] The idea is thus the complement of the one mentioned a little while ago in connection with the unroasted apples of Adam and Eve. Here, as there, we observe C at work stressing the didactic elements of his poem. Alterations such as this may be found throughout the C-text, but particularly in the *Visio* where the subject is frequently social rather than moral man and where A and B in considering things temporal momentarily neglect things eternal. In such cases C is apt to revise in such a way as to prevent his version from ever resembling the purely social document that A and B are sometimes mistaken for.[2]

Another manifestation of the emphasis C placed upon spiritual and moral implications appears obliquely in his tendency to generalize statements that in the earlier texts are specific. As does the matter just discussed, this habit of C's suggests that his attitude toward his work was somewhat different from A's and B's. In a sense, C is more pretentious and more self-conscious. He seems more acutely aware of the eternal value of what he is revising and more determined that his version should not suffer from lack of emphasis on the wider significance. In A and B much of the story—at least in the *Visio*—is told in the manner of one of Aesop's fables and the reader is trusted to see for himself in what way the particular represents the general. C, on the other hand, frequently makes the universal application explicit.

This principle is abundantly illustrated in the incidents involving that most amiable of wicked women, Lady Meed. In speaking of her marriage, the King in A and B is described as saying:

> I shal assaye hir my-self and sothelich appose
> What man of þis molde þat hire were leueste.
> And if she worche bi my witte and my wille folwe,
> I wil forgyue hir þis gilte, so me god help![3]

The passage expresses fairly accurately what we might expect a specific fourteenth-century king to say about a specific woman—provided she were a charming one—who had acted contrary to his wishes. C, adopting the first two lines, alters the last two to fit a larger conception:

> And yf hue wirche wisliche, by wys mennes counsail,
> Ich wolle for-gyue hure alle hure gultes, so me god helpe![4]

C's King does not take upon himself the responsibility of arranging

---

1. Jusserand's interpretation of the line as meaning that the poet was released from bondage upon taking minor orders is forced. See *Mysticism,* pp. 64–5.

2. See especially C's handling of the entire incident of Meed, the passage in Reason's sermon at C, VI, 192–7, and the alteration in C, VI, 177.

3. AB, III, 5–8.   4. C, IV, 7–8.

Meed's life. That is to be left up to a council of wise men. The King is thus a better king than his fellow in A and B, but he is rather less a human being. More significant, however, is the fact that in C the King is more aware of what Meed represents, recognizing her as an old offender, with many entries on the police blotter. In A and B the King, like the Dreamer, seems highly susceptible to Meed's charms, even though he realizes that she is a lady with an evil past. When he reproves her in person, however, he seems worried chiefly by her unauthorized engagement to False and very little by her previous backslidings. His speech of reproval takes but six lines.[5] The same passage in C takes eighteen lines[6] and the King is far more concerned with the general wickedness of Meed, reminding her of her "many guilts" and threatening her with imprisonment unless she amends. Her engagement is merely the last and culminating incident in a lifetime of misdemeanor. The result of this change is that Meed is a more villainous villainess in C than she is in A and B. There is no danger that even the most obtuse reader will get the idea that she is only an occasionally erring woman. And where in A and B there was at least a slight chance that we might become absorbed in the story to the detriment of the moral, C has interspersed throughout little guideposts to keep us on the straight and narrow path.[7] In a similar fashion, the passages in the earlier texts which, because of their topical significance, are apt to attract attention to themselves and to distract it from the lesson they illustrate C handles in such a way as to make their universality more obvious than their topicality.[8]

The Meed incident is particularly full of C's generalizations. In B after the lady is finally disclosed in her true colors, we are told the following about the persons who witnessed the scene:

> Alle riȝtful recorded þat resoun treuthe tolde,
> And [kynde] witt acorded þer-with and comended his wordes.
> And þe moste peple in þe halle and manye of þe grete,
> And leten mekenesse a maistre and Mede a mansed schrewe.[9]

C preserves the first line but continues,

---

5. B, III, 105–10, A, III, 101–06.   6. C, IV, 130–47.

7. C's desire to make the significance of the story of Meed clear is shown also in his addition of C, IV, 317–409, distinguishing between *mede* and *mercede*.

8. See especially the generalizations added to Conscience's charge against Meed, C, IV, 203–12; Meed's generalizations which obscure the account of Edward III's debacle in France, C, IV, 234–58; and the omission of B, III, 188–99. Although in C Meed refers to the same historical incident, and makes some use of historical detail, her words would not recreate the event even for a contemporary, so successfully does C have her oppose generality to generality. See the discussion in Chapter IV, especially pp. 111 f.

9. B, IV, 157–60. I insert *kynde* before *witt* in 158 because it is present in the C-text, the alliteration demands it, and Wit, or Witty, is at this time one of Meed's followers. A, IV, 135–6 varies and does not mention Kind Wit.

> And kynde wit and conscience cortesliche þankede
> Reson for hus ryght speche; riche and poure hym louede,
> And seiden, "we seth wel, syre reson, by þy wordes,
> That meknesse worth mayster ouer mede atte laste."[1]

The approval of "most of the (common) people in the hall and many of the great" becomes that of "rich and poor" generally, who do more than applaud Reason—they come to love him. The effect, which is to take the reader out of the King's Judgment Hall into an ideal world of moral truth,[2] has already been foreshadowed in C's revision of Reason's earlier threat, which reads in B,

> . . . I shal no reuthe haue,
> While Mede hath þe maistrye in þis moot-halle.[3]

In C the second line reads,

> Whyl mede hath þe maistrye þer motyng is atte barre.[4]

The fact that in C we are not concerned with the reign of Reason in England or at Westminster, but in all the world, is borne out in the conversation between Reason and the King that follows the passage just quoted. In A and B Reason's promise of a just rule is thus expressed:

> But if I reule þus ȝowre rewme, rende out my guttes!
> Ȝif ȝe bidden buxomnes be of myne assente.[5]

In C, the promise is this:

> Bote ich rewely þus alle reames, reueþ me my syght;
> And brynge alle men to bowe with-oute byter wounde,
> With-oute mercement oþer manslauht amenden alle reames.[6]

The little kingdom of England is no longer the subject. The speech has become literally universalized to include all the kingdoms of the earth and all the men therein. Simultaneously, the practical provision that Reason stipulates in B—the assent of Obedience—has disappeared as the power of Reason, like his scope, becomes all-embracing.[7]

---

1. C, v, 152–5. Skeat places a semicolon after l. 152, making Conscience and Kind Wit the recipients of the gratitude, but it seems more logical that they are thanking Reason and that the construction parallels that of B.

2. The effect is heightened by C's addition of Conscience, who throughout the *Visio* is a figure of greater prominence in C than he is in B. Characteristic is the addition in these lines of one allegorical figure, Kind Wit, by B, and a second, Conscience, by C.

3. B, iv, 134–5. A, iv, 117–18 varies slightly.   4. C, v, 132.

5. B, iv, 186–7. A, iv, 149–50 varies slightly.   6. C, v, 180–2.

7. One might also cite the generalizing *alle tymes* in C, viii, 212 (compare A, vi, 55, B, v, 574) and in C, ii, 17 (see p. 57, n. 7, above); Piers's promise to go with "all those that wish to live in truth" (C, ix, 57: cf. A, vii, 54, B, vi, 60); his vow to be a "pilgrim at the plow for profit of poor and rich" (C, ix, 111: "poor" only in A, vii, 95, B, vi, 104);

Let us now turn back to matters more closely connected with poetic technique and consider several mannerisms of C that may not have been observed before. In C's introduction the reader will have noticed the repetition that occurs in C, I, 9 and 13,

> And Merueylously me mette, as ich may ʒow telle;

> *   *   *   *   *   *   *

> Al ich saw slepynge, as ich shal ʒow telle.

This habit of repeating a line or half-line at short intervals is by no means rarely exemplified in C. Sometimes, as is probably the case here, where an aging Prospero is nervously undertaking one final fling at the creation of magic and is filled with a sense of responsibility toward his audience, the repetition is at least half deliberate. On other occasions it seems to be accidental. Thus sometimes when C is paraphrasing his original, adding new ideas, he suddenly loses his inspiration and is forced to fill out a line or a passage by repeating himself. A good example of this occurs in the conversation between Meed and the venal Friar who comes to confess her. In the earlier texts he suggests that if she is willing to contribute heavily to the upkeep of the Priory, her soul will be sure of getting into heaven. Meed thereupon promises to be generous in her gifts—so generous, indeed,

> That eury segge shal seyn I am sustre of ʒowre hous.[8]

As C revised the passage his mind seems to have raced ahead of the text, for he has the Friar promise Meed that she will receive not heaven but the prayers of his order:

> In masse and in matyns for mede we shulleþ synge
> Solenliche and sothlich, as for a sustre of oure ordre.[9]

This impresses Meed sufficiently for her to promise a large donation and her promise concludes, as it did in A and B, with her expectation

> Þat euery seg shal see ich am sustre of ʒoure ordre.[1]

The recurrence is apt to jar upon the ear of the reader like a phrase in music erroneously repeated by an inexpert pianist.

---

and C, XII, 214, where Solomon is said to have ruled "all realms" (only one realm in A, XI, 259, B, X, 381 : MS R only). The last may be an unconscious generalization, resulting from a habit of mind.

8. B, III, 63 (A, III, 54 in T, C, IV, 67 in X). The verb in MSS T and X (see n. 1 immediately below) is Modern English *see,* as in the B-text.

9. C, IV, 53-4.

1. C, IV, 67. Skeat reads *shal see, and seye,* which seems an instance of "þ"-sophistication. I follow MSS IX. Another repetition occurs in the same passus, C, IV, 43-4, 48-9 : cf. B, III, 41-2, A, III, 42-3.

Two instances of the same sort occur in C, Passus IX. In the first, the poet is describing the energizing effect of Hunger upon those who were normally reluctant to perform honest work. So heartily did they begin to help in the management of the farm, A and B tell us, that

> . . . þere-of was peres proude and put hem to werke.[2]

C, who expands the description of the useful labor accomplished, tells us this fact twice, once at 197,

> Tho was peers ful proude and putte hem alle to werke;

and then, immediately after an insertion, at 203,

> And peers was proud þer-of and putte hem alle to swynke.

Evidently C here realized that he had repeated himself and tried to introduce variation by making the last word in the second line *swynke*. But the effect is still unsatisfactory. In the same passage we are told by B that the famine made men content with inferior food,

> For þat was bake for bayarde was bote for many hungry.[3]

C in revising incorporates the idea into Piers's plea to Hunger to cease his oppression, a speech that occurs earlier in the action than the line quoted above. Piers asks Hunger's permission to give beans to the hungry,

> And þat was bake for bayarde may be here bote.[4]

The line is virtually repeated immediately afterward in the same context in which it appears in the earlier versions.[5]

A final example will serve as a transition to another of C's peculiarities. In A and B Thought defines Do-Well in the following manner:

> Who-so is trewe of his tonge and of his two handes,
> And þorugh his laboure or þorugh his londe his lyflode wynneth,
> And is trusti of his tailende, taketh but his owne.[6]

C revises—and generalizes—as follows:

> Who-so is trewe of hys tonge and of hus two handes,
> And þorw leel labour lyueþ and loueþ his emcristine,
> And þer-to trewe of hus tail and halt wel his handes.[7]

Here the idea of the proper management of one's hands is repeated within

---

2. B, VI, 200. A, VII, 187 varies in the second half-line.
3. B, VI, 196 (not in A). 4. C, IX, 178.
5. C, IX, 192. See also repetitions at C, III, 120, 145; IV, 77, 115; VII, 253, 286; XII, 8, 82.
6. B, VIII, 80–2 (A, IX, 72–4). 7. C, XI, 78–80.

the space of three lines, its second expression being nonalliterative, so that it seems that C originally intended to write *and of hus two handes* again and checked himself, though unable to find another word to complete the sum of three *t*'s. The idea itself seems to have been on C's mind, for he had already introduced it earlier in the poem, at a point where, in Holy Church's description of a man living in accord with Truth, the A- and B-versions read,

Who-so is trewe of his tonge & telleth none other [8]

This C altered as follows:

For [who] is trewe of hus tonge and of hus two handes.[9]

As he revised the earlier passage the later one came into his mind, since they both have the same first half-line.

The borrowing of a line or half-line from one part of the poem for use in another occurs a number of times in C. Thus A and B in describing Meed's reception at the King's palace tell how a clerk

Toke Mede bi þe Middel and brouȝte hir in-to chaumbre.[1]

C revising, in this case undoubtedly in order to improve the alliteration, wrote that the clerk

Toke mede by þe myddel and myldeliche here broughte
In-to boure with blysse and by hure gan sitte.[2]

The source of the expansion is a later passage in the earlier texts, where the King is said to have sent for Meed

. . . with seriauntes manye,
That brouȝten hir to bowre with blisse and with ioye.[3]

When C came to revise the later passage, he seems to have remembered his earlier borrowing, for he omits the line from its proper place after C, IV, 128.[4]

The habit of lifting an expression from one place for use in another is not confined to borrowings from the B-text. C also borrows freely from himself. For instance, in the Prologue of A and B the pious are said to devote themselves to prayers and penance

In hope forto haue heueneriche blisse.[5]

C makes a slight amplification:

In hope to haue a gode end & heuene-ryche Blysse.[6]

8. B, I, 88 (A, I, 86).   9. C, II, 84 in MSS IX.   1. AB, III, 10.
2. C, IV, 10–11.   3. B, III, 101–02. A, III, 96–7 varies slightly.
4. C, IV, 212 may be an echo of B, X, 17–18.
5. AB, Pro., 27.   6. C, I, 29.

The expression *a good end* is used again at C, III, 35 in Holy Church's description of the rewards of the righteous and at C, XI, 60 in the Friar's valediction to the Dreamer. In neither of these instances does it appear in the parallel passage in AB. Similarly, the phrase *holynesse oþer hendenesse* appears at C, III, 81, a revision of B, II, 76, and again at C, XII, 13, a revision of B, X, 16 (A, XI, 16). The Latin line added by C at II, 144,

> And deye raþere þan to do eny dedlich synne;
> *Melius est mori quam male uiuere.*

is echoed in a C-addition at VIII, 209–10:

> That ys to seye sothliche ȝe sholde raþer deye
> Than eny dedliche synne do. . . .

Moreover, the Latin is repeated at C, XVIII, 40. In A and B the idea appears only in the first passage and then only in translation:

> No dedly synne to do, dey þouȝ þow sholdest.[7]

Related to this self-borrowing[8] is C's use of several favorite expressions. The first of these is the phrase *as it were* with which he qualifies certain statements, much as Cicero prefaces his metaphors with *quasi*. This might be said to indicate a fear on C's part that he will be found guilty of violating the laws of verisimilitude, as if, with rather petty love of literal truth, he were explaining, "This is all just make-believe," like Bottom and his fellows playing before the Duke of Athens. It is probably more correct, however, to regard it as part of a plan to make the simples reader recognize the presence of allegory—an insistence not on the literal truth so much as on the allegorical truth. We have seen one use of the phrase in the very first lines of the C-text, in the preface to the vision:

> Wynkyng as it were wyterly ich saw hyt.[9]

It is employed several times elsewhere to qualify a statement of the poet's sleeping or dreaming, as if he wanted it understood that his was not a usual sort of sleep or a usual sort of dream. Thus, after Lady Holy Church had left him, the poet explains that he

> . . . sauh how mede was maried, metyng as it were,[1]

and before the beginning of Reason's sermon he promises that he will

> . . . seye as ich seih, slepynge, as it were.[2]

---

7. B, I, 142 (A, I, 132).
8. Another echo may be seen in C, IX, 53 and C, I, 138. Both lines terminate speeches.
9. C, I, 11.   1. C, III, 54.   2. C, VI, 125.

At other times he uses the qualifier in such a way as to suggest that the people or things whom he sees in his visions have more than a literal significance. Meed is introduced as follows:

> Ich lokid on my lyft half as þe lady me tauhte,
> And sauh a womman as yt were, wonderlich [y-]cloþed.[3]

Piers, in his allegorical account of the highway to Truth, warns the pilgrims about a certain *brygge as hit were,*[4] while the Tree of Charity is introduced as *an vmbe as hit were.*[5] Possibly the most interesting use of the phrase—so far as the authorship controversy is concerned—occurs in the introduction to the Rat Parliament:

> Thanne ran þer a route of ratones, as it were,[6]

which replaces the B-line,

> Wiþ þat ran þere a route of ratones at ones.[7]

Here the intention is obviously to suggest that these rats are a metaphorical sort of rodent at best and that the reader is not to take them too literally, or to fret himself overmuch if they talk like and about men.[8]

Of even more frequent occurrence is C's use of the words *leel* and *leel(l)ich.* I have counted at random some fifteen appearances of these words in his revisions of nine passus.[9] The words evidently appealed to him not only because the useful variety of meanings they share[1] makes the task of the alliterative poet easier, but because at least one of the meanings expresses an idea close to C's heart. Precisely what this meaning is, it is, oddly enough, difficult to say but it is certain that the same meaning, and a very definite one, is indicated for a number of C's uses of the word. The obvious meaning of *leel,* "loyal," is entirely unsatisfactory, just as is the meaning "Loyalty" which is generally given for the personification Lewte. "Honest," a normal sense of the word, fits a number of C's uses but is also inadequate.[2] My own suggestion is the

---

3. C, III, 8–9. In 9 I read from MS X.   4. C, VIII, 213.
5. C, XIX, 6.   6. C, I, 165.   7. B, Pro., 146.

8. The controversy between Manly and Jusserand about whether C thought that the *segges* of B, Pro., 160 were dogs or men is easily settled if one examines C's opening line in the light of his ordinary use of the phrase *as it were.* The rats are neither altogether rats nor altogether men, but as-it-were rats, a little of both. So are the dogs. See Manly, *CHEL,* II, 38; *MPh,* VII, 131–2; Jusserand, *MPh,* VI, 316–17; *MPh,* VII, 323–4. The phrase *as it were* also occurs in C at IX, 22 and X, 210 and possibly elsewhere.

9. C, I, 88, 146; III, 76; IV, 319, 350; VIII, 196, 238; IX, 255, 262; X, 14; XI, 210, 273; XII, 148, 267; XIV, 69.

1. For the many senses, see *OED, leal,* a. and adv., and *leally,* adv.

2. The meaning "honest" seems undoubtedly the correct one where the words are used in conjunction with labor. See *OED, leal,* a. and adv., A, 1, and C, IV, 350, IX, 255, 262. In these lines the poet is talking in terms of honest work—the sort of work that asks payment in exact proportion to its deserts, or just payment. Though this meaning is closely related to the one discussed in the next two notes below, it is not adequate for all C's uses.

meaning "just," instanced in *William of Palerne* and, in the Old French form *leal,* in Chrestien de Troyes.[3] "Justice," indeed, seems to be the best rendering of *Lewte* in all texts[4] and the quality in which C takes a particular interest. When B describes good bishops as persons

> . . . yblessed, ȝif þei ben as þei shulden,
> Legistres of bothe þe lawes þe lewed þere-with to preche,[5]

C makes them

> Leel and ful of loue and no lord dreden.[6]

When we are told that Kind Wit has made it possible for the common people

> With leel labour to lyue whyl lif and londe lasteth,[7]

we should probably think in terms of honest labor, as practiced by the Village Blacksmith. But when Truth is said to be

> . . . louh as a lombe and leel of hus tonge,[8]

we should most likely think of God's justice rather than His honesty or loyalty. So also when we learn that Truth's house is roofed with *leel-speche.*[9] C's preoccupation with justice is indicative of his moral interest and the frequent appearances of *leel* and *leel(l)ich* in the C-text have the effect of moralizing it. They also, of course, have the effect of reducing

3. See *OED, leal,* a. and adv., A, 3: "Lawful; also, just, fair." Also Wendelin Förster, *Kristian von Troyes: Wörtenbuch zu seinen sämtlichen Werken* (Halle, 1914), p. 168, where *leal* is defined as "rechtlich," "gesetzlich." For *leaute, lealte,* Förster gives "Rechtlichkeit."

4. For the word *lewte* in *Piers Plowman* I suggest that the meaning is a good deal closer to the root meaning "legality" (Latin *legalitas*) than it is to Modern English "loyalty." I should define it as "exact justice; strict adherence to the letter of the law." Thus the character Lewte is first introduced as the lover of Holy Church (B, ii, 21) and the direct antithesis of Meed. Meed stands for inequitable distribution of reward, Lewte for its equitable distribution. It is also Lewte who as umpire informs the Dreamer what he may legitimately tell concerning the abuses practiced by the Friars (B, xi, 89–102), while Holy Church advises the Dreamer to keep silent about the wicked until Lewte becomes judge (B, ii, 47–8). Unpersonified, *lewte* seems almost interchangeable with *law* in the wide sense. C substitutes it for law at iv, 197 (cf. B, iii, 158): "Þoruh which loueday ys lost þat leaute [*B-text:* lawe] myȝte wynne." It is also closely associated with law at C, iv, 450 (B, iii, 292), C, v, 174 (B, iv, 180), and C, xiii, 79 (B, xi, 140). See also C's use of the word at xiii, 92 and elsewhere in the Trajan incident, xiii, 88 and 96. It is curious that in xiii, 88, "Lo, lordes! what leaute dude and leel dome y-used," the word might almost be rendered by "legality" in the sense used by Bunyan: "reliance on works for salvation, rather than on free grace" (see *OED, legality,* 1, b). *OED, loyalty,* gives no meaning of "justice," the closest approach being "lawfulness" as applied to marriage in 1660. One might observe that the adjective *leel* is at least twice used in C (i, 88, x, 14) in connection with bishops, whom the poet consistently regards both as executors of the laws and as judges of the righteous and unrighteous.

5. B, vii, 13–14. A, viii, 13–16 varies.   6. C, x, 14.
7. C, i, 146.   8. C, viii, 196.   9. C, viii, 238.

its concreteness, since they are abstract words[1] and in a number of lines
where C introduces them he may be seen turning the reader away from
the physical and tangible to the spiritual and intangible.[2]

One further point about the narrative technique of the C-revision
should be mentioned briefly. In the Prologue, it will be remembered, C
gives us an exact description of the geography of the Field of Folk:

> Esteward ich byhulde after þe sonne,
> And sawe a toure, as ich trowede, truthe was þer-ynne;
> Wortwarde ich waitede in a whyle after,
> And sawe a deep dale; deþ, as ich lyuede,
> Wonede in þo wones, and wyckede spiritus.
> A fair feld, ful of folke, fonde ich þer bytwyne.[3]

In the earlier texts the picture is not so topographically clear:

> As I bihelde in-to þe est an hiegh to þe sonne,
> I seigh a toure on a toft trielich ymaked;
> A depe dale binethe, a dongeon þere-Inne,
> With depe dyches & derke and dredful of sight.
> A faire felde ful of folke fonde I there bytwene.[4]

A map maker might reasonably criticize this last as misleading. The
tower is "in the east," but the deep dale is at first merely "beneath"—
presumably beneath the tower. It is not for several lines that we learn
that the two are separated by the field lying "between." In C, however,
everything is at once located with precision. And having set the stage
with such pains, C was careful to adhere to the plan of the scene as he
continued his revision. Lady Holy Church, admonishing the Dreamer
and discussing the destination of the righteous and the unrighteous,
promises, in A and B, that

> . . . alle þat worche with wronge wenden hij shulle
> After her deth day and dwelle wiþ þat shrewe.
> Ac þo þat worche wel, as holiwritt telleth,

> *   *   *   *   *   *   *

> Mowe be siker þat here soule shal wende to heuene.[5]

C, however, remembers that from where they are standing the Dreamer
and Holy Church can see both heaven and hell. Hence he has the lady
say,

> Alle þat worchen þat wikkede ys wenden þei shulle

1. C several times uses the adverbial form lamely in the flat sense of Modern English
"really." See *OED, leally,* adv., 2, and C, III, 76, XI, 273.
2. See especially the change at C, I, 88, discussed below.
3. C, I, 14–19.   4. AB, Pro., 13–17.
5. B, I, 126–8, 130 (A, I, 117–19, 121).

After hure deþ-day and dwelle þer wrong ys;
And alle þat han wel y-wroght wenden þey shulle
Estwarde to heuene euere to abyde.[6]

Probably C thought of her as pointing westward "þer wrong ys," and "estwarde to heuene."

There are sufficient examples of this sort of precision in C to justify our crediting him with some interest in accuracy and consistency of details.[7] Ordinarily, however, this interest evidences itself either in changes that involve only a line or two, or in such major changes, affecting the very fabric of the narrative, as C makes in the pardon incident. It is also true that in a number of revisions he achieves precisely the opposite of accuracy and consistency with regard to details, so that one is apt to find oneself stating, with a good deal of conviction, both propositions of a paradox. That is, with respect to certain passages, one may say that C has a careful eye for details. But with certain others, one must say that he shows a wonderful negligence. His negligence appears particularly in passages where he has omitted from his revision something present in the B-text without making adequate adjustment for the omission. Manly long ago noticed and scoffed at C's permitting the Dreamer to refer to the "jangling" between the Priest and Piers when the jangling had been eliminated.[8] A rather worse error appears in C, XI. In the A- and B-texts Wit inserts into the middle of a circumstantial description of the Castle of Caro a digression on the subject of the creation of Adam and Eve. C, revising, omitted the digression but characteristically replaced it with another on the effects of sin.[9] Among the lines he omitted—and failed to replace—were those by means of which B got himself back from the digression to the main topic. The result is that C's return is precipitous in the extreme. He leaps straight from sin to the castle with the AB-line,

Inwitt and alle wittes closed ben þer-ynne,[1]

forgetting that he had omitted the antecedent for *þer-ynne* which, in the earlier texts, is governed by a mention of the Castle of Caro a few lines earlier.[2] Similarly, though in C's account of the Dreamer's quarrel with the mercenary Friar the dispute about the Dreamer's burial in the Priory

6. C, II, 130-3.
7. Miss Day, *MLR*, XXIII, 18-20, cites a number of lines in which she believes C made revisions in order to get minor points straight. See her discussions of B, V, 516 (C, VIII, 154), B, V, 371 (C, VII, 424-5), B, II, 21-2 (C, III, 21), B, IV, 41 (C omits), B, V, 554-5 (C, VIII, 190-1). Some of these seem to me dubious illustrations. The sex of Lewte in B, II, 21 remains troublesome. See Manly, *CHEL*, II, 37; *MPh*, VII, 116-17; Jusserand, *MPh*, VI, 302-03; *MPh*, VII, 316; Chambers, *MLR*, V, 16-17.
8. C, X, 292. See *MPh*, VII, 130.   9. B, IX, 25-51, A, X, 25-41. Cf. C, XI, 150-69.
1. C, XI, 170 (B, IX, 52, A, X, 42).   2. B, IX, 48, A, X, 38.

churchyard is omitted,[3] yet it is referred to at the beginning of C, xvi in a line altered from its B-form.[4] Of inconsistencies such as these there are many instances, of which those mentioned will suffice as illustrations. Inasmuch as C's failures in coherence are somewhat more conspicuous than his successes, I am disposed not to do him the wrong of attributing to him an overwhelming interest in the matter.[5]

Two passages in which C seems to render confusion worse confounded should not be used as examples of his carelessness. The better known of these is the problem of Meed's paternity. In B the text makes False both the father of Meed and her fiancé and, judging by the reading of the passage, I think we may attribute it to the B-reviser himself and not to his scribes, as has been suggested.[6] C changes Meed's father's name from False to Favel in the line where her father is first named.[7] But having apparently amended the mix-up, he reverts to B and gives it upon a second occasion as False.[8] Hence so far as consistency is concerned, C is even less satisfactory than B, in whose text we are free to suppose an incestuous relationship.[9]

The situation is even worse with the two scoundrels who pursue Conscience and Reason to the King's court. In B they are known as Warren Wisdom and his fellow Witty.[1] C initially changes the former to Warren Wiseman and the latter to Wilyman.[2] Just three lines later,

3. B, xi, 62–74. Cf. C, xiii, 16–23.

4. C, xvi, 11. Cf. B, xiii, 9.

5. Even the best artists forget that trifles make perfection, and the celebrated charge that C dealt with B in so chaotic a fashion that he could not have been B becomes weaker and weaker as the examples of authors who have dealt chaotically with their own work pile up. I quote from Albert Feuillerat, *Comment Marcel Proust a composé son roman* (New Haven, 1934), pp. 256–7: "Dans les passages profondément retouchés, il arrive souvent qu'une conversation ou une description soit coupée en deux par l'insertion d'une idée adventive longuement developpée, celle-ci pouvant elle-même donner naissance à des ramifications secondaires jusqu'à ce que l'on perde complètement de vue l'idée interrompue d'où est sorti ce flot d'idées intruses. Les contradictions abondent, présentant d'un même fait des interprétations entièrement différentes, et cela quelquefois dans un même passage. . . . Ces contradictions sont encore plus choquantes quand elles se rencontrent dans le caractère d'un même personnage." Yet I believe that most people would agree that Proust was a careful artist. I am indebted to Professor Menner for calling this example to my attention.

6. A, ii, 20, "Out of wrong heo wox to wroþerhele monye," was revised to B, ii, 25, "For fals was hire fader þat hath a fykel tonge." Jusserand, *MPh*, vi, 304–05, argues that B intended to make Meed's father Favel, but the evidence is poor.

7. C, iii, 25, paralleling B, ii, 25.

8. C, iii, 121: "Þouh fals were hure fader and fykel-tonge hure [bel]syre" (so MSS MIGX). There is no parallel in the earlier texts.

9. The whole question of Meed's paternity was treated at length, in a very literal fashion, by Manly, *CHEL,* ii, 37; *MPh*, vii, 117–21; and Jusserand, *MPh*, vi, 303–05; *MPh*, vii, 316–17.

1. B, iv, 26.

2. C, v, 27. Miss Day, *MLR*, xxiii, 20, believes that the first change was made because C was "distressed at such a dubious character being called Wisdom." Inasmuch as Wisdom appears in Wiseman's place a few lines later in C, the explanation does not seem adequate.

however, he says that these two are hoping to begin a lawsuit against Wilyman, Wittyman, and Warren Wring-Law,[3] so that Wilyman is made out to be about to sue himself. On their arrival in court in B, Warren Wisdom and Witty exchange a part of their names, becoming Wisdom and Warren Witty.[4] But aside from this interchange the two retain their original identities. In C, on the other hand, they suffer a number of metamorphoses. First, at C, v, 66, C pictures Wrong, in trouble with the King, as seeking aid from Wisdom, whom C has presumably eliminated. A few lines later he has the presumably eliminated Witty appear as Wit, in company with Wisdom.[5] The next time the pair appear, Wisdom is once more eliminated in favor of Wiles (Wilyman?), though Wit remains.[6] Next C mentions a character called simply "a wise one," who replaces B's Wisdom,[7] and a moment later he has Wit speak, ignoring Wilyman altogether.[8] Finally he lets the elusive Wisdom reappear once more[9] and omits entirely the last appearance of B's Warren Wisdom.[1]

If we take the two passages literally and try to follow in detail the comings and goings of False and Favel, of Wilyman and Wiseman, then we are forced to throw up our hands in despair: C's negligence amounts to downright incompetence. It is probable, however, that the sudden changes in identity are intentional. All these *w*- and *f*-alliterating personages are of exactly the same sort, indistinguishable in their common desire to make money by misuse of the law. They are the Rosencrantzes and Guildensterns *de petites affaires,* always eager, for promotion or pay, to ingratiate themselves with influential citizens like Meed and Wrong. Their common lack of distinguishing characteristics seems clearly indicated by B's transfer, within a few lines, of the given name *Warren* from Wisdom to Witty. Equally interchangeable—and interchanged—is the epithet *fickle-tongued,* which is applied indiscriminately to False, to Favel, and, in C, to Liar.[2] Though Favel has a long history in French literature and is properly rendered as "Flattery," there is little in *Piers Plowman* to set him apart from either False or Liar.[2a] Civil and Simony, two other scoundrels concerned in the story of Meed, are also indistinguishable—so indistinguishable, indeed, that A and B let them read the same document out loud simultaneously, as if they

3. C, v, 30–1.   4. B, iv, 67.   5. C, v, 72.
6. C, v, 77.   7. C, v, 83. Cf. B, iv, 87.
8. C, v, 87.   9. C, v, 96.   1. B, iv, 154–6.
2. The epithet is applied to False at B, ii, 25, 40; to Favel at B, ii, 78, C, iii, 25; to Liar at C, iii, 6. At C, iii, 121 it becomes personified and identified as Meed's *belsire* (MS P, *syre*). Notice the associations of the words "false," "faithless," and "flatterer" at B, ii, 129, 165; C, iii, 42, 83, 143.
2a. A, ii, 140 has Favel riding on Fair-Speech; B, ii, 165, on Flatterer; C, iii, 43 credits him with flattering speech. For Favel in French literature, see Dorothy L. Owen, *Piers Plowman: a Comparison with Some Earlier and Contemporary French Allegories* (London, 1912).

shared one set of vocal chords.[4] It seems to me that all this is a sort of inversion of the technique employed with Hawkin, who loses any trace of individuality when he confesses to all the sins of the whole community. Here individual members of the community lose their individuality because of their single-minded devotion to a common vice. The same technique is employed in the confessions of the Deadly Sins, where, both in B and C, we have changes of sex and of profession within what purports to be the same sinner.[5] If we can reconcile ourselves to the fact that the poet's intention was not to create realistic characters who would adequately embody a certain vice, but rather to illustrate the prevalence of the vice within the community, we shall be in a better position to understand *Piers Plowman* than if we insist upon looking for the sort of verisimilitude we expect—and do not always find—in Chaucer.

I have set down these peculiarities of the C-revision without interrupting the exposition—except in the case of the last one discussed—by attempting to condone or apologize for such of them as may seem either to impair the literary value of the poem or to suggest that C was a different poet from A and B. It is now time for the prosecution to rest its case and for the defense to take the stand. I shall begin at the beginning, with the first lines of the poem, and with that habit of C's that they are said to exemplify—his "spoiling" of his original.

The chief objection to C's revision of the opening lines of the Prologue is based, apparently, upon his elimination of the natural surroundings in which the poet lies down to sleep—AB, 5–10, which Hall calls "one of the most delightful morsels in our earlier literature."[6] This is the morsel which C rejects, seemingly as a waste of his own and the reader's time. Now the lines are certainly pleasing and it is impossible to·congratulate C for eliminating them. On the other hand, it is not inconceivable that the same mind that wrote the lines should at a later time delete them, for they are not essential or even particularly pertinent to the great plan of the poem. Their appeal is not to the moralist or to the religious-minded, but to the lover of nature and the poetry of nature. And there is little evidence that either A or B or C had anything but a passing enthusiasm for nature. "Middle English poetry," say the editors of *Mum and the Sothsegger,*

as a rule, does not afford long nature-passages, and except in the case of Northern poets, confines itself to imitations of the *Roman de la Rose.* In *Piers Plowman* this traditional opening is reduced to the barest minimum; the mountain and valley and plain of the vision are only mentioned; the poet's interest is in the men on the plain.[7]

4. B, II, 71–3, A, II, 57–9. This minor oddity C does eliminate at C, III, 72–4.
5. Pride in C seems to be both a woman (C, VII, 3) and a man (C, VII, 43). Sloth in B and C seems both a priest (C, VIII, 30, B, V, 422) and a layman (C, VIII, 10, B, V, 401).
6. *MLR,* IV, 4.   7. Day and Steele, *Mum and the Sothsegger,* p. xvii.

One thumbs through the three versions of *Piers Plowman* in an almost vain search for the poetry of nature. Scattered references there are—the longest passage extends for five or six lines in A and B—but nothing is altogether comparable to the beginning of the poem.[8] Hence "the barest minimum" of imitation of the *Romance of the Rose* is the most impressive bit of nature poetry in the thousands of lines of *Piers Plowman*. O monstrous! but one half-pennyworth of bread to this intolerable deal of sack!

Fine though the lines are, they are both traditional and imitative and it is necessary to take this fact into consideration in judging the mind of the man who could bear to omit them. What is traditional and imitative is not likely to be very close to the heart of a truly creative poet such as A, B, and C. Actually, the imitation here seems fairly narrowly limited. If one turns to the opening lines of *Winner and Waster* and the *Parliament of the Three Ages* one may, perhaps, recognize the babbling bourn from which A, the most earthy of all the possible authors of *Piers Plowman,* drew his inspiration :[9]

> In the monethes of Maye when mirthes bene fele,
> And the sesone of somere when softe bene the wedres,
> Als I went to the wodde. . . .[1]

> Als I wente in the weste, wandrynge myn one,
> Bi a bonke of a bourne, bryghte was the sone.[2]

Perhaps A had never seen or heard these lines. But if he had not, he had read countless lines like them. Admirable as is his variation on an old theme, it would be ironical for us to admire it above his more original poetry.

We must be careful not to fall into a sort of sentimental antiquarianism in dealing with *Piers Plowman*. It is a large poem, and it has a large meaning. It is the large meaning that the author or authors wished us to perceive. The poem may, incidentally, contain a number of one-line gems, but if we spend our time admiring these, instead of trying to grasp the broad significance, there is something wrong with our perspective, and A, B, or C would probably not have much patience with us. No more

8. See A, IX, 54–8, B, VIII, 62–7, C, XI, 61–7; B, XI, 356–9, C, XIV, 176–9; B, XV, 94–100, C, XVII, 247–54; B, XVII, 226–8, C, XX, 192–4; B, XVIII, 409–10, C, XXI, 456–7, and the discussion in Day and Steele, *op. cit.,* p. xvii.

9. *Winner and Waster* probably antedates the A-text. See Manly, *CHEL,* II, 43; J. R. Hulbert, "The Problems of Authorship and Date of *Wynnere and Wastoure,*" *MPh,* XVIII (1920–21), 31–40; J. M. Steadman, "The Date of *Wynnere and Wastoure,*" *MPh,* XIX (1921–22), 211–19; Sir Israel Gollancz' edition (London, 1920), preface; and Steadman's review, *MLN,* XXXVI (1921), 103–10. For the date of the *Parliament,* see Gollancz' edition (London, 1915), preface. Oakden, *Alliterative Poetry in Middle English,* II, 51–5, summarizes the evidence for both poems and discusses their relation to *Piers Plowman.*

1. *Parliament,* ll. 1–3.   2. *Winner and Waster,* ll. 32–3.

would Beethoven if we listened to one of his long symphonies for the sake of a few strikingly beautiful bars. In respect to C's revision,of the opening of the poem, it seems evident that he omitted the lines describing the natural scenery because he was in a hurry to get to "the men on the plain." In this race he was not really very far ahead of A and B. It is no surprise, if we assume unity of authorship, to find C in his haste sacrificing what as A he had never found particularly important to his poem.

Besides, he put something in the place of what he left out, even if it was only "four prosaic lines," as Hall called them, "introduced as a sort of argument to the entire vision" :[3]

> Al þe welþe of þis worlde & þe woo boþe,
> Wynkyng as it were wyterly ich saw hyt,
> Of tryuþe & of tricherye, of tresoun and of gyle,
> Al ich saw slepynge, as ich shal ȝow telle.

Whether the lines are really prosaic or not seems to me to depend upon one's bias—whether one prefers nature poetry to the sort of lines that are characteristic of *Piers Plowman*. In any case, it is fair to ask, What is wrong with introducing an argument to the entire vision? That such an argument is needed is, perhaps, proved by the number of readers who stop short of the *Vita,* satisfied that they have read *Piers Plowman.* Let me quote what a recent critic has said about the passage in the C-text which these four lines conclude:

. . . Langland, in the passage just quoted [C, 1, 1–13], showed that he could do what very few modern poets have been able to accomplish—that is, to handle a plain unadorned narrative, bringing out its full implications, without interrupting its natural flow. He succeeded in telling us that his poem was to be a complete survey of human life under the aspect of good and evil (for he saw—"Al the welthe of this worlde and the woo bothe"), without in any way distracting us from the preliminary statement of the circumstances of the poem. And, since we could trust very few of even the greatest of our Romantic poets to do this, we must conclude that it was in itself a considerable achievement.[4]

In short, if we read the whole of C's introductory passage by itself, instead of comparing it piecemeal with A and B, we may both understand what C was trying to achieve and even admire his achievement. That C wanted the reader to concentrate on the significance of the poem, and not go to sleep by the bourn along with the Dreamer, explains his revision. Viewed thus, the revision will not seem a serious debasement of the original.

A good many of the judgments that have been made on the style of the C-text are as reversible as certain patent overcoats. The line,

3. *MLR,* IV, 7.   4. D. A. Traversi, *Scrutiny,* v, 283.

> Al þe welþe of þis worlde & þe woo boþe,

provides a good example. Manly asserted that its author was "funda-
mentally not a poet but a topographer"[5]—though it is difficult to see
what wealth and woe have to do with topography. Jusserand, on the
other hand, admired it, since he felt that it tended to "broaden the spec-
tacle."[6] Traversi, one may conclude from the paragraph quoted above,
is allied with Jusserand. My opinion is that the line is a good enough one
that shows C characteristically revising to point up the moral, but I
should not go a great way either to praise or blame it. It is impossible
not to wonder whether, if the line had stood in the A- and B-texts, any
one would have troubled to disparage it, or, if it had appeared in A and
B and had been omitted by C, whether some one might not have complained that C was spoiling the picture. Even so poetically dubious a
line as

> And sawe meny cellis and selcouthe þynges,

might be said to have its place, since it carries on the thought of its
predecessor,

> Ich wente forth in þe worlde wonders to hure,

into the province of sight as well as of sound, which is what one would
expect. It is, of course, by no means an indispensable line. But if it had
stood in A, should we not have accepted it as an integral part of the
picture?

Miss Day has pointed out as an instance of C's flatness his revision of
B Prologue 89–90.[7] Here the poet, in speaking of priests and their duties,
says that they have received the tonsure in token

> And signe þat þei sholden shryuen here paroschienes,
> Prechen and prey for hem, and þe pore fede.

C, employing anacoluthon, revises,

> Ben chargid with holy churche, charyte to tulie,
> Þat is, leel loue and lif a-mong lered and lewed.[8]

C's version is certainly the more abstract. Yet it gives a wider, more
mature definition of the duties of the clergy and has the decided advantage of introducing the dominant image of the poem, that of the plow,
which tills charity, itself one of the manifestations of the Church. In
another place where C has altered the original in order to bring in the
image of the plow he deserves, I think, some praise. That is when he
changed B's

5. *MPh*, vii, 131.   6. *MPh*, vi, 316.
7. *MLR*, xxiii, 6.   8. C, i, 87–8.

> Souteres and shepherdes, suche lewed iottes,

to

> And lewede leele laborers and land-tylynge peuple.[9]

If ever there is a point in the poem that needs the climactic mention of plowmen, it is here. C alone fulfills the artistic requirement. But of course, because of his alteration in the next line of "the palace of heaven" to "paradise or heaven" critics have been too busy blaming the error to notice the improvement.

Some of the critics of C betray a strange idea of the duties of a poet. Thus Hall abuses C for omitting the "interesting" passage in B, x where Study laments the fact that modern lords and ladies have deserted the great halls of their castles, preferring to eat in privacy.[1] The passage is, certainly, interesting as a commentary on fourteenth-century social customs and we are sorry to see it go. At the same time, it is certainly a digression and not germane to the main current of the conversation. One might, however, let Hall's reproof stand, were it not that he also blames C for the "ineptness" of one of his insertions[2]—the humorous passage in which Holy Church forbears to say why Lucifer betook himself to the north lest she offend northern men.[3] This passage is no more inept than B's digression and can surely claim as valid a *raison d'être*. Hall's criticism of C here seems prejudiced and based upon the notion that medieval poets, in order to be adjudged good in the twentieth century, should have filled their poems with interesting, if irrelevant, pieces of historical information. Somewhat the same notion possibly influences our attitude toward C's elimination of naïveté. It is an agreeable sensation today to look back on the popular superstitions and misconceptions of the fourteenth century and one is apt to attribute to a pedantic turn of mind C's deletion of all traces of them. Yet who of us in our maturity would leave in our work traces of a naïveté about which we had become self-conscious? C worked to be judged by his age, not by all time. I have sometimes thought that even the excellence of B's simile of the child weeping in church might be an accident of the passing centuries— that the simile may, indeed, have become excellent largely because of the influence that Blake and Wordsworth in their love for children worked upon literature, more than four centuries after B wrote the line.[4] In somewhat the same vein, I am disposed to think that the large measure of appreciation accorded to B's famous prophecy,

9. C, xii, 294. Cf. B, x, 460. 1. *MLR,* iv, 6. The passage is B, x, 94 ff.
2. *MLR,* iv, 7. 3. C, ii, 112–22.
4. One is reminded that when Wordsworth wanted to compliment Chaucer for having perceived the natural piety of children he cited the line, "Sweet is the holiness of Youth," which Wordsworth himself had added to the original in his modern rendering of *The Prioress' Tale.* See *Ecclesiastical Sonnets,* ii, xxxi, 1, and Wordworth's *The Prioress' Tale,* ix, 61.

And þanne shal þe abbot of Abyndoun and alle his issu for euere
Haue a knokke of a kynge, and incurable þe wounde,[5]

which C has been blamed for altering so that the *Abbot of Abingdon*
became generalized to the *Abbot of England,* depends fairly largely on
the purely fortuitous circumstance that B's prophecy was literally fulfilled during the Reformation. As students of literature, our interest is
in poets, not prophets.

If we set out, then, to defend C with as much enthusiasm—and, I
admit, with as much bias in the opposite direction—as some have set out
to prosecute him, we might find that there is another side to even his
most drastic and presumably ruinous revisions. But it would be futile to
deny the obvious fact that in a number of places the C-text is inferior
to A and B—less imaginatively appealing, less concrete, less truly poetic,
and less readable. I have listed a number of instances, amounting, perhaps, to a hundred lines, where this is true. I must, however, issue a
warning: the examples I have given have, most of them, been pointed
out before by those who hold with the theory of multiple authorship
and though ordinarily one gets the impression that these are but a selection of examples from a large potential stock, the truth is that they are
the best examples in the whole poem—the only ones, indeed, that stand
on their own feet. In more than 99 per cent of their seven-thousand-odd
lines there is little to choose between B and C. The expression may
differ in the two texts but neither shows any long-sustained superiority.
It is important that this be borne in mind. The fact that C revised a
great many of B's lines and spoiled some of them is frequently stated as
if the spoiling were a constant element in the revision. But if C made the
error of mistaking change for improvement, let us not make the complementary error of mistaking change for decay. The position of B as
the older text exercises sometimes a hypnotic effect on our critical faculties. In order to reattain some measure of critical impartiality we ought to
test each individual judgment of C by assuming, arbitrarily, that C is the
older text and B the revision. If we did this, we should find, I think, our
impression of C's inferiority rather less firm.

On the strength of the fact that actually B is the earlier text, containing none of C's peculiar weaknesses, scholars have come to the conclusion
that B is the best form in which to read *Piers Plowman.* But even this
conclusion is not altogether safe. For the trouble is that C, although he
shows deficiency in imaginative power, also shows, just as often, bursts
of imaginative power that are quite as impressive as anything in the
earlier texts. One could go on at length quoting passages that are as good
as, or even better than, any in B. C has been blamed for omitting one of

5. B, x, 326–7. Cf. C, vi, 177–8. See Coghill, preface to Wells's modern rendering, p.
xxvii; Skeats, *EETS,* iii, lxx. Skeat is careful not to blame C for spoiling the poetry,
but rather the prophecy, of the accuracy of which C could scarcely have been aware.

B's passages on the poor. But many forget that he wrote a passage on the same subject every bit as eloquent:

The most needy aren oure neighebores, and we nyme good hede,
As prisones in puttes and poure folke in Cotes,
Charged with children and chef lordes rente,
That þei wiþ spynnynge may spare spenen hit in hous-hyre,
Boþe in mylk and in mele to make with papelotes,
To a-glotye with here gurles þat greden after fode.
Al-so hem-selue suffren muche hunger,
And wo in winter-tyme, with wakynge a nyghtes
To ryse to þe ruel, to rocke þe cradel,
Boþe to karde and to kembe, to clouten and to wasche,
To rubbe and to rely, russhes to pilie,
Þat reuthe is to rede oþere in ryme shewe
The wo of þese women þat wonyeþ in Cotes.[6]

Though such a passage has its inspiration close to the poet's home, we see that he can also go far afield. Thus the Satan of the C-revision gives the following vigorous command when Christ comes to harrow hell:

Ac rys vp ragamoffyn and reche me alle þe barres
That belial þy bel-syre beot with þy damme,
And ich shal lette þis lorde and hus light stoppe;
Ar we þorw bryghtnesse be blent, barre we þe gates.[7]

In an earlier part of the poem Holy Church thus summarizes her definition of love,

So loue ys lech of lyue and lysse of alle peyne,
And þe graffe of grace and grayþest wey to heuene.[8]

This is a revision of a less pointed passage in B,

Loue is leche of lyf and nexte owre lorde selue,
And also þe graith gate þat goth in-to heuene.[9]

Observe the added detail in the otherwise emasculated confession of Envy,

Sholde no lyf lyuye þat on hus londe passede,[1]

and the expansion in Repentance's account of God's mercy,

6. C, x, 71–83. This fine passage was not mentioned in the literature of the controversy except obliquely by Jusserand, *MPh*, vii, 321, along with other C-additions. Manly appeared to find in C's omission of the similar passage in B (xiv, 174–80) an indication that C did not have the same feelings as B on the subject of the poor. See *CHEL*, ii, 35, and *MPh*, vii, 129–30. Hall recognized the similarity of attitude but did not directly call attention to the C-passage. See *MLR*, iv, 12. Recently Miss Day, *MLR*, xxiii, 6, has given C the credit he deserves in this matter.
7. C, xxi, 283–6. This passage is praised by Miss Day, *MLR*, xxiii, 7.
8. C, ii, 200–01.   9. B, i, 202–03.   1. C, vii, 67.

> For al þe wrecchednesse of þis worlde and wickede dedes
> Fareþ as a fonk of fuyr þat ful a-myde temese,
> And deide for a drop of water; so doþ alle synnes.[2]

Notice the following curious but clear figure,

> For god is def now a dayes and deyneþ nouht ous to huyre,
> And good men for oure gultes he al to-grynt to deþe,[3]

and the following description of the lunatic lollers, who are

> . . . mad as þe mone sitt more oþer lasse.
> Thei caren for no cold ne counteþ of no hete,
> And arn meuynge after þe mone, moneyles þei walke,
> With a good wil, witlees, meny wyde contreys.[4]

In passing, we might also notice C's use of the ancient jingle in the second of the following lines,

> At churche in þe charnel cheorles aren vuel to knowe,
> Oþer a knyght fro a knaue, oþer a queyne fro a queene.[5]

Finally, I invite the reader to read the whole of C's autobiographical passage appearing at the beginning of Passus VI, a few lines of which are quoted elsewhere.[6] This, the poet's *apologia pro vita sua,* contains the most striking of all the bursts of irony in *Piers Plowman,* the more effective since it is largely self-directed.

These passages, some of them of unquestioned brilliancy, afford a strange contrast to the examples that have been given of C's lack of imagination and of his lack of appreciation for imaginative poetry which he saw before him. It is a paradox difficult to resolve. If human nature were as consistent as one might wish it to be, the only way to explain the conflict of opposites in C would be to split him into two writers, one a poetic Dr. Jekyll and the other a prosaic Mr. Hyde. Unfortunately, human nature is not so consistent and it is altogether possible that one man should write so poorly and so well. If C was a different man from A and B, it is difficult to reconcile his two manners, inasmuch as we should expect a revision carried on by a second poet to be all of a piece. Why else make the revision? If, however, C was the same as A and B, we should expect a mixture of the brilliant and the mediocre, since that is just what the A- and B-texts show that their author was. It was, indeed, the mixture of qualities in the A-text that first led Manly to suspect the presence of two poets in its composition. Therefore it seems to me that the mixture of good and bad in C is more reasonably explained by the hypothesis of single authorship than in any other way. There is

2. C, VII, 334–6.   3. C, XII, 61–2.
4. C, X, 108–11.   5. C, IX, 45–6. Cf. B, VI, 50–1.
6. C, VI, 1–101. See the discussion in Chapter VII.

a consistency in the very lack of consistency. Knowing A and B, brilliance mingled with mediocrity is just what we should expect from C.

A few words about the long passage added by C in which Conscience makes his laborious distinction between reward and bribery (*mede* and *mercede*) would not be beside the point.[7] Of all the C-additions, this is probably the least popular and has been the target of an extraordinary amount of abuse which has done serious injury to C's reputation as a poet and thinker.[8] I suggest that its inferiority has been exaggerated. It is quite true that C has chosen a simile from grammar, nowadays considered the driest of all studies, and that the simile is too rigid to be bent to the uses to which C tries to put it, so that the result is not wholly comprehensible. The reader, like the King, would like to know

> What is relacion rect and indyrect after,
> And þenne adiectyf and substantif, for englisch was it neuere.[9]

On the other hand, the passage contains several of the most interesting and clearly expressed of the poet's political tenets and at least one very characteristic figure of speech. In this the King is described as

> . . . haldyng with no partie,
> Bote stande as a stake þat stykeþ in a muyre
> By-twyne two londes for a trewe marke.[1]

This is certainly an ingenious and, on the whole, effective presentation of an idea. I am inclined to feel that the attitude that the entire passage is stupid and senseless amounts to a sort of defense, in that it absolves us of the necessity of bothering about the lines. But if we refuse to bother with them, it becomes apparent that we have no real appreciation for medieval literature and we had better go back to Chaucer, whom we can always praise as the most modern of poets—that is, if we pick the right selections. For the C-passage is blatantly and unblushingly medieval, though possibly less so than many more fashionable passages in the poetry of Donne, and we have no cause to blame a medieval poet for being of his age. It is not impossible to find in the disputed passage both intelligence and imagination, though it is certainly difficult to follow

7. See C, IV, 317–409.
8. Skeat, *EETS*, III, lxxxvi: "A passage of that subtle and simile-seeking character which was no doubt once highly esteemed, but to us seems tedious and puerile." Hall, *MLR*, IV, 7, "The most outrageous case of irrelevant insertion. . . . Poor arid stuff. . . ." Moore, *MPh*, XI, 192, "Quite unintelligible and utterly barren of all interest." Skeat goes on to observe that the passage is so similar to B, XVII, 135–249 that any one who compares the two "may easily see that the writer of one of them would be just the man to write the other." Moore, relying on the force of assertion, says that "the two passages are not really of the same character," and adds that Manly believed the C-passage showed "a quality of dry pedantry in the mind of C which does not appear in the writer (or writers) of the earlier texts." See *MPh*, XI, 191.
9. C, IV, 344–5.   1. C, IV, 383–5.

every one of its convolutions. Since there are a good many other parts of the poem—in all versions—where I find myself in a similar predicament, I should suggest that before we damn the passage as an outrage we make a less hostile attempt to understand it, even if we have to go to school, as Langland did, with medieval grammarians.[2] The elaborate distinction is as characteristic of C, and of B, as *Peter Bell* is of Wordsworth. Who would damn all Wordsworth because of *Peter Bell?* And, since it helps us to understand the poetry of Wordsworth, who would utterly damn *Peter Bell?*

For the other idiosyncrasies of the C-revision some apology, as I suggested earlier, may be made. C's preoccupation with the moral and religious implications of the poem, exemplified in his revision of the Prologue, and his fondness for generalizing its application are at worst minor irritants to those who prefer to sport with Amaryllis in the shade, or with the Dreamer by the bournside. Possibly Samuel Johnson (if he could have been brought to read anything so barbarous as *Piers*) would have preferred the C-text, as did Whitaker, the only eighteenth-century man of letters to express a clear judgment on the subject. Perhaps a time will come when C's emphasis upon broader implications will seem more attractive than the earlier texts' closer adherence to concrete detail. In any case, we must remember that *Piers Plowman* in all its forms deals with matters *sub specie aeternitatis* and to read it without bearing this in mind is to misread it. There is nothing incompatible with the theory of single authorship if in the final version the eternal and universal significance is more conspicuous than in the earlier texts. It was there the whole time and was, in fact, what gave the poem being. C, in emphasizing it, was only doing what A might easily have done and what B, frequently enough, actually had done.

That C is sometimes more guarded in his statements than A and B cannot be denied. I resist, however, attributing this to "caution," at least in the belittling sense of the word. C avoids strong statements, but strong statements are, by their nature, generally inaccurate and unfair. C may have desired to be both accurate and fair. Many doctors, says B, are murderers. Our knowledge of fourteenth-century medical ethics is limited, but it is a safe guess that while faulty prescription and faulty diagnosis caused deaths, few doctors set out to fill the graveyards. C's statement of the situation is fairer than B's, though the profession could still find reason to complain of slander. At other times C's toning down can be explained less easily. But just as one is about to yield a point and grant C's cautiousness, one comes across such a statement as that made

2. The passage becomes somewhat more understandable—or at any rate its purpose does—when read in the light of medieval treatises on Latin grammar such as that published by S. B. Meech on pp. 98–125 of the University of Michigan volume referred to above, p. 46, n. 1.

by Conscience to the King. Meed, Conscience tells him, along with her sister Unsuitable Tolerance,

> Haue maked al-most, bote marie þe helpe,
> Þat no lond loueþ the, and ȝut leest þyn owene[3]—

an example of plain-speaking to royalty unparalleled in A or B. Caution, if that was what C suffered from, has been thrown to the winds.

C's tendency to tone down strong sentiments seems, then, to have been of the same nature as his desire to attain accuracy and coherence in the development of the narrative, to which it is perhaps related. While one part of his mind may have sought after guarded statement, the other part burst forth with the unvarnished truth. Similarly, though one part of his mind may have desired a nice coherence, the other part persisted in a deep-rooted habit of loose, inaccurate composition. In both these matters C seems to be acting very much like A and B. We do not know what inhibitions they had—though I should be disposed to include among them a great reverence for royalty—but we do know that when they became angry, like C they did not spare the feelings of their contemporaries. So far as incoherencies are concerned, neither A nor B is without sin. Witness A's omission of the confession of Wrath and any one of a number of slips by B.[4] The one in B that most delights me is the very line which, in its C-form, I referred to a little while ago as an instance of C's negligence—the line which refers back to the Dreamer's quarrel with the Friar over burial in the Priory churchyard.[5] According to B's account of the quarrel, the Dreamer refused to be buried with the Friars, but according to the line in which he mentions the matter, the Friars refused to let him be buried among them. Concerning confusions like this, one cannot do better than to repeat Jusserand's words, "Such peculiarities are indeed so peculiar as to be, in a way, the author's mark—his seal and signature."[6]

C's habit of repeating lines and half-lines within short passages is largely his own, but there are enough repetitions in B,[7] as well as one or two in A, to make it seem that C's are a logical development. Thus the AB-line in Passus I,

> For-thi chastite with-oute charite worth cheyned in helle,[8]

---

3. C, IV, 209-10.

4. For instance, his inability, inherited from A, to count to seven deadly sins. Chambers, *LMS*, I, 36, points out that in B's list in XIII, 272-457 Gluttony is omitted (though present in R), while in XIV, 215-56 Gluttony and Envy are omitted (though Gluttony is added in R). In Piers's allegory of the Commandments (A, VI, 50-74, B, V, 568-93, C, VIII, 204-31) none of the texts manages to get up to ten.

5. B, XIII, 9. Cf. C, XVI, 11.   6. *MPh*, VI, 297-8.

7. See B, V, 552, 555; IX, 113, 116; X, 118, 125; XI, 45, 49, 51; 343, 345, etc.

8. B, I, 186; Cf. 192 (A, I, 162 in T; cf. 168; C, II, 185). C, curiously enough, deletes the second appearance of the line from its proper place after II, 191.

is repeated after an interval of five lines with the insertion of *such* before
chastite. Repetition of lines or half-lines at longer intervals is instanced
only rather rarely in B, though it does occur.[9] But the fact that C was
addicted to the practice does not lead to the conclusion that he was a
different man from B. Indeed, it suggests quite the opposite. His borrowings are of such a sort as to postulate a remarkably thorough knowledge of B, since what he borrows is often situated in a passus of the
B-text remote from, and occurring later than, the one he is revising. It
is possible that some one other than B had this mastery of the B-text but
it is not likely. So far as C's recurrent use of the word *leel* and the phrase
as it were are concerned, the former, of course, appears with some
frequency in B, while the latter occurs at least once.[1] B, though he does
not seem to have been susceptible to domination by phrases like these,
was not altogether innocent in this respect. One may note his fondness
for the expression *ryȝt so,* which is used in one passage four times within
the space of twenty-five lines.[2] In all these matters it is possible to trace
from B to C a gradual development such as we might expect in one
man's writing. The larger number of repetitions in C is indicative of
lessened facility in composition, although they do not constitute any
serious blemish.

In a previous discussion I tried to show that the three versions of *Piers
Plowman* in respect to alliterative practices resemble nothing so much
as each other. The same may be said of their poetic and narrative techniques. Although in this chapter the emphasis has fallen upon the differences between C and the earlier texts, the fact remains that C is much
more like them than it is like anything else in Middle English alliterative
poetry. None of the versions shares any marked peculiarity with any other
poem that it does not share with the other two versions. On the other
hand, the three versions share certain peculiarities that appear in no
other poem. It was my original intention to demonstrate this and I had
worked out a *modus operandi*. But the demonstration could only be
made by sampling certain lines from the other poems and since this
method is open to the charge of partiality in the selection of samples, I
decided to forego the plan. A good illustration of the differences between
Piers and its contemporaries is provided by *Mum and the Sothsegger*.
As we know, the author of the latter borrowed words, phrases, and
lines from *Piers Plowman* in what seems to have been conscious imitation. Yet individuality will express itself, for the poet of *Mum* devotes
more than fifty consecutive lines to a description of natural scenery,
something that the impatience of our poet made altogether impossible.[3]

9. See B, Pro., 18 and II, 55; v, 467 and VI, 102.
1. For *as it were*, see B, III, 37. The phrase appears elsewhere in Middle English poetry.
See, for instance, *Alexander A,* ll. 568, 766, 784; *Patience,* l. 450.
2. B, XII, 36, 48, 53, 60.   3. See Fragment M, ll. 876–943.

To take another tack, let us look at the following lines in C. They occur in a speech by Liberum Arbitrium which concerns, in general, the wealth of the clergy:

> Alas! lordes and ladies, lewede counsail haue ȝe
> Þat founded beþ to fulle to feffe suche and fede
> With þat ȝoure barnes and ȝoure blod by goode lawe may cleyme!
> For god bad hus blessede, as þe book techeþ,
>> *Honora patrem & matrem, ut longeuus sis, &c.*[4]

This rather obscure passage seems to say: Alas, lords and ladies, you are badly advised when you fief these clerics, who are already too fully endowed, with property that the issue of your flesh and blood may lawfully expect to inherit; for God commanded His apostles, as the Bible tells us, Honor thy father and thy mother. With a rather desperate effort the poet does succeed, a few lines later, in reversing the sense of the fifth commandment so that it will apply to the attitude of parents toward their children. But it is a near thing. The carefree manner in which the poet's logic goes the wrong direction up a one-way street, emerging triumphantly though scarcely legitimately at its destination, seems to me thoroughly characteristic of C, of B, and even of A. The reversal may, indeed, have its explanation in some contemporary Biblical gloss. But even if it does, the glossator's way of thinking is that of the poet of *Piers Plowman* and if it is characteristic of any other poem or poet of the period, I have failed to observe it.

In this chapter I have attempted a partial vindication of the artistic value of the C-text, operating on the principle, which was set forth fully in the first chapter, that the hypothesis of multiple authorship is supported by a low evaluation of the C-text and unity by a higher one. The reader will judge for himself how far the vindication has succeeded. In regard to the actual evidence adduced, it may be said that none of C's peculiarities leads inevitably toward the conclusion that he was a different man from A and B. Certain points, moreover, such as his thorough knowledge of the B-text and the individualistic technique he shares with B in the handling of such characters as False and Favel, Warren Wiseman and Wilyman, strongly suggest that he was the same. That C was at times wanting in poetic facility and poetic imagination is indisputable. On the other hand it is equally indisputable that he was capable of occasional outbursts of vivid and moving poetry which prove that although his imagination was sometimes dormant it was not dead. The fact that in these outbursts his writing is not inferior to that of A and B makes it probable that he was A and B. With such a point of view the lesser peculiarities observed are entirely consistent since a development of idiosyncrasies is usual in an aging writer and those displayed

4. C, XVIII, 55-8.

by C may be explained either as a logical growth of tendencies present in the earlier texts, or as habits to which any poet is susceptible. Hence the evidence drawn from this study does not support the theory of divided authorship and it does support unity of authorship.

IV

The Politics of the C-Reviser

PERHAPS no problem in *Piers Plowman* is more confused than that of the author's (or authors') political attitude. The confusion is twofold. In the first place, published accounts dealing with the poem as a whole give conflicting descriptions of the political sentiments it contains, so that we learn from one report that the author was a staunch democrat who reflected the more radical political thought of his time,[1] and from another that he had no political opinions that would have offended the most rigorous royalist of the fourteenth century.[2] In

1. See Esmé Wingfield-Stratford, *The History of British Civilization* (London, 1928, 2 vols.), I, 260: ". . . one who was the most striking democrat of them all, William Langland"; Ramsay Muir, *A Short History of the British Commonwealth* (6th ed., London, 1937, 2 vols.), I, 141: ". . . in *Piers Plowman* there is a remarkably democratic note to be observed"; Vida D. Scudder, *Social Ideals in English Letters* (Boston, 1898), p. 22: "The first note of the social revolution is heard in its [the poem's] confused echoes" (but on p. 25 Miss Scudder notes that the poet was "at once conservative and radical"); G. G. Coulton, *The Medieval Scene* (Cambridge, England, 1930), p. 158: "Radical as the author is in politics and in religion, he accepts the distinction of classes as God-ordained"; G. C. Homans, *English Villagers of the Thirteenth Century* (Cambridge, 1941), p. 307: "Langland was a sentimentalist. He wrote of Piers Plowman as a left-wing novelist writes of the worker, and for the same reason. His sympathies were with the common man at a time when the conflict between the classes of society was bitter."

2. See Manly, *MPh*, VII, 87: "The political and social views of these poems were, indeed, common views of Englishmen of that day"; Jusserand, *MPh*, VII, 298: agreement with Manly; Jusserand, *Mysticism*, p. 103: "In reality, he [Langland] is, from the religious and social points of view, one of those rare thinkers who defend moderate ideas with vehemence . . ."; C. S. Lewis, *The Allegory of Love* (Oxford, 1936), p. 159: "As a politician, Langland has nothing to propose except that all estates should do their duty. It is unnecessary, I presume, to state that his poem is not revolutionary, nor even democratic"; T. F. Tout, *The History of England from the Accession of Henry III. to the Death of Edward III.* (London, 1905), p. 424: "He is no revolutionist with a new gospel of reform . . ."; G. M. Trevelyan, *England in the Age of Wycliffe* (4th ed., London, 1929), p. 35, mentions Langland's conservative treatment of the fable of the Rat Parliament; Charles Oman, *The Great Revolt of 1381* (Oxford, 1906), fails to include the poet anywhere among the radicals he discusses; see also the sane summary of the poet's political attitude in Kenneth Sisam, *Fourteenth Century Verse and Prose* (2d ed., Oxford, 1937), p. 78. The citations given in this and the previous note are only a fraction of those that might be given for both points of view. In particular one might quote from a large number of historians and literary historians who agree that Langland was a radical. Therefore the second sentence quoted above from C. S. Lewis seems unduly optimistic. For the benefit of those who wish to make a frontal attack on the problem one should mention the following studies of the poem: Heinrich Wiehe, *Piers Plowman und die sozialen Fragen seiner Zeit* (Emsdetten, 1935); D. Chadwick, *Social Life in the Days of Piers Plowman* (Cambridge, England, 1922); and the pioneer work, E. M. Hopkins, "Character and Opinions of William Langland," *Kansas University Quarterly* (April 1894), pp. 233–88.

the second place, there is confusion among the accounts of those who have compared the various texts of the poem, so that we learn from one scholar that B was a good deal bolder than C,[3] and from another that the C-reviser distinguished himself from B "in the emphasis which he places upon the power of the Commons"[4] and this, in an era of only nascent democracy, implies that C was rather bolder than B. There is not even agreement on the matter of the amount of political interest that any one text exhibits, so that we find the same poet being credited with a vital interest in the political movements of his day and with little more than a passing interest in them.[5]

> This were a wikked way but who-so hadde a gyde,

but, as Manly said about himself and Jusserand,[6] the reader is apt to suffer as much from a diversity of guides as from the wickedness of the way.

In this chapter I shall examine several aspects of the problem. In accordance wth the main purpose of this book I shall be interested largely in eliminating, if possible, the supposed discrepancy between B and C by laying the twin ghosts of B's radicalism and C's ultraconservatism. These are ghosts whom the student encounters frequently in the Gothic castle of *Piers Plowman*. They were first raised by Thomas Wright a hundred years ago and for this reason I shall have to base some part of the discussion on the remarks of that pioneer in Middle English studies. Wright formulated the original multiple-authorship theory and the basis for it lay in the divergence he was able to detect between B's and C's political opinions: he even went so far as to suggest that the primary

3. Thomas Wright, *The Vision and Creed of Piers Plowman*, I, xxxiv–xxxv.

4. Sister Mary Aquinas Devlin, "The Date of the C Version of *Piers the Plowman*," p. 318. I am at a loss to understand the reason for Sister Mary Aquinas' statement, which is contained in the published abstract of her dissertation. Justification is doubtless included in the dissertation itself, which I have not seen.

5. See H. deB. Gibbins, *English Social Reformers* (2d ed., London, 1902), pp. 7–8: "In 1377 he [the author] began to expand his poem into the second or B-text. The grief of the nation at the death of the Black Prince, the troublous political events of 1377, and the dissatisfaction of the people with both Edward III. and the Duke of Lancaster, roused Langland once more to write. . . . So he re-wrote . . . his poem . . . , weaving in new thoughts, suggested by the events of the times in which he lived"; Richard Garnett, *English Literature: an Illustrated Record* (London, 1903–6, 4 vols.), I, 96–7: "He takes a keen interest in the politics of his day, and usually sides with the Commons in their disputes with the Crown"; Jusserand, *MPh*, VI, 271: "The author of *Piers Plowman* concerns himself especially with classes of men, great political movements, the general aspirations of the people, the improvements necessary in each class for the welfare of the nation"; see also the remarks of Thomas Wright, referred to in n. 3 immediately above. For the opposite point of view, see Chambers, *Mind*, p. 102: "The light thrown upon contemporary history, however important, was only incidental; the poem as a whole tells the story of the struggle of the human soul"; Manly, *CHEL*, II, 33: ". . . great as is the interest in political theory displayed by the author in the passages inserted in the prologue, this is not one of the subjects to which he constantly reverts."

6. *MPh*, VII, 139.

motive of the C-revision was the toning down of B's radical expressions of political theory.[7] It may seem to some readers that to answer a century-old theory is an empty labor. Yet it must be remembered that Wright was the founder of the tradition of multiple authorship; and, as we have already seen, with such a poem as *Piers Plowman,* which many readers find easier to read about than to read, tradition is of great importance. Furthermore, Wright's premises were repeated—though in a rather oblique manner—by Manly during his controversy with Jusserand[8] and some years later Moore was able to complain, with reason, that no one had ever bothered to answer Wright's arguments.[9] Nor has the situation altered during the thirty years since Moore's article appeared.

One other aspect of the topic also compels our attention in this chapter. The B-text, as every one knows, contains a good deal of what seems to be topical allusion, particularly in the Prologue. Although topical allusion in a poem does not necessarily mean that its author had any great political interest or any marked political bias, the amount and quality of it that have been detected in B by certain scholars leave one with the impression that the B-poet had a lively political interest and strong democratic sympathies. Topical allusion in a medieval poem is, of course, a challenge to scholarly ingenuity, and in the interpretation of allusions we sometimes exert our ingenuity in such a way as to distort altogether the truth about the work under scrutiny. This has sometimes happened to the earlier texts of *Piers Plowman,* ninety-nine one-hundredths of which is far removed from anything political, but which appears in certain accounts as if it were a medieval *Absalom and Achitophel.* It is the more difficult to counteract this impression because of the undoubted use of *Piers Plowman* in one of its earlier forms by the rebels in the most exciting political event of the time—the Peasants' Revolt of 1381.[1] Nevertheless,

7. Wright, *op. cit.,* I, xxxiv–xxxv.

8. See Jusserand, *MPh,* VI, 271–2; *MPh,* VII, 296–8; Manly, *MPh,* VII, 85–8. The enthusiasm of Jusserand's admiration for the sentiments he believed were expressed by B, Pro., 112 13, in which the poet says that the power of the *comunes* made the King's reign possible, produced an unfortunate effect upon the controversy between the two scholars, inasmuch as in the subsequent exchange both managed to give the impression that they considered the B-poet a radical and the C-poet a conservative—the opposite of the fact, so far as B is concerned, as one can see from reading their observations quoted in n. 2 above. The false impression, which arose from a misunderstanding or misinterpretation by Manly of Jusserand's extravagant praise of the lines mentioned, is apt to be extremely misleading to those reading the literature of the controversy for the first time. Actually, Manly did not accept the premise that B was in any way radical, although he seems to have thought that Jusserand did and the argument thus became confused.

9. *MPh,* XI, 193.

1. For a thorough analysis of the use of *Piers Plowman* by John Ball and his fellows, see Burdach, *Ackermann,* pp. 167–203. C. S. Lewis, *op. cit.,* p. 159, n. 1, expresses doubt that Ball was indebted to *Piers Plowman* for the phrases in his famous letter (see *CP,* II, lv) and suggests instead a common source. But Burdach's analysis seems to make the connection very likely. Apparently Trevelyan shared Lewis' opinion: see Manly, *CHEL,* II, 44.

a reputation for being a political commentator with democratic sympathies—which B in particular has acquired—seems, on close examination, altogether unjustified. Since this unearned reputation tends to produce an apparent difference between B and C, who is relatively untopical[2] and scarcely a liberal, I shall, at the end of the chapter, reexamine those portions of the Prologue wherein B's allusions to contemporary political events appear.

The point of departure for a discussion of the politics of *Piers Plowman* and, indeed, the point in which much of the discussion must center, is a well-known passage describing the structure of the kingdom that was introduced into the Prologue by B and revised by C. In the earlier text the poet continues his account of the folk on the field as follows:

> Þanne come þere a kyng, knyȝthod hym ladde,
> Miȝt of þe comunes made hym to regne,
> And þanne cam kynde wytte and clerkes he made,
> For to conseille þe kyng and þe comune saue.
> The kyng and knyȝthode and clergye bothe
> Casten þat þe comune shulde hem-self fynde.
> Þe comune contreued by kynde witte craftes,
> And for profit of alle þe poeple plowmen ordeygned,
> To tilie and trauaile as trewe lyf askeþ.
> Þe kynge and þe comune and kynde witte þe thridde
> Shope lawe & lewte, eche man to knowe his owne.[3]

C paraphrases as follows:

> Þanne cam þer a kyng, knyȝt-hod hym ladde
> [Myght of tho] men made hym to regne;
> And þanne cam kynde witte & clerkus he made,
> And conscience & kynde wit and knyȝt-hod to-gederes
> Caste þat þe comune sholde hure comunes fynde.
> Kyndewit & þe comune contreuede alle craftes,
> And for most [profitable] a plouh þei gonne make,
> With leel labour to lyue whyl lif [on] londe lasteth.[4]

It was chiefly upon C's revision of this passage that Wright based his theory of multiple authorship. Indeed, the revision provided him with the only tangible piece of evidence that he ever produced to support the validity of the theory. "Nobody," he said, "I think, can deny that in this instance the doctrine is stated far more distinctly and far more boldly

2. For C's elimination of topical allusions, which was not, however, consistently carried on, see Skeat, *EETS*, iii, lxviii–lxxi.

3. B, Pro., 112–22.

4. C, i, 139–46. In 140 I substitute the reading of MSS XB2 for P *The muche myȝte of þe men;* MS E, which otherwise resembles P, has *þo* for *þe*. The reading is more sensible, besides being that of two "i"-group MSS. I also adopt the XB2PS reading *profitable* for FE *profit to þe puple,* preferred by Skeat in 145, and XB2 *on* for *and* in 146. XB2 omit 141b–2a accidentally.

in the first text than in the second."[5] To this Skeat was able to reply only that C's revision showed that "the poet grew more conservative in his ideas and more careful in his expressions as he grew older; a result so common and natural that it is not to be wondered at, but may be accepted as the fact."[6] The conservatism of old age was also the only explanation for the change that Jusserand could give to Manly in the course of their extremely confusing exchange of remarks about the two passages. The explanation is, in a sense, adequate; but in admitting that C was more cautious and conservative than B, one leaves the door open to further attacks upon the unity of authorship, since not every one will accept C's advanced age as an excuse for his apparent change of heart.[7] But the extent of the change of heart has been exaggerated and, as we shall see, the explanation of Skeat and Jusserand is necessary only in a very minor way.

Exercising a laissez-faire policy toward the meaning of the word *comune(s)*—that is, permitting the reader to understand by it whatever he will—let us examine the passages as they stand. B we may paraphrase as follows:

Then came, led by his knights, a king whom the power of the *comunes* had caused to reign. And then came Kind Wit, who created clerks in order to advise the king and save the *comune*. King, knighthood, and clergy devised that the *comune* should provide for themselves. The *comune*, with the help of Kind Wit, contrived crafts, and for profit of all the people appointed plowmen to plow and work as an honest life requires. King, *comune*, and Kind Wit created law and justice (*lewte*), so that each man might know his own place.

C may be paraphrased as follows:

Then came, led by his knights, a king whom the power of those men (i.e., the knights) had caused to reign. And then came Kind Wit, who created clerks. Conscience, Kind Wit, and knighthood devised that the *comune* should provide their rations. Kind Wit and the *comune* contrived all crafts, and, for the greatest profit to all, made a plow, in order to live by honest labor while life on land lasts.

The chief differences between these two passages are as follows: (1) C attributes to knighthood, rather than to the *comunes*, the power that enables the king to reign; (2) C omits from the description the part played by clerks in the kingdom; (3) C substitutes Conscience and Kind Wit for king and clergy, though he lets knighthood stand, as members

5. Wright, *op. cit.*, I, xxxv. The toning down of B's radical sentiments was the only motive assigned by Wright for the C-revision.

6. *EETS*, III, lxxix.

7. It was not accepted by Moore, *MPh*, XI, 190–1, who believed that Skeat had evaded the issue raised by Wright.

of the trio that devise that the *comune* should be the providers of rations (precisely who is to receive the rations remains unclear in both texts) ;[8] (4) C omits the summary lines, in which it appears that king, *comune*, and Kind Wit were founders of the law. Of these four changes made by C, the second, while interesting in itself, scarcely affects one's ideas on the radicalism or conservatism of C's politics. The same might be said of the third, which is interesting as an example of C's tendency toward the abstract. It is the first and, to a lesser degree, the fourth which are most relevant to a discussion of C's political attitude. If, as the *Oxford Dictionary* says,[9] the word *comunes* in B's second line means "the third estate in the English . . . constitution; the body of the people . . . represented by the Lower House of Parliament," then C's substitution of *knighthood* represents a serious about-face, emphasized by his omission of B's summary lines in which the *comune* plays so important a part.

We must, however, bear in mind that the lines quoted represent only a very small fraction of the total number of lines in each text and that in a poem as long as *Piers Plowman* we may expect any important idea to be expressed more than once. Therefore I propose to go through B and C in search of other passages that will give us reflections of their authors' sentiments in regard to government and politics, thus making certain that we make no mistake in our interpretation of the passages under examination. According to both B and C in the lines just quoted, the four components of which the kingdom consists are king, knighthood, clergy, and *comune*. Let us examine each of these in turn.

Both B and C consistently present the king as possessed of a triple function: he is the head of law, the defender of his realm, and the defender of the Church. The most specific description of his functions—one which is, incidentally, highly reminiscent of the passage we have just analyzed— occurs in the next-to-last passus of the poem and is, of course, the same in both texts:

> Then cam þer a kynge and by hus corone seide,
> "Ich am a kyng with corone þe comune to reule,
> And holy [kyrke] and clergie fro corsede men to defenden.
> And yf me lackeþ to lyue by, þe lawe wol þat ich take
> Ther ich may haue hit hastelokest, for ich am hefd of lawe,
> And ȝe ben bote membrys, and ich a-boue alle.
> Sitthen ich am ȝoure alre hefd, ich am ȝoure alre hele,
> And holychurches chef help and chefteyn of þe comune.
> And what ich take of ȝow two ich take hit at techynge

---

8. Both texts may be read as saying either that knighthood, etc., devised that the *comune* should feed the devisers, or that knighthood, etc., devised that the *comune* should be self-sufficient. The sense of B119 and C145 suggests that the latter is the better interpretation.

9. *OED, commons,* sb. pl., 1, 2.

Of *spiritus iusticie,* for ich Iugge ʒou alle;
So ich may baldely beo housled, for ich borwe neuere,
Ne craue of my comune bote as my kynde askeþ."[1]

To this admirable definition of royal prerogatives and duties—centering, as it does, in taxation, the very core of the problem of a king's relations with his realm—Conscience gives his full assent, troubling only to stipulate for the King the condition

. . . þat þou conne defende
And reule þy reame in reson, right wel, and in treuthe,[2]

and to remind him that he had power over all property only for the purpose of defense and not for the purpose of self-enrichment.[3] There was no question in the fourteenth century of Stuart absolutism and the divine right of kings: the king was subject to the spirit of the law over which he was the head—subject, that is, to *spiritus iustitiae,* under whose guidance he governed. And, according to B and C,

Spiritus iusticie spareþ nat to spille
Hem þat beoþ gulty, and for to corecte
The kyng, and þe kyng falle in eny þynge gulty.[4]

Presumably, then, a king who ruled unjustly could be removed under common law, although who might act as the agent of common law in his removal is not clear.

As much as his duties in regard to the law, however, B and C stress the king's military function—his position as defender of the realm and of the Church. This appears clearly in the third line of the long passage quoted just above and in several other passages which we shall consider below under the subject of knighthood.[5] In the accomplishment of his mission of defense, a king was, according to C, expected to undergo whatever perils were necessary:

. . . the kynde is of a knyʒt oþer for a kynge to be take,
And among here enemys in morteils bateles
To be culled and ouercome, þe comune to defende.[6]

We are to understand from this that the poet considered kingship not a privilege but a duty—a function rather than an honor—just as is theoretically the case with generals in a modern army.

The agency through which a king accomplished his military mission

1. C, xxii, 467–78 (B, xix, 462–73): *kyrke* in 469 is from MS X for P *church.* For the constitutional background of the passage, see p. 97, n. 6, below.
2. C, xxii, 479–80 (B, xix, 474–5).
3. *Omnia tua sunt ad defendendum, set non ad depredandum,* following B, xix, 476. C, xxii, 481 has *deprehendendum* for *depredandum.*
4. C, xxii, 303–05. B, xix, 298–300 varies in the last line.
5. See also C, xxii, 42 (B, xix, 42): "Hit by-comeþ for a kyng to kepen and defende."
6. C, xviii, 289–91.

was knighthood, the order whose members had the privilege and duty of bearing arms. In the fourteenth century the order included, ideally, all those of noble or gentle birth who met certain financial requirements, both barons (peers) and others.[7] In *Piers Plowman,* knighthood is closely associated with the king both by function and by alliteration and the term is generally used in all texts in its military, chivalric sense, without political connotation. Notice the last lines quoted in the paragraph immediately above and the following, in which, through long association with their subjects, the verbs have taken on an intransitive sense,

> Kynges and knyghtes þat kepen and defenden.[8]

Elsewhere, we are told that

> Kynges and knyghtes þat holy kirke defenden,
> And ryghtfulliche in reames ruelen þe comune,[9]

will pass quickly through purgatory. Piers Plowman agrees to labor for the Knight who is present on Piers's half-acre so long as the Knight will

> . . . kepe holy kirke and my-selue
> Fro wastours and wyckede men þat þis worlde struen.[1]

Lady Holy Church's summary of the duties of knighthood is perhaps the clearest of all:

> Kynges and knyȝtes shoulde . . .
> Ryden and rappe a-doune In reames a-boute,
> And take [*transgressores*] and tyen hem faste,
> Til trewþe hadde ytermenyd here trespas to þe ende;
> And holde with hym and with hure þat han trewe accion,
> And for no lordene loue leue þe trewe partye.
> Trewely to take and treweliche to fyȝte,
> Ys þe profession and þe pure ordre þat apendeþ to knyȝtes.[2]

B and C both attribute to knighthood an honorable and, indeed, august history. Holy Church explains that God, upon creating heaven, made

---

7. See *OED, knight,* sb., 1, 4, a: "In the Middle Ages: Originally . . . , A military servant of the king or other person of rank; a feudal tenant holding land from a superior on condition of serving in the field as a mounted and well-armed man. In the fully-developed feudal system: One raised to honourable military rank by the king or other qualified person, the distinction being usually conferred only upon one of noble birth who had served a regular apprenticeship (as page and squire) to the profession of arms, and thus being a regular step in this even for those of the highest rank." In England, the term *nobility* has come to signify only the peerage, but according to the Marquis de Ruvigny, *The Nobilities of Europe* (London, 1910), p. 1, the "true criterion of 'Nobility,' however, is now, as it has always been, the lawful bearing of arms and, properly speaking, every one bearing duly authorised arms is equally a Noble whether a Peer, Baronet, or Commoner. . . ."

8. C, xxiii, 257 (B, xx, 256).   9. C, x, 9–10. B, vii, 9–10 varies slightly.

1. C, ix, 26–7 (B, vi, 28–9).

2. C, ii, 90–7. The first four lines are the same as B, i, 94–7, but the rest expand the thought of B. MS X reads *transgressores* for P *trespassours.*

ten knightly orders—cherubim, seraphim, and so on down through the order that revolted under Lucifer.[3] Therefore so far as the position of the king and his knights is concerned, fourteenth-century England was following the Divine example, as David the King, according to Holy Church, had done earlier.[4]

The part the clergy were to play in the structure of the kingdom is less clear. Both B and C blame

Bischopes and bachelers, bothe maistres and doctours,[5]

who abandon their proper calling and

Liggen in London in lenten, an elles.
Some seruen þe kyng and his siluer tellen,
In cheker and in chancerye chalengen his dettes
Of wardes and wardmotes, weyues and streyues.[6]

Nevertheless, though he reproves the clergy for deserting their parishioners to take part in the secular government, B, at least, seems to recognize that clerks have a right to such a part. Thus, as we have seen, he explains that Kind Wit made clerks "to conseille þe kynge." Although he omits this detail, C, in another definition of the duties of the clergy, while providing that some should sing masses, says that others should

. . . sitten and wryte,
Rede and receyue þat reson ouhte spende.[7]

Although the precise significance of this is not clear to me, I think that it at least leaves the door open for the clergy to engage in secular activities, which might include those pertaining to the government. It is, however, possible that C differed from B in his attitude toward the clergy in politics, though there is no great body of evidence to call upon. Despite a certain wavering in both texts, I think it safe to say that B and C recognized that the clergy might, *de facto* if not *de iure,* engage in the administration of the country, if only because the clergy had control of the largest body of educated men.[8]

We come now to that vague group known as the *comune.* It is in one's attitude toward this group that one's bias in respect to democratic government will be manifested. But I should like, before plunging into the subject, to emphasize that in their most distinct expression of sentiments

3. C, II, 104–06, B, I, 105–10.
4. C, II, 102–03, B, I, 102–04.
5. B, Pro., 87 (C, I, 85).
6. B, Pro., 91–4 (C, I, 89–92).
7. C, VI, 68–9.
8. A and B describe the King as summoning his Council "of clerkis and of erlis" (B, IV, 189, A, IV, 152; C omits). The problem of the clergy's part in the government is complicated by the fact that all three texts use the word *clergy* in two senses: to refer both to persons in the Church and to all learned persons, lay or ecclesiastical. For example, the character Clergy seems the personification of learning in general.

in regard to democracy, B and C seem to agree, and seem to agree in displaying a strong bias against it. The only reason that may be sensibly assigned to B's insertion, and C's retention, of the Rat Parliament in the Prologue[9] is a dislike on their part of the idea of rule *by* the people—in the sense in which President Lincoln used the phrase. In the first place, the people are pictured, in the Rat Parliament, as scarcely capable of mustering the strength to check the injustices of a bad ruler.[1] But more significant is the fact that the mouse "þat moche good couthe" apparently speaks for the poet when he asserts, most emphatically, that the assembled rodents are incapable of ruling themselves.[2] Furthermore, if we heed the mouse's warning that every man should "wite wel his owne"—a phrase that inevitably associates itself with the reason B elsewhere gives for the creation of law[3]—it appears that the poet did not think that the removal or repression of an unjust ruler was one of the prerogatives of the unjustly ruled; rather, he seems to have thought that they should continue to "suffre," even though their suffering might be acute. In the Rat Parliament we find no answer to the question which came up a little while ago concerning who should enforce common law in respect to the king. Certainly it is not people in the mass.

We can make a direct attack upon the attitudes of B and C toward the political function of the majority of the people through a study of the contexts in which the word *comune(s)* is used in the two texts. But in doing this, we must be careful that we know, as precisely as possible, what the word signifies—a requirement that is the more urgent because, in its modern form *Commons,* the word has acquired, in a self-consciously democratic age, a sort of emotional fungus that is apt to obscure the value it possessed in the fourteenth century. I list here what seem the three pertinent definitions given by the *Oxford Dictionary* for the term as it applies to groups of persons:

1. The third estate in the English . . . constitution; the body of people, not ennobled, and represented by the Lower House of Parliament.[4]

2. The common people, the commonalty; the lower order, as distinguished from those of noble or knightly or gentle rank.[5]

3. The common body of the people of any place; the community or com-

9. C, I, 165–215, B, Pro., 146–207.

1. C, I, 191–4, B, Pro., 176–9.

2. B, Pro., 200 (C, I, 215): "For had ȝe rattes ȝowre wille ȝe couthe nouȝt reule ȝowre-selue." For *wille* the C-MSS read *reed* and *reik*. The last is probably correct. See notes by C. T. Onions, *MLR*, III (1907–8), 170–1; *MLN*, XXIII (1908), 231; G. T. Flom, *MLN*, XXIII, 156–7; A. G. Mitchell, *MedAev*, VIII (1939), 118–20.

3. B, Pro., 207. Cf. B, Pro., 122.

4. *OED, commons,* sb. pl., I, 2. The general definition given by *OED* for the plural (1) is "common people; community."

5. *OED, commons,* sb. pl., I, 1.

monalty; . . . sometimes, the commonwealth or state, as a collective entity.[6]

Considered loosely, these definitions are not dissimilar. We have met the first before, applied to the word *comunes* in the second line of the B-passage which precipitated this whole discussion. It is the first sense that predominates in the modern word *Commons* and which gives it that emotional overtone I spoke of a moment ago. And it is chiefly in the direction of its modern value that the first sense distinguishes itself from the second and third, for it connotes the *homo politicus,* the man capable of taking an interest and a share in the government of his community, and inevitably suggests to the twentieth-century mind the long struggle which that group now known as the third estate endured before it became the dominant element in a democratic England. The second sense seems social, or even feudal, since it excludes knights of the shire, while, in the fourteenth century, the first sense given above includes them. The second sense coincides with the definition given for the third estate in the older medieval system.[7] The third sense I have listed (unlike the other two, which are given for the plural *commons,* this is given for the singular *common*) is neither political nor social but civil, for it may include all the people of any community—the entire citizenry, regardless of rank. Inasmuch as numerically the common people make up the greater part of any civil community, it is obvious that the second and third definitions will, in certain contexts, tend to be interchangeable. But both are sharply divided from the first in respect to political connotation. Let us see under what circumstances B and C use the word *comune(s)* in each of these several senses.

I have counted some seventy-one uses of the noun as applied to groups of persons in the two later texts of *Piers Plowman*—thirty-eight in C, thirty-three in B.[8] In a majority of these, the word evidently has no political connotation at all—that is, it does not connote the modern House

6. *OED, common,* sb., 1. Under this word, 2, *OED* gives substantially the same sense as for the plural in the preceding note. It is necessary to deal with both singular and plural because of this semantic interchangeability and because the MSS deviate in reproducing the forms. See p. 105, n. 7, below. It should be observed that the poet also uses the plural in the sense "provisions or expenses in common." See *OED, commons,* sb. pl., 11, and C, 1, 143b for examples.

7. See *OED, estate,* sb., 6: "In England the 'estates' as represented in Parliament were originally 1. Clergy; 2. Barons and Knights; 3. Commons." For the position of knights of the shire in the third estate in the fourteenth century, see references cited on p. 109, n. 2, below.

8. The list is as exhaustive as I have been able to make it, although I may have missed one or two examples. The following are peculiar to B: Pro., 113, 115, 121, 143, 187; III, 77 (with A, III, 68); IV, 151; IX, 88; X, 29; XII, 292; XIII, 262, 266. The following are peculiar to C: I, 95, 147; IV, 207, 378, 381, 388; VI, 20, 75, 182, 187; IX, 84; X, 10; XVI, 11; XVII, 359; XVIII, 216, 291, 310. The following are common to both texts: C, I, 143, 144 (B, Pro., 117, 118); C, IV, 202, 472 (B, III, 163, 314); C, V, 76, 161, 176 (B, IV, 80, 166, 182); C, VI, 181 (B, V, 49); C, XVI, 169 (B, XIII, 169); C, XXII, 155, 214, 381, 393, 409,

of Commons—but refers either to the entire commonwealth or to the great body of common people socially considered. Let us begin with illustrations of the first of these two senses. The clearest example occurs in the C-line,

Lo! in heuene an hy was an holy comune[9]—

which, though not a part of Holy Church's description, already mentioned, of the governmental arrangement of heaven, follows out her ideas very closely and introduces a second reference to Lucifer's disruption of the holy kingdom. The word undoubtedly has this same meaning of "commonwealth" in the C-lines in which Conscience tells the King that the land in which Meed is tolerated will not endure long without producing various social evils of a sort "to destroy the *comune*."[1] Similarly, when B and C describe the Jewish priests as asking the guards of the Sepulchre to tell the *comune* that Christ's body had been stolen by a band of apostles, it is undoubtedly the community, or commonwealth, of Jerusalem that is meant by the word.[2] In Conscience's long disquisition on Meed in the C-text, when we learn that a king may claim the *comune* at his will, just as the *comune* may claim law, love, and justice of a king, we may suspect a political sense; but when, a few lines later, we are told that most of the people in the kingdom care only for their own profit, even though the king and the *comune* have to bear the cost of their avarice, it seems more likely that the *comune* is the commonwealth and not either the common people or the third estate in the political sense.[3] In modern times we might say that many people cheat on their income-tax returns, not caring whether the commonwealth is the loser thereby. Similarly, in the long B- and C-passage which I quoted above in my discussion of kingship, the *comune* is mentioned three times: the King is to rule it, he styles himself chieftain of it, and he asks of it only what he requires in order to fulfill his function.[4] Again, there is a possibility that the King is referring to the political commons, or even to the common people generally, but the presumption seems more strongly in favor of the secular commonwealth as a whole, as contrasted with the spiritual commonwealth, Holy Church. We may notice this contrast in the line in which the King announces himself as

---

418, 453, 468, 474, 478 (B, xix, 150, 209, 377, 389, 405, 414, 448, 463, 469, 473); C, xxiii, 30, 78 (B, xx, 30, 77). So far as I can ascertain, the word occurs only twice in A: at iii, 68 (B, iii, 77), and at A, xi, 219. In this list I include only the noun, and only in its primary meanings. There are a number of instances of the adjective, of which I mention only the following: B, ii, 57, C, iii, 58, "Knights, clerks, and other common people"; C, iv, 245, "A kingdom that is conquered through common help": B, iv, 123, C, v, 119, "Until the King's Council be all common profit." Here the meaning seems to approach the genitive of the noun: "of the community." See also p. 98, n. 4, below.

9. C, vi, 187.   1. C, iv, 207.
2. C, xxii, 155, B, xix, 150.   3. C, iv, 378, 381, 388.
4. C, xxii, 468, 474, 478; B, xix, 463, 469, 473.

. . . holychurches chef help and chefteyn of þe comune,[5]

and in his references to "you two"—the clerical organization on the one hand, the lay organization on the other.[6] The same meaning seems the correct one for the several other lines in B and C in which kings and knights are described as defenders of the *comune*[7] and in the speech in B in which Imaginative tells the Dreamer that formerly wit and wisdom were treasure to "kepe with a comune."[8]

The commonwealth, or, more narrowly, the community, seems to be the correct meaning of the word in those lines in C in which a character is described as addressing a moral speech to the *comune*,[9] or in which, in both texts, the entire *comune* is called upon to witness to a certain fact.[1] In this use the word apparently connoted for the poet all the people whom he was addressing—the men on the plain, or the *comune* of middle-earth. This seems also to be the sense when the *comune* is accused, in B, of treating fellow Christians worse than Jews treat fellow Jews,[2] or, in both texts, of ignoring Conscience and the cardinal virtues[3] and of degenerating into avarice through the influence of Lady Meed.[4] And so also, I suspect, when in both texts Grace advises Piers and Conscience to summon all the *comune* into Piers's barn, so that Grace may distribute treasure to "all sorts of five-witted creatures"—surely a universal term.[4a] It is probably all the people of the community who, in the last passus of the poem, are called into Unity by Conscience[4b] and who earlier have asked, naïvely, whether they should pay their debts before going to shrift.[4c] And it is the purity of these same people which, along with clerkly purity, has been made responsible for the Church's standing in holiness.[4d] Finally, it is the entire community whom Reason has in mind when, in C, he asks whether the Dreamer knows any trade "þat to þe comune nedeþ."[4e]

At other times the second definition cited above—"the common people"—seems more fitting. Thus in C the Dreamer finds, to his grief,

5. C, xxii, 474 (B, xix, 469).

6. In the Lytlington (*Liber Regalis*) coronation *ordo*, which came into being during the fourteenth century, the king is described as *ecclesie catholice . . . defensor, fidei christiane dilatator, ac regni sui et patrie . . . protector*. See L. G. W. Legg, *English Coronation Records* (London, 1901), p. 82. For the history and use of this *ordo*, see P. E. Schramm, *A History of the English Coronation*, L. G. W. Legg, tr. (Oxford, 1937), pp. 80-1, 170-2.

7. C, vi, 75, x, 10, xviii, 291.   8. B, xii, 292.   9. C, i, 95, 147.

1. C, v, 76 (B, iv, 80). In this instance, Peace asserts that the *comune* is aware of his innocence, and it is possible that the reference is to the common people, who were particularly susceptible to the sort of wrong Peace has suffered. But I am disposed to think he means that the entire kingdom is aware of his injury.

2. B, ix, 88.   3. C, xxii, 453, B, xix, 448.
4. C, iv, 202, B, iii, 163.   4a. C, xxii, 214 ff., B, xix, 209 ff.
4b. C, xxiii, 78, B, xx, 77.   4c. C, xxii, 393, B, xix, 389.
4d. C, xxii, 381, B, xix, 377.

4e. C, vi, 20. This definition for the word here and at C, vi, 75 is given by J. R. R. Tolkien in his glossary for Sisam's *Fourteenth Century Verse and Prose*.

that bodies of "poure comune" may not rest in the churchyards of rich Priories[1] and B calls the Bible to witness the iniquity of rich lords who are unkind to the *comune*—the common people, whom the lords callously let starve.[2] The feudal meaning of the word is indicated in certain contexts where *comune* is contrasted with the other classes. Thus we learn that the man who has true charity may, according to C, become master of king, *comune,* and clergy (B: king, queen, and *comune*),[3] though it is possible here that the *comune* signifies the secular organization, in contrast with the spiritual. Elsewhere C tells us that if knighthood, Kind Wit, *comune,* and Conscience love one another, bishops will lose their lordship :[4] here the reference is surely to the common people as a class. Mayors and mace-bearers, described by B as means between the extremes of king and *comune,* probably intervene between king and common people,[5] though again the meaning of commonwealth is not impossible. Finally, the social sense is probably meant in C's statement that Jews believe that Jesus was a "japer" among the *comune*[6]—a commoner who asserted that he was a king.

In several of these instances the reader may justifiably feel that I have urged one definition or the other too arbitrarily. But the two meanings so far discussed are, as I have said, difficult to keep separate semantically and the poet may not always have distinguished clearly in his own mind according to modern dictionary definitions. There are a number of other instances where I am unable to make up my mind which sense is pertinent. Thus I am uncertain whether, in B, Hawkin has difficulty in feeding the entire community, or just the common people ;[7] and the same problem confronts us in respect to the statement, made in both texts, that the world is lost unless Conscience feeds the *comune*.[8] When B describes the King's clerks as construing Reason's riddle for the King's profit, but not for the good of his soul or for the comfort of the *comune,*[9] we may probably choose either of the two definitions without getting into serious trouble ; and so when Meed mourns because the *comune* in the King's Court call her a whore.[9a] In all these uses, however, it is at least possible to construe *comune* as signifying the entire community.

The survey thus far has not given us much to go on if we expect the poet (either B or C) to display decided democratic bias. In the first place, according to my interpretation, none of the uses of *comune* we have examined seems to possess any political connotation, since each of them seems to refer either to the commonwealth or to the common people

1. C, xvi, 11.   2. B, x, 29.   3. C, xvi, 169, B, xiii, 169.

4. C, xviii, 216. B, xv, 515 varies, making *comune* an adjective modifying *conscience.* I suspect that C has the original reading.

5. B, iii, 77, A, iii, 68.   6. C, xviii, 310.   7. B, xiii, 262, 266.

8. C, xxii, 409, B, xix, 405.   9. B, iv, 151.

9a. C, v, 161, B, iv, 166. The line in its C-form and C, i, 143 suggest that C enjoyed playing upon the word.

in a nonpolitical sense. In the second place, however, even if I am wrong in some of my interpretations and the reader is able to detect a political connotation that I have missed, we have still found no trace in either B or C of any democratic bias. Nor have we found evidence that either possessed any different bias from the other. If when the King says that he is chieftain of the *comune* he means the political third estate, one can scarcely detect any admiration for the power of that estate on the part of the poet. And if, when C says that the *comune* may claim certain qualities of a king, he is referring to the Commons in the modern sense, then he is expressing no individual sentiment, since we have already seen that he and B agree that a king exists solely for the sake of his function, which is to rule his kingdom justly. But let us continue with the examination.

There remain seven instances of the word *comune* wherein, on first sight at least, it appears as if the poet actually did intend a political connotation and in certain of them we might detect a distinct democratic or antidemocratic bias. The first of these occurs only in the B-text, shortly after the conclusion of the passage describing the structure of the kingdom. The reader will recall that a Lunatic implores the King to rule justly. Then an Angel, speaking in Latin,

> . . . for lewed men ne coude
> Iangle ne iugge þat iustifie hem shulde,
> But suffren & seruen,[2]

admonishes the King to conduct his administration in such a way as to show greater respect for mercy than for strict justice. To this a Goliard, also using Latin, opposes a pair of verses calling for strict justice. At this point, the poet tells us,

> . . . gan alle þe comune crye in vers of latin,
> To þe kynges conseille, construe ho-so wolde—
> *"Precepta Regis sunt nobis vincula legis."*[3]

Who is this learned *comune?* We have seen from our earlier investigations that the King is head of law. The Angel and the Goliard have just given advice on how the King should interpret the law—how he should act in accordance with *spiritus iustitiae*. Now the *comune* intrudes a remark which seems to say that, regardless of how the King interprets the law, his decisions are binding upon his subjects. Without gratuitously reading something into the speech, it is difficult to find in it any reference to a politically constituted third estate. The *comune* addresses the King's Council (which seems to be the name by which our author usually referred to the legislative body of the kingdom)[4] and it seems to speak

2. B, Pro., 129–31.   3. B, Pro., 143–5.
4. The poet several times uses *parlement* in what seems to be its modern sense, "the Westminster Parliament." See A, IV, 34, B, IV, 47, C, V, 45, where Peace is described as coming into the "parliament" and putting up a bull. According to *OED*, *parliament*,

not as a participant, even through representatives, but as an excluded party.[5] The word seems to be used loosely to include the entire community of England, all of the members of which are equally bound by the King's *praecepta*. On the other hand, if one insists upon finding a political connotation, one must observe that in any case the Commons is described as being entirely subject to the royal will[6]—scarcely an accurate picture of the situation in England in the last quarter of the fourteenth century.

A second reference to the *comune* occurs shortly thereafter, during the Rat Parliament, whose undemocratic lesson we have already noticed. The articulate mouse, reviewing the fiasco that overtook the conspiracy against the cat, counsels "alle þe comune" to let the cat go his own way.[7] Once again the reference seems to be to the entire community—or possibly to the common people en masse[8]—rather than to any political estate represented in the royal council. As in the last instance, the noun is modified by the adjective *alle,* which tends to extend the meaning beyond the assembly the mouse is addressing. It should, moreover, be noticed that the mouse advises his audience to suffer the foibles of their sovereigns and that is precisely what the *comune,* in the lines quoted in the last paragraph, has indicated its practice to be. Further, the Angel is introduced with lines defining the lot, if not the duty, of lewd men as to "suffer and serve." Nor does the poet advance any criticism of this lot, either as that of the *comune* or as that of lewd men. If there is any reference to a political body, it is not a flattering one.

At the end of the incident of Lady Meed, the King resolves to have legality in law and to punish wrong. Conscience then warns him,

sb. 1, 3, b, this is the earliest example of the modern technical sense. See also C, v, 185, where the word replaces the definition, given by A, iv, 152, B, iv, 189, of the King's Council as consisting of "clerks and earls." Skeat, however, glosses as "conference."

5. On the relationship of King's Council to Parliament shortly after the poet's time, *The Cambridge Medieval History* (Cambridge, England, 1911–36, 8 vols.), vii, 481–2, explains as follows: "By the end of Richard II's reign there are to be distinguished, first, a small efficient body of ministers, in part administrative experts, meeting almost daily, directing the day to day government of the kingdom; second, the Great Council of the magnates, summoned under the Privy Seal; and third, Parliament, summoned under the Great Seal. Parliament is still an aspect of the Council, and is in theory and for some purposes one assembly, but its two parts are fairly sharply defined." I am under the impression that the poet thought ordinarily in terms of the Council in its narrower senses.

6. G. R. Owst, "The 'Angel' and the 'Goliardeys' of Langland's Prologue," *MLR,* xx (1925), 275, construes these lines as expressing a "wistful hope and confidence in the strong personal rule of the monarchy." I fail to detect the wistfulness. As Cyril Brett, "Notes on Old and Middle English," *MLR,* xxii (1927), 261, says, the sense is merely that the king's commands are the guides of the people.

7. B, Pro., 187.

8. Wells, in the notes to his translation, p. 285, says that the rats represent nobles. But while this is partially correct, it is incorrect to speak of the fable without mentioning the fact that the poet also speaks of "small mice with them, more than a thousand," and that these mice must stand for the common people. See B, Pro., 147, C, i, 166.

. . . but the comune wil assent,
It is ful hard, bi myn hed, here-to to brynge it,
Alle ʒowre lige leodes to lede þus euene.[9]

At first sight this looks like a party-chairman's warning: the Commons is a powerful political factor and if you don't watch out, it will spoil your plans. But actually all Conscience is saying to the King is that it is difficult to rule a country unless the people of that country—the *comune*—are willing to cooperate. This sentiment is reinforced, a few lines later, when Reason agrees to undertake the governance of the kingdom only on the condition that the King will order Obedience to be of Reason's "assent"[1]—the very word which was used, in the B-text, in connection with the *comune*. To the enthusiastic democrat this interpretation will seem very tame. Yet it is in accord with one of the most ancient principles in the English constitution. One of the oldest of the English coronation *ordo*'s—the second recension of Dunstan's[2]—provides that the king, after receiving the crown, shall terminate the ceremony by delivering to the people present a mandate consisting of three *praecepta*. Later these *praecepta,* augmented by a fourth, became the several parts of the king's oath. But in earlier times they formed the contract, mutually subscribed to, which regulated the relations between the king and his subjects. In the first of the *praecepta,* in its early form, the king is not mentioned: he merely decrees *ut eclesia dei et omnis populus christianus ueram pacem seruent in omni tempore.*[3] To this the people present at the ceremony were expected to reply *amen* and, as Schramm observes,[4] in the response "there is involved, as in a legislative act, the assertion of the willingness of the people to support the King in the execution of the *praecepta,* for he cannot do so of himself." Conscience, therefore, is restating an old constitutional point.[5] If he had told the King that it would be difficult to raise money for a war without the assent of the *comune,* we should be justified in understanding a political reference. But the King's only desire is to rule justly and the *comune,* if it is meant to be understood politically, appears as a potential hindrance to good government, a body capable of obstructionist tactics. I doubt that the word here means anything less than the entire commonwealth, comprising all the estates of the realm.

In the B-version of Reason's sermon the King is urged

9. B, IV, 182–4. C, V, 176–8 renders the first half-line "with-oute þe comune help," which *OED, without,* C, conj., 2, construes as a clause rather than as a prepositional phrase. The explanation for these lines may possibly apply also to B, XX, 30, C, XXIII, 30, which I noticed too late for inclusion in the discussion above.

1. B, IV, 187, A, IV, 150.

2. For the *ordo* itself, see Legg, *op. cit.,* pp. 3–9. For its identification, see Schramm, *op. cit.,* p. 233, item 4.

3. Legg, *op. cit.,* p. 9.   4. Schramm, *op. cit.,* p. 180.

5. For an example in Walsingham of the survival in the fourteenth century of an outmoded coronation form, see below, p. 117.

. . . þe comune to louye,
It is þi tresore, if tresoun ne were, and triacle at þi nede.[6]

Here again we should be ill-advised to assume a reference to a political
third estate. Reason is urging the King to love the community which he
has the responsibility of managing, just as a few lines later he advises
the Pope to have pity on the Church, which the Pope is responsible for
managing.[7] The treason referred to could scarcely be that of the Commons in the modern sense, but must, rather, be that of the treacherous
barons with whom any medieval king was surrounded. It should be
observed that the C-revision makes explicit what is implicit in B. After
altering the lines quoted so as to omit treason, C goes on to speak of the
need for unity in the kingdom and shows how disunity, in the person of
Lucifer, broke up the holy *comune* of heaven.[8] The emphasis on love
recalls the advice that Reason has, in C, already given the King—namely,
to let love take the place of his merchants, bishops, Lombards, and Jews[9]
on whom the actual King, Richard II, was then relying for his finances.

In the C-addition to the given name of Piers's son, the following new
line, among others, is introduced,

Consaile nat þe comune þe kyng to displese.[1]

If we read too hastily, we might mistake this for a bit of conservatism on
C's part, inasmuch as it does not appear in B. But the line is only an
expansion of an idea which is present in B and which derives from a
combination of several verses in the Gospel of St. Matthew:[2] *Super
cathedram Moysi sederunt scribae et pharisaei. Omnia ergo quaecumque
dixerint vobis, servate et facite;* and, from the Sermon on the Mount,
Nolite judicare, ut non judicemini. Thus the B-text reads,

His sone hiȝte suffre-þi-souereynes-to-hauen-her-wille-
Deme-hem-nouȝte-for-if-þow-doste-þow-shalt-it-dere-abugge.[3]

C retains these two lines, adds the one quoted above, and then goes on
to elaborate on the first quotation from Matthew:

Ne hem þat han lawes to loke lacke hem nat, ich hote,
Let god worthe with al, as holy writ techeþ;
   Super cathedram moysi sedent, et cetera;
Maistres, as þe meyres ben, and grete men senatours,
What þei comaunde as by þe kyng contrepleide hit neuere,
Al þat þey hoten, ich hote heyliche, thow suffre hem;
By here warnyng and worchyng worch þow þer-after;
   Omnia que dicunt, facite & seruate;
Ac after here doynge do þow nat. . . .[4]

---

6. B, v, 49–50. C, vi, 181–2 gives the second line, "For þe comune ys þe kynges tresour,
conscience wot wel."   7. B, v, 51–2. C, vi, 192–7 elaborates.
   8. C, vi, 183–91.   9. C, v, 187–94.   1. C, ix, 84.
   2. Matthew 23.2–3; 7.1.   3. B, vi, 82–3.   4. C, ix, 85–91.

I quote the entire passage because I think it is probably the fullest statement in *Piers Plowman* of the author's political beliefs, so far as they concern the lower classes. That the word *comune* here means flatly the common people is proved—if any proof is necessary—by the fact that the A-poet had already used the same word unequivocally in this sense in association with the same verses from Matthew that C is here elaborating. The word occurs when the Dreamer in A interrupts Scripture's discourse to inquire whether kingship and knighthood are not Do-Well:

> For I haue seize it myselfe & siþþen red it after,
> How Crist counseilliþ þe comune & kenneþ hem þis tale,
> *Super cathedram moisi sederunt principes.*[5]

According to the Vulgate, Christ was speaking *ad turbas et ad discipulos suos*[6]—the common people. Hence there seems to be no recognition of a political *comune* and the lesson derived from Christ's words both by B and C is that the common people should be obedient to their superiors—should not, indeed, try to wield any political power.

We revert now to an earlier part of the poem. In Conscience's harangue to the King concerning Lady Meed there appear, both in B and in C, lines which predict that a time will come when

> Shal noþer kyng ne knyȝt, constable ne meyre
> Ouer-cark þe comune ne to þe court sompne.[7]

Skeat glosses these lines, "Kings and knights shall not oppress the commons," which is a perfectly fair statement so long as we recognize what is meant by *oppress* and by *commons*. *Ouer-cark* may, indeed, be properly rendered "oppress" in the Latin sense, since it means "overburden."[8] The word here derives, I imagine, from the same set of verses in Matthew that we discussed in the previous paragraph. Christ says of the scribes and Pharisees (Langland's *principes*) that they fashion *onera gravia et importabilia, et imponunt in humeros hominum.*[9] We have already seen, however, that it is not the part of the over-burdened to cast down their loads but to carry them. This part of Conscience's speech is a prophecy of the Second Coming, when all government and governing classes will be superseded by the rule of *on berne*[1]—namely, Christ; and at that time—and not until then—the *comune*, the common people, will find relief. A hint of sympathy for the lot of the common man there certainly is in the lines, for the duty of suffering is not an

---

5. A, XI, 218–19.   6. Matthew 23.1.

7. C, IV, 471–2. B, III, 313–14 varies in reading *Ouer-lede* for *Ouer-cark*. I take this to be scribal deviation.

8. *OED, overcark*, v., defines the word in this line as meaning "to burden with excessive charges; to oppress." The only other instance of the word is in *Cursor Mundi,* which *OED* explains as meaning "to overcharge, overweight."

9. Matthew 23.4.

1. C, IV, 477. B, III, 319 reads, less happily, *one baroun.*

agreeable one; but there is no expectation that there will come a time of
self-rule by a politically minded Commons.

We are left with one further example of the word. In the C-text,
Liberum Arbitrium explains of a personified Charity that

> Among þe comunes in court he comeþ but selde,
> For brawelynge and bacbytynge and beryng of false wittnesse.[2]

In this case the word is used to signify community, but probably in a
more technical sense than we have before encountered. Liberum Arbitrium has just explained under what circumstances Charity is willing
to come into the King's Court; he now describes his attitude toward the
Common Court. Although the sense is not specifically recorded in the
Oxford Dictionary, comunes here seems to be a translation of the Latin
communitates, the singular of which, according to Bishop Stubbs,[3] was
used to denote an organized body of the freemen of shires or towns; and
the court referred to is the court of the *communitas,* represented by the
County Court. The poet refers to these *Common Courts* on two other
occasions, employing the adjectival *comune*.[4] But though the word here
is, in essence and historically, political, it is not the same thing as the
Commons in the parliamentary sense, which was, according to Stubbs,
the *communitas communitatum,* a union of organized bodies of freemen.[5]

We return now to the B-lines,

> Þanne come þere a kyng, knyȝthod hym ladde,
> Miȝt of þe comunes made hym to regne,

with what I think must be a somewhat chastened attitude. One is reluctant to take exception to the *Oxford Dictionary* and in this case also
to the opinion of Jusserand, who found in these lines a splendidly isolated
reference to "the grandeur of the internal reform that had been going
on in England during the century: the establishment on a firm basis of
that institution, unique then, and destined to be imitated throughout the
world, . . . the Westminster Parliament."[6] But we have found nothing
in our examination to encourage us in a belief that the poet—either as B
or as C—recognized the existence of a political third estate, or, if he did,
that he in any way admired it. The lines, as Jusserand interpreted them,
are not only, as he says, unique in fourteenth-century Europe, they are
unique in *Piers Plowman,* which poses a rather more serious problem,
since they contradict what the author says elsewhere on a number of

2. C, xvii, 359–60.
3. William Stubbs, *The Constitutional History of England* (Oxford, 1896–1903,
3 vols.), ii (4th ed.), 174–5.
4. At C, iii, 22, Meed is said to be undoing Holy Church's teaching "in kynges court
& in comune court," and at C, iv, 476 (B, iii, 318) Conscience prophesies that "Kynges
court and comune court" will become but one court.
5. Stubbs, *op. cit.,* ii, 175.   6. *MPh,* vi, 272.

occasions. But if *comunes* does not signify the lower house of Parliament, how are we to interpret the lines?

One might, I suppose, on no very good evidence, take the easy way out and ascribe the words *þe comunes* to an error on the part of the archetypal B-scribe, suggesting that he read the phrase *þo men* (now preserved in the "i"-group MSS of the C-class) as *þe cõe,* the form in which the word was frequently written, as may be seen from the numerous instances of Skeat's printing "*comune.*" But though the two groups of letters have the same length, it would probably still be necessary to attribute definite intention to the scribe, who would also have had to convert into the plural the word which he had mistakenly understood. One scarcely knows how to treat the singular-plural alternations of *comune* in a poem with a textual history such as *Piers Plowman*'s. In the printed texts of B and C, the plural is very rare. Furthermore, there is a fairly high degree of correspondence in its use among the MSS of each class.[7] In Skeat's editions, the plural occurs three times: in the B-line now under discussion, once in the A-text (where, in the corresponding line, B has the singular)[8] and once in C, with, apparently, the technical sense that I discussed in the last of the examples of the uses of *comune(s)*. The plural is the form that one would, possibly, expect to find for the sense "House of Commons";[9] and, if one were pursuing the argument that the word is of scribal origin here, one might instance the fact that this is the only plural form in Skeat's or Wright's B-text, along with the fact that the word in this line is the earliest of the *Oxford Dictionary*'s examples for the sense under discussion, as evidence for one's theory. But the argument is both slippery and reversible. In any case, we cannot alter readings just because we find them embarrass-

7. With respect to the singular and plural in B-MSS, W agrees with Skeat's text (L) throughout, except that it omits XIII, 169, not in L but printed by Skeat from R. Cr (Crowley) has the plural in Pro., 113, like LW, but also in Pro., 115, 117, 118, 121, 143, 187, as well as in v, 49, where in every case LW have the singular. Elsewhere Cr agrees with LW. MSS YOGCC2 are available to me for only the first fifteen of the B-text's thirty-three uses of the word. Of these MSS, YC agree with LW throughout; G except at III, 77, where it has the plural; O except in Pro., 143, III, 77, 163, v, 49, where it has the plural; C2 is like O, except that it has the plural at Pro., 187 as well. MS B, available to me as a B-text for only eight examples, those in III–v, is like LW. For further data on III, 77 see next note. With respect to C-MSS, X follows Skeat's P in thirty-six out of the thirty-eight cases, everywhere except for a plural at I, 143 and a singular at XVII, 359, where P has the opposite. MS B2, available as a C-text for only the first four examples, follows P. MSS UDYP2ERMQSFKGN, available in Carnegy's critical text for nine examples, those in IV–v, follow PX except that P2 has the plural at IV, 207, G the plural at IV, 378, and M the plural at IV. 381—only three divergences in 117 opportunities. I failed to examine MS T on this subject.

8. A, III, 68, B, III, 77. Readings for these lines are available in *EETS*, IV, 835–46 for seventeen B-MSS and fourteen A-MSS. In the B-group, the singular form appears in twelve MSS: LMRYCBBmCotCrWHmCr5; the plural in five: GOC2FHt. In the A-group, the singular appears in four MSS: RJH3K; the plural in nine: VHEUTH2WDL. MS A reads *comouneris.*

9. See *OED*, commons, sb. pl., 1, 2, but compare *common*, sb., 2.

ing; if we could, *Piers Plowman* scholarship would degenerate into an anarchy of guesswork. We must work with what we have.

What we have, I think, is a pair of lines in which the author assures us that the rule of a king depends upon the power of the commonwealth. We have already seen what idea the poet had of the function of a king. Hitherto I have been reluctant to call it either conservative or radical, contenting myself with pointing out that his attitude toward the *comune* was certainly not extremist. It is time to say now that the poet's attitude was also that to which Edward III and Richard II publicly subscribed and which was, indeed, an established part of the English Constitution. The fourth question which, since the ascension of Edward II, has been asked, in one form or another, of every prince by the officiating bishop, reads, in the original Latin: *Concedis iustas leges et consuetudines esse tenendas, et promittis eas per te esse protegendas, et ad honorem dei roborandas quas uulgus elegerit secundum uires tuas?*[1] In the French translation, in which, possibly, the oath was more widely known, the question reads: *Sire, graunte vous à tenir & garder les Loys, & les Custumes droitureles, les quiels la Communauté de vostre Roiaume aura esleu, & les defendrez & afforterez, al honur de Dieu, à vostre Poer?*[2] As Stubbs says, the French *communauté,* rendering the Latin *vulgus,* can refer only to all three estates of the realm.[3] In this oath we have, perhaps, the explanation of why, without self-contradiction, the B-poet could say of the king that

> Miȝt of þe comunes made hym to regne,

comunes rendering, as we have seen that its singular form often does in *Piers Plowman,* the idea expressed in the related French *communauté.* The reference is not to that group which we associate with the House of Commons but to the whole commonwealth. The fourth question in the coronation oath also explains the purport of the summary lines in the B-passage,

> Þe kynge and þe comune and kynde witte þe thridde
> Shope lawe & lewte, eche man to knowe his owne.

The laws *quas uulgus elegerit—les quiels la Communauté aura esleu—* govern even the king.

The ritual of the coronation ceremony itself, as it came to be performed during the fourteenth century, supports this interpretation. At some point during the service—according to the *Liber Regalis* before the king actually takes his oath, but according to accounts of Richard's

---

1. Legg, *op. cit.,* p. 88. In the official account of Richard's coronation, *idem,* p. 147, the words *iuste et racionabiliter* were inserted between *uulgus* and *elegerit.* See Schramm, *op. cit.,* pp. 212–13.

2. See Thomas Rymer, *Foedera* (London, 1703–35, 20 vols.), III, 63.

3. Stubbs, *op. cit.,* II, 175.

coronation, immediately afterward[4]—the bishop offers the king to the *collaudatio* of the onlookers. The Lytlington *ordo* of the *Liber Regalis* describes the ritual as follows :

Metropolitanus siue episcopus regem coronaturus per quatuor partes dicti pulpiti plebem alloquatur ipsorum inquirens uoluntatem et consensum de dicti principis consecracione. Rege interim in sede sua stante atque ad quatuor partes dicti pulpiti dum pontifex plebem alloquitur se uertente, quibus ut moris est consencientibus atque uoce magna unanimi proclamantibus, fiat fiat et uiuat Rex, nomen dicti regis gratissime nominitant.[5]

The author of the *Anonimalle Chronicle* describes the bishop's question in the *collaudatio* at Richard's coronation as follows : . . . *le dit erchevesqe demanda les communes sils vodroient assenter et tener le prince Richarde lour roy.*[6] The vexed problem of exactly what the *collaudatio* means in terms of constitutional law does not interest us here. What does interest us is the fact, for which there is ample evidence, that each person present at, or hearing an account of, a coronation might come away with the impression that his own assent had been instrumental in the making of a king. Collectively, these individual witnesses, whether barons, burgesses, or poor commoners, had been the plebs of the Latin text, *les communes* of the French and, I suggest, *þe comune* or *þe comunes* of *Piers Plowman,* whose sanction had been required.

This seems the most satisfactory and reasonable explanation of the B-passage. So far as the plural form of *comunes* is concerned, we have several courses of action. The plural may, according to the *Oxford Dictionary,* mean "commonalty,"[7] though in the *Piers Plowman* MSS this meaning is ordinarily attended by the singular. On the other hand, it might be possible to relax the strictures, laid down above, concerning emendation, so that one might alter a single letter, particularly since the MSS do show occasional writings of the plural for the singular of this word. Or, taking the word as it stands, it would be possible to explain it as meaning a federation of those communities referred to above in the last of the examples of the use of the word *comune(s)* : that is, a *communitas communitatum* which does not, however, in this case connote the modern Commons, but rather the three estates of which the realm consists. In any case, it seems virtually certain that it is the entire nation that B is crediting with the power that puts a king upon his throne.

The meaning "commonwealth" may hold good throughout the passage

---

4. H. T. Riley, ed., *Thomae Walsingham Historia Anglicana* (London, 1863–64, 2 vols.), I, 333. See Schramm, *op. cit.,* p. 171.

5. Legg, *op. cit.,* p. 85.

6. V. H. Galbraith, ed., *The Anonimalle Chronicle, 1333–1381* (Manchester, 1927), p. 110. For the significance of the ritual, see Schramm, *op. cit.,* index under *collaudatio*.

7. *OED, commons,* sb. pl., I, 1. For the general definition of the plural, see above, p. 94, n. 4.

in B. Kind Wit made clerks to save the *comune*—probably to insure the spiritual salvation of the population, the foremost duty of clerks, as we learn both from Imaginative and from Anima (Liberum Arbitrium). When king, knighthood, and clergy are said to have devised that the *comune* should provide for themselves, the sense may still be that of the entire nation. There is some reason here, however, for assuming a contrast among the three classes, so that the word *comune* may carry its second connotation "the common people." But when the *comune* is described as contriving crafts with the aid of Kind Wit, the reference seems to be once again to the community. And so, as we have seen, when the *comune* is credited, along with king and Kind Wit, with the invention of law.

Wright was correct in saying that C's revision of the passage is less distinct that B's original, although the more important part of his assertion, that C was less bold, cannot be admitted without some qualification. We have ample evidence that in their opinions on government as expressed elsewhere, B and C are indistinguishable. Yet it is undeniable that C's removal of the king-making power from the entire community, and his vesting it in knighthood, does betray a form of caution—even though, from our study, we should scarcely find reason to feel surprise if the C-line had stood in B. An explanation for C's alteration lies at hand. As I have said, by a strange quirk of fate, *Piers Plowman* was used by the revolutionists in the uprising of 1381, apparently as propaganda for their movement and certainly as part of the code in which they communicated with one another. Assuredly the author, a moderate and a traditionalist, if not a reactionary, could not have approved of this use of his poem and must, indeed, have been considerably embarrassed by his unwitting mésalliance with John Ball. The line in B which mentions the might of the *comunes,* even though it is capable of a perfectly innocuous interpretation consonant with the poet's political beliefs, is also capable by the enthusiastic democrat—and by a good scholar like Jusserand—of an interpretation which might, obliquely, give support to the participants in an affair like the Peasants' Revolt. The C-revision, though made at a certain sacrifice in breadth of conception, is unequivocal. So far as the historical accuracy of the two versions is concerned, it is interesting that each reflects a point of view current in the fourteenth century. Thus the continuator of Knighton's chronicle tells us, almost echoing the B-text, that Richard II ascended to the throne *jure hereditario ac etiam voto communi singulorum;*[8] while Walsingham states that Edward II *successit . . . non tam jure haereditario quam unanimi assensu procerum et magnatum.*[9] Chronologically and in terms of liberality, C's is the more archaic point of view, but quite possibly the writers

8. J. R. Lumby, ed., *Chronici Henrici Knighton* (London, 1889–95, 2 vols.), II, 125.
9. Riley, *op. cit.,* I, 119.

of both chronicles were speaking with reference to generalities of constitutional theory, rather than with reference to any individual reign. C's emphasis on the importance of knighthood is consistent with the impression that both he and B give us in the remarks of Holy Church. Therefore the only element in C's alteration for which we must apologize is the loss of breadth of conception, and for this we can at least partially excuse him on the grounds that no man wishes to associate himself, even accidentally, with a political movement for which he has not the slightest sympathy.[1]

The importance C accords to knighthood is emphasized by his treatment of the rest of the passage on the state's structure, for the knights, collectively, make up the only mortal element that is assigned a share in distributing the individual duties to the kingdom. At one time I thought that C's preoccupation with knighthood might be interpreted as indicating his awareness of the Commons' political strength. Such power as the embryonic House of Commons possessed was largely concentrated in the knights of the shire[2] and it seemed to me possible that, if *comunes* in the B-text was to be understood in its modern sense, then C might, in his revision, have been thinking of the knights of the shire under the term *knighthood*. The author of *Mum and the Sothsegger* has a good deal to say about the Commons, but ordinarily he writes in terms of its most influential component, the knights of the shire.[3] If this interpretation were correct, there would be no question of C's having been more conservative than B, since *knighthood* would be no more than a sort of synonym for *Commons*. But the evidence shows that C (and B) thought of knighthood not politically but in its old chivalric sense and this conception of knighthood seems, in both texts, to be derived from its august origin in the newly created heaven of God the Father. It is a spiritual, rather than a political, notion of government that both B and C seem to possess. C permits a chivalric knighthood to share with Kind Wit and Conscience—whom C introduces into the passage—in drawing the blueprint for the kingdom. In so doing, he is displaying his accustomed tendency toward abstraction, as well as striving to justify a rather old-fashioned idea by giving it spiritual sanction, since Kind Wit and Conscience are spiritual qualities. We should observe, however, that the hint for this course of action lay in B, who had introduced Kind Wit. C was merely developing B's thought when he superimposed Conscience upon the description of the kingdom.

The most significant phrase for understanding B's and C's idea of

1. We must remember that John Ball was convicted on the evidence of a letter filled with phrases probably derived from *Piers Plowman*, and certainly reminiscent of it, and was thereafter *tractus, suspensus, et decollatus*. See Riley, *op. cit.*, II, 34.

2. See Stubbs, *op. cit.*, II, 540, 648; Tout, *op. cit.*, p. 436; Trevelyan, *op. cit.*, p. 14.

3. Whom he calls *knyȝtis of þe comunete*: see Fragment R, IV, 41. He uses *comunes*, probably in its modern sense (*OED, commons*, sb. pl., I, 2) at IV, 60 and again at IV, 18,

earthly government is probably that brief one which has been mentioned before, "Each man to know his own."[4] Without risk of error, one may add the word *place* or *part* in order to make the phrase meet the requirements of modern idiom: each man, and therefore each class, should know and keep his own place. The part of the common man was to suffer— "to suffer and serve," as B says of the uneducated of the country. The part of the clergy was to advise and, more important, to show the population the way to spiritual salvation. The part of knighthood was to defend. And the part of the king was to lead his knights in the preservation of the realm and of the Church and to execute the law under the guidance of *spiritus iustitiae*. The result of each man's doing his duty would be unity, a sort of unity exactly equivalent to that envisioned, in the last two passus, for the Church. This is the ideal for the *comune*— the commonwealth. By what sanction these definitions of duties exist is the endless problem of political theorists. Langland was not, however, a political theorist but a religious poet. The sanction he assigns is that of the eternal spiritual qualities that exist within each man: in B it is Kind Wit alone, in C it is Kind Wit and Conscience. Characteristically, the poet finds the answer to governmental problems, as to all others, in the heart of man. Translated into terms of politics, this conception puts him neither to the right nor to the left, but in the very center, like his own king

> . . . haldyng with no partie,
> Bote stande as a stake þat stykeþ in a muyre
> By-twyne two londes for a trewe marke.[5]

The curious paradox that caused Langland, a political moderate, to become associated with the Peasants' Revolt and, among literary historians, with the more radically democratic elements of his age, is not, let me hasten to add, caused solely by the fact that *comune(s)* is an ambiguous word. For the paradox is exactly paralleled by another one, which caused Langland, a religious moderate, to become associated with that most drastic of ecclesiastical events, the Reformation. The explanation for both these paradoxes lies in the quality of the poet's thought. Christianity points out that the path to spiritual salvation lies through the heart of the individual—*cor hominis*. Saturated with Christian thought, the poet saw everything in terms of it and, as I have just said, found that the path to political salvation lay through the same country as the path to spiritual salvation. Even though the details and formulas of his religious and political thought are conservative and traditionalist,

4. B, Pro., 122, 207. The phrase almost seems an echo of the statute *Quo Warranto*, enacted in 1278 by Edward I, and thus paraphrased in part by *The Cambridge Medieval History*, VII, 394: "We must find out what is ours, and is due to us, and others what is theirs, and due to them."

5. C, IV, 383-5.

his doctrine of the individual tends inevitably toward the radical. It is this, along with the violence that he displays in castigating those in positions of responsibility for their shortcomings, that causes the curious dichotomy in his thought which makes it possible for intelligent critics to come to such conflicting conclusions as those quoted in the first two notes to this chapter. If every individual is important, then great groups of individuals are so much the more important and, willy-nilly, barriers begin to break down. In his emphasis on the individual, Langland was in advance of his own church and of his own nation—and, indeed, of himself. It is this element in him which makes it possible for us to place him among the early humanists and which makes his poem so much more than just another Middle English religious piece.

Before concluding this chapter, let us turn briefly to the matter of allusion to contemporary political events in B and C. As I have noted above, B, particularly in the Prologue, has been suspected of introducing into his poem a number of these references, some of which would make him appear, contrary to the evidence we have assembled, a man of democratic sympathies. C, on the other hand, seems to exhibit few such references. Let me preface my remarks by affirming that the identification of topical references is an interesting and valuable labor. But there are conditions. The labor is valuable only so long as the identifications fit the known facts without our having either to read between the lines or to pervert the obvious sense in order to achieve our ends. Nor can one condone the practice of seeing topical reference everywhere—even in those parts of the poem where the poet is dealing with universals, *sub specie aeternitatis.* Finally, with *Piers Plowman* at least, even in those passages where topical allusion is indisputably present, we must be careful not to concentrate on the allusion to such an extent that we ignore any independent meaning the passage may have, or to adopt too readily the attitude that it means nothing unless we can identify the reference.

This last rule is particularly important because its violation has a bad effect on our idea of C, who sometimes revises B's topical passages in such a way as to strip them of much of their concrete detail, leaving in them only an echo of topicality. In these cases we are, unless we exercise caution, apt to find C altogether meaningless. Let us take an example which is, happily, removed from the troublesome sphere of politics. According to all three texts, in Lady Meed's spirited defense of her actions—or rather, in her spirited counteroffense against Conscience—she brings up the subject of the English campaigns in Normandy under Edward III and tries to show that Conscience was responsible for their eventual failure, while she herself would, if permitted, have insured their success.[6] In A and B it is obvious that she is referring to a specific campaign—probably that of 1360, which preceded the Treaty of Bretigny, although this identifi-

6. C, IV, 232–65, B, III, 185–207, A, III, 180–201.

cation has been questioned. In the C-version, while Meed is still referring to the French wars in general, there is no detail by which we can possibly identify any particular phase of them. Having stated so much, one might go on, as others have,[7] to make the usual complaints against C—that he has blurred the earlier texts' clear picture, or that he has misunderstood his original, or any one of a number of ready-made charges. But before doing so, one must ascertain the relevance, in any of the texts, of the Norman wars to the dispute between Meed and Clergy. The answer is perfectly clear and has already been given by Father Dunning in his study of the A-text.[8] Meed asserts that if she had been marshal of the King's men she would have continued to fight to victory and made every participant in the campaign a rich man, individual prosperity being, of course, the essence of Meed's motivation. But, she says, since Conscience's council prevailed, the King withdrew and only he became the richer thereby, and not much the richer at that. Conscience does not deny the charge and the King, at least tacitly, confirms it. Therefore it follows that Meed is speaking the truth and I do not see how we can escape the conclusion that Conscience—and the poet—considered the Norman venture a war of aggrandizement if not of aggression, which the King had no justifiable reason for undertaking and which he was right in liquidating. This lesson, which is the real reason the subject was ever brought up in the first place, is even clearer in C than it is in A and B, regardless of the fact—or because of the fact—that the historical details are less clear. Every one would like to know what campaign the poet had originally in mind and whether Lady Meed stands for Alice Perrers. But these matters are secondary and we must be careful, in handling them, that we do not do injustice to C, or even to A and B.[9]

Let us return to political events. The happy hunting ground for al-

7. Hall, *MLR*, IV, 5, abuses C for omitting the passage about the "dim cloud," using terms which would suggest that it was C's duty to record contemporary history, not to write a poem on the salvation of the soul.

8. T. P. Dunning, *Piers Plowman: an Interpretation of the A-Text* (Dublin, 1937), pp. 94-5.

9. Bernard Huppé, *PMLA*, LIV, 37-64, presents, largely on the basis of topical allusion, some excellent reasons for dating the A-text some years later than 1362. The most telling part of his discussion concerns the resemblance of Lady Meed in A to Alice Perrers, and I am disposed to accept his conclusions, as modified by J. A. W. Bennett, *PMLA*, LVIII, 566-72, for a *terminus a quo* of about 1370. The subtlety of many of Huppé's arguments is, however, excessive, and one gets the idea, incorrect I am sure, that the A-poet was criticizing the conduct of the Norman wars rather than the wars themselves. Thus, pp. 62-3, Huppé tries to show how Conscience (most unhappily identified with John of Gaunt) throws back upon Meed (Alice Perrers) and upon the King (Edward III) the blame for the great military failure of 1373 which Meed had tried to place upon Conscience. It is difficult to see that Conscience has any interest in the failure as such. He thoroughly disapproves of the entire war, which is, as Huppé admits, presented as an expression of Meed's venality. Such an analysis as Huppé gives presumes in the A-poet a topical interest that is, in other respects, unbelievably well hidden, and the effect of the analysis is to do injury to a correct understanding of A and, in comparison, of B and C.

lusions to these is in the B-addition to the Prologue, where we have in rapid succession the description of the structure of the kingdom, the speeches of the Lunatic, the Angel, the Goliard, and the *comune,* and the fable of the Rat Parliament. Combined with other evidence, the fable makes it likely that the addition to the Prologue was composed after the meeting of the Good Parliament in 1376, for, as has been conclusively shown,[1] the fable was used by Thomas Brunton, Bishop of Rochester, in a sermon delivered at the time the Parliament was in session and the poet, avid reader and hearer of sermons, may well have derived it from Brunton. It is in connection with the Bishop that a topical allusion has been identified in such a way as to do violence to a correct understanding of the poem. G. R. Owst, who has done Middle English studies a great service in showing the influence of medieval sermons upon the literature of the time, has suggested that in the Angel of the B-Prologue is to be seen Bishop Brunton and in the Goliard is to be seen Sir Peter de la Mare, speaker of the lower house in the Good Parliament.[2] Both of these persons were staunch democrats. Brunton had used the fable of the rats in his sermon in order to make clear to the Parliament what it should not do in regard to curbing the royal powers—that is, he advised it not to make the same mistake the rats made in failing to execute their plans. De la Mare had so heeded the advice that, when the reaction to the work of the Good Parliament set in, he was imprisoned as a reward for his vigorous action. Owst suggests that our poet took Brunton for his hero and here introduces him—as the Angel—speaking in behalf of the people because they, being lewd, "*cannot* speak for themselves, in their own defence."[3] Peter de la Mare was prompted "by the prelate's courageous example" to take a strong stand against royal abuses and, according to Owst, as the Goliard he echoes the speech of the Angel.[4] Finally, the lines which terminate the set of speeches in B,

> And þanne gan alle þe comune crye in vers of latin,
> To þe kynges conseille, construe ho-so wolde—
> "*Precepta Regis sunt nobis vincula legis,*"[5]

give a picture, Owst believes, of the Commons standing at the back of de la Mare "like a supporting chorus," expressing their "wistful hope and confidence in the strong personal rule of the monarchy."[6]

1. See Owst, *MLR,* xx, 274. The connection between Brunton's sermon and Langland's fable had been pointed out by Dorothy L. Owen, *Piers Plowman: a Comparison with some Earlier and Contemporary French Allegories,* pp. 86–7. Eleanor H. Kellogg, "Bishop Brunton and the Fable of the Rats," *PMLA,* L (1935), 57–68, dates the sermon May 18, 1376. The Good Parliament sat from April 28 to July 6, 1376.

2. *MLR,* xx, 273–5. Owst's article is reprinted in an expanded form, without reference to Brett's objections (see below), in his book, *Literature and Pulpit in Medieval England* (Cambridge, England, 1933), pp. 576–88.

3. *MLR,* xx, 273, n. 4.   4. *Idem,* p. 275.
5. B, Pro., 143–5.   6. *MLR,* xx, 275.

If all this were true, one would have to concede to B a strong democratic bias, and, since C omits the speeches of the Goliard and the *comune,* assigning the Lunatic's speech to Kind Wit and the Angel's to Conscience, one would also have to admit that C had blunted, if he had not altogether spoiled, the fine democratic edge of B's lines. Furthermore, one would have to explain how it happens that B reversed himself so rapidly that immediately after this passage he was able to expound the undemocratic lesson of the Rat Parliament.

But the identifications cannot be correct. One has only to read the passage carefully to perceive their basic fallacy, which Cyril Brett has pointed out.[7] The Angel's speech is as follows:

> *Sum Rex, sum Princeps, neutrum fortasse deinceps;—*
> *O qui iura regis Christi specialia regis,*
> *Hoc quod agas melius, iustus es, esto pius!*
> *Nudum ius a te vestiri vult pietate;*
> *Qualia vis metere, talia grana sere.*
> *Si ius nudatur, nudo de iure metatur.*
> *Si seritur pietas, de pietate metas!*[8]

Whereupon the Goliard is introduced as follows:

> Thanne greued hym a Goliardeys, a glotoun of wordes,
> And to þe angel an heiȝ answered after,
> *"Dum rex a regere dicatur nomen habere,*
> *Nomen habet sine re, nisi studet iura tenere."*[9]

Brett makes clear the basic conflict between the two speakers. The former is urging upon the King mercy in his justice—*pietas,* which can only be translated, despite Owst's assertion to the contrary,[1] as "mercy." The Goliard, who "grieved" the Angel, is urging strict *ius.* The conflict, according to Brett, is a common one in medieval thought and, as we shall see, was particularly appropriate at the time B was writing. Since Brunton and de la Mare were allies, while the Angel and the Goliard are adversaries, Owst's identification breaks down. Furthermore, in the Angel's speech there is nothing democratic, unless the Christian virtue of mercy is the exclusive property of democratic ideology. Nor is it likely that Langland would have chosen Brunton for his hero, since, upon the evidence, the two had opposite political ideas and used the Rat Parliament

7. *MLR,* XXII, 261–2.

8. B, Pro., 132–8. C, I, 152–7 varies in reading *Hoc vt agas* for the less intelligible *Hoc quod agas* in B134, inserting *&* before *esto,* and by omitting B137.

9. B, Pro., 139–42. C omits.

1. *MLR,* XX, 275, n. 1. See Brett, *MLR,* XXII, 261. *DuCange* lists "miseratio, misericordia," as the first two meanings of *pietas.* In his original article, Owst asks, "Need we follow Skeat in translating Langland's 'pietas' as 'mercy'?" In the restatement in his book, *op. cit.,* p. 581, n. 3, he says, "There seems no very good reason for following Skeat here in his translation of Langland's 'pietas' as 'mercy.'"

for opposite purposes. Finally, Owst's interpretation of the speech of the *comune,* while ingenious, is by no means inevitable. It is somewhat less forced to take it to mean that, regardless of Goliard and Angel, the *comune* was bound by the King's interpretation of law. It is my point that the identification of topical allusions in this case does violence both to B, since it perverts the sense of that text to meet the ends of the identification, and to C, since it produces a nonexistent discrepancy between B and C. Yet despite Brett's conclusive answer, Owst's identification has been repeated recently by a serious historian² — a multiplication of error.

Although B probably did have in mind certain contemporary events when he was writing the passage, the basic idea does not depend upon our identifying the reference in order to be fully realized and C's revision expresses the same sense in a somewhat simplified form. This is true also of the Rat Parliament. It is certain that in B the cat who is to be belled stands either for Edward III or John of Gaunt—I incline to the latter, though good cases have been made out for either³—while the rat of renown probably denotes Peter de la Mare. But in C, who preserves, in this case, the same set of characters, any topical allusions must have been lost because of the passage of time. Nevertheless, the fable makes as good sense in C as it does in B and makes perfectly good sense in both, even though we are unable to make any identifications at all. For it expresses the poet's disapproval of a Parliament's usurping the king's function of government, and it must be interpreted in this way, regardless of what contemporary allusions we find in it in B. Thus, though I am impressed by what Huppé and Bennett⁴ say about the political relevance of the fable to the years of the Good and Bad Parliaments, and though it seems entirely likely that the poet derived it from the sermon of Brunton in May, 1376, I cannot agree with the inference they make that the fable was told ironically and that "the irony would have been pointless if the failure of the Good Parliament had not been plain to all by the time of writing."⁵ There is no reason that we cannot take the fable straight, without irony, though we must admit that if, as Huppé and Bennett suggest, it was first written shortly after the Bad Parliament, it would acquire a certain extra measure of pointedness. But the fable, unlike its putative irony, would not have been pointless at any time, for it expresses a timeless attitude toward the problems of government. This is suf-

2. See Anthony Steel, *Richard II* (Cambridge, England, 1941), pp. 30-1. Steel's acceptance of Owst's theory, combined with his own observation of Langland's conservatism (see his interpretation, p. 37, n. 1, of the lines B, Pro., 112-3: "They do not enshrine any political theory") causes some confusion in his treatment of the poet's politics.

3. For the theory involving John of Gaunt, see Skeat, *EETS,* II, iv; Huppé, *StPh,* XXXVIII, 34-40; Bennett, *MedAev,* XII, 57-9. For the theory involving Edward III see Jusserand, *Revue Critique* (October 25, 1879), pp. 313-19, translated, with Skeat's comments and acceptance, *EETS,* IV, 877-83; also *CP,* II, 17.

4. See the references in the preceding note.

5. Bennett, *MedAev,* XII, 58. See Huppé, *StPh,* XXXVIII, 36.

ficiently attested by its long and honorable history as a fable: according to Baum,[6] it was in currency in Asia Minor as early as the sixth century and was repeated again and again throughout medieval Europe, being told a number of times in England in the fourteenth century before Bishop Brunton's sermon. Surely every time the story was told contemporary political events did not prompt its use. Some narrators were, however, probably lucky enough to have events mold themselves to fit the story, for it is the nature of a fable to have recurrent topicality, universal reference—thus the Bad Parliament justified Brunton. But it was probably as much for the universal as for the specific reference that B told the story in the first place and it was altogether for the universal that C retained it.

Nevertheless, I do not wish to overstate the case against the identification of topical allusions and to make the poet out as altogether blind to what was going on about him. His additions to the Prologue undoubtedly do allow us to see behind them the background of contemporary events. Bennett finds that the B-lines,

> Þanne come þere a kyng, knyȝthod hym ladde,
> Miȝt of þe comunes made hym to regne,

and those following, suggest "the beginning of a new reign"[7]—rather than the end of an old one as Jusserand believed.[8] I am in entire agreement with Bennett that the passage describes Richard II at the very beginning of his reign, though I am unable to agree with the statement that the lines quoted are "a fitting allegorical description" of Richard's induction "as heir apparent, into the order of knighthood (the Garter)," on April 23, 1377.[9] For if this particular ceremony—at which Richard's royal grandfather was present—were in the poet's mind, he could scarcely have used the word *king,* since to do so would have been to cry prematurely, "The King is dead. Long live the King!" On the other hand, I see no reason why Bennett's alternate suggestion—in which he seems to have less confidence—that the lines describe Richard's coronation cannot be accepted. The ceremony took place on July 16, 1377 and, according to the official account of it, on the day before, St. Swithin's Day, the king issued from the Tower of London in order to make his progress to Westminster Abbey (where he spent the night), *vna cum ingenti multitudine procerum Magnatum Militum et Armigerorum in secta sua se circumdancium*[1]—an almost exact equivalent of the first B-line.

6. P. F. Baum, "The Fable of Belling the Cat," *MLN,* xxxiv (1919), 462–70.

7. *MedAev,* xii, 57.

8. *Revue Critique* (October 25, 1879), p. 315.

9. *MedAev,* xii, 57. Bennett cites *The Anonimalle Chronicle* (see p. 107 above), but does not discuss the meaning of French *communes* and the possible significance to the interpretation of B, Pro., 113.

1. Legg, *op. cit.,* p. 145.

Not only the tone of the passage describing the kingdom but also the purport of the four speeches which, in B, follow it suggest the beginning of Richard's reign. The Lunatic's prayer,

> Crist kepe þe, sire kyng, and þi kyngriche,
> And leue þe lede þi londe so leute þe louye,
> And for þi riȝtful rewlyng be rewarded in heuene![2]

while it would not be without application at any time during a given reign, would have especial pertinence at the beginning of one, since it seems to contain a gratulatory as well as a monitory note. The speeches of the Angel and the Goliard also are the sort commonly given in advance of the execution of a project and the tenor of all three speeches suggests an awareness, on the poet's part, of the provisions of the coronation oath. We have already seen how that oath may be used to explain the reference in B to the might of the *comunes*. In it is also implicit the background of the conflict between *pietas* and *ius* which is reflected in the Angel's and the Goliard's speeches. The third question which, according to the Lytlington *ordo,* the officiating bishop asked the king to answer reads as follows: *Facies fieri in omnibus iudiciis tuis equam et rectam iusticiam et discrecionem in misericordia et ueritate secundum uires tuas.*[3] It was to this question that Richard actually responded.[4] But more ancient forms of coronation seem to have been still in circulation even at the time that the Lytlington *ordo* had replaced them[5] and Walsingham, indeed, reports Richard's coronation according to an older form. Thus he describes Richard as swearing that he would not be a *personarum acceptor,* that he would make fair judgment between man and man, *et praecipue misericordiam observaret, sicut sibi suam indulgeat misericordiam clemens et misericors Deus.*[6] It is possible that the B-poet had got hold of some such oath as the one Walsingham was using—in addition to a more modern *ordo*—for the last Latin passage quoted seems directly echoed in the third line of the Lunatic's prayer and even more strikingly in the last three lines of the Angel's speech. Furthermore, the emphasis that was placed upon mercy in the coronation—at an earlier time, if not at the coronation of Richard—is reflected in Walsingham's version of the opening of the ceremony: *Deus, humilium visitator, qui nos tua misericordia consolaris, praetende super famulum tuum, Regem nostrum, misericordiam tuam, ut per eum tuum in nobis adesse sentiamus adventum.*[7] The B-poet's Angel seems to have been a student of coronation *ordo*'s.

2. B, Pro., 125-7 (C, I, 148-50). 3. Legg, *op. cit.,* p. 88.
4. See official account, *idem,* p. 147. 5. See Schramm, *op. cit.,* p. 88.
6. Riley, *op. cit.,* I, 333.
7. *Idem,* p. 332. The Lytlington *ordo* has *sancti spiritus illustracione* for *tua misericordia,* and *graciam tuam* for *misericordiam tuam.* See Legg, *op. cit.,* p. 87. Walsingham was using an older *ordo.*

Even the *comune*'s cry,

> *Precepta Regis sunt nobis vincula legis,*

is perhaps explicable against the background of a coronation. I have already had occasion to mention the fact that, in the second recension of St. Dunstan's coronation *ordo,* what later became the oath of the king appeared in the form of a mandate to the people consisting of three *praecepta,* to which the people were expected to reply *amen.*[8] If, among his wanderings, the B-poet encountered a copy of this *ordo,* the meaning of the *comune*'s cry becomes apparent. The first part of the B-addition is an allegorical coronation and in this line the people are answering the question—which actually was put to them at the coronation of Richard II—whether they wished to consent *ad habendum ipsum Regem et dominum suum ligeum et ad obediendum ei tanquam Regi et domino ligeo.* To this question, we are assured, the people *vnanimiter consenserunt.*[9]

Having tried to establish that there is no real need, so far as the sense is concerned, to identify such characters as the Angel with any contemporary of the poet's, I shall now reverse my ground and attempt such an identification with the Angel himself. On the day before his coronation, Richard II made his *processus* from the Tower of London to Westminster Abbey. His route lay along the Cheapside where the populace had erected in his hor or many elaborate ornaments. Among these was a wonderful tower, a turret on each of its four corners, and fountains of wine emanating from two of its sides. And, according to Walsingham, *in summitate castelli . . . positus erat angelus aureus, tenens auream coronam in manibus, qui tali ingenio factus fuerat, ut adventanti Regi coronam porrigeret inclinando.*[1] It may well have been this golden angel, inclining to proffer Richard the crown, who inspired the B-poet's Angel that "lowed to speke in latyn." On the other hand, the golden angel and B's Angel may have both been merely representatives of a long tradition of angelic participation in coronation ceremonies. St. Adamnan in his life of St. Columba recounts circumstantially how a persistent angel caused Columba to crown Aidan as king—the first recorded English coronation.[2]

This examination of the topical background of the B-addition "haþ don

---

8. Legg, *op. cit.,* p. 9.

9. *Idem,* p. 147. Against the interpretation given here is the fact that the poet describes the *comune* as addressing the King's Council—who might, however, be identified as the *proceres, magnates, et clerici* that surrounded the king at his coronation.

1. Riley, *op. cit.,* I, 332. The *Anonimalle Chronicle* (Galbraith, *op. cit.,* p. 108) gives a slightly different account: *et enmy la dite toure fuist fait une petit clocher et amount le clocher fuist esteaunt une aungelle portaunt une corone dore et moustraunt al dit prince pur luy comforter.*

2. The story is repeated in Legg, *op. cit.,* pp. 1–2. As Miss Kellogg, *PMLA,* L, 67, n. 31, observes, the "warning spoken by an angelic voice is a literary commonplace," appearing in a number of Langland's contemporaries, including Wycliffe. It originates, apparently, in the story of Constantine's donation.

me lepe" from my main subject, the C-revision. But if we accept the premise that B was writing at the time of the coronation of Richard II, then several of C's alterations become easier to understand. The C-revision was accomplished probably during the eighties, when any optimism that may have been generally felt at the time of Richard's accession would have had time to dissipate in the disorder of the Peasants' Revolt—even though the worst was not to come for some time. The King whom the B-poet, expressing an ideal of unity, had said was made to reign by the power of the commonwealth had not yet shown any signs of being capable of inspiring unity; and possibly there was something of discouragement in the poet's alteration of his idealistic line.[3] In re-working the passage containing the four speeches to the King, C omitted the conflict between *ius* and *pietas*—the Goliard and the Angel—possibly because the kingdom had been experiencing very little of either and, whereas the poet still favored *pietas,* he would do nothing to discourage a tendency toward *ius,* in any form whatsoever. In any case, the conflict between the two would have less pertinence if presented in the middle years of an ineffective reign: it was no time to be splitting hairs. The omission of the *comune's* one-line speech is less easy to explain. To be sure, C might have cut it out on the grounds that it referred originally to the coronation and was hence no longer topical; but C was not always scrupulous to keep his topical references up-to-date, even negatively by omitting them when they had lost their point. Possibly in the *comune's* cry he had originally envisioned the same ideal of unity as that discussed above; and since the ideal was not realized, he deleted the line expressing it. But even though none of these explanations is altogether satisfactory— and they do not, I admit, altogether satisfy me—we should observe that the C-revision of the passage, in the general direction of its thought, is the same as in B: politically no less, and no more, conservative.

In this chapter we have found reason for believing that the discrepancy between B's and C's political views, one of the foundation stones in the tradition of multiple authorship, does not in actuality exist and that the political cautiousness that Wright saw in C as compared with B, and that Skeat and others admitted, is, therefore, largely illusory. Moreover we have seen that this "discrepancy" tends to become exaggerated by certain of the interpretations given to the topical allusions in A and B, and that if we remain aware of the universal application of *Piers Plowman,* which interested the poet far more than the specific, the differences between the texts disappear. So far as the actual nature of the poet's politics is concerned, they seem to have had a decidedly middle-of-the-road tendency and to have agreed with, if they were not actually derived from, the several coronation oaths that were known to fourteenth-century Eng-

3. A similar explanation was offered by Jusserand, who understood B's lines to refer to the House of Commons. See *Mysticism,* p. 57.

land. Familiarity with these explains not only the direction of the poet's politics, but also his sudden interest in politics in the B-addition to the Prologue. Finally, from a study of the political opinions and allusions of B and C we have found no evidence for assuming independent authorship of the two texts. Indeed, the harmony that exists between them suggests that they are the work of one poet.

V

The C-Reviser and the Occupations of the Folk on the Field

A Feir feld ful of folk fond I þer bi-twene,
Of alle maner of men, þe mene and þe riche,
Worchinge and wondringe as þe worlde askeþ.[1]

IT was to the A-poet that the vision of the Field of Folk was first given and, though his later dreams—and those of B and C—seem to have taken him far and wide, it is nevertheless true that with the exception of one excursion to hell he never succeeded in getting out of sight of the Field of Folk.[2] Even that most mystical of localities, the garden in which the Tree of Charity grows, turns out to be named Cor Hominis, and the reader finds that the Dreamer, instead of journeying spirally away from the field, has actually been on it the whole time. Thus the most restless, other-world-seeking poet of his time turns out to be almost as earth-bound as Chaucer and without the services of Chaucer's eagle.

The poet's preoccupation with the folk on the field—a preoccupation that is equally apparent in all three texts—offers us an easy method of tracing the development of his ideas and of studying the changes that took place in them, or, where no development took place, of observing their consistency. In its literal content the Prologue of the poem, like Chaucer's Prologue, amounts to little more than a catalogue of men, listed according to their earthly occupation—plowing, preaching, begging, singing for their suppers, trading, catering, praying—while the last passus of the *Visio,* in which the provisions of Piers's pardon are disclosed, offers a judgment on the practical and spiritual values (the poet hardly distinguishes between the two) of many of the *modi vivendi* that are described in the Prologue. But while the Prologue is Alpha, the last passus of the *Visio* is by no means Omega in this matter, for, as is characteristic of *Piers Plowman,* not all the questions that have seemingly been answered by the pardon stay answered for the poet, and he reverts to some of them again and again. In this chapter I shall review the opinions expressed in the A-, B-, and C-texts on a number of occupational groups. In doing this, my aim will be to show the homogeneity of the

1. AB, Pro., 17–19 (C, I, 19–21). I give the A–reading.
2. See H. W. Wells, *PMLA,* XLIV, 129: "With the exception of the Harrowing of Hell the poet avoids all scenes that belong to another life than that of this world."

ideas in the three versions, whether these ideas remain static or undergo change.

The most interesting development of an idea may, I think, be observed in the attitude displayed in the successive texts toward minstrels, and a large part of the discussion will be devoted to that subject. But the manner in which several other occupations are treated, whether or not any real growth or change is perceptible, is also of interest and this chapter would not be complete without some consideration of them. Let us begin by classifying occupations according to the way they are regarded in the poem.

The classification may be limited to three groups. In the first of these may be placed those occupations which, although they are capable of being abused, are indisputably reputable and wholesome: physical labor, particularly farming; spiritual labor, consisting in the cultivation of the Lord's vineyard by the clergy, secular and regular—bishops, priests, monks, friars, hermits; and civil and military labor, that of kings and knights. In the second group may be placed those occupations which, while they are in the main wholesome and reputable, entail a kind of occupational hazard that brings many practitioners into evil ways: the best examples are trade, the law, and medicine. To the third group may be assigned those occupations which either entail so great an occupational hazard that an honest practitioner is rarely if ever encountered, or which are by their very nature evil: the occupations of pilgrim, palmer, beggar, pardoner, juryman, commissary, sheriff, summoner, and various petty officials of Church and state. With this last group, as with certain members of the second, it is often difficult to tell whether the poet condemns the occupation per se, or condemns it because of its attraction for thieves and rascals. For instance, as we shall see, there are honest beggars, but they do not beg professionally and the profession itself is damned. In the possibility of an honest sheriff or summoner the poet may have believed, but we shall look long in *Piers Plowman* before we find an example of one. One occupation, that of minstrels, I have not included in any group, wishing to let classification wait until a thorough examination of the topic has been completed.

Let us look at the first group. So much has been said of kings and knights in the previous chapter that it is unnecessary to repeat that the two latest texts, at least, maintain a consistent point of view toward them, or to explain what this point of view is. The members of the subgroup called physical labor are, in the appropriate guise of plowmen, the first persons that the poet notices in his catalogue of folk.[3] The vice to which laborers are susceptible is, naturally enough, idleness. This is brought out by the fact that the poet mentions wasters immediately after describ-

3. AB, Pro., 20–1 (C, I, 22–3): "Some putten hem to þe plow, pleyed ful selde, In settyng and in sowyng swonken ful harde."

ing honest laborers[4] and, in the passus containing the plowing of Piers's half-acre, by the introduction of Waster.[5] The attitude toward honest laborers is the same in all texts:

> Alle lybbyng laboreres þat lyuen with her hondes,
> Þat trewlich taken and trewlich wynnen,
> And lyuen in loue and in lawe, for her lowe hertis
> Haueth þe same absolucioun þat sent was to peres,[6]

while those who do not live up to such a standard become automatically classed with dishonest beggars, who are excluded from the terms of Truth's pardon.

Despite the great importance of physical labor to the fundamental doctrine of the poem, comparatively little analysis is made of it. The reason for this is not hard to find. The poet believed firmly in the principle that the readiness with which one may obtain salvation varies with the degree of responsibility attached to one's secular activity. Thus, while

> Souteris & seweris, suche lewide iottis,
> Percen wiþ a pater noster þe paleis of heuene,[7]

we have it on the authority of St. Augustine that

> Arn none raþere yrauisshid fro þe riȝte beleue
> Þanne arn þise grete clerkis þat conne many bokis.[8]

It is "þise grete clerkis"—the clergy, regular and secular, who act as the Lord's stewards—rather than those who will be held to less strict account that most interest and trouble the spirit of the poet.

There is not time here to make a full survey of the passages dealing with the clergy's duties and shortcomings, and indeed to do so would be needlessly to repeat a large portion of the poem itself. It may be said in general that in all texts the clergy is represented as the means by which mankind is to attain salvation and is, therefore, the most important of all occupations possible to men of this world. In view of the overwhelming importance of this calling, it would be well to glance briefly at the poet's attitude toward the various branches of the clergy. We shall begin with the regulars.

In the medieval conflict between the two large divisions of the regulars, A, B, and C all obviously take part with the monks against the friars, as, indeed, did Chaucer, if we may judge by the portraits in his Prologue. But this partisanship, as Skeat observed long ago,[9] amounts to no blind

---

4. AB, Pro., 22 (C, I, 24): "And wonnen that wastours with glotonye destruyeth."
5. B, VI, 154 ff., A, VII, 140 ff., C, IX, 149 ff. Along with Waster is introduced a Britoner, a fellow of the same character.
6. B, VII, 62–5 (A, VIII, 64–7). C, X, 58–60 paraphrases.
7. A, XI, 301–02. B, X, 460–1, C, XII, 294–5 vary slightly.
8. A, XI, 297–8. B, X, 456–7, C, XII, 290–1 vary slightly.
9. *EETS*, I, xxxviii: ". . . while he satirizes the friars, he seems not much more friendly to the monks."

loyalty, and if the poet directly praises life "in cloistere or in scole"[1]
and pictures Wrath as incapable of disrupting the harmony of the monas-
tery,[2] he still recognizes—as, I believe, Chaucer did—the perilous path
that monasticism, through its avarice and its worldliness, its inobedience
to rule, is taking, and he has Clergy (and Reason) utter that famous
prophecy which was so disastrously fulfilled.[3] On the other hand, with
the friars he is almost universally severe, frequently making them the
villains of his piece or the butts of his jokes. In this point of view there
is no change or development in his attitude from one text to another.
Recently an attempt has been made to assign a new date to the composition of B partly on the basis of the supposed increase in bitterness B
shows in dealing with the friars.[4] But this increase seems largely the
result of the operation of the laws of statistics. B is more than three
times as long as A, and since the subject of friars is a recurrent one, B
contains, naturally, about three times the amount of bitterness that A
shows. Actually, the poet's chief reason for hating the friars was originally expressed in the Prologue of the A-text and was left virtually unchanged in B and C. The Dreamer beholds all four orders of friars
preaching to the people for the good of their own bellies and interpreting
the Gospel in whatever way will most benefit themselves. Many of them,
the poet says, can dress themselves as they please, inasmuch as they get
a good price for their merchandise, which consists of the carefully adjusted penances they assign in their confessionals :

> For sith charite haþ be chapman and chief to shryue lordes,
> Many ferlis han fallen in a fewe ȝeris.
> But holychirche and hij holde better togideres,
> The moste myschief on molde is mountyng wel faste.[5]

That is, the comfortable confessions—which Chaucer also comments
on—given by oversympathetic and avaricious friars are destroying the
very fabric of the Church and, through it, of all society. This thought is
fully developed in the last lines of B and C, where the "Frere with his
phisik" is described as drugging Contrition himself, the spiritual quality
most necessary for salvation.[6] Nothing could be more disastrous than the
disruption of the Church and, since the poet sincerely believes that the
friars are accomplishing such a disruption, he does not spare them.

Hall suggested that C was more stringent in regard to friars than

1. B, x, 301 (R only) (C, vi, 154).   2. B, v, 169–81, C, vii, 151–63.
3. B, x, 291–330, C, vi, 144–80.
4. See A. Gwynn, RES, xix, 1–24, especially p. 1 : "Reading through the B-text in
Skeat's edition with an eye to the contemporary controversy between the friars and the
secular clergy, I was surprised to note how sharp is the difference between Langland's
criticism of the friars in the A-text and the very much more polemical tone of the
B-text." The passages Gwynn cites in evidence do not seem impressive.
5. B, Pro., 64–7. A, Pro., 61–4, C, i, 62–5 vary, A only slightly.
6. B, xx, 307-84, C, xxiii, 309-86.

A and B and found in this increased stringency evidence for multiple authorship. B, he says, "had a good word to say for the 'pore freres' even when most discredited,"[7] while C displayed no such generosity—a belief Hall endeavored to support by citing C's omission of several lines in B, Passus xv. Anima, who has been talking about the excessive wealth of the regulars—monks, canons, and friars—finds occasion to ask who, nowadays, performs the text of the Psalm, *Dispersit, dedit pauperibus.* The question is rhetorical and Anima furnishes his own answer:

> If any peple perfourme þat texte, it ar þis pore freres!
> For þat þei beggen abouten, in buildynge þei spene,
> And on hem-self sum and such as ben here laboreres,
> And of hem þat habbeth þei taken and ȝyue hem þat ne habbeth![8]

Hall found these lines a "memorable testimony to the good done by the friars"[9]—which is, perhaps, a memorable example to poets of the peril of making jokes. For, as Skeat's exclamation points are probably intended to suggest, the lines are nothing but a humorous gibe at the friars. The context concerns, as I have said, the wealth of the regulars and their interminable building programs, to complete which they perpetrated such parodies of their spiritual function as the poet has described in the confession of Lady Meed. Anima is here moved to remark, with a bitter sort of mirth, that at least the building programs have an incidental benefit, since they support artisans and friars—just as some one might say that thieves have a wholesome influence on the economy, since they keep money in circulation and relieve unemployment. C, probably because he feared, with some justification, that some one might miss the point, altered the lines.

Nevertheless, both B and C do have a good word to say about friars, ideally if not in the flesh, and it is for this reason that I have had the temerity, which must have puzzled some readers, to class friars among the occupations regarded as in the main wholesome. The pertinent lines appear in the speech of Liberum Arbitrium (Anima) concerning the whereabouts of that allusive person, Charity:

> And in a freres frocke he was yfounde ones,
> Ac it is fer and fele ȝeres, in fraunceys tyme.[1]

These lines, which are as hauntingly effective as any in the poem, give us the clue to the poet's true conception of the ideal which was theoretically that of the mendicant orders. That ideal is charity itself. And

> . . . sith charite haþ be chapman and chief to shryue lordes,

7. *MLR,* iv, 7.   8. B, xv, 321-4.   9. *MLR,* iv, 12.
1. C, xvii, 352-3. B, xv, 225-6 varies and is less effective, probably as a result of scribal deviation.

the entire structure of the Church (which is also charity) is in danger.
Therefore Church and friars must purge themselves. As C writes,

> Bote holy churche & charite choppe a-doun swich shryuers,
> The moste myschif on molde Mounteþ vp faste.[2]

Charite here stands for the mendicant orders—*hij,* meaning the friars,
in the B-text. The real reason for the poet's bitterness is not partisan and
is the same in A, B, and C. He hates the friars because, given the highest
of ideals, they have sunk to the vice most destructive of charity, namely,
avarice.

The principle which holds that the greater the ideal, the more pernicious the failure to live up to it, appears consistently throughout the
texts in application to the secular clergy. And while the poet's bitterness
is visited upon the parochial clerks for their ignorance and for the desertion of their parishes—

> Persones and parisch prestes pleyned hem to þe bischop,
> Þat here parisshes were pore sith þe pestilence tyme,
> To haue a lycence and a leue at London to dwelle,
> And syngen þere for symonye, for siluer is swete[3]—

a rather greater amount of vituperation is expended upon bishops, who
are responsible for the conduct of their flocks here on earth and will be
called to account for it in the next world. Manly was able to detect in the
C-text an inclination "to tone down criticisms of bishops and the higher
clergy,"[4] but a careful study of significant references to bishops in all
texts reveals no great discrepancies.[5] The episcopacy is everywhere susceptible to more or less gratuitous insult. It is true that in two places
C omits or modifies a stinging reference. Thus, according to A and B,
among the vehicles that were fashioned to carry Meed's fellowship to
London is one consisting of various minor ecclesiastical officials yoked
together and saddled with silver

> . . . owre synne to suffre,
> As auoutrie and deuorses and derne vsurye,
> To bere bischopes aboute, abrode in visytynge.[6]

Elsewhere Meed is pictured as blessing

> . . . þise bisshopes þeiȝe þey be lewed.[7]

2. C, I, 64–5.   3. B, Pro., 83–6 (A, Pro, 80–3, C, I, 81–4).
4. *CHEL,* II, 40.
5. The most important references in B and C are as follows: B, Pro., 78, C, I, 76;
B, Pro., 87, C, I, 85; B, II, 176; B, III, 148, C, IV, 186; B, IV, 124, C, V, 120; B, V, 298, C,
VII, 345; B, VII, 13, C, X, 13; C, X, 255; B, VIII, 94, C, XI, 92; B, IX, 89; C, XI, 191; B,
XI, 303, C, XIV, 124; B, XV, 239, C, XVII, 363; B, XV, 515, C, XVIII, 216; B, XV, 538. Some
of these lines begin passages of considerable length. As has been observed elsewhere, C
insists much more than B upon bishops' not standing in fear of great lords.
6. B, II, 174–6. A, II, 150–1 varies, but is still offensive to bishops. Cf. C, III, 185 ff.
7. B, III, 148 (A, III, 144). Compare C, IV, 186: Carnegy reads, however, like B.

The first of these passages C rewrites omitting the bishops, while in the second many C-MSS insert *negh* before *lewed*—a rather grudging concession to episcopal literacy. On the other hand, C adds a longer, more vigorous, and far more responsible passage of reproof to bishops in which he likens them to negligent shepherds and promises the inefficient ones hell-fire, not only for their own sins, but for the sins of their flock.[8] One might suppose that an actual fourteenth-century bishop would fail to find himself flattered either by B or by C. The consistent asperity with which bishops are handled is, as I have said, of the same origin as that cast upon the friars. At its most elevated level, the episcopacy is Do-Best of all.[9] If they did as they should, God would grant bishops

> To be peeres to a-posteles, alle puple to ruele,
> And deme with hem at domes day boþe quike and ded.[1]

But when, through worldliness, they fall short of their ideal, the poet rewards them with his vituperation. The same is true of his treatment of even higher ecclesiastical officials. Unsuitable Tolerance is Meed's sister and no friend of the poet's, and the result of his austere idealism is that, whereas he has the highest respect for the office of pope, the bishop of bishops and Christ's vicar on earth, for contemporary flesh-and-blood popes, as for cardinals, he seems to have had little respect of any sort.

Toward the independent regulars, hermits and anchorites, the attitude is likewise consistent throughout the texts, although there is a good deal more material on the subject in C than in A and B, even if there is no alteration in attitude. We first meet hermits on the Field of Folk. In fact, rather curiously, we meet them twice. On the first occasion the poet presents honest hermits, who live in prayer and in penance, hoping to obtain the bliss of heaven. These are such as

> . . . holden hem in here selles,
> And coueiten nought in contre to kairen aboute,
> For no likerous liflode her lykam to plese.[2]

The second, dishonest type of hermit which is implied in these lines we meet a few moments later:

> Heremites on an heep With hoked staues,
> Wenten to Walsyngham and here wenches after.[3]

These great loafers have become hermits only through a desire for

8. C, x, 255–81.

9. C, xi, 92–3: "Dobest bere sholde þe bisshopes croce, And halye with þe hoked ende ille men to goode." B, viii, 94–5 varies slightly. For the recurrence of the image, see Coghill, *MedAev*, ii, 126–8, under *Dobest*.

1. C, x, 20–1. B, vii, 16–17, A, viii, 18–19 vary.

2. AB, Pro., 28–30 (C, i, 30–2).   3. B, Pro., 53–4 (A, Pro., 50–1, C, i, 51–2).

singularity and for an easy life. The poet keeps the two types of hermit carefully distinct. Thus Piers promises to feed

> . . . ancres and heremytes that eten noȝt but at nones,[4]

while the good-for-nothing sort are pictured, a few lines afterward, as seizing spades and working furiously in order to repel the onslaughts of Hunger.[5] To these passages, which he takes over without significant change from A and B, C adds two long diatribes against

> > . . . lewede eremytes,
> That loken ful louheliche to lacchen mennes almesse,
> In hope to sitten at euen by þe hote coles,[6]

and against

> . . . eremites þat en-habiten by þe heye weyes,[7]

who lead a pleasant and profitable social life. Furthermore, C alludes again to these "lewede heremytes" in his own autobiography.[8] The invective here seems motivated not only by the breach between the ideal of St. Anthony and the practice of fourteenth-century hermits, but also by some experience in the poet's life which gave him an especial bias. C admits that he resembled, in a striking way, the very persons whom he has been at such pains to label "lollers" according to what he conceived to be correct etymology.[9] Yet he is very eager that we should distinguish between them and himself, even though we, like Reason, may have some difficulty in so doing. Despite this increased interest in hermits, particularly in bad ones, C's attitude is at heart the same as A's and B's. It differs only in being more personal.

The second group of occupations mentioned at the beginning of this chapter—those that entail a certain moral and spiritual hazard for their practitioners—need not detain us long. In the main, the poet's treatment of them is consistent and conventional. We are first introduced to merchants on the Field of Folk:

> And somme chosen chaffare, they [cheueden] the bettere,
> As it semeth to owre syȝt that suche men thryueth.[1]

In the confession of Avarice there is in all texts a vivid description of a cheating merchant[2] and it appears that cheating, along with a disposition to keep shops open on Sundays and holy days, is the occupational hazard

---

4. B, vi, 147 (C, ix, 146). A, vii, 134 virtually repeats A, Pro., 28.
5. B, vi, 190–3. A, vii, 177–8, C, ix, 183–7 vary.
6. C, x, 140–2.   7. C, x, 188.
8. C, vi, 2–5.   9. C, x, 213 ff.
1. AB, Pro., 31–2 (C, i, 33–4). I give the reading of MS W in B31.
2. B, v, 188–231, A, v, 107–145, C, vii, 196–233.

incurred by tradesmen. Therefore Truth will not grant them pardon *a poena et a culpa:*

> For þei holde nouȝt her halidayes as holicherche techeth,
> And for þei swere by her soule and "so god moste hem helpe,"
> Aȝein clene conscience, her catel to selle.[3]

But so long as they trade fairly, and make distribution of their profits in good works, Truth, and the poet of all three texts, bear them no ill will and promise them heaven at the last. The only difference between C and the earlier versions in this matter is C's elaboration, upon lines already laid down in A and B, of a passage castigating dishonest retailers.[4]

The occupational hazard pertaining to law is somewhat greater than that which imperils merchants, for lawyers

> Pleddeden for penyes and poundes þe lawe,
> And nouȝt for loue of owre lorde vnlese here lippes onis.[5]

The result of this niggardliness, which when it is enforced against the poor amounts to simony, is that lawyers have the smallest share in the pardon of any occupational group, although they do have some share and are not, like dishonest beggars, altogether excluded.[6] For all three texts state that such lawyers as are willing to donate their services to the poor may expect salvation. That other historically much-damned profession, medicine, receives no mention either in the Prologue or in connection with the pardon. Doctors appear only fleetingly in Hunger's speech of advice to Piers.[7] In A Hunger asserts that there are more liars in the profession than genuine leeches, while, as we have seen, in B he says that many doctors are murderers and in C, more moderately, that the profession is not distinguished for honesty. All three agree that doctors increase the death rate. Despite the variation in force of expression, the basic sentiment is constant: good doctors exist but in small numbers. Perhaps we should recall here that in B and C the friar who completes the disruption of Unity masquerades as a doctor.

We come now to the third group of occupations—those which are *sui generis* unwholesome, or which attract men of such a disreputable character that they lose all traces of honesty. Not much interest attaches to the poet's attitude toward the majority of these. Most are mentioned only once or twice and always in an unflatteringly unambiguous con-

---

3. B, VII, 20–2 (A, VIII, 22–4, C, X, 24–6). For similar passages in the sermon literature, see Owst, *Literature and Pulpit in Medieval England*, pp. 338–49 (lawyers); pp. 349–51 (doctors); pp. 352–61 (merchants).

4. C, IV, 77–114. Cf. A, III, 67–77, B, III, 76–86.

5. B, Pro., 212–13 (A, Pro., 86–7, C, I, 161–2).

6. B, VII, 39–61, A, VIII, 45–63, C, X, 44–57.

7. A, VII, 260–1, B, VI, 275–6, C, IX, 296–7. The cobbler of Southwark and Dame Emma of Shoreditch should not be included in a discussion of doctors since their pretensions to leechcraft are magical, not medical. See B, XIII, 340, C, VII, 83.

text. The problem presented by the poet's opinion of beggars is, however, a real one which is interesting in itself and which has furnished some fuel to the devouring fire to which C's reputation has been subjected. As treated in *Piers Plowman,* mendicancy must be considered in two ways : first, in relation to the mendicant himself, and second, in relation to the community which supports him. The first point is complicated by the fact that, although B and C assure us that

> Þe boke banneth beggarie and blameth hem in þis manere :
>   *Iunior fui, etenim senui; et non vidi iustum*
>   *derelictum, nec semen eius querens panem,*[8]

all three texts allow for the existence of justifiable mendicancy.

Concerning beggars of both sorts A, B, and C are equally clear, even though in the Prologue we meet only evil ones :

> Bidders and beggeres fast about ȝede,
> With here bely and her bagges [bratful] ycrammed.[9]

The souls of mendicants of this sort, who the poet says

> Fayteden for here fode, fouȝten atte ale,[1]

are doomed, for according to Piers's pardon

> Beggeres ne bidderes ne beth nouȝte in þe bulle,[2]

if their begging is voluntary and not forced upon them. If, on the other hand,

> . . . þe suggestioun be soth þat shapeth hem to begge,[3]

then they are excusable, since

> . . . olde men & hore þat helplees ben of strengthe,
> And women with childe þat worche ne mowe,
> Blynde and bedered and broken here membres,
> Þat taketh þis myschief mekelych, as meseles and othere,
> Han as pleyne pardoun as þe plowman hym-self.[4]

On this much the texts agree, and on the strength of C's eloquent expansion of the last passage it is fair to say that he felt as deeply as A and B that there might be just cause for begging.

Whatever discrepancy there is among the texts appears in the handling of the second point in the problem of begging—the mendicant in relation

---

8. B, vii, 88. C, x, 162 gives a second Latin quotation.

9. AB, Pro., 40–1 (C, i, 41–2). For B's *of bred ful* I give the AC reading.

1. AB, Pro., 42 (C, i, 43).   2. B, vii, 66 (A, viii, 68, C, x, 61).

3. B, vii, 67 (A, viii, 69, C, x, 62).

4. B, vii, 99–103 (A, viii, 83–7). C, x, 175–86 elaborates. If the Church did its full part, no one would have to beg. See C, xi, 182–4, B, ix, 66–70. But this does not alter the principle under discussion.

to the community that supports him. The question arises, Should one dispense charity to all beggars, or simply to those that one knows are deserving? This is first broached by Piers, who asks Hunger,

Of beggeres and of bidderes what best be to done?[5]

Piers knows that dishonest beggars work only when forced to do so by Hunger, and yet Piers would like to see them always earning their own living. But they will not, and since Piers has been taught that all men are brothers and that each should help the other, he is in a quandary. Hunger's sage answer to Piers's question is recorded in all three texts:

Bolde beggeres and bigge þat mowe her bred bi-swynke,
With houndes bred and hors bred holde vp her hertis,
[A-bane] hem with benes for bollyng of her wombe;
And ȝif þe gomes grucche, bidde hem go swynke.[6]

Thus Hunger tells Piers to give charity to all beggars, but to show some discrimination, giving less generously to those who appear capable of work. Honest beggars should, however, be helped without hesitation. With this response the A-poet is content, for the subject is not brought up again. In B, however, it recurs. Coghill has suggested in an interesting note that B,[7] reading the A-line in which Hunger urges Piers to help those

Þat neodi ben, or naket, and nouȝt haue to spende,[8]

was induced by the word *nouȝt* to think of its cognate *naughty,* in the sense of "wicked," and thus rewrote the line to read

That nedy ben, and nauȝty, helpe hem with þi godis.

Whereupon the subject of discrimination in charity, presumably settled, came up again briefly. B went on to settle it for the second time:

Loue hem and lakke hem nouȝte, late god take þe veniaunce.[9]

That is, give to the wicked, leaving it up to the Lord to punish them. As Miss Day has pointed out, when C came to revise these lines, he so altered them that all mention of the naughty is removed and the result is that in this particular part of Hunger's speech only deserving beggars

5. B, VI, 206 (A, VII, 192, C, IX, 210).
6. B, VI, 216–19 (A, VII, 202–05, C, IX, 224–7). I substitute the reading of A (in MS H) and of C for B *Abate* in B218. The word *a-bane* I do not take to mean "poison," as Skeat does (*EETS,* IV, 169), but rather "fortify." See *Purity,* l. 620, where Abraham offers the Lord "a morsel of bred to banne yor hertte," which renders Genesis 18.5, *Et confortate cor vestrum.* See R. J. Menner's note to the line in his edition (New Haven, 1920).
7. Nevill K. Coghill, "Langland, the 'Naket,' the 'Nauȝty,' and the Dole," *RES,* VIII (1932), 303–09.
8. A, VII, 212. Cf. B, VI, 226.   9. B, VI, 227.

appear as proper recipients of charity.[1] According to the venerable principles of parallel-text reading, C has omitted a sentiment of which he disapproves.

In the following passus of B and C the whole subject is brought up again in connection with the provisions of the pardon. A is content to have Truth grant salvation to honest beggars, damnation to dishonest ones. He observes that the latter sort are

> . . . Fals with þe Fend and defraudeþ þe neodi,
> And eke gyleþ þe ȝiuere al aȝeyn his wille.[2]

B for some reason felt that the last clause needed elaboration, for he added,

> For if he wist he were nouȝte nedy he wolde ȝiue þat an other,
> Þat were more nedy þan he, so þe nediest shuld be hulpe.[3]

The ignorance of the giver then reminded him of Cato's instruction, *Cui des, videto,* the ungenerous purport of which, however, is contradicted by Gregory's *Non eliges cui miserearis,* of which B straightway thought. After a characteristic debate with himself, B decided in favor of Gregory. "Give to every one,"

> For wite ȝe neuere who is worthi, ac god wote who hath nede.[4]

But not altogether satisfied that the subject has been exhausted, B goes on to resolve the whole question by putting the full responsibility on the beggars, who, he promises, will be damned if they accept charity they do not need.

When C revised the passage he followed B down through the mention of Cato's teaching and then went on to summarize Gregory's, without mentioning him by name, in the single line,

> Wot no man, as ich wene, who is worthy to haue.[5]

Following this he launched into that passage on the sorrows of the poor from which I have already quoted—a passage which, incidentally, tends to give the lie to the last line quoted. At the end of the passage, C returns to the subject of begging, exclaiming as follows:

> Ac beggers with bagges, þe whiche brewhouses ben here churches,
> Bote þei be blynde oþer broke, oþer elles be syke,
> Þauh he falle for defaute þat faiteþ for hus lyf-lode,
> Reccheþ neuere, ȝe ryche, þauh suche lorelles steruen.

---

1. Mabel Day, *"Piers Plowman* and Poor Relief," *RES*, VIII (1932), 445–6. See C, IX, 232–5. Manly, *CHEL*, II, 35, notes that "instead of the indiscriminate almsgiving insisted upon by B, C distinctly condemns it." Manly cites C, X, 71–281, but ignores Hunger's advice.

2. A, VIII, 71–2 (B, VII, 69–70). C, X, 64–5 varies slightly.

3. B, VII, 71–2.   4. B, VII, 78.   5. C, X, 70.

> For alle þat han here hele and here eyen syghte,
> And lymes to laborye with, and lolleres lyf vsen,
> Lyuen a-ȝens godes lawe and lore of holy churche.[6]

The conclusion seems inescapable that C is in disagreement with B on the subject of the treatment of beggars, both upon the evidence of the passage inserted and upon the evidence of the B-lines omitted. Miss Day, filling in the picture of C as a staunch believer in discriminate charity (a picture which, she says, though it differs "radically" from her idea of B, proves nothing about the authorship), quotes one other passage from C that I have neglected to mention.[7] It is a part of Hunger's advice to Piers, added by C and occurring several pages after that passage in Hunger's speech that has already been discussed. The lines quoted by Miss Day are the following:

> Alle þat greden at þy gate, for godes loue, after fode,
> Parte with hem of þy payn, of potage oþer of souel,
> Lene hem som of þy loof þauh þou þe lasse chewe.
> And þauh lyers and lacchedrawers and lolleres knocke,
> Let hem abyde tyl þe bord be drawe, ac bere hem none cromes.[8]

But I fear that this is a case of illustrating Conscience's parable about *Omnia probate: bonum tenete*. For the passage as quoted is not complete. There is another line which, when taken with its two predecessors (all three form one sentence in Skeat's edition), modifies the thought considerably:

> And þauh lyers and lacchedrawers and lolleres knocke,
> Let hem abyde tyl þe bord be drawe, ac bere hem none cromes,
> Til alle þyn nedy neihebores haue none ymaked.[9]

Now if, as seems likely, *none* here means "lunch,"[1] although one must concede that the lines still urge discrimination in charity, the lesson is perfectly obvious that one should feed all beggars, the deserving first and fullest, the undeserving later and less daintily. In short, C is merely repeating the advice that Hunger has already given in all three texts:

> Bolde beggeres and bigge þat mowe her bred bi-swynke,
> With houndes bred and hors bred holde vp her hertis.

The fact is that C's opinion is no more at variance with B than it is with C. B urges one to give to all beggars. C urges one to give to all beggars and to let dishonest beggars starve. If we found the former piece of advice only in lines that C had taken over intact from B, we might suggest that the transfer was accidental and that C did not realize what

6. C, x, 98–104.   7. *RES*, viii, 446.
8. *Idem*, p. 445. The lines are C, ix, 285–9.   9. C, ix, 288–90.
1. See Skeat's glossary. Also *OED*, noon, sb., 3, where this line is used to illustrate the meaning "mid-day meal,"

he was doing. But the two passages in which C expresses himself most clearly, and on opposite sides of the same question, are both entirely new to the C-text and must have been the result of conscious labor. This fact, while it requires some explanation, largely vitiates whatever conclusions one may be tempted to draw from C's omission of certain B-lines. An inference *a silentio* must yield before direct statement. The passage in which C's Hunger urges charity for all beggars effectually replaces the omitted lines in which B's Hunger does the same thing. It replaces them, but it does not have a parallel location, a fact that should warn us not to rely too heavily on parallel-text reading.

The reason for the conflict of opinions in C becomes more evident if we read the C-text as a whole and not through the dark glass of B. The C-passage in which C advises the rich to let healthy beggars starve follows, as we have seen, the moving passage on the sorrows of the poor. In the course of those lines the poet says that our needy neighbors

> . . . beth abasshed for to begge and wolle nat be aknowe
> What hem needeþ at here neihebores at non and at euen.[2]

And he goes on to speak of the little that would relieve them:

> . . . a ferthyng-worth of muscles
> Were a feste for suche folke, oþer so fele Cockes.[3]

It is against this background that we must read what follows. The deserving poor, ashamed to beg, are the needy neighbors of the rich and a little would bring them great comfort, if the rich but recognized their need. But instead the rich feed professional beggars. The implication is that Gregory's comprehensive spirit of charity is not enough. The rich ought actually to seek out those who are really needy—to assume responsibility for helping where help is badly needed. This is a positive rather than a negative interpretation of *Cui des, videto*. Angered by the injustice of misdirected charity, the poet, deeply sympathetic with honest poverty, breaks out in a vehement condemnation of professional mendicants. The result is certainly confusing in terms of logic, but dramatically it is perfectly harmonious—more human, perhaps, than strictly Christian, but understandable enough. And since B, when he came to weigh the question, as he did more than once, of whether or not to help the undeserving, teetered precariously on the seesaw between Gregory and Cato, and seemed for a time as likely to take sides with the schoolbook as with the Pope, I suspect that it was B who eventually became the C who tried once more to achieve a balance and succeeded in doing so only by taking each side alternately.[4]

2. C, x, 86–7.   3. C, x, 94–5.
4. Miss Day, *RES*, VIII, 445–6, also cites as instances of C's illiberality his omission of B, x, 189–206, his alteration of B, xv, 164 (C, XVII, 300), and his insertion of C, XII, 29–30. The first passage in B is advice to return evil with good, which is at least implicit

In one respect, however, C's interest in begging does seem different from A's and B's. Like his interest in hermits, to which it is related, it is both greater and more personal. Thus he introduces and discusses at length a new class of deserving beggars whom he calls by the curious name of God's minstrels. With these we shall deal later. On the personal side, the C-poet describes himself as being taken by Reason for a beggar and even admits the justice of the identification, although he attempts to make a distinction. To Reason's accusation,

> . . . for an ydel man þow semest,
> A spendour þat spende mot, oþer a spille-tyme,
> Oþer beggest þy bylyue a-boute at menne hacches,
> Oþer faitest vp-on frydays oþer feste-dayes in churches,
> The whiche is lollarene lyf[5]—

which would put the poet squarely in the class with dishonest beggars— C replies in such a way as to excuse himself :

> And þo þat fynden me my fode vouchen saf, ich trowe,
> To be welcome whanne ich come oþer-whyle in a monthe,
> Now with hym and now with hure, and þus-gate ich begge
> With-oute bagge oþer botel, bote my wombe one.[6]

Despite this plea, Conscience concludes that

> . . . it semeth nouht parfytnesse in cytees for to begge.[7]

Defeated in his attempt to find in Reason and Conscience some sanction for what seems to have been a mendicant sort of existence, the poet goes about the business in a slightly less candid way with Liberum Arbitrium. After the latter's initial description of Charity, the Dreamer exclaims,

> Were ich with hym, by crist, . . . ich wolde neuere fro hym,
> Þauh ich my by-lyue sholde begge a-boute at menne hacches.[8]

He then quickly asks a question about Charity which precipitates Liberum Arbitrium into a further discussion. In the course of this there appears a line which is taken over from B, indeed, but which gains added point in the C-context. Charity, says Liberum Arbitrium, appears in a number of guises,

---

in the emphasis C puts on loving one's enemy at C, XVI, 141. The second passage in B is a line which describes Charity as "gladde with alle gladde and good tyl alle wykked," which C paraphrases, "glad with alle glade as gurles þat lauhen alle, And sory when he seeþ men sory." What C is doing is developing B's hint and translating Rom. 12.15, St. Paul's definition of charity: *Gaudere cum gaudentibus, flere cum flentibus.* A line or so later C says that Charity cannot even conceive of men's doing evil. C's insertion at XII, 29–30, which says that the deserving poor should be helped before people who have no need, precisely parallels B's sentiments at B, VII, 71–2, quoted above.

5. C, VI, 27–31.   6. C, VI, 49–52.   7. C, VI, 90.
8. C, XVII, 334–5.

Ac biddyng as a beggere by-heold ich hym neuere.[9]

The passage closes with several lines, also adapted from B, in which the incompatibility of Charity and beggars is further emphasized.[1] The poet seizes upon these to reopen the subject, asserting that there is no man alive who does not sometimes borrow

Oþer beggeþ oþer byddeþ, beo he ryche oþer poure.[2]

But Liberum Arbitrium will not be swayed and answers the assertion by recounting the lives of Paul the Hermit, St. Anthony, Egidius, and others who neither borrowed nor begged, but were sustained by God's help and their own labor. The precise relationship between the poet and begging is not clear. I shall revert to the subject briefly in my last chapter. For the present it is enough to observe that C, despite his violent strictures on dishonest begging, seems to have had a wry desire to justify something that closely resembled what he deplored. Although this is a new development in the thought of *Piers Plowman,* it is a development in the opposite direction from what we have been led to expect. I cannot see that it affects the theory of single authorship adversely.

We come now to the subject of minstrels. It is significant that in the Prologue C preserves the same attitude as A and B toward all the occupations except that of minstrelsy. That is why, at the beginning of the chapter, I was reluctant to assign minstrelsy to any of the three categories I set up. In the Prologue of A and B there are two sorts of minstrels, just as there are two sorts of hermits :

And somme murthes to make as mynstralles conneth,
And geten gold with here glee, synneles, I leue.
Ac iapers & iangelers, Iudas chylderen,
Feynen hem fantasies and foles hem maketh,
And han here witte at wille to worche ʒif þei sholde.[3]

C, on the other hand, mentions but one class of minstrels and they are wicked :

9. C, XVII, 349 (B, XV, 221).   1. C, XVII, 369–71, B, XV, 251–2.

2. C, XVIII, 2. That these remarks are probably not aimed at the friars is indicated by Liberum Arbitrium's characterization of St. Francis as Charity at C, XVII, 352–3.

3. AB, Pro., 33–7. A34 in MS T reads *giltles I trowe,* and was adopted by Skeat into his edition of A (V omits the line), as it had been adopted by Wright and Owen Rogers into their editions of B. Skeat thought that *giltles* was probably correct for B, although all B-MSS, along with A-MSS UHD, read *sinless.* See *EETS,* II, 388. OC2 of the B-class read *not synles.* The alliterative pattern *aaaxx* is so common in A and B that it is not unlikely that *sinless* was what the poet wrote. See Schumacher, *Studien über den Stabreim in der mittelenglischen Alliterationsdichtung,* p, 25. In A36, TV have *Founden,* UH2 *fynden,* for B-text *Feynen.* C-text has *fynde.*

And somme murthes to make as mynstrals conneþ,
Þat wollen neyþer swynke ne swete, bote swery grete oþes,
And fynde vp foule fantesyes[4]—

and so on, as in the passage quoted above. This is one of the most abrupt reversals of opinion in the C-text and has caused a good deal of comment.[5] The suggestion has even been made that the reading of a bad B-MS caused C to say the direct opposite of what he felt.[6] Let us examine the problem at first hand.

From what is said in the Prologue, we should expect in the course of the poem to find A and B differentiating between two sorts of minstrels, praising the virtuous and rebuking the evil, while we should expect C's remarks on the subject to be altogether derogatory. That is what we should expect if consistency were the virtue of the three texts. Actually, what we do find is that A and B, as often as not, tend to disagree with what they have postulated in the Prologue, as, indeed, does C with what he has postulated, although his disagreement takes the opposite direction from A's and B's. Thus all texts agree and disagree with themselves and each other. But for this striking lack of consistency there is probably a good reason.

The first mention of minstrels after their introduction in the Prologue occurs, in all three texts, in the description of the headlong flight of Meed's bridal party. All took refuge from the King's officers, including Liar who

> . . . was nawhere welcome for his manye tales,
> Ouer al yhowted and yhote trusse.[7]

Yet despite his unpopularity Liar was given shelter by several un-savory groups of persons—pardoners, physicians, grocers, friars, messengers, and minstrels. So far as C is concerned, this is consistent. But A and B might have had the courtesy to qualify the minstrels with some phrase explaining that they were bad minstrels, so that we should not be confused. A second reference follows soon afterward in the earlier

4. C, i, 35-7. Note that the phrase *grete oþes* seems to derive from B, x, 50, A, xi, 37, where C omits it.

5. Wright, *The Gentleman's Magazine* (April 1834), p. 390, notes that in C the "account of the minstrels is very confused." This is perhaps the earliest example of an error that has become fairly prevalent—that of trying to read several versions of the poem simultaneously. There is nothing confused about C's account of the minstrels: they are a bad lot, and that is an end to the matter.

6. Miss Day, *MLR*, XXIII, 7, conjectures that C was revising from a corrupt text of B which, like MSS OC2, read *not sinless* in B34 and that, dissatisfied with the alliteration, he revised to improve it, while retaining the sentiment, which was "not his general opinion of minstrels," but one that "was dictated to him by his text." Elsewhere Miss Day describes C as careful to remove incongruities that appear in the earlier texts, yet here we find him manufacturing incongruities because of a slavish adherence to a bad MS.

7. B, ii, 217-18. A, ii, 193-4, C, iii, 227-8 vary slightly.

texts. Conscience, upbraiding Meed before the King, submits the following indictment:

> . . . she is tikel of hire taile, talwis of hir tonge,
> As comune as a cartwey to eche a knaue þat walketh,
> To monkes, to mynstralles, to meseles in hegges.[8]

Again minstrels are not graced by the company they keep. C, whom we should expect to approve of the sentiment, strangely alters the last line so that the minstrels are omitted:

> To monkes and to alle men, the meseles in heggys.[9]

Miss Day implies that the motive for the change was to get the minstrels out of bad surroundings,[1] but it is possible that C was merely yielding to that urge to generalize which is characteristic of him. In any case, A and B are inconsistent with the Prologue, since they neglect to qualify the minstrels as bad. So is C, if we may make an inference *a silentio,* though in the opposite way from A and B.

Although the lines may indicate the trend of the poet's thought, it would, of course, be foolish to lay much stress upon them. I pause over them only because they illustrate the basic fallacy in the classic statement that A was brilliantly consistent, C the reverse, and B somewhere in between, and also because one of the passages has been used in a study damaging to C's reputation. The truth is that both sets of lines include with the minstrels several occupations, such as that of monk, of which the poet approves. Apparently he did not feel it necessary to explain that he meant only bad monks and bad minstrels. Let us proceed to something less equivocal.

The next significant mention of minstrels in the A- and B-texts appears at the beginning of Dame Study's speech on modern customs. Her theme is that wit and wisdom are no longer considered of any value except as instruments in effecting the circumvention of the barriers that justly impede acquisition of riches. By one of those slippery trains of thought from which Study is no more free than the authors of A, B, and C, she gets herself into a consideration of modern minstrelsy. In the A-text, she quotes Jeremiah, *Quare via impiorum prosperatur, bene est omnibus qui praue et inique agunt?*[2] and then abruptly plunges into the subject:

> Ac he þat [haþ holy writ ay] in his mouþe,
> And con tellen of Tobie And þe Twelue Apostles,

---

8. B, III, 130–2 (A, III, 126–8).   9. C, IV, 169.   1. *MLR,* XXIII, 7.

2. Jeremiah 12.1, as quoted in A XI, 23. The Vulgate reads *praevaricantur* for *praue,* and this is the reading of B, x, 25, which, however, gives the first question as *Quare impij viuunt?* In both texts Study attributes the quotation to Job. Apparently the poet confused Jeremiah with Job 21.7: *Quare ergo impii vivunt, sublevati sunt, confortatique divitiis?* Because of its mention of riches, the version of Job is perhaps more appropriate to the sense of B.

And prechen of þe penaunce þat Pilatus wrouhte
To Iesu þe Ientil þat Iewes to-drowe
On Cros vppon Caluarie, as Clerkes vs telleþ ;—
Luytel is he loued or leten bi þat such a lessun Redeþ,
Or Daunseled or Drawen forþ, þis Disours witen þe soþe ;
For ȝif Harlotrie ne Holpe hem þe bet (haue God my soule !)
More þen Musyk or Makyng of Crist,
Wolde neuer kyng ne kniht ne Canoun of Seynt poules
Ȝeuen hem to heore ȝeres-ȝiue þe value of a grote.[3]

Having indulged in this unexpected outburst (why should Dame Study, with weightier matters on her mind, become so exercised about the degeneration of minstrelsy?), she sums up as follows :

Ac murthe and mynstralcye amonges men is nouthe
Leccherye, losengerye, and loseles tales ;
Glotonye and grete othes, þis murthe þei louieth.[4]

From the handling of the passage in A we can make out at least the reflection of the differentiation between two kinds of minstrels that we had originally expected to find. Although neither of them is called by the name given them in the Prologue, both sorts are under discussion here, the good (the Prologue's *mynstralles*) in the first passage and the bad (the Prologue's *iapers* and *iangelers*) in the second passage and in the eighth line of the first. Apparently what A meant by the mirth-making, sinless minstrel of the Prologue was the pious entertainer who can tell of Tobit and the Apostles. But though he reverts to the twofold classification of the Prologue, A seems to be at a loss for terms which will keep the two types distinct. *Minstrel,* his original word, is too comprehensive and, as we have seen, fits too readily into an evil context. What is the correct name for those whom A would now exempt from censure ? He does not seem to know.[5] A new term is needed.

Leaving A for a moment, let us look at B's treatment of the same passage. B has Dame Study approach the subject in what seems a more self-controlled manner than A. Instead of letting the topic of minstrels share equal stress with others more important, B subordinates it to a broader discussion of the proper expenditure of wealth. Having quoted Jeremiah, Study applies his gloomy question to rich lords who lead evil lives. One manifestation of their wickedness may be observed in the unworthy guests upon whom they choose to lavish their hospitality (we are once more getting close to the conflict between Cato and Gregory) :

3. A, XI, 24–34. In 24 I give the reading of MS T, which agrees with B, x, 32 and C, XII, 31.

4. B, x, 48–50 (A, XI, 35–7 in T). I quote B because the A-passage as Skeat prints it is full of Vernon misreadings. MS T has it correctly.

5. In A30 Dame Study calls upon "these diseurs" to witness to the truth of her remarks, and perhaps the diseurs are intended to represent virtuous entertainers, though elsewhere the word has no good connotation. See A, VII, 50, B, XIII, 172.

> Harlotes for her harlotrye may haue of her godis,
> And iaperes and iogeloures and iangelers of gestes.[6]

Study then goes on to speak of the man who has Holy Writ ever in his mouth and paraphrases the long A-passage quoted above, keeping the substance but expending considerably more venom on wicked minstrels. B either referred to the Prologue or had it in mind as he revised. The two-line quotation I have just given uses almost the same terms as the Prologue,[7] and in the course of her speech B's Study speaks of

> . . . þo þat feynen hem folis and with faityng libbeth,[8]

which is a clear echo of B Prologue 36,

> Feynen hem fantasies and foles hem maketh.

Largely because of these echoes, B is more specific than A in regard to the wicked minstrels, whom he calls by a variety of names. But like A he puts no name to his good minstrels, merely implying that he considers them genuine minstrels when he says that their opposites

> . . . conne namore mynstralcye ne musyke, men to glade,
> Than Munde þe mylnere of *multa fecit deus!*[9]

The clear and confident distinction of the Prologue is, however, absent. B is also in need of a new term.

A has no more to say on the subject, but B turns to it at least once more. When, in Passus XIII, Patience, Conscience, and the Dreamer meet Hawkin (Activa Vita), they recognize him, even before he announces himself, as a minstrel.[1] And Hawkin is an even stranger sort of minstrel than any we have hitherto had described to us and a remarkably unsuccessful one:

> Couthe I lye to do men laughe þanne lacchen I shulde
> Other mantel or money amonges lordes mynstralles.
> Ac for I can noither tabre ne trompe ne telle none gestes,
> Farten, ne fythelen at festes, ne harpen,
> Iape ne iogly, ne gentlych pype,
> Ne noyther sailly ne saute, ne synge with þe gyterne,
> I haue none gode gyftes of þise grete lordes.[2]

It is fortunate that Hawkin has a secondary occupation as a waferer.

The reason for Hawkin's being presented as a minstrel is not clear, but the identification is definite, and is restated by Conscience after

6. B, X, 30-1.   7. See B, Pro., 35: "Ac iapers & iangelers, Iudas chylderen."
8. B, X, 38.   9. B, X, 43-4.
1. See B, XIII, 221: "Þei mette with a mynstral, as me þo þou3te." Two lines later Hawkin's first words are: "I am a mynstral."
2. B, XIII, 228-34.

Hawkin's long confession.[3] It is certainly true that the passage quoted contains a criticism of minstrelsy as practiced. Chambers describes Hawkin as a "purveyor of honest entertainment" and goes on to observe, "In the very first page of the A-text, in the vision of the Field of Folk, the author had gone out of his way to commend honest minstrelsy. . . . The poet now repeats the same doctrine here."[4] Yet this purveyor of honest entertainment is capable of none of the professional tricks with which minstrels entertained their audiences. In fact, the list of things Hawkin cannot do forms one of the most inclusive catalogues of the functions of a fourteenth-century minstrel in Middle English poetry.[5] Hawkin's honesty as an entertainer is as great as his unpopularity, of which it is the cause. It looks as if the B-poet, faced for the second time with the problem of defining worthy minstrelsy, characteristically dodged the issue by defining bad. While he reverts to the Prologue in referring to the honest entertainer as a *minstrel,* the term is not distinctive and, indeed, B seems to deny Hawkin in the name of virtue the very arts necessary to any minstrel, honest or dishonest. In the Prologue reputable entertainment is associated with the idea of making *murthes,*[6] and Dame Study uses the words *murthe* and *musyke* as if they carried no evil connotation. Where A was clear on definitions if not on terms, B seems confused on definitions and to some extent on terms.

Two problems confront us in B and one in A. First of all, the earlier texts display that sort of verbal confusion—or ambiguity—which the reader has encountered with Lady Meed and which we shall meet again with Recklessness. For want of a couple of terms that would distinguish the evil in Meed from the good, the security of the whole kingdom was threatened. For want of a couple of terms that would distinguish good from bad minstrels and minstrelsy, the A- and B-poets perplex their readers. The minstrel-japer distinction of the Prologue was a laudable start but it failed to hold up. As much as the poet might have liked them to be, minstrels and japers were not distinct *genera.* Minstrels constituted a *genus* of which japers, unhappily, were the dominant species— so dominant that they virtually preempted the entire *genus.* The logic of majority-rule indicates in what direction the second problem lies—a problem that is manifest in B much more than in A. Since most flesh-

3. At B, xiv, 26-7 Conscience promises Hawkin that there will "no mynstral be more worth amonges pore & riche, Þan Haukynnes wyf þe wafrere with his *actiua vita.*" The sudden mention of Hawkin's wife is odd. Is Hawkin being so generalized as to comprehend the female representatives of active life?

4. *Mind,* p. 151.

5. The passage quoted is the most informative cited from poetry by Wilhelm Grossmann, *Frühmittelenglische Zeugnisse über Minstrels* (Brandenburg, 1906), pp. 58–66.

6. In its good sense in *Piers Plowman, mirth* seems either to be synonymous with "music" (see *OED, mirth,* sb., 3, b), or to signify gratification in a religious sense (*ibid.,* 1). In its bad sense it seems to connote jest and laughter, general jocularity, and ridicule (*ibid.,* 4).

and-blood minstrels are dishonest and do not scruple to use the lowest of tricks to please their hearers, the opprobrium which transfers itself readily from the majority of practitioners to the whole body also tends to transfer itself from the majority of the arts of entertainment to the whole body. Thus among the things that Hawkin cannot do and—if we are right in assuming from the context that his lack of talents is all to the good, morally speaking—the things he should not do are included the playing of musical instruments and the telling of stories. Yet these are the arts we should expect—have been led to believe, indeed—were practiced by innocent entertainers. Expressed differently, the fact seems to be that the B-poet has come around to a belief that all minstrelsy, except perhaps for a very special pious sort, is evil.

Let us see what the C-poet did to resolve this problem. We may come to him by what is, perhaps, B's last reference to minstrels. After C's wholesale condemnation of the profession in his Prologue, his next significant treatment of the topic comes at the end of the last of the confessions of the Deadly Sins in a passage which, at least in part, is taken from Hawkin's confession in B, xiii. At the conclusion of Sloth's confession, or Hawkin's confession of sloth in the B-text, the narrator inquires, What leads a man to sloth? and then goes on to give himself a long answer. Sloth develops when a man is not sorry for his sins, fails to accomplish penance enjoined by a priest, gives no alms, does not fear sin, is faithless and lawless, breaks holy days,

> And haþ no lykynge to lerne ne of oure lord hure,
> Bote harlotrie oþer horedom oþer elles of som wynnyng,
> Whan men carpen of cryst oþer of clennesse of soule,
> He wext wroþ, and wol nat huyre bote wordes of murthe.[7]

This leads the poet off to the subject of "fool sages, flaterers, and lyers," whom rich men entertain to the detriment of their own souls. For, the poet warns them,

> In ȝoure deþ-deynge ich drede me sore
> Lest þo manere men to moche sorwe ȝow brynge.[8]

The reader will perceive the similarity between this idea and the treatment given by B to Dame Study's monologue.

Immediately following the lines just quoted, in the C-text and in MS R of the B-class, occurs a passage that concerns minstrels specifically. In the present state of our knowledge of the MSS we cannot be sure whether this passage was originally written by B and taken over by C, or whether it was written by C and copied from a C-MS into the archetype of R.[9] It does not make much difference here whether the passage

7. C, viii, 75–8. B, xiii, 416–18 varies somewhat. Note that *murthe* has now taken on an evil sense.

8. C, viii, 86–7 (B, xiii, 426–7).   9. See Appendix C, note on MS R.

represents B's last effort to clarify his ideas on minstrels or C's first effort to do the same. The lines begin,

> Clerkus and knyʒtes welcomeþ kynges mynstrales,
> And for loue of here lordes lithen hem at festes;
> Much more, me þenkeþ, riche men auhte
> Haue beggers by-fore hem whiche beþ godes mynstrales.[1]

The poet proceeds to define "God's minstrels," of which there are three sorts, just as there are three sorts of evil guests mentioned in the preceding passage. The first is,

> Þe poure for a fol sage, syttynge at þy table;[2]

the second,

> . . . a lered man, to lere þe what oure lord suffrede;[3]

and the third,

> . . . a blynde man for a bordiour oþer a bedreden womman,
> To crye a largesse by-fore oure lorde, ʒoure goode loos to shewe.[4]

The poet assures the rich that

> Thuse þre manere mynstrales maken a man to lauhe;
> In hus deþ-deynge thei don hym gret comfort.[5]

G. R. Owst, in his study of medieval sermon literature, prints excerpts from a sermon by John Bromyard that is similar in purport to the passage under discussion.[6] The same application is made of the idea of minstrelsy: it is better to give alms to the deserving poor than to entertainers, for the former will bear witness to your charity upon your

1. C, VIII, 97–100 (B, XIII, 437–40 in MS R only).
2. C, VIII, 104 (B, XIII, 444 in R).   3. C, VIII, 105 (B, XIII, 445 in R).
4. C, VIII, 108–09 (B, XIII, 448–9 in R).   5. C, VIII, 110–11 (B, XIII, 450–1 in R).
6. Owst, *op. cit.*, pp. 300–01. The passage occurs in the *Summa Praedicantium*. Enormously valuable as his book is in filling out the background for much Middle English literature, I feel that many of Owst's judgments in respect to the influence of the sermon collections on the poem are extremely dubious. In particular his repeated statement, p. 549, that the poem "represents nothing more nor less than the quintessence of English medieval preaching gathered up into a single metrical piece of unusual charm and vivacity," seems a remarkable distortion of the facts. It would be as valid to say that medieval preaching is no more than a dispersion of the ideas contained in *Piers Plowman*, or that the later fourteenth century is no more than a development in the sphere of historical fact of the common ideas of *Piers Plowman* and medieval sermons. One religious-minded society produced ideas which had their reflections on history, literature, and sermons, and it is absurd to try to make of the preacher a horse to pull the "long cart" of everything else. Furthermore, while many of the poem's single ideas are illustrated by, and possibly derived from, the sermons, there is nothing in the latter that explains the large plan of its great allegory—a piece of synthesis (even admitting it is synthesis) which quite transcends the sum of its parts. Owst puts the makers into the pulpit, while the poets are left as mere stenographers in the congregation. To call Manly's observation that the *Piers Plowman* poet "presents the veritable interior of an English ale-house in the fourteenth century, with all its baseness and its gross hilarity" (*CHEL*,

death. One difference, however, between Bromyard's treatment and our poet's is that the preacher does not mention a learned man as a substitute for minstrels. Therefore there is a chance that, even if the main lines of the reasoning are conventional and derivative, the poet has added something of his own in the learned man. The poor and the maimed are not, of course, real entertainers but metaphorical ones. The learned man, on the other hand, performs the minstrel's chief function in that he is articulate—he can even

> . . . fiþele the, with-oute flateryng, of goode fryday þe geste.[7]

It is probable that the poet sees him not as a purely figurative entertainer but as an actual reciter—the sort of minstrel who might have rehearsed *Purity* or *Patience* or even *Piers Plowman* at the homes of such rich men as were also pious. Indeed, the learned man might well be the very minstrel that Dame Study has in mind.

In this strict limitation of the minstrel's repertory to religious subjects we may have B's ultimate definition of honest entertainment, a definition in which C followed him. But although the definition is certainly less comprehensive than we should expect from the A- and B-Prologue, it is developed upon lines very carefully laid down in the A-text, in Dame Study's long speech. For it is she who, while allowing for mirth and music, first emphasizes the religious function. Furthermore, in the expression *God's minstrels* B—or perhaps C—finally succeeded in finding the right term for the entertainers of whom the poet approved. Since the group is a very limited one, C was able with full consistency to alter the lines in the Prologue in the way he did. After all, the average minstrel was, according to A, B, and C, a social evil. In much the same way Bishop Cobham in his *Penitential,* after carefully classing minstrels in three groups, and the third group into two subgroups, finds only that the second subgroup of the third group is blameless. All the rest are pernicious. In Cobham's description of the virtuous minority there is a striking similarity with the good minstrels of *Piers Plowman.* Cobham, who calls them *ioculatores,* says that they *cantant gesta principum et vitam sanctorum, et faciunt solatia hominibus vel in aegritudinibus suis vel in angustiis, et non faciunt innumeras turpitudines.*[8]

The subject of God's minstrels is illuminating enough to pursue further. C reverts to it again in Passus x, in the same passage in which he advises the rich to let healthy beggars starve. Immediately after giving that piece of advice, he makes an exception :

---

ii, 18) a "facile interpretation" (Owst, *op. cit.,* pp. 434–5) is probably the ultimate *reductio ad absurdum* of historical scholarship. Apparently Langland was so busy listening to sermons that he was able to come to know the sights and sounds of the world around him only through the lurid descriptions given by the pulpiteers.

7. C, viii, 107 (B, xiii, 447 in R).

8. Quoted from E. K. Chambers, *The Mediaeval Stage* (Oxford, 1903, 2 vols.), ii, 262.

And ȝut arn þer oþer beggers, in hele, as hit semeþ,
Ac hem wanteþ here witt, men and women boþe,
Þe whiche aren lunatik lollers and leperes a-boute,
And mad as þe mone sitt more oþer lasse.[9]

These are the special objects of God's attention, for

. . . suthþe God hath þe myghte
To ȝeuen eche a wyght wit, welthe, and his hele,
And suffreþ suche so gon, hit semeþ, to myn Inwitt,
Hit arn as hus aposteles, suche puple, oþer as his priuye disciples.[1]

Therefore men should give them refuge:

For hit aren murye-mouthede men, mynstrales of heuene,
And godes boyes, bordiours, as þe bok telleþ.
Si quis uidetur sapiens, fiet stultus ut sit sapiens.
And alle manere mynstrales, men wot wel þe soþe,
To vnder-fonge hem faire by-falleþ for þe ryche,
For þe lordes loue and ladies þat þei with lengen.
Men suffren al þat suche seyn and in solas taken,
And ȝut more to suche men doth er þei passe,
Gyuen hem gyftes and gold for grete lordes sake.
Ryght so, ȝe riche, raþer ȝe sholde, for sothe,
Welcomen and worsshepen and with ȝoure goode helpen
Godes mynstrales and hus messagers and hus murye bordiours.[2]

These are a rather different type of God's minstrel from those discussed before. In the earlier description only one of the three substitutes for minstrels was capable of exercising the professional function, but the lunatic lollers, although the poet tells us that they do not preach, as did those similar wanderers Peter and Paul, are at least sometimes articulate. For

. . . meny tymes hem happeþ
To prophecien of þe puple, pleyinge, as hit were.[3]

9. C, x, 105–08.
1. C, x, 115–18. A. S. Jack, "The Autobiographical Elements in Piers the Plowman," *JGPh*, III (1901), 406, says that the poet "nowhere recognizes two classes of wanderers, the one excusable and the other not." Jack forgets God's minstrels.
2. C, x, 126–36. Miss Day, *MLR*, XXIII, 7, cites 128–33 as evidence of C's favorable opinion of minstrels in general. I am disposed to believe, however, that this passage gives us little idea of how he felt. It *by-falleþ* to the rich to entertain minstrels not for the minstrels' sake but for the sake of the lords and ladies *þat þei with lengen*—which I take to mean for the sake of those who are the minstrels' patrons. The passage seems exactly equivalent to C, VIII, 97–100, B, XIII, 437–40, quoted above. There the poet says that clerks and knights welcome King's Minstrels for love of their lords—the minstrels' and their own. Therefore men should welcome God's minstrels, not so much for the sake of the minstrels as for the sake of God, their common Lord. In both passages it is the love of a higher authority, whether great lord or God, that prompts the giving of hospitality to their representatives.
3. C, x, 113–14.

What form the prophecies took, or how they were spoken, we are not told. But the poet evidently valued them.[4]

The phrase *God's minstrels* is an interesting one. It evidently derives from the legends that grew up during the Middle Ages around the lovable figure of St. Francis of Assisi. According to Brother Leo, the author of the *Speculum Perfectionis,* a collection of stories about him, St. Francis was the composer of a song, the *Cantus Fratris Solis,* and delighted in thinking of his mission on earth in terms of minstrelsy. Leo writes that after he had composed his song,

. . . spiritus ejus erat tunc in tanta consolatione et dulcedine quod volebat mittere pro fratre Pacifico qui in saeculo vocabatur rex versuum et fuit valde curialis doctor cantorum, et volebat dare sibi aliquos fratres ut irent simul cum eo per mundum praedicando et cantando Laudes Domini. Dicebat enim quod volebat ut ille qui sciret praedicare melius inter illos prius praedicaret populo, et post praedicationem omnes cantarent simul Laudes Domini tamquam joculatores Domini.

Finitis autem laudibus volebat quod praedicator diceret populo: "Nos sumus joculatores Domini et pro his volumus remunerari a vobis, videlicet ut stetis in vera paenitentia." Et ait: "Quid enim sunt servi Dei nisi quidam joculatores ejus qui corda hominum erigere debent et movere ad laetitiam spiritualem?"[5]

Joculatores Domini: the word *ioculator* was the common Latin rendering for the English *minstrel*[6] and the phrase, probably handed down through the Franciscan preachers, appears in the C-text literally translated as *God's minstrels.* The poet was probably aware of the tradition, for he mentions the resemblance of the lunatic lollers to Peter and Paul, whom St. Francis was imitating, and in making it clear that they do not

---

4. Either of two senses of the word *prophesy* will fit the description of the lunatic lollers. See *OED, prophesy,* v., 1: "To speak by (or as by) divine inspiration, or in the name of a deity; to speak as a prophet"; 1, b: "To utter predictions, to foretell future events (by inspiration, or generally)." The first sense fits the more readily, particularly with reference to St. Francis' *ioculatores Domini* (see next note, and text above it). But the second describes the sort of prophecy popular in the thirteenth and fourteenth century, such as those attributed to Thomas of Erceldoune and those we meet in *Piers Plowman* (B, IV, 113–33, C, V, 108–30; B, X, 317–30, C, VI, 169–80; B, VI, 322–32, C, IX, 344–55), and may possibly apply also to the lunatic lollers. The satirical character of the poet's prophecies has, I think, been exaggerated. At least one of them deals with the solemn subject of the Second Coming, an event which was commonly thought to be about to occur in the near future: see Burdach, *Ackermann,* pp. 314–51, *passim.* Perhaps the poet really visualized himself as a prophet and his poem as a prophetic writing. Its tone suggests a poet who felt confident that he was speaking according to the will of God—one of God's minstrels.

5. Brother Leo, *Speculum Perfectionis,* Paul Sabatier, ed. (Paris, 1898), pp. 197–8. E. K. Chambers, *op. cit.,* I, 46, n. 4, quotes part of this account without reference to *Piers Plowman.*

6. E. K. Chambers, *op. cit.,* II, 230: ". . . generic *ioculator* is the normal mediaeval Latin term for the minstrel in the widest sense."

preach[7] he is evidently emphasizing a departure from an established concept. His familiarity with the tradition should make us careful not to assume that he had the same attitude toward lunatics as Wordsworth's, which seems more sentimental than respectful. To Langland, the articulateness of the lunatic lollers was important. Whatever words they uttered were of divine origin and in the pious Franciscan tradition they were actual minstrels.

So much for the development that C gives to the subject of minstrels.[8] We have seen that A, who made an explicit distinction in the Prologue, discovered, when he tried to revert to that distinction later in the poem, that he had involved himself with certain ideas for which he lacked terms. B fell heir to something of the same difficulty, and in his text the problem became complicated by an increased austerity in his attitude toward minstrelsy. Somewhere between his revision of Passus x and his composition of Passus XIII he seems to have come to believe that none but the most pious sort of minstrelsy was morally sanctionable. Either he or C did, however, succeed in phrasing this highly limited function in a term borrowed remotely from St. Francis. C, recognizing that A's and B's introduction of the subject in the Prologue was ambiguous, simplified it in the direction toward which their later thought was tending. But it is possible to simplify the expression of one's thought without in any way simplifying one's thought and C, having deleted the distinction between two types of minstrels, had partially to retract. Probably he felt that God's minstrels were so unlike the majority of fourteenth-century minstrels that no serious contradiction was involved. Once he had settled on the notion of God's minstrels, C proceeded to develop it in the curious way we have seen, getting farther and farther away from the reality of everyday entertainment but still developing an idea that was implicit in A and B.[9] In view of what we have seen, one is tempted to put minstrelsy in the second category of occupations mentioned at the beginning of this chapter—those which, while they may be basically wholesome, contain a grave occupational hazard. In this case, however, the occupational hazard is so overwhelming that virtually no practicing minstrel escapes it and as a result the profession in general is condemned.

The imagery of minstrelsy is extraordinarily profuse in *Piers Plowman*. So far as I know, no other fourteenth-century English poem contains an equivalent amount. Whether they approve or disapprove, all

---

7. See C, x, 112.

8. C retains only a small part of Dame Study's remarks on minstrels, taking advantage of the sense of B to reopen the subject of discrimination in charity.

9. The possibility of a class of persons who must beg because they are incapable of supporting themselves on account of "witlessness" (a class briefly described at B, IX, 66–70) was recognized, at least by implication, in the A-Prologue in the lines describing the evil minstrels who make themselves appear as fools despite the fact that they have "wit at will" to work if they so desire. See AB, Pro., 37, C, I, 38.

three texts exhibit a pronounced interest in the profession. It is the fifth mentioned in the Prologue, itself a significant fact, inasmuch as there must have been far fewer minstrels than members of any of the other occupational groups listed. As Chambers says, the A-poet went out of his way to commend honest entertainers, and throughout A, B, and C there are a good many casual references to the subject. Some of these, like the following from B, are probably of ecclesiastical derivation:

> Lesyng of tyme, treuthe wote þe sothe!
> Is moste yhated vp erthe of hem þat beth in heuene,
> And sitthe to spille speche þat spyre is of grace,
> And goddes gleman and a game of heuene;
> Wolde neuere þe faithful fader his fithel were vntempred,
> Ne his gleman a gedelynge, a goer to tauernes![1]

The same may be true of Piers's advice to the Knight not to spend his time listening to idle tales or his substance entertaining harlots,[2] which reflects the conventional ecclesiastical attitude expressed by Cobham: *Histrionibus dare nichil aliud est quam perdere.*[3] It is, perhaps, the poet's growing sensitivity to the ecclesiastical point of view that explains the dichotomy which begins to appear in the B-text. But strong as the Church's influence may have been on the poet's thought, a number of his references to minstrelsy seem individual and even personal. Let us examine some of these.

Love, Lady Holy Church tells the Dreamer in the A-text,

> . . . is þe leuest þing þat vr lord askeþ,
> And eke þe [plante] of pees; prechet in þin harpe
> Þer þou art Murie at þi mete whon me biddeþ þe ȝedde.[4]

As Hall pointed out,[5] the lines bring to mind the story of Caedmon, except that the Dreamer is receiving a theme for a song, not the gift of song itself. And, for the moment at least, the poet seems to be thinking of himself—or rather, Holy Church is thinking of the Dreamer—as if he were a minstrel. The allusion is, perhaps, one of those conventional ones employed by many poets, merely expressing the poetic mission in figurative language. We do not know whether the A-poet literally

1. B, IX, 98–103.
2. B, VI, 52–6, A, VII, 46–50, C, IX, 48–52. It is interesting that C, revising this passage in which A and B describe Piers as telling the Knight to shun all tales except those of wisdom and wit, liberalizes to give sanction to tales of bounty, battles, and truth—a sanction derived, perhaps, from such a statement as Cobham's, quoted on p. 144 above.
3. E. K. Chambers, *op. cit.*, II, 263. See *idem*, I, 38–41, 55–9, for a summary of the ecclesiastical attitude toward minstrelsy.
4. A, I, 136–8 (BC omit 137b–8). In A137 *plante* is the reading of MS T. V reads *playnt*, but see C, II, 149, *plonte*.
5. *MLR*, IV, 1–2.

followed Holy Church's advice at supper, but we do know that he followed it allegorically in his poem.

I have already noted the abruptness with which Dame Study, in the A-text, comes to the subject of minstrelsy. "Wherefore," she asks with Jeremiah, "doth the way of the wicked prosper?" Then, with no clear connection, she continues her discourse by remarking that the man who is always ready to speak of Holy Writ enjoys no popularity, and she is off on minstrels. The turn is the more surprising because the logic of the speech seems to require quite a different group of persons to be mentioned. The wicked whom Dame Study has been discussing are apparently influential perverters of wisdom and wit, crafty counselors who can "counterfeit deceits," conspire wrongs, and arrange lovedays with which to baffle justice. The antithesis to these wicked people we should expect to find in an influential man who uses his intelligence righteously, and though a minstrel may be both righteous and wise, the fact that Dame Study chooses to speak of a mere minstrel seems odd. The only way in which she can make him fit into the context is by introducing wicked minstrels, whom she equates with the unrighteous counselors she has been talking about. The relation is thus established deviously, by a sort of backward logic.

We may, of course, ascribe this coming-about to an incompetent helmsman. Or we may, on the other hand, try to discover how and why it took place. In the preceding passus (A, x) the Dreamer, seeking Do-Well, has been granted a one-sided audience with Wit, to whom he was introduced by Thought. Wit, discoursing on Do-Well and related topics, reaches a semicolon, if not a full stop, at the end of A, x. In the first lines of the next passus, Dame Study appears with the suddenness of a dream. Wonderfully wroth with her husband for dispensing wisdom

> To Fayturs or to Fooles þat Frentik ben of wittes,[6]

she tells him to hold his tongue. She then exercises the wifely prerogative of wagging her own for some eighty-five lines, addressing all her remarks to her husband and heaping insult upon the Dreamer both explicitly and by keeping him in the third person. Her theme is, as we have seen, the perversion of wit—or, in context, of Wit—while the precipitating cause of her discourse is her conviction that the Dreamer has come to pick Wit's brain of ideas which he may then convert into cash. Her sudden leap into the subject of minstrelsy seems motivated by her taking, or mistaking, the Dreamer for a minstrel of some sort and, since she is a suspicious woman, for a minstrel of the worst sort. The theme of righteous and unrighteous entertainment, once she gets into it, remains dominant throughout her tirade. The Dreamer is, by

6. A, xi, 6. T reads *flatereris* for V *Fayturs*.

implication, likened to every sort of person whose livelihood might depend on an ability to provide entertainment at mealtimes, whether by parodying the scholastics or by telling indecent stories.[7] The precise nature of the Dreamer's occupation she does not seem to know, except that it is related to minstrelsy and is undoubtedly impious. In his desire to know about Do-Well she sees only a selfish motive. He is one of those who

> . . . fyndeþ forþ fantasyes vr feiþ to Apeyre,[8]

and hence a specialized type of dishonest minstrel, a member of the class who, according to the Prologue,

> Founden hem Fantasyes and fooles hem maaden.[9]

By the conclusion of her speech—in the last lines of which, incidentally, she brings the whole matter to rest on the head of the hapless Dreamer—both Wit and he are stupefied. But from Wit the Dreamer gets a furtive signal to try to ingratiate himself with Dame Study. The Dreamer thereupon makes a tactful three-line speech and she, with a kind of April changeability, suddenly becomes all good nature, promising to tell the way to the home of Clergy and Scripture who, she is sure, can explain the nature of Do-Well. Great is the Dreamer's joy:

> Þenne was I as Fayn as Foul on feir morwen,
> Gladdore þen þe gleo-Mon [þat gold haþ to ȝifte].[1]

Perhaps again the image is no more than accidental or conventional. But in view of what has gone before, it is possible that the author is setting the seal on the scene with an appropriate figure from minstrelsy, personally applied.[2]

In revising the poem, the B-author cut out the significant passages which tend to associate the Dreamer with minstrelsy. For instance, the line in Holy Church's speech, discussed above, disappears and the speech of Study is rewritten so that the theme becomes the misuse of riches, rather than the misuse of wit, although it still contains references to entertainers of various sorts. But in identifying Hawkin as a minstrel the B-poet seems to betray his preoccupation with the subject, as well, perhaps, as his tendency to connect it with himself. It is impossible to

---

7. Otto Mensendieck, in his studies of the autobiographical elements in the *Vita,* finds that Study's remarks are directed at the poet's education. He does not mention minstrelsy. See *Charakterentwickelung und ethisch-theologische Anschauungen des Verfassers von Piers the Plowman* pp. 15–18, and *JEGPh,* ix, 408–14.

8. A, xi, 63.   9. A, Pro., 36.

1. A, xi, 109–10: 110b is from MS T, which agrees with B, x, 154, C, xii, 104.

2. In the passage A, xi, 24–34 Study leaves as an excuse to the malpracticing minstrels the fact that unless they indulged in low tricks they would starve to death. In this A shows more sympathy than B does when he revises the passage, for all traces of the excuse are removed in the later text.

accept the theory which would identify the poet with Hawkin,[3] but it is difficult to read the Hawkin passage without suspecting the presence of a number of personal references. Moreover, it is significant that B should have made the typical representative of active life primarily a minstrel and only secondarily a provider. We should expect him to be, like his master Piers, a provider above all things. There may be some explanation for this in the conduct of the allegory but I do not know what it is. For the present I am disposed to believe that in Hawkin the poet put something of himself, and that Hawkin's minstrelsy is an oblique instance of his tendency to associate himself with that profession.

It is the C-text, however, which shows this tendency most clearly and in a most interesting, not to say curious, form. For the assimilation of poet to minstrel follows precisely the development in the idea of minstrelsy that we have already examined. The reader will recall the picturesque descriptions that the poet writes of himself in B and C, and his frequent references to a mental unbalance—an apparently sporadic lack of "inwit." After the disappearance of Imaginative he says that he

> . . . awaked þere-with, witles nerehande,
> And as a freke þat [fey] were forth gan I walke
> In manere of a mendynaunt many a zere after.[4]

Later, at the termination of the Hawkin incident, the poet found himself in a similar distracted condition:

> And so my witte wex and wanyed til I a fole were,
> And somme lakked my lyf, allowed it fewe,
> And leten me for a lorel and loth to reuerencen
> Lordes or ladyes or any lyf elles,
> As persones in pellure with pendauntes of syluer;
> To seriauntz ne to suche seyde nouzte ones,
> "God loke zow, lordes!" ne louted faire,
> Þat folke helden me a fole, and in þat folyc I rauced.[5]

And finally, after the Samaritan leaves him he wakes to find himself confused and unable to adjust himself to life:

> Wolleward and wete-shoed went I forth after,
> As a reccheles renke þat of no wo reccheth,
> And zede forth lyke a lorel al my lyf tyme.[6]

To these instances one might add that of the Lunatic who in the B-Prologue utters a pious wish to the King. Skeat first suggested that the Lunatic was the poet himself, "a lene þing with-alle,"[7] and I see no reason to reject the suggestion.

3. See Allan H. Bright, "Langland and the Seven Deadly Sins," *MLR*, xxv (1930), 133–9. Also his *New Light on "Piers Plowman,"* pp. 69–71.

4. B, xiii, 1–3 (C, xvi, 1–3). In B2 I read MS B *fey* for Skeat's *fre,* thus assimilating to the C-text. 5. B, xv, 3–10. C omits.

6. B, xviii, 1–3. C, xxi, 1–3 varies slightly. 7. B, Pro., 123. See *CP*, ii, 15.

Both B and C, then, assure us that the poet is, at times, like the lunatic lollers "mad as þe mone sitt more oþer lasse,"[8] and that, like them, he leads the life of a mendicant. Nor are these the only similarities between himself and those he calls alternately lunatic lollers and God's minstrels. He resembles them in the very form which his distraction takes. For one of God's minstrels,

> . . . þauh he mete with þe meyre amyddes þe strete,
> He reuerenceþ hym ryght nouht, no raþer þan anoþer,[9]

while the poet, as we have just seen, was equally loath to salute the great men that he met by the way. God's minstrels are described as "privy disciples" of the Lord, so that we should expect to find them carrying out His instructions: *Nolite portare sacculum, neque peram, neque calceamenta, et neminem per viam salutaveritis.*[1] Apparently the wet-shod poet dedicated himself, literally or metaphorically, to the same mission. Just as God's minstrels

> . . . arn meuynge after þe mone, moneyles þei walke,
> With a good wil, witlees, meny wyde contreys,[2]

so the poet, in imagination at least, is endlessly wandering over the countryside. If we may adopt the reading of the more reliable C-MSS, the oft-quoted line in which it appears that he lives both in and on London actually reads,

> And ich lyue in londone and [vp-londe] bothe.[3]

This is what we should expect of so restless a person, even though he had presumably settled down in a cottage in Cornhill. Even in the very manner in which the poet tries to distinguish himself from professional beggars he assimilates himself to the lunatic lollers,

> For þei bereþ no bagges ne none botels vnder clokes,
> Þe whiche is lollaren lyf,[4]

while he himself, trying to escape the charge of being a loller, assures Reason that he begs

> With-oute bagge oþer botel, bote my wombe one.[5]

Finally, God's minstrels, being "in hele," at least look as if they could do a day's work. When Reason accosts the poet, the first question he

---

8. Skeat's note to C, x, 108, *EETS*, IV, 189, "And more or less mad, according as the moon sits," does not, perhaps, make it sufficiently clear that the lunatics are mad in proportion as the moon waxes and wanes, the phrase *more or less* modifying the moon, not the lunatics.   9. C, x, 122–3.
    1. Luke 10.4. Quoted in part after C, x, 123.   2. C, x, 110–11.
    3. C, vi, 44. For P *on londone* I read MS I *vp-londe*. X reads *oþe londe*.
    4. C, x, 139–40.   5. C, vi, 52.

asks is why he is not earning his own living, so obviously "in hele" does he appear.[6]

Precisely how we are to evaluate this constant association and assimilation of poet to minstrel, carried on through all three texts and through certain alterations in the concept of minstrelsy, is a problem that lies for the most part outside the scope of this book. It is possible that Langland was, at least in his youth, a minstrel of sorts. Our knowledge of fourteenth-century minstrelsy is far from complete and our ideas of the profession are, I believe, unduly influenced by a romantic, Sir Walter Scott picture which probably makes the suggestion in the last sentence offensive to certain readers. But we have it on Cobham's and Langland's word that there were a few pious minstrels who wrote and spoke on religious subjects and we certainly have sufficient examples of the works they might have read aloud or recited. Harold Whitehall once gave a very convincing demonstration of the auditory value of the A-text,[7] and I find it difficult not to believe that it was written by some one accustomed to giving public readings, who knew how to write in order to make the most of oral effects. It is true, however, that B and C lack on an increasing scale oral appeal, so that if Langland was a minstrel, it was probably only in his youth.

It is interesting that when one works through the poem in an attempt to discover what sort of minstrel the poet could have been, one encounters a number of things reminiscent of the goliardic tradition—and this, despite the fact that the tradition itself and *Piers Plowman* are worlds apart. As a matter of fact, the relationship was first remarked upon by Thomas Wright: "It will be seen that the Latin poems attributed to Walter Mapes, and the collection of Political Songs, form an introduction to the Vision of Piers Ploughman. It seems clear that the writer was well acquainted with the former, and that he not infrequently imitates them."[8] Traces of the goliardic tradition may be observed primarily, of course, in the satire on the Church. They appear also in the strange self-revelations that we have reviewed in this chapter, the passages where the poet half-bitterly, half-humorously, emphasizes his own disreputability. One may see them in the occasional obscenities, such as that personally pointed one in the last, most serious passus of the poem.[9] And the long search for Charity, which the Dreamer has never known before

6. Cf. C, x, 105, "And ȝut arn þer oþer beggers in hele, as hit semeþ," with C, vi, 7, "whenne ich hadde myn hele," and 10, "In hele and in [inwitt]" (where P has *vnite* for XI, *inwitt*). Another similarity between the Dreamer and the lunatic lollers is suggested by C, vi, 83, "For in my conscience ich knowe what crist wolde þat ich wrouhte," and C, x, 138, "For vnder godes secre seel here synnes ben ykeuered."

7. In a paper delivered before the Middle English Language and Literature Division of the Modern Language Association of America, December 28, 1946. See *PMLA*, lxi (1946), 1364.

8. *The Vision and Creed of Piers Ploughman*, i, xiii.

9. B, xx, 192-7, C, xxiii, 193-8.

nor behind, seems to echo one of the favorite themes of the more serious goliardic poems. For Charity appears to the Dreamer, not among the hierarchy,

> But on the road from Jericho,
> I come with a wounded man.[1]

Finally, the poet's self-portrait at the beginning of C, VI reminds one of the first stanza of the most brilliant of the goliardic works, the *Confessio* of the Arch Poet:

> Estuans intrinsecus
> ira vehementi
> in amaritudine
> loquar mee menti:
> factus de materia
> levis elementi
> similis sum folio
> de quo ludunt venti.[2]

In our poet's apology to Reason, who is, after all, but a part of his own mind, there is something of this inward seething, as in his life there was a similar instability.

The resemblance is one that may easily be pushed too far. Nevertheless, we must remember that any clerk in minor orders, such as the poet was,[3] without a regular position in the Church and leading a life that took him from place to place, would necessarily come to know members of the goliardic group and might, indeed, more or less appear to be one of them. Sir Edmund Chambers notes of the goliards that "most of them were probably at least in minor orders. But practically they lived the life of the minstrels. . . ."[4] If Langland was ever a minstrel, he was probably a clerical one. It is possible that his minstrelsy was of a very elementary sort, consisting merely of reading his own works to an audience. Concerning the relations between an author and his public in the fourteenth century we are, with certain exceptions like Lydgate, about whom we know almost everything, even more ignorant than we are about minstrels in general.[5] But probably the distinction between

1. Translation by Helen Waddell, *The Wandering Scholars* (3d ed., Boston, 1929), p. 188, of the final lines of poem xciii, *Carmina Burana*, J. A. Schmeller, ed. (4th ed., Breslau, 1904), p. 51. Cf. the Dreamer's observation about the elusiveness of Charity, B, xv, 147 ff., C, xvII, 284 ff., and his meeting with the Samaritan, B, xvII, 48 ff., C, xx, 47 ff.

2. Version given by Helen Waddell, *Mediaeval Latin Lyrics* (London, 1929), pp. 170 ff. Another version, with variant readings, appears in Max Manitius, *Die Gedichte des Archipoeta* (Munich, 1913), pp. 24 ff.

3. See Chapter VII.

4. E. K. Chambers, *op. cit.*, I, 60. Though the great age of the goliards was past, their descendants, or those whom the Church considered their descendants, were still in existence, as is proved by the decrees against them issued at Arezzo in 1350, Prague in 1355, and Magdeburg in 1370. See Helen Waddell, *The Wandering Scholars*, p. 270.

5. H. S. Bennett, "The Author and His Public in the Fourteenth and Fifteenth Centuries," *Essays and Studies by Members of the English Association*, XXIII (1937), 7–24,

author and minstrel, at least among men without patrons, broke down, and I am inclined to believe that Langland, in his youth, was one of the irregulars of minstrelsy, of whom there seem to have been thousands :[6] a vagrant poet, wandering over the Field of Folk and coming to know those merchants and messengers, monks and friars, goliards and parish priests, beggars and laborers, rich and poor who meet together in the pages of his poem.

The literal interpretation of the poet's references to minstrelsy is, however, something of a side issue. He may merely have figured himself in such terms. What is chiefly interesting to us here is that the apparently conscious assimilation of himself to a minstrel appears as well in C as in A, and follows closely an individualistic development in the concept of minstrels exhibited in the three texts : first, an honest, plausible, idealistic entertainer and ultimately an apostolic-Franciscan *ioculator Dei*. The development of the assimilation, paralleling exactly the development of the conception, seems to me to point strongly to one author for all three texts. If, as I am disposed to believe, in the references to minstrelsy there is involved something more than a sustained metaphor, then unity of authorship becomes assured. But even if we are to understand the references only on the figurative level, it is still difficult to understand how one or two men could so astutely have fitted themselves into the psychological pattern of the original poet. For them to have done so would, indeed, have been the most laborious act of forgery— and multiple forgery at that—ever recorded.

In this chapter we have reviewed the attitudes toward the callings of men in the world that are displayed in the three texts of *Piers Plowman*. In certain cases we have been able to find no alteration in attitude. In others, apparent alterations turn out not to be real. And in still others, notably beggars and minstrels, we have noted a genuine alteration, or rather development. In no case, however, has there been any change so abrupt as inevitably to suggest the presence of a different author. With minstrelsy, moreover, the development in thought is accompanied by a secondary development in association so harmonious as definitely to suggest unity, rather than multiplicity, of authorship. Even if we state the case negatively, we are left with the conclusion that an examination of the attitudes toward worldly occupations does nothing to support the theory of divided authorship.

---

makes clear the gaps in our knowledge. For the system of patronage, see also K. J. Holzknecht, *Literary Patronage in the Middle Ages* (Philadelphia, 1923).

6. E. K. Chambers, *op. cit.*, I, 54, cites an early fourteenth-century restrictive decree issued by the Crown which, "in view of the number of idle persons who 'under colour of mynstrelsie' claimed food, drink, and gifts in private houses," limited entertainment of minstrels to such as were unambiguously professionals. The number of irregulars is suggested by the variety of alternate names listed by Chambers, I, 74–5 : *fabulator, narrator, fableor, conteor, gestour, disour,* and *segger.*

VI

Changes Affecting the Interpretation of the Religious Allegory

1. *Introductory: The Three Ways of Life*

BEFORE we can begin this chapter it is necessary to make sure that the reader will not be misled by its title. The topics that are to be discussed here are some of the alterations by C which seem to affect the interpretation of the religious allegory as set forth in the B-version; or better, which affect my interpretation of B's allegory. The phrase "the interpretation of the religious allegory" suggests that a widely accepted, all-inclusive interpretation of B is in existence. But this is not true, although, of course, there do exist studies that are of great value in putting one on the road to a satisfactory interpretation. Of these I make considerable use in the following pages; but it is not likely that any of their authors would lay claim to having settled, once and for all, the problem of the religious significance of the B-text of *Piers Plowman*. Even the best doctors disagree. Furthermore, none of them has turned his attention to C. As a result, any one who undertakes a comparative study of B and C is forced, first of all, to choose among several varying interpretations of B; second, to put his own construction upon the meaning of C; and, finally, to compare the various aspects of these largely homemade interpretations. This fact will, of course, foster in the reader a healthy suspicion of the findings of one whose book supports the single-authorship theory, since such a partisan might well be expected to present interpretations minimizing the discrepancies between the texts. In an endeavor to allay this suspicion I have chosen to deal with several of those alterations by C which seem most drastic and far-reaching. Moreover, I shall for the most part eschew debate on the question of authorship, limiting myself to an attempt to make clear, if I can, that C's revisions are intelligent and intelligible. The C-poet's creative deficiencies have, as we have seen, been rather widely celebrated, and it would be at least a minor contribution to show that, in his conduct of the religious allegory, these deficiencies have been exaggerated.

The reader will recall that in all three versions the poem is divided into two main parts: the *Visio de Petro Plowman* proper and the so-called *Vita de Do-Well, Do-Bet, et Do-Best*. In B and C the second part is subdivided into three sections, one for each member of the triad. The entire poem, in all its versions and in all its sections, concerns, as I believe every one will agree, a search for the road or roads that lead to salvation. In the *Visio* this search is considered under its social and moral aspects: the seeker is man-in-society, and it is with the problem of social man that the greater part of the material deals. The second part is less easy to characterize and less general agreement as to its meaning exists. Although according to the colophons of B and C the *Vita* purports to take up the three kinds of life one at a time, the lines of demarcation between them, as well as the exact shape that any one life assumes, are far from clear.[1] In two extremely suggestive articles H. W. Wells,[2] confining himself to the B-text, has pointed out the resemblance of Do-Well, Do-Bet, and Do-Best to the active, contemplative, and mixed lives as set forth by various medieval writers—most clearly, perhaps, in fourteenth-century England by Walter Hilton.[3] N. K. Coghill, in a study based partly on Wells's first article, has endeavored to show that Piers Plowman in his appearances in the B-text embodies each of these lives in turn.[4] Do-Bet and Do-Best he embodies in the appropriately entitled sections of the *Vita,* while he appears as Do-Well in the *Visio*. The section named (or, in reality, misnamed) Do-Well, wherein Piers makes no appearance, amounts to a moral consideration of all three lives.[5] Coghill differs from Wells in emphasizing the vocational nature of the three sorts of life, finding them illustrative of the laity, the clergy, and the episcopacy respectively.[6] Wells, with the agreement of Chambers,[7] makes a less restrictive definition, preferring to regard them as mental states which are possible in varying degrees to any man, whatever his vocational status.[8]

Chambers, whose last summary of the B-text provides the nearest thing we have to an accepted interpretation, adopts the more important conclusions of Wells and Coghill, adding them to his own considerable findings and synthesizing, to some extent, Wells's, Coghill's, and his own interpretations where they tend to vary from one another.[9] Thus he accepts Wells's theory of the significance of the three lives and Coghill's suggestion that Piers embodies each of these lives in turn; but he rejects

1. For the colophons of B and C, see p. 29, n. 7 and 8, above.
2. In *PMLA,* XLIV, 123–40, and LIII, 339–49.
3. In two treatises, the *Scala Perfectionis* and the *Epistle on Mixed Life*. The former has been edited from various MSS by Evelyn Underhill (London, 1923); the latter, from MSS Thornton and Vernon, by C. Horstman[n], *Yorkshire Writers: Richard Rolle of Hampole, an English Father of the Church, and His Followers* (London, 1895–96, 2 vols.), I, 264–92. The ideal of the active and contemplative lives was, of course, commonplace in medieval thought. That of the mixed life was considerably less common. See Wells, *PMLA,* XLIV, for references. For a general discussion of the lives in their relation to the poem, see Chambers, *Mind,* pp. 102–06.
4. See *MedAev,* II, 108–35, especially p. 111. 5. *Idem,* p. 114.
6. *Idem,* pp. 130–3. 7. Chambers, *Mind,* p. 127.
8. Wells, *PMLA,* LIII, especially pp. 345–7.
9. *Mind,* pp. 102–06, 127–8, etc.

Coghill's strict vocational interpretation and defines more clearly than Wells the moral and spiritual characteristics that the B-poet associates with each of the lives. Much of Chambers' summary is taken up with showing the connection between the A- and B-texts, a most important and acute piece of analysis which falls, however, outside the boundaries of the present discussion.

The first serious modification of the Chambers-Wells-Coghill interpretation to be forthcoming is that suggested by Professor Howard Meroney who, in a paper which has not yet been published as I write this,[1] has pointed out that Do-Well, Do-Bet, and Do-Best might be interpreted not so much as exemplifying Hilton's three lives or the mental states underlying them, but, more in the mystic tradition, as portraying the purgative, illuminative, and unitive conditions of the soul—a triad which, it must be admitted, was just as common in medieval times as the other. Meroney's suggestion seems a most fruitful one and I regret that I cannot refer to a published version of it. My study of *Piers Plowman,* however, inclines me to agree with the premise that we must look beyond a strict Hiltonesque interpretation of Do-Well, Do-Bet, and Do-Best in order to arrive at a satisfactory explanation of the poem. The specific use I shall make of Meroney's suggestion will be to try to explain by means of it the obscurity which cloaks much of the *Vita* and in particular the section on Do-Well. This obscurity, which exists in all three versions, seems to be caused by the fact that the poet is dealing, simultaneously, with at least two, and possibly more, distinct triadic notions. That means that from one point of view—the point of view expressed by some of the personifications the Dreamer encounters—the commonly accepted hypothesis may be quite correct: Do-Well equals the active life, Do-Bet the contemplative, and Do-Best the mixed. But from another point of view, the subject of the *Visio* is the active life of society, while the *Vita* is concerned with the more subjective and more contemplative life of the individual in his search for perfection: this life itself is divided into three sections, Do-Well standing for the initial stage in the journey, Do-Bet for its medial stage, and Do-Best for its ultimate stage. These stages may be equated with the purgative, illuminative, and unitive conditions of the soul, or, possibly, with other similar triune concepts. For the moment I should like to defer the matter of attaching specific labels in order to emphasize my conviction

---

1. The paper was delivered before the English I Section of the Modern Language Association of America on December 30, 1946. See *PMLA,* LXI (1946), 1373, for an abstract which does not, however, do justice to the paper. I am deeply indebted to Professor Meroney for setting in motion in my mind certain trains of thought that are developed here, though I am afraid that the direction in which I have carried them may be entirely different from the one he contemplated—unhappily a frequent, if not inevitable, occurrence in *Piers Plowman* studies. For anything that he may consider a misuse of his ideas that I have made in this chapter my apologies are due him.

that the *Vita* handles two basically different concepts at the same time and sometimes in the same terms. The chief difference between the concepts is that the first, as applied to the life of the individual, seems to develop in a sequence from outwardness (the active life) to inwardness (the contemplative life) to inward-outwardness (the mixed life), while the second develops in a sequence of three stages of inwardness, all of which, of course, have also appropriate outward manifestations and all of which are, incidentally, open to men of all vocations. To give a specific example, when Wit explains that

> Trewe wedded libbing folk in þis worlde is dowel,[2]

he is referring to the active life in all its externality. But when the Dreamer, blushing with shame at his scolding from Imaginative, exclaims,

> To se moche and suffre more, certes, . . . is dowel![3]

the reference is to an inward state, the first stage of a more contemplative life. A similar instance occurs when Conscience, in the B-text, defines Do-Well as contrition:[4] the person to whom this definition is made, however, is Hawkin, the type of the active life and hence of one sort of Do-Well.

The double purpose, or, if one will, the cross-purpose, is present in all three texts and particularly in the Do-Well section of B and C. An important difference between these two later texts is, as I see it, the fact that in the former the larger share of the emphasis seems placed on a definition of Do-Well as the external active life, while in the latter the emphasis is so shifted as to effect a definition of Do-Well which seems to encompass the spiritual qualities appropriate to the first of the three stages in an inward, contemplative life. How the C-poet accomplished this shift, particularly in his revisions of the *Visio* and the section entitled Do-Well, will form the basis for a part of the discussion which follows.

If this sort of interpretation seems too complicated, one can only answer, Then so is *Piers Plowman*. I think that we err when we try to pin the poet down to any single system of theological thinking. No one has ever made an effective case for his having been a learned man, subjected to the strict discipline of a coherent philosophy;[5] indeed, it seems generally agreed that he was not much more than an avid and indiscriminate reader and an equally avid listener, both to sermons and

2. B, IX, 107. 3. B, XI, 402. 4. B, XIV, 16-18.

5. Miss Hort at one time believed that Langland had some sort of systematic theological training, but she later gave up the idea. See Greta Hjort [Hort], "Theological Schools in Medieval England," *Church Quarterly Review,* CXVI (1933), 201-18, especially p. 201, n. 1; G. G. Coulton, same title, *idem,* CXVIII (1934), 98-101; and Miss Hort's *Piers Plowman and Contemporary Religious Thought,* pp. 43-59.

serious conversation.[6] Therefore it does not seem likely that there can be found for the body and arrangement of his ideas any precise, all-inclusive source, or even any very satisfactory analogue. At times one can scarcely refrain from thinking of him as an intellectual catchall. Thus the expert in the philosophy of St. Thomas will notice in *Piers Plowman* much that is Thomistic; students of Christian mysticism will observe many mystical elements; and those who are familiar with the esoteric backwashes of medieval thought will perceive odds and ends left over from the most recondite, and least orthodox, of the Fathers. At a time when all religious ideas came, from the analogy of the Trinity, in groups of three, the poet seems now and then to have tried to demonstrate the congruity of quite dissimilar triangles. For his learning and the tendency of his mind were not systematic but eclectic. He exercised the free choice, the *liberum arbitrium,* of an artist who from the vast spectrum of contemporary thought borrows whatever colors will best illumine his own basic ideas. And despite what I have written above, I venture to think that these basic ideas are in themselves relatively simple. It is in the guises and disguises they assume that the difficulty lies. In essence, the C-text of *Piers Plowman* is, I conceive, rather like a huge elaboration of an incident in the life of Christ that St. Matthew recounts in a few verses:

Et ecce unus accedens ait illi: Magister bone, quid boni faciam ut habeam vitam aeternam? Qui dixit ei: Quid me interrogas de bono? Unus est bonus, Deus. Si autem vis ad vitam ingredi, serva mandata. Dixit illi: Quae? Jesus autem dixit: Non homicidium facies; Non adulterabis; Non facies furtum; Non falsum testimonium dices; Honora patrem tuum et matrem tuam; et, Diliges proximum tuum sicut teipsum. Dicit illi adolescens; Omnia haec custodivi a juventute mea; quid adhuc mihi deest? Ait illi Jesus: Si vis perfectus esse, vade, vende quae habes et da pauperibus, et habebis thesaurum in caelo; et veni, sequere me. Cum audisset autem adolescens verbum, abiit tristis; erat enim habens multas possessiones.[7]

6. See Chambers, *Mind,* p. 100: ". . . *Piers Plowman* is the work of a well-educated man, not however very learned. . . . Langland's mistakes . . . show that his knowledge of Latin was rather limited. But he has enough Latin to get along, and, it would seem, some French." *Idem,* p. 104: "Langland, a poor clerk in Fourteenth-Century London, probably had access to few books; we are deceiving ourselves if we suppose that he had read all that an expert in medieval theology has read to-day. His knowledge must have been largely derived from what he heard in sermons, or got from conversation with other men." Miss Hort in her book, *op. cit.,* pp. 58–9, concludes a study of the poet's theological learning by observing "that Langland at some stage of his life had lived among people who knew much more theology than that contained in the books we know him to have read, and who talked with him and instructed him in theology." See also G. G. Coulton, *Medieval Panorama* (Cambridge, England, 1938), pp. 143–5.

7. Matthew 19.16–22. The parable was cited in connection with *Piers Plowman* by Chambers, *Mind,* p. 124, and by Professor Meroney, to whom I owe my use of it, at the beginning of his original paper. The poet alludes to the verses in his discussion of patient poverty, C, XIII, 166 and B, XI, 265.

It is this incident that the poem in its basic structure most resembles; and it is this incident that is acted out in many forms in the great drama in which the Dreamer asks again and again what he must do that he may have eternal life. The two main sections of the poem deal with the first and second of Christ's answers respectively. The *Visio,* with its picture of contemporary society, deals, much of the time by contrast, with the practical and social aspects of the first response: *Keep the commandments.* The *Vita,* a consideration of the degrees of perfection attainable by the individual, is a dramatization of the second response, which begins, *If thou wilt be perfect.* As Chambers has observed, it is "the enormous step from the first to the second" of Christ's precepts that Piers makes when, in the B-text, having torn the pardon, "he resolves that he will cease from sowing, that his plough henceforth shall be of prayer and penance, that tears shall be his meat day and night and that he will take no more thought for the morrow than the fowls of the air."[8] Like the young man in Matthew, Piers goes beyond the first answer; but unlike the young man, he is willing to act upon the second. With this transition, the tone of the poem alters. Social well-being, while never in any sense forgotten, tends to become more and more subordinate to the well-being (and better- and best-being) of the spirit of the individual.

2. *The* Visio: *Piers Plowman and the Pardon*

Concerning the nature of C's revision of the *Visio* I have made some general remarks elsewhere. Most of his alterations either are minute, or take the form of long insertions which, while they may affect the movement of the poem, do not affect the meaning of the allegory. It is only at the very end of the *Visio* in the incident[9] that involves Piers, the Priest, and the pardon sent from Truth[1]—the incident by which is accomplished the "enormous step" from the first to the second of Christ's precepts—that the C-poet makes his first drastic revision, one that seems to change the entire course of the allegory.

Let us look at the incident as it is recorded in the B-text. The author having concluded his review of the clauses of Truth's pardon,[2] a priest

8. *Mind,* p. 124. 9. A, VIII, 90–124, B, VII, 106–37, C, X, 282–91.

1. Chambers, *Mind,* p. 117, apparently relying on B, VII, 38, C, X, 42, where Piers is said to have purchased the bull, and on the THU-readings *purchace* and *purchasen* in A, VIII, 3, says that Truth bade Piers "purchase a pardon from the Pope," rather than sending him a pardon directly. See Coghill's discussion of the problem in his Gollancz lecture, *The Pardon of Piers Plowman* (London, 1945), pp. 17–19. It is my belief that, although for purposes of realism the Pope is somehow involved as an agent in the transaction, the poet tended to regard the pardon as coming direct from Truth to Piers. The lines on which the interpretation depends are A, VIII, 1–3, 8, 21, 25; B, VII, 1–3, 8, 19, 23, 38, 104; C, X, 1–3, 8, 23, 27, 42, 59, 184. There seems to be an increasing tendency from text to text to omit the Pope and make the transaction direct.

2. Though the pardon consists of only two lines, the discussion of its clauses and marginal annotations and of Truth's secret letter to the merchants takes up much of a

appears abruptly and asks to see the pardon itself, so that he may construe it to Piers "in English." The Dreamer, standing near, sees that the document consists of just two lines: *Qui bona egerunt, etc.* The Priest, who apparently recognizes the lines as coming from the Athanasian Creed,[3] exclaims that he can find no pardon except the common promise of heaven to the good and hell to the wicked. Piers, acting in "pure teen," tears the pardon asunder, quoting the Twenty-third Psalm: *Si ambulavero in medio umbrae mortis, non timebo mala.* He then resolves to cease from his labors, citing Christ's words to the disciples, *Ne solliciti sitis,*[4] and calling upon the Gospel to witness that God will provide for His own. The Priest exclaims superciliously at Piers's learning. The two exchange angry remarks and the scene fades out with the Dreamer explaining that as

Þe prest and perkyn apposeden eyther other,[5]

their words awoke him and he found himself, at evening, meatless and moneyless on Malvern Hills.

Probably no single incident in the A- and B-texts of *Piers Plowman* is more puzzling than Piers's angry tearing of the pardon: puzzling, indeed, to the logical mind, but, as Jusserand pointed out,[6] artistically as effective a scene as the poem provides. The pardon incident is not only the climax of the *Visio* but the point where the transition from the *Visio* to the *Vita* begins; and its importance is emphasized by the vigor with which it is presented. What proves surprising is not Piers's rejection of the life he has been leading[7] (for in this the young man in the Gospel had set a precedent), but the violence of his rejection, exhibited in his tearing of the pardon.[8] For this there seems to be no satisfactory

passus in all texts. In A and B the expositor seems to be the poet himself, but in C Piers is involved in at least part of the exposition. See C, x, 159–60, where Piers is described as saying that loliers are not included in the bull.

3. The real source of the lines is not given by Skeat. See Burdach, *Ackermann,* p. 267, n. 1; Chambers, *Mind,* p. 118; Coghill, *op. cit.,* p. 19, n. 2. The last-named says that the Priest "gives no sign of recognition that the Pardon is nothing but a quotation from the Athanasian Creed." But does not his derogation of the pardon as such spring from an awareness of its source?

4. Matthew 6.25 and Luke 12.22.   5. B, vii, 138 (A, viii, 127). C, x, 292 varies.

6. *MPh,* vi, 315: "This is one of the grandest, if not the grandest scene in the poem, the most memorable, even for us to-day, the culminating point of the work."

7. Despite Piers's assertion that he will not work *so* hard nor be *so* busy about his livelihood, his resolution to reject active life has the effect on the reader of being absolute and unequivocal. See B, vii, 117–29, A, viii, 102–16.

8. Piers's anger is explained differently by virtually every critic. See Coghill, *op. cit.,* pp. 19–20; Dunning, *Piers Plowman: an Interpretation of the A-Text,* pp. 145–52; Chambers, *Mind,* pp. 118–21. All solutions depend on reading between the lines, since the poet makes no explanation. I am disposed to believe that Piers's anger has a twofold cause. It is aroused by the Priest because he is supercilious and insulting and because, being an ecclesiastical bureaucrat, he refuses to recognize that the promise of the Creed is as effective as any pardon ever granted by the Pope. And Piers's anger is aroused by

logical explanation in the narrative itself. It is possible that the poet was carried away by the dramatic force of his poem and forgot, for the moment, the remoter ramifications of its allegorical significance. The brilliantly visualized scene brings to fullest realization the humanity of both Piers and the Priest—a simple, honest laborer reacting vigorously to a disappointing explanation given him by a disagreeable, probably sophistical, man of education and authority. Somehow, though we do not understand the reason for it, we are able to sympathize with Piers's tearing of the pardon, as well as with his subsequent, or even concomitant, anger with the Priest. Indeed, the passage is so dramatically apt that only after thinking back does one recall, with a shock, that the pardon Piers has torn was sent to him by Truth and may possibly, if Coghill's surmise is correct, represent the Atonement.[9] Even then, most readers would prefer to keep the scene as it stands and undergo the shock of Piers's seeming ingratitude, rather than have a less vivid presentation. And apparently the B-poet, when he came to revise A, felt that the incident was dramatically if not allegorically pertinent, so that he not only retained it but even elaborated the contention between Piers and the Priest.

C in his revision omitted the tearing of the pardon altogether, a change which, while it may have stored up treasure for him in the heaven of the pious, has probably reaped him little praise from the less scrupulous reader. The motive behind this change was undoubtedly the same that seems to have underlain a number of C's alterations: the desire to rid the poem of elements that might be misconstrued by the ignorant or might give offense to the learned—a desire which in C reflects, perhaps, the belated self-consciousness of a poet who has received recognition from the more or less august for an enterprise directed at the more or less humble. But although he obliterated what could be construed as a serious flaw (would an obedient servant of Truth tear a pardon procured for him by the agency of his master?), the C-reviser diminished the artistry of the scene by staling its freshness and blurring its immediacy. And unfortunately the alteration, having achieved an improvement in logic

---

the pardon itself because Piers is disappointed in it, having apparently expected some larger, less commonplace sanction for his manner of life. Thus Piers finds himself in virtual agreement with his antagonist. In Piers's angry disappointment it is necessary to assume a transfer from the poet to Piers of that latent dissatisfaction with Do-Well and the active life which becomes explicit when Do-Well is found in the honest minstrel Hawkin the Active Man, who is guilty of all the sins in the catalogue, and when the cure for the sins of Do-Well is shown to be in the contemplative life of Do-Bet.

9. See especially Coghill, *op. cit.*, pp. 17–20. I am unable to agree that the pardon is the Atonement—that is that the pardon represents the *act* of the Atonement allegorically. Nevertheless, the *fact* of the Atonement is, of course, not far away from the poet's thought, since it is through the Atonement that man receives pardon of any sort, and since the Creed is, in one aspect, an expression of faith in the efficacy of the Atonement. But Piers's pardon seems but to confirm a particular phase of this efficacy and not its whole.

if not in art, did not stop there. Along with the tearing of the pardon C eliminated the whole quarrel between the Priest and Piers, during which, in the earlier texts, Piers makes his resolution to cease from sowing and to devote himself to a contemplative life. As both Chambers and Burdach, independently of one another, have pointed out,[1] this resolution of Piers's is a vital signpost that directs the reader on the safe way to the *Vita*. It is, indeed, our only indication that from this point on the poem will concern less and less the active life of society and more and more the contemplative life of the individual. Thus it is the connecting link between the two parts of the poem. C takes down the signpost. His Piers neither rejects the one life nor vows to take up the other. The reader is, apparently, left to shift for himself.

In order to explain this omission at all satisfactorily, we must look back over the earlier passus of the poem to a passage which has the same form in the B- and C-texts. At the conclusion of the confession of the Deadly Sins the Dreamer tells us that

> A thousand of men þo thrungen togyderes;
> Criede vpward to cryst and to his clene moder
> To haue grace to go with hem treuthe to seke.[2]

The significance of the pilgrimage which the folk on the field thus abruptly initiate has not, I think, been properly appreciated. All these sinners, these protagonists of the worldly life whose shortcomings have just been fully set forth, spontaneously make a vow which at least suggests a renunciation of their way of living: a single-minded search for God. To the modern reader the pilgrimage may seem no more than an allegorical representation of the sinners' desire to mend their ways; but to the medieval reader it probably meant a good deal more than that. Despite his love for allegory, the medieval reader was able to take the Gospels literally; and the Gospels leave no doubt about the cost that must be defrayed by the soul that would devote itself to seeking God.

Go and sell that thou hast, and give to the poor, and thou shalt have treasure in heaven: and come and follow me. . . . He that findeth his life shall lose it: and he that loseth his life for my sake shall find it. . . . Take no thought for your life, what ye shall eat, or what ye shall drink; nor yet for your body, what ye shall put on. . . . Martha, Martha, thou art careful and troubled about many things: But one thing is needful. . . . If any man come to me, and hate not his father, and mother, and wife, and children, and brethren, and sisters, yea, and his own life also, he cannot be my disciple. . . . Whosoever he be of you that forsaketh not all that he hath, he cannot be my disciple. . . .[3]

1. *Mind,* p. 124; *Ackermann,* pp. 269 ff., 309–10.
2. B, v, 517–19. C, viii, 155–7, A, v, 260–3 vary, C but slightly.
3. Matthew 19.21; 10.39; 6.25; Luke 10.41–2; 14.26, 33.

To undertake a single-minded search for God was to abandon the active life and to take up the contemplative.

The suggestion of the abandonment of the active life is, perhaps, no more than that. None of the Biblical texts I have quoted appears in this portion of the poem. Yet surely the "great multitudes" whom Christ warned to count the cost before they should undertake to follow Him[4] must have been in the poet's mind as he wrote. But on the Field of Folk there is no Messiah—no one who can tell the pilgrims about the path to Truth until Piers Plowman puts forth his head and offers to lead them.[5] Piers declares that he has known and served Truth for many years and that he is well acquainted with the road to his house. The road, as Piers describes it, is little more than the commandments in allegory. It is, indeed, the same road that Christ pointed out to the young man in answer to his first question, the road upon which the representative of the active life may pass to salvation.[6] For the moment the suggestion that the pilgrimage represents a rejection of the active life seems altogether denied. Yet we must bear in mind that the pilgrimage is never actually performed.[7] Before Piers can start out, he must plow and sow his half-acre. The accomplishment of that task is described in the following passus, and at its conclusion Truth procures Piers his pardon and instructs him

> To taken his teme and tulyen þe erthe.[8]

Furthermore, Truth bids Piers

> . . . holde hym at home and eryen his leyes,
> And alle þat halpe hym to erie, to sette or to sowe,
> Or any other myster þat myȝte pieres auaille,
> Pardoun with pieres plowman treuthe hath ygraunted.[9]

From these lines the only conclusion I can draw is that Truth has anticipated the pilgrimage and has, in effect, canceled it, so that the

---

4. Luke 14.28: "For which of you, intending to build a tower, sitteth not down first, and counteth the cost, whether he have sufficient to finish it?"

5. A, vi, 28, B, v, 544, C, viii, 182.

6. For the moral aspect of Piers's instructions, see Coghill, op. cit., p. 14; Dunning, op. cit., p. 121; Chambers, Mind, p. 124. Dunning says that "Piers, in describing the way to Truth, first shows that Truth can only be reached by an observance of the entire Christian moral law, as interpreted by the Church." Chambers calls Piers's instructions "a dull and wooden allegory of the Commandments."

7. Carnegy, The Relations between the Social and Divine Order in William Langland's "Vision of William concerning Piers the Plowman," p. 8, says that the search for Truth "consists in setting the pilgrims to work on the half-acre," and cites in corroboration Chambers, MLR, v, 13: "Piers' guidance of the pilgrims actually consists in setting them all to work." But while the plowing is, indeed, all the guidance Piers provides, it is not the fulfillment of the search. As Dunning says, op. cit., p. 128, the "ploughing episode is definitely said to precede the pilgrimage; and the pilgrimage, in point of fact, is never made. . . ."

8. B, vii, 2 (A, viii, 2, C, x, 2).

9. B, vii, 5–8 (C, x, 5–8). A, viii, 5–8 reads Pope for treuthe in 8.

pilgrims, led and in a sense typified by Piers, may remain at home and perform the world's work. The pardon promised them accords active life full expectation of salvation. By implication, Truth seems here to recognize what Piers fails to recognize when he so readily explains the way to Truth's dwelling in an allegory of the commandments. The pilgrimage to God, undertaken here on earth, consists in something more than obedience to the tables of the law. It entails a complete rejection of the world's business. And in this instance Truth orders the pilgrims, through Piers, to remain sons of Martha rather than to undertake to imitate their cousins, the sons of Mary. Mary's life may be better, or best, but Martha's is still good and, according to a basic statement of faith, is worthy of salvation. Piers, however, possibly reflecting a spiritual experience of the poet's, seems to have believed that the active life would be accorded some sanction greater than that of the Creed—a comparative or a superlative, instead of a flat positive. It is perhaps his realization of his own error in regard to the value of the virtuous life of Do-Well—which he has earlier described to the pilgrims in allegorical terms—that causes the anger in which he tears the pardon.[1] That life is not good enough. Piers suddenly resolves to take an altogether different path to Truth from the one which he has said that he knows so well.

I should be no friend to *Piers Plowman* if I were to point out inconsistencies in one version merely in order to make another seem, by contrast, superior—or less inconsistent. Therefore when I assert that in the A- and B-texts when Piers resolves to cease from sowing he acts directly contrary to the instructions that he has received from Truth, who stands for God, I do not do so in order to derogate from the merit of the earlier versions—which is, in any case, sufficiently well-established so that the derogator has to work against great odds. Indeed, I wonder how many readers have noticed this inconsistency, or, if they have, how many have let it affect their pleasure in the poem. But I suggest that, to a poet who had come to esteem his Christian responsibility more highly than his artistic responsibility, a passage which pictured the poem's hero, the old and faithful servant of Truth, as disobedient to him in respect to a quite definite instruction, might seem to require emendation.[2] Granted that the criticism is a quibbling one, since in either way of life Piers is serving God directly, still we are dealing with a period when both poets and their readers could quibble with the best, and readers who read for elevation rather than pleasure might well take offense—probably had taken offense—at the A- and B-texts. For this reason C's omission of Piers's resolution, as well as of his tearing of the pardon, seems logical.

Yet, as I have said, Piers's resolution provides us with a necessary

1. See p. 162, n. 8, above.
2. Perhaps the phrases *so harde* and *so bisi* in Piers's resolution were intended to soften the possible shock of his disobedience upon the reader.

signpost in our search for the truth of *Piers Plowman*. Did C give us anything in its stead? The answer is, I think, in the affirmative. If we turn back to the conclusion of Piers's speech explaining his conception of the way to Truth, we shall find that in all three texts three persons—an ape-keeper, a pickpocket, and a wafer-seller—decide emphatically not to go on the pilgrimage, since they feel that they would not find any relatives at Truth's home.[3] But Piers urges them to persist, saying that a maid named Mercy lives there, who is related to all sinful men. With these remarks A and B close the incident and terminate a passus. But in C Piers's statement about Mercy is followed by objections from other persons and these, on first sight, seem a needless continuation of those already made.

> "ʒe, *villam emi*," quaþ on, "and now most ich þudere,
> To loke how me lykeþ hit," and tok hus leue at peers.
> Anoþer a-non ryght nede seyde he hadde
> To folwen fif ʒokes, "for-thy me by-houeþ
> To gon with a good wil and greiþliche hem dryue;
> For-þy ich praye ʒow, peers, paraunter, yf ʒe meteþ
> Treuthe, telleþ to hym þat ich be excused."
> Thenne was þer on heihte actif, an hosebounde he semed;
> "Ich haue ywedded a wyf," quaþ he, "wel wantowen of maners;
> Were ich seuenyght fro hure syghte synnen hue wolde,
> And loure on me and lyghtliche chide and seye ich loue anoþere.
> For-þy, peers plouhman, ich praye þe telle hit treuthe,
> Ich may nat come for a kytte, so hue cleueþ on me;
> *Vxorem duxi, et ideo non possum uenire.*"[4]

But this is more than a continuation of the earlier objections. The lines are, of course, a direct paraphrase from St. Luke's account of the Parable of the Unwilling Guests,[5] which concerns those who would "eat bread in the kingdom of God." It is in the same chapter of the Gospel that Christ advises the persons in the multitude to count the cost before they decide to become His disciples, warning them that they must first renounce all that they have.[6] Thus the unwilling guests are equated with those who have counted the cost and found it too great—who have determined, in short, to persist in the active life. The C-text lines immediately following those quoted read as follows:

> Quaþ contemplacion, "by crist, thauh ich care suffre,
> Famyn and defaute, folwen ich wolle peers."[7]

Only those who are ready to forsake the world and to suffer care, hunger, and want will come, after long pilgrimage, to the banquet of the Lord.

---

3. A, vi, 118–26, B, v, 639–51, C, viii, 283–91. B adds a pardoner and a prostitute, whom C omits.

4. C, viii, 292–304.
6. See p. 165, n. 4, above.

5. Luke 14.18–20.
7. C, viii, 305–06.

And, as the C-poet makes clear, these are the practitioners of the contemplative life.

These inserted lines, which show that the pilgrimage does indeed entail a renunciation of active life, are also the signpost that C introduced into his version in order to point out to the reader the direction which his poem is, sooner or later, going to take. To claim any great artistry for the inserted signpost would be difficult. It is, in the first place, rather inconspicuous and we come to it some time before we get to the most bewildering crossroads. Then too, it makes the three practical men of business who reject the pilgrimage because it is a renunciation of active life seem possessed of sounder theological learning than Piers, whose description of the highway to Truth has been little more than an outline of the virtuous active life. Furthermore, although three worldly characters withdraw from the pilgrimage, a large number of their fellows continue on it, at least to the extent of performing the preliminary step, the plowing of Piers's half-acre. Nevertheless, when we consider the number of incongruities in all versions of *Piers Plowman,* these do not seem too serious. C's paraphrase of Luke accomplishes, though less forcefully, the same purpose as Piers's resolution in A and B to cease from his labor; and it does so without making Piers seem disobedient. In all texts Truth affirms the active life. Despite this, in all texts the reader is given to understand that the active life is inadequate—in A and B through Piers's resolution, in C through Contemplation's. It is possible that C was here writing, consciously or unconsciously, as a gloss upon B: the introduction of "one hight Active" would cause the reader familiar with B to recall Hawkin's confession, with its full and unequivocal demonstration of the inadequacy of active life, and this recollection would suggest the proper interpretation to put upon the new lines.

As I have said, no pilgrimage is accomplished in the *Visio,* but the *Vita* is, in a very real sense, nothing but a pilgrimage shared by the Dreamer and Piers Plowman himself. The stages in Piers's advancement on this journey in the *Vita* are not defined in terms of human motivation. He alters from one epiphany to another not by an act of will but by a mystical transition. In the A- and B-texts his renunciation of the active life is given a sort of dramatic impetus by his anger—no real motivation but something which very nearly replaces it. In C, this is lacking and the transition to his next manifestation is accomplished, like his later transitions, without explanation or intensification of the narrative. Thus Piers is like the young man in Matthew who goes on, apparently without reason, to ask a second question when he might well have been fully satisfied by the answer he received to his first.

3. *Do-Well: Recklessness, Hawkin, and Piers*

We come now to the *Visio de Do-Well,* that most elusive of all the sections of the poem. The A-text poet apparently conceived it not as a discussion of Do-Well alone but as a discussion of Do-Well, Do-Bet, and Do-Best.[8] It was the B-poet who tried, without marked success, to shape it in such a way as to fit the title *Visio de Do-Well,* while the C-poet seems to have had another try at the same business,[9] with, possibly somewhat more success. Since a consideration of all the multitudinous revisions in this part of the poem is hardly possible in such a book as this, I shall limit myself to the question, as applied to C, of what Do-Well is. This is the question which, in all texts, the Dreamer asks again and again and to which he gets answers from virtually all hands. Yet none of the explicit definitions that he hears succeeds in satisfying him or the reader, so that we are forced to search beyond the explicit for an implicit definition. For the B-text the most commonly accepted interpretation is, I suppose, that expressed by Chambers: Do-Well is the active life, embodied here by Hawkin, Activa Vita,[1] just as in the *Visio* it was embodied, though on an ideal level, by Piers. There is much evidence for this theory and it would be difficult to refute it. I have, however, already mentioned my belief that the Do-Well section contains two not wholly congruent ideas considered simultaneously: on the one hand Do-Well as the external active life, on the other Do-Well as the first stage of the internal contemplative life—on the one hand the moral and social, on the other the spiritual. As Dunning has shown, this contrast between moral and spiritual definitions is perceptible in the A-text, where Wit and Study present one side, while Thought and Clergy present the other.[2] It is also present in the B-text, where, however, the personifications do not so neatly express one point of view or the other.[3] And it is present in the C-text. In the definition—not so much expressed as achieved by an accumulation of effects—that C accepts for Do-Well lies, as I have said, the chief difference between the

8. MSS TUDH2 agree in closing Passus VIII of the A-text with a colophon suggesting that the subsequent part of the poem will concern Do-Well, Do-Bet, and Do-Best together. Thus T reads, in part, *incipit vita de do-wel do-bet et do-best secundum wyt et resoun.* The next two passus are labeled in TH2 *de dowel, &c.,* while U omits, probably accidentally, *&c.* The abbreviation is also omitted after the heading of Passus XII in URJ. See *EETS,* I, xxv, 137*; *EETS,* IV, 857. Dunning, *op. cit.,* pp. 167–84, argues that the A-*Vita* is complete. Though I cannot agree with his major premise, he does make it clear that A treats all three lives together.

9. While the headings of B- and C-MSS vary greatly, the presence of individual sections for Do-Well, Do-Bet, and Do-Best are clearly indicated. See Skeat's footnotes.

1. *Mind,* pp. 149 ff.

2. Dunning, *op. cit.,* p. 173: ". . . the three 'lives' mentioned by Thought as Dowel, Dobet and Dobest, are not subjective but objective states of perfection or well-doing." *Idem,* p. 174: "Wit . . . defines Dowel, Dobet and Dobest as subjective states of perfection or well-doing." See *idem,* pp. 178–9, for Clergy's and Study's definitions.

3. Dunning, *idem,* pp. 191–2, notes that B obfuscates Wit's definition.

B- and C-texts in the Do-Well section. In B, the solution is found in the person of Hawkin, the moral aspect of Do-Well. But in C, it is worked out in Do-Well's spiritual aspect as the first stage in the contemplative life which he must pursue who would be perfect. What the name of this stage is we shall see shortly.

We have long been accustomed, in literature, to hearing wisdom spoken from the mouths of fools and idiots. Yet we can hardly help being shocked when the approaches to a highway leading toward perfection are shown to us by some one bearing the deplorable name of Reckless-ness. But this is precisely what occurs in the C-text. In the B-version, Recklessness appears apparently just in order to give the Dreamer some bad advice (which the Dreamer follows) and then disappears, having spoken a total of eight lines.[4] He seems to be merely another one of those reprehensible characters that surround Fortune, a suitable fellow for Childishness and the trio who, according to St. John, make up the sum of things in this world—Lust of the Flesh, Lust of the Eyes, and Pride of Life.[5] Thus Chambers is fully justified in referring to Recklessness as one of the "sins of passionate youth."[6] In C, Recklessness appears in the same company earlier than he does in B[7] and takes over all the Dreamer's monologue about predestination, the salvation of the heathen, and the value of learning—the famous rebellious monologue with which the A-poet broke off the poem.[8] In C Recklessness then gives the Dreamer the bad advice[9] and afterward, becoming as it were coalesced with the Dreamer, follows the advice in the Dreamer's person.[1] He reappears after the interlude of the pursuit of Fortune and, still inhabiting the Dreamer's body, harangues Clergy steadily for five hundred lines.[2] Of this speech part is new in the C-text, while the rest is, in B, assigned by Skeat to Lewte,[3] though on doubtful evidence. The B-poet, or possibly an early B-scribe, left out the speaker's identity. In C, however, the speech is expressly assigned to Recklessness, although the assignment is made at its end rather than at the beginning.[3a]

The most arresting thing about this speech is its extremely eloquent praise of the virtues of patience and poverty, or, to be more accurate, the virtue of patient poverty. One should, perhaps, hyphenate the expression, since the noun and adjective seem to combine to make one distinct idea. I shall, however, follow the poet's lead and refer to "patience" and "patient poverty" as meaning, in this context, the same thing. The poet himself seems clearly to have been following the lead

---

4. B, xi, 33–40.   5. 1 John 2.16.   6. *Mind*, p. 134.
7. At C, xii, 195, in time to rejoin B at B, x, 375, more than a hundred lines before his appearance in B.
8. A, xi, 250–303, B, x, 372–474, C, xii, 200–303.   9. C, xii, 304–09.
1. Cf. C, xiii, 4 with xiii, 12. In the first line, Covetousness-of-Eyes gives Recklessness advice which in the second line the Dreamer follows.
2. C, xiii, 88 through xiv, 128.   3. See *EETS*, ii, 176, sidenote to xi, 148.
3a. See C, xiv, 129, and Skeat's note, *EETS*, iv, 278.

of the author of *Patience* in yoking the two virtues thus inseparably, although, inevitably, he is less clear than his forerunner on how the two virtues come to be yoked under a single *significatio*.[5] No speech in *Piers Plowman* is more filled with New Testament quotations and New Testament paraphrases on the subject of apostolic poverty than this of Recklessness. In rapid succession we get Matthew, Mark, Luke, and John— Gospel and Epistles—as well as Paul[6] and, though Skeat does not mention it, a good bit from the fifth chapter of the Epistle of James.[7] Indeed, the passage would serve as a guide book for any one who is looking for authority to cast his burdens upon the Lord and to renounce all anxiety for the affairs of this world. By the same token, the passage is a storehouse of quotations that set forth the distinction between the active and contemplative lives, although the poet lays the emphasis not on the two lives but on poverty and riches. Thus even the story of Mary and Martha is used, not in its classic medieval sense to illustrate Christ's preference for the contemplative life, but to illustrate the superiority of a life of patient poverty over a life of wealth.[8] In both B and C the speech is an excellent one. But in C, where there is added the well-sustained metaphor of the merchant and the messenger, the poet attains an even greater degree of eloquence than is apparent in the B-text.

It is this speech which, I believe, first sets the reader upon the trail leading to C's definition of Do-Well: patient poverty, the first stage in the soul's journey to perfection. Though the idea has never been without influence on the earlier conduct of the poem, it receives here its fullest expression and, as we shall see, holds the stage for most of the remainder of Do-Well in the C-text. But before we can continue on the path to perfection, we must pause to consider the nature of the traffic policeman who set us upon it. Who, and what, is Recklessness? An obvious explanation may be based upon the etymology of his name. Recklessness is the quality of not caring. In English, and in Middle English, the sense of the noun seems to have been universally pejorative.[9] But the sense

5. See *Patience*, ll. 1–60. The relationship has not, of course, been established, but seems to me highly probable. See Menner, ed., *Purity*, pp. xxix–xxx, and *Patience*, H. Bateson, ed., (2d ed., Manchester, 1918), pp. xxiv–xxviii, with which compare his first edition (1912), pp. 20–5, 67–70.

6. Matthew 19.29 at C, xiii, 159; 19.21 at xiii, 166; Mark 16.16 at xiv, 87; 12.43 at xiv, 98; Luke 14.12 at xiii, 102; 10.40 at xiii, 136; 10.42 at xiii, 139; 14.33 at xiii, 170; 12.20 at xiii, 215; John 8.34 at xiii, 111; 12.24 at xiii, 178; 16.20 at xiii, 207; ii Corinthians 6.10 at xiv, 4; Galatians 6.2 at xiv, 78; i John 3.14 at xiii, 98; James 2.10 at xiv, 122; and the part of the Athanasian Creed which forms Piers's pardon at xiii, 118.

7. Cf. James 5.10–11 with C, xiv, 20–5; 5.11 with xiii, 200–03. C, xiii, 198–9 closely translates James 5.7. The apostrophe to the rich at xiii, 219 ff. echoes James 5.1 ff.

8. C, xiii, 135–9, B, xi, 242–6. The poet concludes the story of Mary and Martha by observing (B), "Ac pouerte god put bifore and preysed it þe bettre."

9. See *OED, recklessness*, and *reckless*, a. The use of the adjective in *Gawain and the Green Knight*, l. 40, seems, however, to point to a nonpejorative sense in Middle English. Arthur's court is described as indulging in "reckless" mirths—surely innocent merriment, though carefree.

of the verb upon which the noun is ultimately formed is less one-sided. *To reck* (Middle English *recchen*) means, among other things, "to take heed for," "to be anxious for," and might conceivably be used to translate the Latin *esse solliciti* in the phrase, "Take no thought for the morrow."[1] By extension of this meaning into that of the derived noun, recklessness might come properly to be ascribed to the apostles who, casting their burdens upon the Lord, forbore to suffer anxiety for worldly things. Such, indeed, is Burdach's conception of the character in *Piers Plowman*.[2] And, upon the basis of Recklessness' speech on patient poverty, this seems to be what the character came to mean for the C-reviser.

Such a development of the personification we meet in the B-text is, to say the least, unexpected, for in B there is no quality apparent in Recklessness that would make us admire him. And, strangely enough, C, when in his elaboration of B he first introduces Recklessness, takes some pains to make him appear as bad as possible. Thus he describes him as speaking "in ribaldry" and repeats a rumor to the effect that he is kinsman of Sir Wanhope.[3] The mention of wanhope, however, may be a clue leading to a solution of the problem of what C was about. Chambers has shown that the A-poet broke off his poem in despair—wanhope—because he was unable to solve the riddles posed by predestinarianism and the dogma concerning the damnation of the righteous heathen.[4] In the statement of these riddles, the central question seems to be, What sort of men are, in God's eyes, most worthy to receive His saving grace? Arbitrarily and, indeed, recklessly, the poet makes several rapid conclusions: since learning (Clergy) is historically seen to be no more attractive to grace than is ignorance, it follows that the will of God is inscrutable; and since the will of God is inscrutable, one may as well take a chance and lead one's life as one's will, or even whim, dictates.

1. See *OED, reck,* v., 1, b. The word is not used for Matthew 6.34 in either Wycliffe Bible, where the locution *be busy* is preferred. The poet, however, uses *reck* in precisely the same sense at C, XVII, 315, where Liberum Arbitrium says of Charity that "of rentes ne of richesses . . . reccheþ he neuere."

2. I had developed my theory of the character of Recklessness before I realized that it had already been put forward by Burdach, who (*Ackermann*, p. 310) describes Recklessness as "die 'Sorg- und Sorgenlosigkeit,' die nicht rechnet und zählt und frei ist von der Unruhe der Gewinnsucht." Burdach continues: "In der Komposition des ganzen Werkes spielt ihr Auftreten und ihre Ermahnung eine vorbereitende Rolle, die künstlerisch wohl durchdacht ist. Von allen Reden, die den mit ihr erscheinenden Personifikationen in den Mund gelegt werden, ist keine mit dem Grundproblem des Gedichts enger verwachsen als ihre weitgreifende Belehrung über die Prädestination und namentlich über den Segen der Armut, über das Verderbenbringende des Reichstums. Durch drei Passus des Gedichts führt sie das Wort. Ihr umfassendes Lob der Armut weist hin auf das Vorbild, das Christus in seiner menschlichen Niedrigkeit gegeben hat." Burdach normally deals with the poem through the B-text and gives notice when he is speaking in terms of C. In this case, however, although presumably he is discussing B, the context indicates that he thinking of C, since it would be difficult to apply his remarks to B's Recklessness. Burdach does not consider the seamy side of the character.

3. C, XII, 198-9. Later he is "in a rage." See XIV, 129.

4. *Mind*, pp. 130-1.

In this mood the poet broke off the A-text and in this mood in the B-text the Dreamer conducts his unfortunate experiment with Fortune. When he returns to his search, with his fingers burned, the question of who is worthy to receive the grace of salvation is once more introduced. But now there is advanced a positive, instead of a negative, argument. Grace is given to the man who, like Trajan, is filled with love and justice, or to the man who imitates in his life the patient poverty of Christ. (The poet of *Piers Plowman*, like the poet of *Patience*, seems to have possessed the virtue of poverty.) We might observe that in the reopened argument of B Clergy still is not presented as being especially attractive to grace, but the inferiority of learning is now presented less for its own sake than in order to exalt patient poverty:

> Ac grace ne groweth nouȝte but amonges lowe;
> Pacience and pouerte þe place is þere it groweth.[5]

Poverty—patient poverty—is the chief means to grace and Recklessness in C seems to have the same sentiments toward Clergy and Scripture that the poet has in B, even though these are not directly expressed in the earlier text.

> Ac me were leuere, by oure lorde, a lippe of godes grace
> Than al þe kynde witt þat ȝe can boþe, and connynge of ȝoure bokes.[6]

Who is actually responsible, in the B-text, for the long speech which carries on the reopened discussion of grace—the speech on patient poverty? Despite its ascription by Skeat to Lewte, and despite the ambiguous line that follows its conclusion, I am convinced that the passage really belongs to the Dreamer. And so, apparently, was Chambers.[7] If this ascription is correct, then the B-text helps us to explain the change that Recklessness' character undergoes in C. In B one man advances a certain argument, draws a rash conclusion from it, acts upon his decision—foolishly, as it turns out—and then, chastened, returns to the argument in order to draw from it a more constructive conclusion. But it is the same man all the time—the Dreamer, or the poet himself. In C, precisely the same thing occurs, only the man is called Recklessness. If we turn from an objective to a subjective consideration of his character we may see that, just like the man of the B-text, Recklessness fulfills a separate one of his potentialities (even if they are only etymological

---

5. B, XII, 62–3. C, XV, 24–9 alters and expands the lines into a consideration of preventing grace. See George Sanderlin, "The Character 'Liberum Arbitrium' in the C-text of *Piers Plowman*," *MLN*, LVI (1941), 453 and n. 13, for a discussion of the change.

6. C, XII, 226–7. This sentiment is, in C, echoed by Conscience, who tells Clergy at C, XVI, 179–80, "Me were leuere, by oure lorde, and ich lyuye sholde, Haue pacience parfitliche þan half þy pack of bokes!"

7. *Mind*, p. 136: "Then our dreamer goes on to contrast with this standard of patience and poverty the avarice and ignorance of priests."

potentialities) in each of the two phases of the discussion of grace: first the recklessness of wanhope, second the reck-less-ness of St. Francis. He is an entity with extension in two directions, while a human being is an entity with extension in an infinite number of directions. One does not ordinarily label each of the various extensions of a man, but one may of a personification. For us, with our natural tendency to regard all personifications as static, and with some years of bitter experience with reckless drivers behind us, the essential unity of Recklessness may be hard to perceive. But if nowhere else, we should be able to see it in the ragged clothes in which he first stands forth:[8] they are, on the one hand, the badge of a man who doesn't give a damn; and, on the other, the banner of the apostles whom Christ ordered to take but one coat with them on their travels.[9]

It is impossible to guess exactly why C made the change. The reader who compares the B- and C-versions of Do-Well will notice that most of B's autobiographical material, particularly in the section dealing with Imaginative, is omitted from the later version, so that it would be impossible to derive from C what Chambers derived from B relative to the A-poet's reasons for abandoning the poem after the third passus of Do-Well. Those biographical details are not necessary to the main sense of the poem and at first glance, in the present matter, it looks as if C were pursuing a policy of omitting biography by having the Dreamer swallowed up by Recklessness. But any one who uses that explanation after observing the magnificent abandon with which Recklessness is identified with the Dreamer is giving C credit for less skill than he deserves. The two characters are fastened together with transparent tape. C was careful that the reader should see through it and perceive at once the Dreamer and Recklessness.[1] Though pointing out a joke that only oneself has seen is a risky business (and from the solemnity with which *Piers Plowman* is sometimes handled, pointing out humor in it at all might be considered offensive), I suggest that C was having a sort of double-edged joke, first in the loose identification of the Dreamer with Recklessness, second in the surprising development of Recklessness from one who is made to appear a very bad actor to one who exemplifies, to some extent, the virtue of patient poverty. I do not think that Joyce was the first artist to discover that a pun might both be entertaining and at the same time accomplish a serious purpose. It occurs to me that just as in Do-Bet the poet rings the changes on charity through Liberum Arbitrium (Anima in B), the Tree of Charity, the Samaritan, and, ultimately, Christ, so here he is beginning to ring the changes on patient poverty in the person, as well as through the words, of Recklessness. As we shall see, he goes on to develop the idea fully in the character of

8. See C, xii, 195.   9. Mark 6.9; Luke 9.3.   1. See p. 170, n. 1, above.

Patience and in Piers. Recklessness, then, introduces a dominant theme of Do-Well.

After this detour during which we have examined Recklessness, let us return to the highway to perfection and investigate patient poverty in its relation to that strangely unsuccessful minstrel, Hawkin the active man. In both B and C we come to Hawkin by way of the banquet given by Conscience in honor of the fat Doctor of Divinity, a social event which the Dreamer and a new acquaintance of his, Patience, are permitted to attend. Although the two texts diverge in significant ways, the dominant theme throughout the banquet scene is, in both, patience: *Patientes vincunt.*[2] With this virtue Conscience is so impressed that he vows to accompany the character bearing its name in order to learn its nature at first hand.[3] And so, after dinner, the two depart, accompanied, of course, by the Dreamer. Straightway they encounter Active, or, as he is more frequently called in B, Hawkin. With this encounter the two texts diverge altogether. In B, Hawkin makes his long confession that includes instances of each of the deadly sins in turn. Following this, Conscience, acting as Hawkin's confessor, speaks of contrition, confession, and satisfaction (defining them, incidentally, as Do-Well, Do-Bet, and Do-Best).[4] Then Patience begins to speak and, employing the phrase *Ne solliciti sitis*[5] which Piers had used after the Priest impugned his pardon, promises that, given an opportunity, he himself will feed Hawkin and those who rely on Hawkin for provisions, if the penitent will renounce the life he has been leading. Twice again we hear the phrase *Patientes vincunt.*[6] Patience goes on to emphasize the importance of contrition, confession, and satisfaction[7] and then, after an interruption by Hawkin, launches into a long speech in praise of poverty, terminating with the nine *distinctiones paupertatis.*[8] Hawkin is overcome with grief, apparently because Patience has made him feel the futility of his way of life. He laments for his existence, asking why, after his baptism, he

> . . . ne hadde ben ded and doluen for doweles sake![9]

And the Dreamer awakes to the sound of Hawkin's lament.

It is, as I have said, generally agreed that in Hawkin, the representative of the average sort of active life, the Dreamer of the B-text finally comes to know Do-Well and what he had thought would be gold turns out to be mere dross. Twice before the Dreamer has favored active life over any other means of salvation: once when it was exemplified in

2. The phrase occurs at B, XIII, 134, 171; C, XVI, 138, 157; also at B, XIV, 33, 52; C, XVI, 255. Skeat, *EETS*, IV, 308, connects it with Matthew 10.22, *qui autem perseveraverit usque in finem, hic salvus erit,* and with similar expressions in the Cato books. See Burdach's interesting note, *Ackermann,* p. 226, n. 1. See also the verses from James quoted on p. 180, n. 2, below.

3. C, XVI, 184, "With pacience wol ich passe, parfitnesse to fynde."

4. B, XIV, 16–21.　　5. B, XIV, 33.　　6. B, XIV, 33, 52.

7. B, XIV, 81–96.　　8. B, XIV, 103–319.　　9. B, XIV, 321.

Piers and once when the Dreamer's inability to solve the riddle of grace had driven him back toward his earlier conclusion.[1] But Hawkin's devastatingly complete confession, along with his lament, seems to settle once and for all the question of the value of the active life : if it is Do-Well, then we must Do-Bet. The phrase *Ne solliciti sitis* serves, as it has before, as a signpost pointing toward a contemplative life. Thus in the B-text Hawkin's confession is the essential element that gives dramatic validity to the direction the poem is about to take : the search for Do-Bet.

The C-reviser makes a drastic simplification of the Hawkin incident. In the first place, the entire confession is omitted, or transferred to the confession of the Deadly Sins in the *Visio*. The incident thus ceases to be a climactic representation of the inadequacy of active life and Hawkin, instead of embodying Do-Well, tends to become just another character like Clergy, holding a place in the poem merely in order to serve as a foil to patient poverty. This transformation is accomplished directly. Whereas in the B-text Patience does not begin to speak until after Hawkin's long confession and until after Conscience has told the penitent about the importance of contrition, confession, and satisfaction, in C Patience takes the stage almost immediately.[2] Hawkin, in his introductory speech, tells of the duty he has of providing food for all mankind. This leads him, by a somewhat devious path, to assert that the degeneration of the people of Sodom was caused by an overabundance of edibles. Patience at this point shows himself quite the opposite of his name :

> "Pees !" quaþ pacience, "ich praye þe, syre actyf !
> For þauh neuere payn ne plouh ne potage were,
> Prude wolde putte hym-self forþ þauh no plouh erye.
> Hit am ich þat fynde alle folke and fram hunger saue,
> Thorgh þe heye helpe of hym þat me hyder sente."[3]

Having maneuvered the conversation around to where he wants it, Patience starts off on a long speech on his favorite theme, a speech which parallels, though sometimes very roughly, the passage assigned to him in the B-text. In the course of the revision C removes most of the emphasis that B placed on the three parts of penitence. In place of Conscience's clear definition of Do-Well as contrition, Do-Bet as confession, and Do-Best as satisfaction, Patience makes a rapid definition which seems intended to equate the sum of the two triads rather than their parts.[4] Furthermore, where in B the relation between penitence and patience is not clear, C makes an effort to express it :

> *Cordis contricio, oris confessio, operis satisfactio;*
> These thre with-outen doute tholen alle pouerte,

1. See A, xi, 293–303, B, x, 452–74, C, xii, 286–303.
2. Hawkin begins to speak at C, xvi, 194, Patience at C, xvi, 234.
3. C, xvi, 234–8. 4. See C, xvii, 25–32.

And lereþ lewed and lered, heh and louh to knowe,
Ho þat doþ wel oþer bet oþer best a-bouen alle.[5]

C's alterations seem to place the emphasis squarely upon patient poverty. In B, patient poverty also figures prominently. Thus it is patient poverty, which is obviously understood as a manifestation of a contemplative life, that is recommended as a cure for the evils attendant upon active life.[6] But in B this theme shares the poet's attention on a more or less equal basis with penitence and with Hawkin's active life. In C, however, patient poverty is the paramount theme and the others are reduced to the barest minimum. This shift in emphasis, occurring as it does at the end of the vision where, if ever, we should expect to find Do-Well defined, suggests to me that the C-reviser intended to accomplish an almost complete redefinition of Do-Well: instead of the active life, Do-Well is patient poverty. Some one may excusably object here that this is all a sort of verbal quibble, since if patient poverty is better than the active life in both texts, why may not the former play Do-Bet to the latter's Do-Well in C as well as in B? Reduced to grammatical terms, the objection is, indeed, unanswerable. But there are two other reasons against it: the first I shall glance at briefly in my remarks on Do-Bet; the second, which is rather more formidable, will be found in C's presentation of the banquet scene, to which we shall now turn.

I have already had occasion to mention Coghill's theory that Piers Plowman embodies Do-Well, Do-Bet, and Do-Best in turn. That Piers should do so—though not, I am sure, vocationally—was, I think, the intention of the C- as well as of the B-poet. Yet in C Piers makes an appearance in the section concerning Do-Well, whereas B excludes him from this part of the poem. His appearance occurs during the banquet scene, where, in the B-text, he is only mentioned.[7] The banquet begins in much the same manner in both texts. Patience appears at the gate, is welcomed by Conscience, and is seated with the Dreamer at a side table reserved for the socially unelect. While the Doctor of Divinity[8] at the head table stuffs himself with rich dainties, Patience and the Dreamer are served sour loaves of *agite penitentiam* and other allegorical foodstuffs. The Dreamer, his resentment at this disparate treatment at first held in check by Patience, is finally allowed to ask the Doctor his usual question about the three lives. The answer that he receives is really not a bad one, but the Dreamer in furious indignation hurls it back into the teeth of the speaker. Desperately trying to make conversation in this inclement social atmosphere, the host Conscience asks Clergy for his

5. C, XVII, 33-5.
6. See especially B, XIV, 28-33, where Patience promises to feed mankind if Hawkin foregoes his endeavors in that direction.
7. B, XIII, 21-219, C, XVI, 26-184.
8. Wells on p. 297 of his translation indicates that Clergy and the Doctor of Divinity are the same character. But the distinction is clearly made at B, XIII, 198-9, C, XVI, 176-7.

definition of Do-Well, Do-Bet, and Do-Best. But Clergy requests that he be excused from answering, since Piers Plowman has impugned all learning except love alone, taking for his text *Dilige deum et proximum* and *Domine, quis habitabit*. At this moment, in the C-text, Piers—who we did not know was present at the banquet—suddenly begins to speak, saying,

>   *. . . pacientes uincunt.*
> By-for perpetual pees ich shal preoue þat ich seide,
> And a-vowe by-for God and for-sake hit neuere,
> That *disce, doce, dilige deum* and thyn enemye;
> Hertely þou hym helpe emforth þy myȝt,
> Cast hote coles on hus hefde of alle kynde speche,
> Fonde þorgh wit and with worde hus loue for to wynne,
> And ȝif hym eft and eft euere at hus neede;
> Conforte hym with þy catel and with þy kynde speche,
> And leye on hym þus with loue tyl he lauhe on þe;
> And bote he bowe for þis betynge, blynd mote he worthe![9]

Having thus spoken, Piers vanishes so quickly and mysteriously that no one knows where he has gone. Reason, who only in C attends the banquet, disappears in search of him.

Now if what I have said about C's identification of patient poverty is true, and if Coghill's conclusions about the significance of Piers's epiphanies may be applied to the C-version, then Piers should represent patience here. And, indeed, that seems to have been the author's intention, for he prepares us for such an identification—ambiguously and in a rather misty way—with the lines introducing Patience:

> Pacience as a poure þyng cam and preide mete for charite,
> Ylike to peers plouhman as he a palmere were.[1]

Since Patience is like Piers, it is quite in keeping with the poet's usual way of thinking that Piers should be patience. Furthermore, Piers's speech is, of course, based upon that of Patience in the B-text.[2] It is, however, undeniable that this speech concerns charity. In order to account for this apparent inconsistency, we have to turn back to B. After Clergy's refusal to discuss Do-Well, Conscience calls on Patience, observing that

> Pacience hath be in many place and perauntre cnoweth
> Þat no clerke ne can, as cryst bereth witnesse;
> *Pacientes vincunt, &c.*[3]

That is, since Patience is successful—and knows what no clerk (Clergy) knows—perhaps Patience can help us out with a definition of Do-Well.

9. C, xvi, 138–48.   1. C, xvi, 33–4.
2. Cf. C, xvi, 138–48 with B, xiii, 136–47. 3. B, xiii, 133–4.

And that is precisely why, in C, Piers is qualified to speak: *Patientes vincunt,* he says, "The patient are successful." Hence,

> By-for perpetual pees ich shal preoue þat ich seide.

The explanation for Piers's special knowledge about charity lies in the fact that he is himself patience, to which special insight, particularly in regard to charity, is given. The idea that patience is the ground in which charity grows—suggesting St. Paul's definition, *Charitas patiens est, beniana est*[4]—is of course repeated many times in *Piers Plowman,* but nowhere expressed more clearly than in the B-lines which describe the Tree of Charity,

> Patience hatte þe pure tre and pore symple of herte,
> And so, þorw god and þorw good men, groweth þe frute charite.[5]

In the banquet scene we have an implicit representation of the patience-charity relationship. Though Piers speaks—prophetically, as of something to be realized in the future—of charity, he is patience. And if we may apply Coghill's theory to the C-text, then Piers is here embodying Do-Well and Do-Well is patience. Reason, as I have said, goes off in search of Piers, while the other dominant personification, Conscience, utterly rejecting the claims of Clergy, goes off with Piers's *alter ego,* Patience, in order to find perfectness.[6] The Dreamer has good company in his search for Do-Well.

Burdach has pointed out in the Epistle of James a possible source for the banquet scene.[7] Reproving his flock for admiring riches rather than poverty, James says that in their meetings they accord greater honor to a man wearing a golden ring and a clean garment than they do to a poor man, giving the one a prominent place and the other at best a stool. That the poet had, perhaps, the Epistle in mind as he wrote the incident seems also indicated by the fact that the Epistle repeats, shortly after the lines concerning the rich and poor man, a text similar to *Dilige deum et proximum,* which Clergy ascribes to Piers Plowman.[8] Following Burdach's lead one finds, as I have observed before, that the discussion of patient poverty in *Piers Plowman* bears many echoes of the Epistle—which may, indeed, have shared with *Patience* responsibility for the inseparable yoking of poverty with patience.[9] The verse which Burdach

---

4. 1 Corinthians 13.4.   5. B, XVI, 8–9.
6. C, XVI, 178–84. Conscience's repudiation of Clergy is less conditional in C than in B and further enhances the importance of patience.
7. *Ackermann,* p. 224 and n. 2. James 2.2 ff.   8. C, XVI, 135. See James 2.8.
9. See p. 171, n. 7, above. The fifth chapter of the Epistle of James begins (1–6) with a dire warning to the rich, and then continues (7–11) with instructions to James's brethren to be patient. Although the brethren are not expressly said to be poor, there is a strong implied contrast between them on the one hand and the rich on the other, and it would be easy to read into the Epistle praise of patient poverty, rather than solely of patience.

suggests may have provided the seed from which the Tree of Charity in Do-Bet grew seems also, along with its companion verse, to have reference to the present matter :

Patientes igitur estote, fratres, usque ad adventum Domini. Ecce agricola expectat pretiosum fructum terrae, patienter ferens donec accipiat temporaneum et serotinum. Patientes igitur estote et vos, et confirmate corda vestra, quoniam adventus Domini appropinquavit.[1]

A little later the prophets, in particular Job, are put forward as examples of true patience and suffering.[2] It occurs to me that Piers in his epiphany as C's Do-Well may, in the anagogical sense, stand for the prophets who waited patiently for the coming of Christ—the coming, that is, of charity, the all-comprehending importance of which Piers has vowed that he will prove and which, in the person of Christ, he does prove in Do-Bet. Traces in the poem of the historical view of Joachim of Flora have been noted before.[3] It is my suggestion that just as in Do-Best Piers is St. Peter in the era following the coming of Christ, and in Do-Bet the human nature of Christ himself at the time of the Incarnation, so here he may stand for the prophets in the era before Christ's coming. And just as morally charity proceeds from patience, so anagogically charity was the end of patience, in that the coming of Christ was the fulfillment of the prophets' patience—the fulfillment of the law. So Do-Bet springs from Do-Well.

4. *Do-Bet: Piers, Liberum Arbitrium, and Anima*

It is generally agreed, I believe, that the subject of B's *Visio de Do-Bet* is charity and that, for all practical purposes, B's definition of Do-Bet is charity.[4] That the same is true of the C-version of Do-Bet will become apparent as we examine the major changes that C made in his revision of the section. But aside from the major changes, there is one aspect of C's revision that should receive some comment here. We have seen how in B one of the cures for the ills of active life was found in patience, which in turn produces charity. In going from the Do-Well of the active life to the Do-Bet of charity, therefore, the B-poet did not allot any special section for a consideration of patience by itself. What he did do was constantly associate it with its fellow virtue, charity, both at the end of Do-Well and at the beginning of Do-Bet. The C-poet, however, shifted

1. James 5.7–8. See Burdach, *Ackermann*, p. 221 and n. 2.
2. James 5.10–11: "Take, my brethren, the prophets, who have spoken in the name of the Lord, for an example of suffering affliction, and of patience. Behold, we count them happy which endure [cf. *patientes vincunt*]. Ye have heard of the patience of Job, and have seen the end of the Lord; that the Lord is very pitiful, and of tender mercy."
3. See Wells, *PMLA*, LIII, 349.
4. See Chambers, *Mind*, p. 154; Burdach, *Ackermann*, pp. 195, 311.

the definition of Do-Well from active life to patience, and in so doing he enabled himself to cover the subject of patience completely before turning to charity—to effect a logical separation of the two virtues while retaining, of course, the sense of their relationship. This fact accounts for several rather surprising changes. Thus where in the B-version of Do-Well Hawkin is permitted to ask where Charity dwells, C, who is presenting patience as Do-Well and wants to save charity for Do-Bet, alters the question to read, "What is perfect patience?"[5] Similarly, where in Do-Bet Anima gives examples from the lives of the saints to show the importance of patient poverty, C, who apparently felt that the topic had already been adequately treated, altered the passage so that these examples serve merely to prove that it is impossible for any one who would live in charity to make his living by begging.[6] And when B describes the Tree of Charity initially as a tree of patience from which grows the fruit charity, C omits the lines.[7] But we must bear in mind that these are not alterations in doctrine but rather rearrangements of material. Once again we must be careful not to misunderstand C by adhering too closely to the parallel-text method of reading the poem.

We come now to the major alterations made by C in the *Visio de Do-Bet*. Probably the most interesting of these is the omission of Piers Plowman from the dream which has to do with the Tree of Charity. Before we proceed to a discussion of this, however, we should call to mind that in the B-text Piers makes two appearances in this part of the poem: one as proprietor of the garden in which the tree grows and another as Christ during Holy Week.[8] The second appearance occurs in the last passus of Do-Bet. The poet, who has experienced a long, unhappy waking interval after the dream in which he converses with the Samaritan, finally goes back to sleep to find himself in Jerusalem on the first Palm Sunday. There he tells us that he saw

> One semblable to þe samaritan & some del to Piers þe plowman,
> Barfote on an asse bakke botelees cam prykye.[9]

Faith, standing at a window, cries, "Hail, Son of David!" The Dreamer, bewildered, asks Faith what is taking place and who it is that is going to joust in Jerusalem. "Jesus," Faith answers,

> And fecche þat þe fende claymeth, Piers fruit þe plowman.[1]

"Is Piers here?" the Dreamer exclaims. Faith replies,

> Þis ihesus of his gentrice wole iuste in piers armes,
> In his helme & in his haberioun *humana natura.*
> Þat cryst be nouȝt biknowe here for *consummatus deus,*

5. Cf. B, xiv, 97–8 with C, xvi, 276.
7. B's lines are quoted on p. 179 above.
9. B, xviii, 10–11.
6. Cf. B, xv, 263–6 with C, xviii, 1–8.
8. B, xvi, 21 ff. and xviii, 10 ff.
1. B, xviii, 20.

In Piers paltok þe plowman þis priker shal ryde:
For no dynte shal hym dere as *in deitate patris*.[2]

These lines, which stand almost unaltered in the C-text,[3] clearly identify Piers with Christ—but, we must note, not with the divine nature of Christ but with Christ's human nature, with the Son of Man, not the Son of God. In one sense, since Christ did take mankind's and Piers's nature, Piers may be said to represent Christ, for Christ was not part God and part man, but wholly God and wholly man. But in another sense, and perhaps the more important one, Piers stands for no more than all mankind in the era between the Creation and the Incarnation, the mankind whose nature Christ took. Thus we must not lose sight—as it is probable the poet never did—of the mystical doctrine which comprehends simultaneously the duality and the unity of Christ's nature, the doctrine that is most effectively presented in the lines quoted above.[4]

In the B-text, a suggestion that Piers is to be identified with Christ is made much earlier in the poem, even before Piers's introduction as proprietor of the Tree of Charity. In his dream following that of the confession of Hawkin, the Dreamer encounters a strange tongueless and toothless person who introduces himself with nine names, the most important of which seems to be Anima.[5] Anima discourses upon various topics related to the general subject of patience and charity. The latter, upon the Dreamer's request, Anima defines as a person of so agreeable a nature that the Dreamer's enthusiasm is roused:

"By cryst, I wolde þat I knewe hym," quod I, "no creature leuere!"[6]

To this Anima rejoins in the next line,

With-outen helpe of Piers plowman . . . his persone seestow neuere.

"Do clerks know him?" the Dreamer asks.

"Clerkes haue no knowyng," quod he, "but by werkes and bi wordes.
Ac piers þe plowman parceyueth more depper

2. B, XVIII, 22–6.

3. Before B, XVIII, 22, C adds at XXI, 20, "*Liberum dei arbitrium* . . . for loue haþ vndertake That þis iesus, etc."

4. The nature of Piers's metamorphoses are discussed at length by Burdach, some of whose observations are of extraordinary interest. See especially *Ackermann*, pp. 304–05, 311–14. The background of Langland's conception of the character is carefully considered, *idem*, pp. 314–57. Burdach is most insistent that Piers remains distinct from the divine nature of Christ: "Immer aber bleibt *Piers plowman* von der göttlichen Natur Christi unterschieden." *Idem*, p. 312. Mention should be made of another interesting study of Piers's significance, that by H. W. Troyer, "Who Is Piers Plowman?" *PMLA*, XLVII (1932), pp. 368–84. In many respects Troyer seems in accord with Burdach. I agree entirely with his statement, p. 371, "The unity of the Piers symbol lies . . . in the humanness of all of its variants. Piers is man." But I find it hard to believe that within the unity of the symbol there is so much variety as Troyer suggests.

5. B, xv, 13 ff.   6. B, xv, 189.

What is þe wille and wherfore þat many wyȝte suffreth,
Et vidit deus cogitaciones eorum."[7]

Anima then gives two examples of men who successfully conceal from the general public the fact that they have not charity, concluding,

Þere-fore by coloure ne by clergye knowe shaltow hym neuere,
Noyther þorw wordes ne werkes but þorw wille one.
And þat knoweth no clerke ne creature in erthe,
But piers þe plowman : *petrus, id est, christus.*[8]

These three mentions of Piers certainly seem to accomplish his identification with Christ, and I think that many of us find it difficult not to agree with Skeat in his note to the second passage, "Here *Piers the Plowman* is completely identified with *Jesus Christ.*" [9] Assuming that the identification has been made, we must also go on to admit that it may emphasize the divine rather than the human nature of Christ. The first passage may, indeed, be read as meaning that charity will never have corporeal existence on earth until Christ assumes Piers's nature, but the other two, in citing Christ's ability to see into the hearts of men, seem to be dealing with an attribute of God rather than of man.

If we accept the identification, we should, in reading on in the B-text, be fully prepared upon our next meeting with Piers to recognize him as Christ. The meeting occurs in the dream-within-a-dream in which the Dreamer is permitted to see the Tree of Charity.[1] The allegory is, as the reader will recall, extremely elaborate. Piers, proprietor of the Garden of Heart where the tree whose fruit is charity grows, has farmed out the land to Liberum Arbitrium. The tree itself is supported by three props, which represent the three persons of the Trinity. Piers explains that against the attacks of the world and the flesh he defends the tree by means of the first two props, God the Father and God the Son. Against the devil Liberum Arbitrium, Piers's lieutenant, is sometimes effective in his own right. And against a concerted attack by the world, the flesh, and the devil, Liberum Arbitrium uses the third prop and pulls down the devil with the aid of grace and the Holy Ghost. After receiving this exposition from Piers, the Dreamer starts to question him about the tree upon which the three props grew. Piers answers brusquely that the tree is called the Trinity and indicates that further questions upon that subject are unnecessary. The Dreamer then expresses curiosity about the fruit of the Tree of Charity, which is now seen to represent the con-

---

7. B, xv, 192–4. Cf. Matthew 9.4; Luke 11.17.   8. B, xv, 203–06.
9. *EETS,* iv, 347, note to B, xv, 193.
1. See B, xvi, 1–89 and cf. C, xix, 1–123. Miss Day, *RES,* iii, 333–4, argues that the source of the tree is in Duns Scotus' *De Rerum Principio.* But the tree in Duns is not much more like the tree in the poem than is the tree in St. Augustine (see *Migne,* xxxiv, 379–80), which Burdach describes, *Ackermann,* pp. 285–7. The history of trees in religious allegory seems very complex. See Burdach's note, *idem,* p. 285, n. 2.

ditions of human life, although earlier it had consisted of charitable works. At the Dreamer's request, Piers causes some of the fruit to fall, and the fruit lying thus scattered on the ground is recognized as the Old Testament prophets. These the devil gathers together and bears away to limbo, unopposed. Whereupon Piers, once again acting in "pure teen," seizes the second prop, *Filius Dei,* and strikes out after the thief, thus precipitating the Incarnation. The dream then dissolves into a vision of the Nativity.

It is difficult to adhere steadily throughout this account to an identification of Piers with Christ, even if we limit the identification to Christ's human nature. One could hardly deny that there is some awkwardness in hearing Piers, if he stands for Christ, explain to the Dreamer,

> Þanne sette I to þe secounde pile *sapiencia dei patris,*
> Þat is, þe passioun and þe power of owre prynce Ihesu.[2]

Piers's action in bringing down the fruit himself also seems strange if he is indeed the Savior. Furthermore, though the scene begins, apparently, in an allegory depicting the spiritual condition of man in the fourteenth century, thirteen hundred years after the Atonement, it ends, with no explicit transition, in an allegory depicting the condition of man between his fall in Eden and the birth of Christ—who alone could rescue the souls of the patriarchs and prophets from Satan. Therefore at the end of the vision when he strikes out with the second prop, Piers could not very well represent the human nature of Christ, since Christ had not yet assumed human nature, although he could represent the human nature which Christ was to assume, or, less effectively, the second person of the Trinity before the Incarnation. The latter, however, seems sufficiently symbolized by the second prop. On the other hand, since a few lines later the poet uses the phrase *plenitudo temporis,* one might argue that he had in mind St. Paul's statement, *At ubi venit plenitudo temporis, misit Deus Filium suum,*[3] and that Piers stands for God the Father. I do not know what conclusion to draw from the statement that Piers taught the Christ child leechcraft. The point is a doctrinal one, with its roots heaven knows where. The concept does, however, suggest a separation between two parts of Christ's nature and possibly means that Piers has at length assumed the form of Christ's human nature. Another explanation has, however, been offered.[4]

2. B, xvi, 36–7.   3. B, xvi, 93, C, xix, 127. See Galatians 4.4.

4. Miss Day, *RES,* iii, 334, identifies Piers in his capacity as Christ's instructor as the Logos and traces the conception to Duns Scotus. But it seems contrary to the evidence to take Piers as the divine rather than the human part of Christ. In C it is Liberum Arbitrium who teaches Christ. According to Miss Day, *MLR,* xxiii, 23–4, C misunderstood B's Scotist conception of Piers when he permitted him to be replaced by Liberum Arbitrium, who is introduced as man's free will and therefore could not rightly act in place of the Logos. The point about the "misunderstanding" is valid only if we allow

It is obvious, of course, that allegory must not—indeed cannot—be read with the intellect alone, but must be interpreted by a sympathetic imaginative process. Even so, we cannot altogether ignore the demands of logical consistency, and it is necessary for us to make as much sense as possible of what we read. The Christ-Piers identification does not fit the vision of the Tree of Charity and it seems necessary to modify our views. An alternate interpretation has been put forward by Burdach, who, in his commentary on the poem, insists that the B-lines which seem to accomplish the identification of Piers with Christ, and in particular the Latin phrase, *Petrus, id est, Christus,* do not do so at all. On the evidence of I Corinthians 10.4, wherein St. Paul says of the water-giving rock from which the tribes of Israel drank, *petra autem erat Christus,* and on the evidence of what Burdach calls an old "speculation" that St. Peter is a source of life for men's souls, Burdach hazards the belief that the reference is not so much to Christ as to St. Peter.[5] That is, Piers is identified not with Christ but with Peter, who had received from Christ some of His effectiveness as a source of spiritual life. So far as the ability to see into men's hearts is concerned, Burdach denies that it is an exclusively divine attribute, since it was also given to the prophets.[6] Unfortunately, the details of Burdach's reasoning are not altogether clear, nor does he cite any medieval authority in support of his theory. Wells, however, seems to have arrived at the same conclusion independently, although he does not develop the argument.[7] The suggestion is extremely attractive, inasmuch as it enables us to continue to regard Piers as a man throughout the vision of the Tree of Charity and gets around some, if not all, of the difficulties enumerated in the last paragraph.

With Piers as a man, it becomes possible to reinterpret the vision. Miss Owen and Burdach have suggested, independently, that the scene

the identification of Piers with the Logos in B, which seems to me arbitrary. See Sanderlin's explanation of C's change, *MLN,* LVI, 452–3; also p. 187, n. 4, below.

5. *Ackermann,* pp. 311–12. Because Burdach's line of reasoning is obscure and possibly capable of another interpretation, I reproduce it here in full: "Hier fällt nun auch einem Blitzlicht gleich das Wort: *Petrus id est Christus.* Das darf man nicht verstehen, als sollte damit die Identität des Pflügers Peter mit dem göttlichen Heiland behauptet werden. Man darf es auch nicht einfach herleiten aus einem Willkürakt der Mystik, d. h. der in Typologie und Tropik schwelgenden, allegorisierenden Auslegung, die bekannt ist als interpretatio mystica. Vielmehr ist hier mit Petrus der Apostel Petrus gemeint auf Grund von 1. Cor. 10, 4. Und dieser Gleichsetzung des Menschen Christus mit dem in der Wüste Lebenswasser spendenden Fels, den der Stab des Moses öffnete, liegt eine alte vielverzweigte Spekulation zugrunde, die auch neben und nach Paulus fortlebte bis ins Mittelalter hinein. Der Apostel Petrus ist ein Quell des Lebens für die Gemeinschaft der menschlichen Seelen, die Gott suchen." Burdach goes on to say that the donation of Constantine was believed to have deprived Peter's successors of Peter's capabilities. This would explain why clerks are unable to recognize charity. See also *idem,* p. 341.

6. *Ackermann,* p. 312, n. 1.

7. See Wells, *op. cit.,* p. 298, where he says that the phrase, *Petrus, id est, Christus,* "almost certainly" refers to the Pope.

is not, as I have described it, twofold, giving first an allegory of the state of man after the Incarnation and then an allegory before the Incarnation, but a single allegory dealing with the pre-Christian era.[8] Such an interpretation is strongly supported by the image of the Trinity as three similar shafts—an image derived from the legends concerning the prehistory of the cross.[9] Nevertheless, there are several serious obstacles to its acceptance, the most troublesome being the mention of the Passion in Piers's description of the second prop, the wisdom of God the Father.[1] On the other hand, the part of Piers himself is somewhat clarified. He is mankind, or rather that elevated portion of mankind which includes the patriarchs and prophets—Moses, Abraham, David, Adam, and the others who prefigured Christ before the Incarnation just as St. Peter became Christ's vicar after the Ascension. The pre-Christian elements are perhaps enhanced by the earlier allusion to the rock which Moses smote to bring forth water (*Petrus, id est, Christus,* or *petra autem erat Christus*) and the later one to the tree of the Trinity, from which grew both the rod with which Moses smote the rock and, ultimately, the cross itself.[2] Considered in association with such details, the scene as an allegory of the pre-Christian era seems fairly satisfactory, if also extremely subtle. Piers is a man throughout, or at least until the moment when he hits out after the fiend with the second prop, thus beginning the Incarnation. At that moment he is, probably, still man, but man about to enter into a combination with God and hence almost divine himself. The poet comes close to the doctrine of deification.[3] After the moment when Piers's anger is aroused he ceases to be human nature in isolation and becomes the human nature of Christ, the Son of

8. See Owen, *Piers Plowman: a Comparison with Some Earlier and Contemporary French Allegories,* pp. 123-4, and Burdach, *Ackermann,* p. 228: "Die Vision des Lebensbaumes umfasst also nur das Leben der Menschheit bis zum Erlösungswerk Christi."

9. For the prehistory of the cross, see the references listed by Skeat, *EETS,* IV, 373-4, and by Burdach, *Ackermann,* p. 229, n. 1. Particularly interesting is the study, cited by Burdach, by Wilhelm Meyer, "Die Geschichte des Kreuzholzes vor Christus," *Abhandlungen der philosophisch-philologischen Classe der königlich bayerischen Akademie der Wissenschaften,* XVI (1882), II, 101-66. The best English version of the legend is that of the expanded Northern Passion, edited from MS Harleian 4196 by Richard Morris under the title "The Story of the Holy Rood," in *Legends of the Holy Rood,* EETS, 46 (London, 1871), pp. 62-86.

1. B, XVI, 36.   2. See Richard Morris, *op. cit.,* p. 74, ll. 439-56.

3. Miss Hort, *op. cit.,* p. 81, speaks of another passage in the poem as "suggestive of the paradox that man, if he remains man, ceases to be man; while if he tries to live according to the divine spark which is in him, he will become more than man, though still remaining man. But Langland has not pursued this line of thought to its conclusion—it would have led him straight on to the mystical doctrine of deification." And concerning B's conception of *Liberum Arbitrium* (discussed below) she notes, p. 115: "And again . . . we see how near Langland came to the doctrine of deification; the only thing wanting is its explicit formulation. Nothing . . . is good except a good will, because a good will is God himself." This is even more true of the C-text, in which Liberum Arbitrium, man's free will, becomes Libera Voluntas Dei. See C, XIX, 118-25 and the discussion below.

Mary who, herself human, nevertheless gave birth to the Son of God.

There remains the objection that if Piers is to be understood as man in the vision of the tree, then man is thrice represented—once in Piers, once in the fruit of the tree, and once by Liberum Arbitrium, man's free will. With respect to the first two, it is possible to regard Piers as the abstract ideal of the prophet-patriarch and his fruit as the souls of individual men. But this still leaves in doubt the part of Liberum Arbitrium. Up until the end of the vision, Liberum Arbitrium is described as performing much of the defense of the tree. What this division of labor between Piers and free will signifies I do not clearly know. One might suppose that Piers, inasmuch as he can make use of the first two persons of the Trinity, might also make use of the third; or, conversely, since Liberum Arbitrium can avail himself of the third prop, that he might also use the other two.[4] Twentieth-century inability to comprehend fourteenth-century allegory possibly accounts for some of our bewilderment, but one wonders whether it was not shared by a good many unsubtle, literal-minded medieval readers—whether, indeed, the incident of the Tree of Charity as it dictated itself to the B-author in terms of poetry is altogether susceptible of satisfactory rational explanation. The allegory seems too complex, too crowded. Although Burdach's interpretation of the phrase *Petrus, id est, Christus* lacks the documentation I should like to see supporting it, it is, I believe, substantially correct. But even though it clears up some of the difficulty, there are still a number of curiously shaped pieces that do not fit into the puzzle. Piers remains ambiguous and even redundant. One can only conclude that in his composition B got hold of an idea of such poetic splendor that he became blinded to its remoter ramifications and particularly to its extension into the field of logic.

We have had cause to notice before a strongly apparent tendency in the C-poet to shut the doors to uncertainty that B left open and to confine the sense of the poem within the walls of logic. Probably in no other part of *Piers Plowman* did B leave more doors open than in the vision of the Tree of Charity and no more strenuous effort in shutting them was required of C anywhere else. His revision was drastic. Instead of redefining Piers more clearly and setting forth in exact terms his relation to Liberum Arbitrium, C took the bold step of eliminating Piers altogether and replacing him by his former coworker, Liberum Arbitrium.

4. While grace, which is sought by man's free will, is considered an attribute of the Holy Ghost, I cannot find that in orthodox thought it was ever held to be exclusively the attribute of the Holy Ghost, and in C Liberum Arbitrium avails himself of all three props of the Trinity. Miss Day, *MLR*, xxiii, 23-4, objects that "man's free will could not have brought into action the power of the Father and the passion of Christ." Sanderlin, *MLN*, lvi, 451-3, suggests that C held with St. Anselm that *liberum arbitrium* is a faculty that seeks rectitude as its end, and hence that there is nothing wrong with representing a self-perfecting (or self-perfected) will as using all three piles to attain this end, or as acting as Christ's instructor.

Nor does the attempt to cast light on obscure matters stop there. The conversation between the Dreamer and his Instructor about the tree upon which the three props of the Trinity grew, a pluralizing of the tree image that threatens to turn the garden into a forest, is omitted.[5] That the Tree of Charity is also the Tree of Human Life is made evident at the very beginning of the vision, where the tree is given the name Imago Dei;[6] in B, this transition from one aspect of the tree to another is unlabeled. Since Piers is entirely replaced by Liberum Arbitrium, the division of labor between the two necessarily disappears. Also deleted is the puzzling statement that Liberum Arbitrium alone may sometimes suffice to ward off the devil, and the companion statement that the third prop is brought into use against the combined attacks of world, flesh, and devil. Moreover, the substitution of Elde for the proprietor of the garden as the agent in knocking down the apples seems a happy one.[7] Finally, with the elimination of Piers the problem of whether the incident is a pre- or post-Christian allegory becomes less insistent. I believe, however, that one can read it as a pre-Christian allegory without encountering too many inconsistencies. In all these alterations C seems to be endeavoring to get rid of difficulties; and if we grant that Liberum Arbitrium is a proper substitute for Piers, the incident as it is told in the C-version seems, on the whole, more intelligible than it does in B.

Clarification, however, must be judged as much by what is introduced as by what is deleted, and Liberum Arbitrium is a personage whom most of us find every bit as puzzling as his predecessor, and who certainly would win no popularity contest for characters in *Piers Plowman*. For all his changing significance, we are apt to feel at home with Piers himself, always recognizing in him (as, I am sure, the author intended us to do) the simple farmer to whom Truth sent a pardon. Liberum Arbitrium, on the other hand, is a formidable creation who owes his existence to scholastic theology—a not very ingratiating paternity. Of course C did not have to go far to find him, since he was already there, prefabricated by B, as Piers's lieutenant in the garden. All C had to do was promote him, albeit to a rank we might not suspect him worthy to receive—from Piers's lieutenant to Active's leader.[8] Let us examine his qualifications for this promotion in order to determine what was in C's mind when he made the substitution of Liberum Arbitrium for Piers.

St. Bernard of Clairvaux, discussing in their relationship to man the three types of freedom that God possesses perfectly—freedom of counsel,

---

5. We should observe that under discussion in B, xvi, 55–63 is an entirely different tree from that over which Piers is watching. It is upon this second tree that the props of the Trinity grew.

6. C, xix, 6–7. "Euene in þe myddes an ympe, as hit were, þat hihte *ymago-dei*, graciousliche hit growede."

7. Cf. C, xix, 106 with B, xvi, 75.

8. C, xvii, 158: "Thenne hadde actyf a ledere þat heyhte *liberum arbitrium*."

freedom of enjoyment, and freedom of choice—makes the following observations which seem pertinent to an understanding of C's conception of the character of Liberum Arbitrium:

Puto autem in his tribus libertatibus ipsam, ad quam conditi sumus, Conditoris imaginem atque similitudinem contineri: et imaginem quidem in libertate arbitrii, in reliquis autem duabus bipartitam quamdam consignari similitudinem. Hinc est fortassis, quod solum liberum arbitrium sui omnino defectum seu diminutionem non patitur, quod in ipso potissimum aeternae et incommutabilis divinitatis substantia quaedam imago impressa videntur. Nam, etsi habuerit initium, nescit tamen occasum, nec de justitia vel gloria capit augmentum: nec de peccato sive miseria detrimentum. Quid aeternitati similius, quod non sit aeternitas?[9]

Now I do not think that the C-poet was in any way directly acquainted with the theology of Bernard, although Skeat records two quotations from the Saint in *Piers Plowman*.[1] But I am entirely certain that some such doctrine about the will as this—whether Bernard's or some other medieval theologian's—transmitted, probably, through other minds, not all of them accurate, was known to the poet and that his creative imagination had grasped some of its essentials. According to the Bernardine system, *liberum arbitrium,* man's free will, or free choice, as it is better translated, is that part of man which bears the impress of the image of God to which man was created.[2] Although man has lost through sin some of the likeness originally inherent in the image, he may, by proper spiritual exercise, restore it. In the C-text, the Tree of Charity, which is also the Tree of Human Life, bears another name: Imago Dei, the Image of God. Indeed, it is by this name that the tree is first known. And if, acting upon this hint, we read the passage while associating Liberum Arbitrium with a Bernardine concept of the will,[3] the scene in the Garden of Heart will become more comprehensible and more suggestive. As Imago Dei, the tree signifies mankind. Simultaneously it signifies charity, the first example of which, so far as man is concerned, was his own creation by a loving God. The three props signify, of course, the Trinity. And the intermediary who can call upon the Trinity for defense against man's enemies is that faculty in man by which he most nearly approaches

9. *Migne,* CLXXXII, 1016. From chap. ix of Bernard's treatise, *De Gratia et Libero Arbitrio.*

1. At C, XII, 165, B, XI, 2; C, XVII, 221, B, XV, 59.

2. For a discussion of this point, see Étienne Gilson, *The Mystical Theology of St. Bernard,* A. H. C. Downes, tr. (New York, 1940), pp. 45–54.

3. Sanderlin, *MLN,* LVI, 453, n. 14, has pointed out that Liberum Arbitrium's self-description at C, XVII, 177, "a wil with a reyson," recalls St. Bernard's definition: *Porro voluntas est motus rationalis. . . . Habet sane, quocunque se volverit, semper rationem comitem, et quodammodo pedissequam: non quod semper ex ratione, sed quod nunquam absque ratione moveatur.* See *Migne,* CLXXXII, 1003. From chap. ii of *De Gratia.*

the Deity, Liberum Arbitrium, who in his very nature bears the image of God, the full likeness of which he may yet restore.

Another Bernardine concept may have been present in the C-poet's mind when he decided to make Liberum Arbitrium, rather than Piers, proprietor of the Tree of Charity. We must never forget that the poem as a whole amounts to a long, many-sided consideration of the problem of salvation. The scene in the Garden of Heart provides in a very real sense the turning point in the poem. Hitherto, the discussion has dealt in general and specific terms with a wide variety of topics related to the problem of salvation: with grace, with predestination, with the status of the heathen both before and after Christ, with the relative merits of learning and ignorance, the active life and patience. But from the moment the Holy Ghost speaks in Mary's ear the poem begins to deal with the first great cause of salvation, both directly in the Incarnation and in the organization whose aim is to perpetuate the effects of the Incarnation, the Church. The central figure in the turning point is Liberum Arbitrium. There is a peculiar appropriateness in the choice of this character if we suppose the poet to have been familiar, in one form or another, with a conception like Bernard's of the role *liberum arbitrium* plays in salvation:

Quid igitur agit, ais, liberum arbitrium? Breviter respondeo: Salvatur. Tolle liberum arbitrium, et non erit quod salvetur: tolle gratiam, non erit unde salvetur. Opus hoc sine duobus effici non potest: uno a quo fit; altero cui, vel in quo fit. Deus auctor est salutis, liberum arbitrium tantum capax: nec dare illam, nisi Deus; nec capere valet, nisi liberum arbitrium. Quod ergo a solo Deo, et soli datur libero arbitrio; tam absque consensu esse [*al.* effici] non potest accipientis, quam absque gratia dantis. Et ita gratiae operanti salutem cooperari dicitur liberum arbitrium, dum consentit, hoc est dum salvatur. Consentire enim salvari est.[4]

As George Sanderlin has said in an interesting but all too brief note on C's Liberum Arbitrium, the passage in C's vision of the tree is "an allegory of the cooperation of grace and free choice in the defense of the righteous soul against evil."[5] It is also, of course, something more than this. But viewed solely as an allegory of grace and free will it fits perfectly into its position in the poem.

With a Bernardine Liberum Arbitrium the scene in C unrolls comprehensibly and even with certain artistic improvements over the B-version. The description of the use of the three props is given in its simplified form, with Liberum Arbitrium as the agency that makes use of all three. The elaboration of the discourse concerning the fruit of the tree we could do without; still, it is characteristic of C while cleaning up B's canvas to smear his own a little. The truly impressive moment comes after Liberum Arbitrium, at the Dreamer's request, has bidden

4. *Migne,* CLXXXII, 1002. From chap. i of *De Gratia.*   5. *MLN,* LVI, 453.

Elde shake down some fruit from the tree. The devil is lurking in readiness, and as soon as the fruit falls he gathers it up and bears it away to limbo. And while the Dreamer's eyes, like our own, are on the fiend, a great alteration has taken place in Liberum Arbitrium:

> Þenne meuede hym mod *in maiestate dei,*
> Þat *libera uoluntas dei* lauhte þe myddel shoriere,
> And hitte after þe fende, happe hou hit myghte.
> *Filius,* hy þe faders wil, flegh with *spiritus sanctus,*
> To ransake þat rageman and reue hym hus apples,
> Þat fyrst man deceyuede thorgh frut and false by-heste.
> And þenne spake *spiritus sanctus* in gabrielis mouthe
> To a mayde þat hihte marie . . . .[6]

The sudden transformation of Liberum Arbitrium from man's free will to God's free will, paralleling what in the B-text I take to be the development of Piers from human nature to the almost divine nature that Christ was about to assume, has its own special grandeur. Doubtless such a transformation would find no sanction in Bernardine epistemology. Yet the creative mind, translating a mystical system into concrete images, could, if it so desired, render the metamorphosis easy. All one has to do is to make man's free will a sharer in the divine free will, a step that seems logically to follow Bernard's question, *Quid aeternitati similius, quod non sit aeternitas?*

I do not wish to imply that C superimposed upon the B-text a Bernardine idea of the will without taking into consideration what B's original idea of the will was. Liberum Arbitrium had, after all, been introduced by B, and there is reason to suppose that when C developed the character in the manner we have seen he was well aware of what it had meant to B. In order to show this, let me refer to an excellent analysis that has been made of the part Liberum Arbitrium plays in B. Miss Hort, discussing the significance of the vision of the Tree of Charity, makes the following comments:

The most important thing about man is his free will; it is that which is his final guard against evil. While man is in the process of growing into perfect charity, he is supported and helped by the power of God and by the wisdom of God; but when he is at length near his attainment, then the only thing that can help him and preserve him from sin is his own free will. He who sins against the Holy Ghost is he who sins of his own free will, by deliberate choice. However, free will can only overthrow the evil one by grace and through the help of the Holy Ghost.[7]

Miss Hort goes on to observe that the relation between free will and the Holy Ghost is not clear in the B-text. She believes, however, that the obscurity may be cleared up. The poet, in a later passage, identifies the

6. C, XIX, 118–25. See p. 186, n. 3, above.   7. Miss Hort, *op. cit.,* pp. 113–14.

Holy Ghost as the free will of the Father and the Son.[8] If we relate this fact to those already given us, we arrive at the conclusion that the B-poet "uses the term Liberum Arbitrium for the Holy Ghost in man, and that the meaning of the whole passage is that Liberum Arbitrium, the most important thing about man, is the Holy Ghost; that it is the Holy Ghost in man, helped by the Holy Ghost outside man, which finally leads man to salvation."[9] The identification of Liberum Arbitrium with the Holy Ghost is, as Miss Hort notes, apparently idiosyncratic and C omits it, along with the special connection between the two in the vision of the tree. He retains, however, more than a little of B's individuality and in particular B's tendency to deify free will—Active's "leader," as C calls it. This is apparent when Liberum Arbitrium becomes, without explanation, Libera Voluntas Dei—a transition which, whatever its relation to the Bernardine doctrine, would seem to have required impetus from elsewhere.[1] In B, man partakes of divinity in the possession of free will, which is the portion of the Holy Ghost that resides in him. In C, man also partakes of divinity in the possession of free will, which is, apparently, itself a portion of the free will of God. It needs only to introduce into C B's definition of the Holy Ghost as the free will of God to bring the two texts into complete agreement. And even though C omits this, we certainly have a striking resemblance between them, since things equal to the same thing are equal to each other. We should observe, therefore, that on the matter of the almost unlimited importance of Liberum Arbitrium, B and C are in accord, despite C's drastic revision. This suggests to me that B's conception of free will, as well as C's, derives ultimately from some doctrine similar to that of St. Bernard.

It is time to speak briefly about C's substitution of Liberum Arbitrium for B's Anima as the character who serves in the capacity of Prologue to Do-Bet. The explanation for this alteration provides us, I believe, with one more reason for the substitution of the same character for Piers and at the same time illustrates C's tendency to develop the poem upon lines already laid down in the B-text. Let us first recall that the dominant theme of Do-Bet is charity and then let us turn to B to find how charity is there defined. The definition is drawn from Anima by the Dreamer's somewhat cynical question through which he lets us know that his name is Long Will. Charity, Anima explains, is a childish thing,

> With-outen fauntelte or foly, a fre liberal wille.[2]

---

8. B, XVI, 220–4: "Þus in þre persones is perfitliche manhede, Þat is, man & his make & moillere her children, And is nouȝt but gendre of o generacioun bifor Ihesu cryst in heuene, So is þe fader forth with þe sone, and fre wille of bothe; *Spiritus procedens a patre & filio;* Which is þe holygoste of alle, and alle is but o god."

9. Miss Hort, *op. cit.,* p. 115.

1. Miss Day, *MLR*, XXIII, 24, seems to object to this development in the character of Liberum Arbitrium. But for Langland's tendency toward the doctrine of deification, see p. 186, n. 3, above.   2. B, XV, 146.

A free, liberal will: the phrase seems almost to be a punning translation of *liberum arbitrium,* as if the poet, along with later translators,[3] realized the inadequacy of the English "free will" to render the full sense of the Latin and took advantage of the relation between the adjectives *liber* and *liberal* to point his own translation in the direction of charity. The importance of the will as the emotional faculty, the faculty capable of experiencing love, is further emphasized by the B-poet in the repeated statement of Anima that charity is to be seen only in the will and hence is perceptible to none but Piers. It seems likely that the C-poet, desirous of emphasizing charity to the utmost, took the hint from B to make Liberum Arbitrium, the emotional faculty of the soul, serve as the prologue to a dramatization of charity. In adopting B's notion of the will as the love-making faculty C was also following the lead of the theologians, including Bernard,[4] from whom either B or C might have derived it. What C failed to do was to have Liberum Arbitrium expressly define himself as the seat of love—the sort of failure that is typical of both B and C. Nevertheless, if we again call into service the axiom that things equal to the same thing are equal to each other, then Liberum Arbitrium seems an appropriate person to play the part he does in Do-Bet.

The substitution is attended, however, by one superficially troublesome alteration and by another which seems more serious. The first of these occurs in the introductory speech by the Dreamer's interlocutor in the vision preceding that of the Tree of Charity. In the B-text the interlocutor, Anima, calls himself by nine names which describe the faculties of the soul according to a catalogue that goes back at least as far as Isidore of Seville,[5] from whom B directly quotes. Because of its antiquity we are apt to think of the catalogue as an invariable entity, like a listing of the forty-eight states of the Union. Thus C's addition of a name not included in B's list, Liberum Arbitrium, the most important of all the names in C, may seem to us, as it did to Skeat,[6] a violation of the laws of common sense. But we err if we assume that Isidore's catalogue formed any generally accepted summary of the soul. Alcuin, for instance, has another catalogue that varies in important respects from Isidore's,[7] and Sanderlin has pointed out that the list in C is exactly the same as that appearing in John of Damascus,[8] as reputable an authority as Isidore. I do not think that the change suggests that C was a partisan of a dif-

---

3. See G. B. Burch, ed., *St. Bernard's The Steps of Humility* (Cambridge, 1940), pp. 13–14; also *The Treatise of St. Bernard, Abbat of Clairvaux, concerning Grace and Free Will,* W. W. Williams, tr. (London, 1920), p. xi.

4. Burch, *op. cit.,* p. 12.   5. See Skeat's note to C, xvii, 201, *EETS,* iv, 338.

6. *Ibid.:* "It is hard to see how all these various names can be applied to Free Will."

7. Skeat, *ibid.,* gives a Middle English translation of Alcuin's catalogue.

8. *MLN,* lvi, 450–1. Sanderlin quotes the pertinent passage from John of Damascus as follows: *Libero ergo arbitrio appetit, et libero arbitrio vult et scrutatur, libero arbitrio inquirit et iudicat; libero arbitrio disponit, libero arbitrio eligit, et libero arbitrio impetum facit et libero arbitrio agit et operatur semper in his que secundum naturam sunt.*

ferent school of theological thought from B. Lists of the faculties of the soul seem to have been popular in medieval times and were apparently used as exercises in intellectual virtuosity. Thus a translation of Alcuin's appears in isolation in Lambeth MS 306;[9] the B-poet's sufficiently delighted Drayton that he turned it into an amiable, if rather implausible, sonnet;[1] and one John Cok took the trouble to copy C's in its entirety.[2] Possibly B found Isidore's in isolation in some MS or other and the same happened with respect to C and John Damascene's. Furthermore, while the catalogue B used may have been the best he could find, it does not, we should observe, really fit the requirements of the B-text. *Liberum arbitrium,* which turns out to be "the most important thing about man," is omitted, and the list does not even contain a good substitute. For no one, I think, would be willing to accept *animus,* the closest thing to will in the B-list. C was fortunate in running across the description he did, for what he needed—and what B needed, too—was a description wherein *liberum arbitrium* should appear as a universal power of the soul. And this, as Sanderlin has said, is precisely what John Damascene's description provides.[3]

The second alteration is more difficult to explain, inasmuch as it seems to involve a genuine doctrinal difference. In B, Anima tells the Dreamer that love, which exists only in the will, may not be perceived in works. In C, Liberum Arbitrium, who as will is the seat of charity, tells the Dreamer that love may be perceived in works and even emphasizes the fact.[4] Now it may be that this is a direct change of heart. On the other hand, C may have been driven to the alteration by the exigencies of logic: whereas it is proper for Anima to say that charity is perceptible only in the will, there is something rather awkward in having will say the same— the subtilization approaches absurdity. Actually, B's insistence upon the invisibility of charity seems an aberration from his normal trend of thought, since nowhere else does he even suggest that there is any flaw in the doctrine of good works. Furthermore, it is interesting that C, who affirms the value of works as an index of charity, is able to take over without modification B's description of charity—that is, his description of the external forms that charity takes. Thus B, having denied the validity of works as an index, is forced by logic to drop the subject then and there or else implicitly to deny his denial. It was the second of these courses that he chose to pursue.[5] I do not know what the source of B's

9. Originally printed by F. J. Furnivall, *Political, Religious, and Love Poems,* EETS, 15 (rev. ed., London, 1903), p. 65.   1. Reprinted by Skeat, *EETS,* IV, 338.

2. See Carleton Brown and R. H. Robbins, *The Index of Middle English Verse* (New York, 1943), p. 119, item 745.   3. *MLN,* LVI, 450.

4. Cf. C, XVII, 339, "Ac þorw werkes þou myght wite wher forþ he walkeþ; *Operibus credite,*" with B, XV, 203–04: "Þere-fore by coloure ne by clergye knowe shaltow hym neuere, Noyther þorw wordes ne werkes, but þorw wille one."

5. The description of Charity in B, XV, 210–52 is, of course, necessarily objective: Charity is known by his works.

idea was; it seems to be a curious, rather perverse extension of one of St. Paul's observations, "Though I bestow all my goods to feed the poor, and though I give my body to be burned, and have not charity, it profiteth me nothing."[6] C, however, was able to find a scriptural passage of equal authority and straightforward sense to support his point of view : *Operibus credite,* the means by which Christ told His followers that they might recognize His divinity.[7] Whatever the motive for it, C's alteration seems to have improved the logic of B and to have made the poem more consistent with what both B and C show elsewhere were the dominant tendencies of their thought.

Reading the C-version of the *Visio de Do-Bet* with a sympathetic rather than a hostile heart, it is possible for one to work out sensible explanations for the alterations that C made. Of artistic improvement there may not be a great deal and the lover of poetry will probably still prefer the B-version of Do-Bet. But taken as a thing in itself, the C-version should prove esthetically satisfying, and if we possessed only C's Do-Bet we should still be aware that we had a splendid piece of Middle English poetry. Furthermore, even on a comparative basis, the lover of clarity might prefer the later text. Let us take as a single illustration C's handling of Piers. Back in Do-Well, in the banquet scene, we were given a glimpse of him prophesying charity while representing, apparently, patience. Piers then passes from the poem for a long time. During the last passus of Do-Well and the earlier ones of Do-Bet we hear nothing about him except a single fugitive reference made by Liberum Arbitrium. This replaces B's three emphatic, and misleading, couplings of Piers with Christ which culminate in the phrase *Petrus, id est, Christus;* it consists of the single suggestive Latin line (also in B), *Et vidit deus cogitationes eorum,* following the statement that Piers has most perfect knowledge of charity.[8] We do not, in C, have to worry whether or not this identifies Piers with Christ, for when Piers finally takes the stage again it is in one body with Christ. Meanwhile the discussion has treated charity—Do-Bet—on various levels: through Liberum Arbitrium, the faculty which is alone capable of love; through the Tree of Charity, which reflects God's love for man in the relation between free will and salvation; in the Incarnation, when Christian charity came to earth; in the Samaritan, who as a symbol of charity becomes one with Christ and Piers Plowman; and ultimately in the Atonement, the supreme act of charity. It is in the Atonement that Piers is seen again. After the long interval since he appeared as Do-Well he reappears as Do-Bet. The patience is rewarded, the law fulfilled, and Piers, who had impugned all learning but love and truth, has made good his promise,

6. 1 Corinthians 13.3.
7. John 10.38.
8. C, xvii, 337.

> . . . ich shal preoue þat ich seide
> And a-vowe by-for God and for-sake hit neuere.

5. *Summary*

Near the beginning of this chapter I spoke of the similarity of the structure of the C-text of *Piers Plowman* to the incident recounted by St. Matthew concerning the rich young man who asked Christ two questions about salvation. I suggested that the first of the two answers he received—*Keep the commandments*—formed the subject of the *Visio de Petro Plowman,* while the second, beginning *If thou wilt be perfect,* formed the subject of the *Vita de Do-Well, Do-Bet, et Do-Best;* and that the first section of the poem dealt with the moral and social aspects of life, while the second dealt with its spiritual aspects. In the study of C's revisions of the religious allegory I have tried to show, among other things, that C's interest in active life virtually ended with the conclusion of the *Visio* and that the *Vita* takes up in turn various stages of a contemplative life. The first of these stages is patience (Do-Well) and the second charity (Do-Bet). It is time to face the issue which I originally avoided of trying to equate these stages of contemplative life with some known medieval triad comprehending the steps by which the soul may attain perfection.

I have presented at some length the evidence for believing that the C-poet was familiar with certain manifestations of a theological system similar to St. Bernard's, and it is to Bernard that we may look for analogue to the C-text's steps to perfection. According to the thinker who represents perhaps the fullest flowering of the contemplative school, the anagogic path consists of the three steps of humility, charity, and unity.[9] It is a peculiarity of the poet that in his long discussion of the first step he only occasionally describes it in terms that associate it directly with humility. Nevertheless, the names by which he calls the first step, poverty and patience, are aspects of humility—practical aspects of humility, one might say. St. Bernard was thinking in terms of monks,[1] with whom the problem of poverty, at least theoretically, did not occur. But the author of *Piers Plowman* was not, I am sure, a monk, and was endeavoring to point out the path of perfection not to monks but to any one who was interested in finding it. Therefore his translation of humility into the more objective patience, and retranslation of patience into the undeniably objective patient poverty, seems only natural. With charity, there is no similar problem, except that the poet of C emphasizes its external aspects more than the theologian does. For the final step on the path, unity, we are left without guidance: the C-poet made no alterations

9. See Burch, *op. cit.,* pp. 101–07. This book contains a most useful summary of St. Bernard's epistemology.   1. *Idem,* p. 1.

in the *Visio de Do-Best*. Perhaps he was satisfied with it as it stood; or perhaps he died before he could undertake its revision. I incline toward the second alternative. As it stands, Do-Best does not seem to contain much that is suggestive of the vision of God of St. Bernard. Nevertheless, in the section as it stands there are elements suggestive of the unitive condition of the soul, just as in B's Do-Well there is a good deal about patience and in B's Do-Bet the main theme is charity. Specifically, there is the constant repetition of the word *unity*, even though it usually signifies the Church.[2] But I am unable to make much out of this. Progress along the anagogic path is, of course, a gift of grace, both in Bernard and in *Piers Plowman*. As the poem ends in the B-text, and hence in C, this progress seems to have stopped short of its goal:

> "Bi cryste," quod conscience þo, "I will bicome a pilgryme,
> And walken as wyde as al þe worlde lasteth,
> To seke Piers þe plowman þat pryde may destruye,
> And þat freres hadde a fyndyng þat for nede flateren,
> And contrepleteth me, conscience; now kynde me auenge,
> And sende me happe and hele til I haue piers þe plowman!"
> And sitthe he gradde after grace til I gan awake.[3]

Perhaps if the C-poet had lived he might have had grace to continue on the path.

With respect to the question of authorship, the evidence considered in this chapter establishes nothing conclusive for either theory. It is altogether possible that a second poet should have revised the religious allegory of B in the manner we have seen. But if there was a second poet, the evidence points to his having been one of large capacities, both intellectual and artistic—a worthy successor to B. Furthermore, he seems to have had an extraordinarily thorough knowledge and understanding of the poem that he was rewriting, since the majority of his revisions have their source and their sanction in B. On the negative side, there is no evidence that C in any way perverted the meaning of the poem so that B would not have approved of it, no question of two different schools of theological thought. Rather, C developed lines of thought that were latent in B. St. Augustine's comment on certain discrepancies between the synoptic Gospels is perhaps relevant here: *Nihil obstat narrandi diversitas, ubi eadem dicuntur, maxime quum quisque evangelistarum eo ordine credat se dicere, quo Deus voluit.*[4] If we alter *evangelistarum* to *poetarum,* the remark seems applicable to B and C. Since the similarities between the texts far outweigh the differences, even where drastic re-

---

2. See C, XXII, 330 ff., B, XIX, 325 ff. Especially significant are the lines B, XX, 211–12 (C, XXIII, 212–13): "... I comsed to rowme Thorw contricioun & confessioun tyl I cam to vnite." Professor Meroney first called my attention to this passage.

3. B, XX, 378–84 (C, XXIII, 380–6).

4. Quoted from *Corpus Iuris Canonici*, E. L. Richter, ed. (Leipzig, 1922, 2 vols.), II, 913.

vision has taken place, I believe that we have to deal with but one poet, who remained ever discontent with what he had accomplished and, to the end of his life, kept striving to write in the way God wished—*eo ordine quo Deus voluit.*

VII

The Poet: Biographical Material

THE reader of *Piers Plowman* is almost inevitably seduced into making speculations about its author, so curiously provocative and attractive is the personality that casts its shadow upon every page of the poem. Indeed, for the modern reader the strong sense of personality is one of the poem's greatest charms. The poet seems to have been incapable of artistic aloofness. As a result, his personality, immensely verbose, self-consciously picturesque, ironical and realistic, tactless and inquisitive, playful yet savagely sincere, becomes, to a very large extent, his poem. This is true of all three texts but is, perhaps, most applicable to C, in which we have the poet's most candid bit of autobiography.[1] In a book dealing with the C-text I find it virtually impossible not to devote some pages to the author, and I propose in this chapter to discuss some of the probabilities of his life.

Biographical accounts by Skeat, Jusserand, Chambers, Coulton, and others are already in existence[2] and it may seem that to add another to the list, when almost all available facts have already been set forth, is either to make needless repetition or to multiply myths. Nevertheless I believe that the extant portrait of the poet, while essentially correct in its general outline, might benefit from being retraced with a heavier pencil. One's individual judgment will probably always be the final arbiter in settling the question of whether or not to accept as fact the biography of the poet, but previous accounts have either omitted or have dealt too briefly with certain historical evidence which tends to confirm the accuracy of the portrait and which should be taken into consideration in forming a final judgment. It is this evidence that I propose to adduce here, using it to illuminate the portrait that others have drawn.[3] I shall suggest only the most minor changes in essentials. My hope is that a somewhat less tenuous picture of the possible author may enhance his probability as well.

It will, of course, be necessary to speak of the poet in the singular number and hence it is suitable to give him a name. Of a choice of several,

1. C, VI, 1–104.
2. See Skeat, *EETS,* IV, xxxi–xxxii, and *CP, II,* xxxii–xxxviii; Jusserand, *Mysticism,* pp. 86–102; Chambers, *Mind,* pp. 167–8; Coulton, *Medieval Panorama,* pp. 143–8; also Coghill's introduction to Wells's translation, pp. vii–xi, and Bright's *New Light on "Piers Plowman."* The last has interesting suggestions, but much of it seems far-fetched.
3. In this chapter I am particularly indebted to Coulton's brief but most suggestive study (see note above), which called my attention to Lyndwood.

William Langland seems the best.[4] Hitherto, partly because it was convenient and partly because I wanted to attain some semblance of scientific detachment, I have tried to refer to the poet only anonymously or alphabetically—though, like cheerfulness upon the would-be philosopher in Boswell, Langland was always breaking in. Any such effort is now abandoned: William Langland will be spoken of as the single author of the three versions of *Piers Plowman*.

There is little point in going over much-trodden ground again and it will suffice to note here that the evidence, both internal and external, points to the name William Langland as the author:[5] William, because the Dreamer remains constantly Will throughout all parts of the poem[6] and because that is to whom it is ascribed by colophons in a number of MSS of all classes,[7] by a note written on MS E[8] and by a note written on MS Hm 128 which also gives the alternate *Robert;*[9] Langland because of the possible anagram at B, xv, 148[1] and because that is the name given by the notes on MSS E and Hm 128, as well as by Bale.[2] Actually, the name is now no more than a point of focus for scholarship, since nothing has yet been turned up concerning the historical William Langland.[3] Even if it were possible to prove beyond a shadow of doubt that the author of even one of the texts was William Langland, we should not be much farther along in *Piers Plowman* studies than we are now.

The best starting point for a discussion of the author's life, and the focal point for a discussion of his occupation, is the well-known passage in the C-text to which reference has already been made. In the earlier

4. Alternate names include William Langley, Robert Langland, William de Rokayle, and William de Colewell. For the first two, as well as other alternatives, see Skeat's summary, *CP*, II, xxvii–xxxii. For the third, see Oscar Cargill, "The Langland Myth," *PMLA,* L (1935), 36–56. For the last, see Bright *op. cit.*, especially p. 42.

5. For a complete summary of the evidence, see J. E. Wells, *A Manual of the Writings in Middle English, 1050–1400* (New Haven, 1916), pp. 250–2.

6. In the A-text at VIII, 43, IX, 118, XII, 51; in B at V, 62, VIII, 124, XV, 148; in C at II, 5, VII, 2, XI, 71. Also at A, XII, 89, 99, 103 (as numbered in *CP*, I), but the author of these lines may have been John But.

7. Most of the colophons mentioning Will appear at the point of division between the *Visio* and the *Vita*. They are of two types, those reading *Willelmi* and those (MSS C2UDXH2YIT) reading *Willelmi .W.* What the *.W.* stands for has not been satisfactorily explained. See J. E. Wells, *op. cit.*, p. 251; Skeat, *EETS*, I, xxv, 102; II, 121; III, xxxvii, 176, 179; Carnegy, *An Attempt to Approach the C-Text of Piers the Plowman*, p. 24.

8. MS Trinity College, Dublin, D.4.1 (C-text): *Memorandum, quod Stacy de Rokayle, pater Willielmi de Langlond, qui Stacius fuit generosus, et morabatur in Schiptone under Whicwode, tenens domini le Spenser in comitatu Oxon., qui praedictus Willielmus fecit librum qui vocatur Perys Ploughman.* Quoted from *CP*, II, xxviii, n. 1.

9. MS Huntington Library Hm 128 (formerly Ashburnham 130): "Robert or william langland made pers ploughman." See *EETS*, II, xxii. According to R. B. Haselden and H. C. Schulz in a note in *HLB*, VIII, 26–7, the inscription is of the sixteenth century. For the possible origin of *Robert*, see Skeat, *EETS*, II, xxviii, n. 3, and Chambers in Bright, *op. cit.*, pp. 24–5.   1. "I haue lyued in londe, . . . my name is longe wille."

2. *Robertus Langelande, sacerdos, ut apparet.* . . . See *EETS*, I, xxxiv–xxxv.

3. For information about Langland's putative father, Stacy de Rokayle, see Cargill, *PMLA,* L, 46–56; Bright, *op. cit.*, pp. 35–7.

versions, and especially in B's Do-Well section, we find scattered references to the events of Langland's life and hints about his character,[4] but all these stray notes are assembled, expanded, augmented, and made explicit in the C-passage—probably an insertion made after the completion of the first revision of the passus in which it stands, as we have already seen.[5] Let us examine these biographical details that the poet, suddenly interrupting the sequence of his visions after the dream of Lady Meed, saw fit to entrust to his reader.

Briefly, they are these. Langland, at least at one time, lived in a small house in the Cornhill district of London, along with Kit, who is elsewhere identified as his wife (his daughter Calote is not mentioned here, though she is introduced later in C and also in B).[6] He was accustomed to go about clothed like a loller, probably in long drab homespuns,[7] but he was not popular with London lollers, whom he treated as Reason taught him—probably with scorn and distrust.[8] At the time when he had been sound of mind and body[9] he had been reluctant to work and liked nothing better than the good life of drinking and sleeping. He considered himself, or pretended to consider himself, too weak for farm work and too tall for manual labor that involved stooping. As a youth he had been put to school by his father and his friends and he had there learned the meaning of Holy Writ. The only life he had found satisfactory since his friends died was that which he lived in his long clothes. He made his living by saying prayers for the souls of those who supported him. He was welcomed to the houses of his benefactors when he came to visit them once a month or so. These visits, he admitted, amounted to a sort of begging, but he carried no bag or bottle as a professional beggar did and hence "begged" only for his immediate board. He was a clerk of the Church, having received the tonsure. Finally, he admitted that much of his life had been wasted.

To attempt to test the historical authenticity of any of the details of fourteenth-century life given us by *Piers Plowman* would seem, at the very least, an act of ingratitude. Among social historians, if not among students of English literature, the poem is accorded high rank as an original source of information concerning medieval England.[1] What-

4. For a complete list of internal references, see J. E. Wells, *op. cit.*, pp. 252–3.

5. See Chapter II above.

6. Kit and Calote are identified at B, xviii, 426, C, xxi, 473. Reference is made to the Dreamer's wife again at B, xx, 192, C, xxiii, 193.

7. Or russet. See C, xi, 1 (A, ix, 1, B, viii, 1): "Thus robed in russett ich romede a-boute."

8. Skeat renders C, vi, 5, "For ich made of þo men as reson me tauhte," by, "For I composed verses about those men, etc." See *EETS*, iv, 87. I agree with Sisam, *Fourteenth Century Verse and Prose*, p. 233, that this is a forced translation.

9. Skeat reads for C, vi, 10, "In hele and in vnite on me aposede," but the reading of MSS IX, *In hele and in inwitte*, seems preferable. The latter doublet occurs at C, xi, 180.

1. See, for instance, the indices of the following under *Langland* and *Piers Plowman*:

ever we believe to be the truth about the author's identity, we must regard him as something of an expert on his times. Similarly, though we may deny the existence of any connection between the person described in the preceding paragraph and the author, we can hardly deny that the description was applicable to some one living in medieval London. As Coulton says, it is *ben trovato,* if not *vero.*[2] Yet curiously enough, ever since Wright's remarkably bad guess that it was "intended as a satire against the mendicant friars,"[3] a number of critics, including some influential ones, have persisted in regarding the passage as an obscurely motivated description of no one in particular. To several of these I shall refer below. At the moment I propose to discuss several of the details of the description in the light of contemporary material. It is not my aim to show that Langland knew what he was talking about; rather I should like to make sure that we know what he was talking about and, so far as possible, to deprive those who would misunderstand or ignore the passage of the excuse that the portrait it paints is too fanciful for analysis. The three points with which I shall be chiefly concerned are Langland's position as a clerk of the Church, his position as a married clerk, and his means of livelihood. On none of these matters, probably, would a fourteenth-century reader have required commentary. But the most common facts of one generation sometimes become more obscure with the passage of time than those more recondite, and today we know a good deal more about medieval bishops, of whom there were relatively few, than we do about minor clerks, of whom there were thousands.

Langland tells us that he was a clerk and, since he also tells us that he was a married man, we are fairly safe in assuming that he was a clerk in minor orders.[4] But what was a clerk in minor orders? The best source of information, on the canonical side, is Bishop William Lyndwood's heavily annotated collection of the ecclesiastical statutes enacted under the Archbishops of Canterbury—the vast *Provinciale,* prepared during the early years of the fifteenth century.[5] According to Lyndwood, there were seven or nine clerical orders, depending on how one chose to define

---

L. F. Salzman, *English Life in the Middle Ages* (London, 1926) ; Jusserand, *English Wayfaring Life in the Middle Ages,* L. T. Smith, tr. (2d ed., London, 1920) ; D. M. Stuart, *Men and Women of Plantagenet England* (New York, 1932) ; G. G. Coulton, *Social Life in Britain from the Conquest to the Reformation* (Cambridge, England, 1919) ; and Miss Chadwick's *Social Life in the Days of Piers Plowman,* which is based upon the poem.

2. Coulton, *Medieval Panorama,* p. 143.

3. *The Vision and Creed of Piers Ploughman,* II, 514.

4. It is evident from C, VI, 53 ff. that the poet had received the tonsure. The possibility of his having been a priest is discussed below.

5. For editions, see article on Lyndwood in *DNB.* I have used that published at Oxford in 1679 under the title *Provinciale (seu Constitutiones Angliae),* to which I give in parentheses page and note references. After extensive legal and diplomatic experience under Archbishop Henry Chichele of Canterbury, Lyndwood became, in 1442, Bishop of St. David's. The *Provinciale* was completed in 1433.

the word *order* (*ordo*). The holy orders, all agreed, included priest, deacon, and subdeacon; to which some added bishop at the top of the hierarchy. The minor orders included acolyte, exorcist, lector, and ostiary; to which some added psalmist, or first tonsure, as the lowest of all.[6] The word *psalmist* as a synonym for *first tonsure* (*tonsuratus*) seems to have come into being as a result of the practice of assigning to those who had received only the first tonsure the task of reading aloud the Psalms prescribed for various church services.[7] According to one point of view, only when the *tonsuratus* had been given this assignment did he become a member of a clerical order. But according to Lyndwood, so long as any *tonsuratus* preserved his tonsure and wore garments distinct from those of the laity, he was entitled to benefit of clergy (*privilegium clericale*)[8] and hence continued to enjoy the most important secular privilege accorded to the medieval clergy—immunity from arrest by the secular arm in connection with most types of crime and the right to trial before ecclesiastical courts.

In theory, then, there were five possible grades that a clerk in minor orders might occupy in the Church. English practice, however, seems to have cut this number down to three at the most and, for practical purposes, to two: the highest, acolyte, and the lowest, first tonsure. A survey of the ordination lists contained in the published Bishops' Registers of the fourteenth century[9] has revealed to me not a single mention of lectors or ostiaries and only one mention of exorcists. The latter occurs in the register of Bishop John Gilbert of Hereford, who, on May 19, 1380, ordained six exorcists at Bromyard Church.[1] This is in contrast to the

6. *Provinciale*, Bk. III, Tit. I (p. 117, n. c).

7. *Ibid.* Also Guilelmis Durantis, *Rationale Divinorum Officiorum* (Venice, 1485), Bk. II, "De Psalmista": *Psalmistatus quandoque tonsoratus vocatur. . . . Dictus est autem psalmista a psalmis dicendis sive ab officio canendi prout sub lectore dicetur.* According to J. Tixeront, *L'Ordre et les ordinations* (Paris, 1925), p. 102, there had originally been no such thing as a *tonsuratus* divorced from one of the four other minor orders. Possibly the office of psalmist was devised to do away with the anomalous class of *tonsurati* after it had uncanonically come into being.

8. *Provinciale*, Bk. II, Tit. 2 (p. 92, n. e); also the definition of clerical privileges, *idem*, Bk. I, Tit. 14 (p. 68, n. t). For the legal rights and immunities enjoyed by the clergy, see R. Génestal, *Le Privilegium fori en France du décret de Gratien à la fin du XIVe siècle* (Paris, 1921–24, 2 vols.).

9. Space does not permit a listing of all the published Bishops' Registers. See, among others, the publications of the Canterbury and York Society (Dioceses of Canterbury, Carlisle, Hereford, Lincoln, London, Rochester, Salisbury, and Winchester); of the Somerset Record Society (Bath and Wells); of the Hampshire Record Society (Winchester); of the Sussex Record Society (Chichester); of the William Salt Archaeological Society of Staffordshire (Lichfield and Coventry); of the Surtees Society (York); of the Worcestershire Historical Society (Worcester); of the Surrey Record Society (Winchester); the Cymmrodorion Record Series (St. David's); and the series for Exeter edited by F. C. Hingeston-Randolph and O. J. Reichel.

1. *Registrum Johannis Gilbert, Episcopi Herefordensis, 1375–1389*, J. H. Parry, ed. (London, 1915), p. 144. There is no record of the further advancement of these exorcists. A century later (1486), Bishop John Martin of St. David's also ordained a number of exorcists, but these were straightway advanced to the position of acolyte. See *The*

thousands who were ordained acolyte or were given the first tonsure.[2] Elsewhere in the registers, particularly in dimissory letters, a clear distinction is made between acolytes and *tonsurati*,[3] but I have been able to find no cleric identified as a member of one of the other minor orders. Middle English literature seems equally silent. The *Oxford Dictionary*, while it records English forms of *acolitus* as early as 1000 and throughout the fourteenth century, gives no instance of *lector* before 1483, none of *exorcist* in the technical sense before 1560, and none of *ostiary* until after 1432. *Benet,* a synonym for *exorcist,* occurs in the technical sense in Wycliffe, and *reader,* a synonym for *lector,* occurs as early as 961 and several times before Wycliffe but does not seem in any example to refer unequivocally to a specific clerical order.[4] Finally, it should be observed that Lyndwood's discussion of the minor orders, except when he is talking about acolytes and *tonsurati,* does not leave one with the impression that the canonist knew the subject fully at first hand, for he relies heavily on such earlier and un-English legalists as Henry of Segusia.[5] It seems likely, therefore, that with respect to the minor orders, fourteenth-century English practice deviated widely from that outlined in canon law.[6]

The virtual disappearance of the orders of lector, exorcist, and ostiary was probably due to the practice of ordination *per saltum.* Originally a clerk was expected to pass through several of the minor orders on his way to holy orders, and he was obliged to spend a definite term as either exorcist, lector, or ostiary before he could become acolyte, and another term as acolyte before he could be ordained subdeacon.[7] But these in-

Episcopal Registers of St. David's, 1397–1518, R. F. Isaacson, ed. (London, 1917–20, 3 vols.), II, 483, 489, 499, 509, etc.

2. See, for example, the ordination lists in the registers of John Trillek, Thomas Charlton, William Courtenay, Simon Sudbury, John Halton, Lewis Charlton, John Gilbert, and John Trefnant, published by the Canterbury and York Society.

3. Thus William Wykeham, in issuing dimissory letters, carefully notes that Richard Gomfrey and William Elstoke are acolytes, while Hugh de Buckynhulle has only the first tonsure. See *Wykeham's Register,* T. F. Kirby, ed. (London, 1896–99, 2 vols.), I, 283.

4. See *OED* under nouns mentioned. *Exorcist* occurs in Wycliffe in reference to an expeller of evil spirits, but the sense is nontechnical.

5. See *Provinciale,* Bk. III, Tit. I (p. 117, n. *c*). Henry of Segusia, called Hostiensis, flourished about 1255. See M. Buchberger's *Lexikon für Theologie und Kirche* (Freiburg, 1930–38, 10 vols.) IV, 934.

6. Miss E. K. Lyle, *The Office of an English Bishop in the First Half of the Fourteenth Century* (University of Pennsylvania, 1903), p. 121, remarks that it is "quite certain that the minor orders, that of acolyte excepted, had fallen into disuse." Tixeront, *op. cit.,* p. 92, says that in sixth- and seventh-century Rome "les acolytes prirent de plus en plus d'importance. Les exorcistes cessant d'exercer leurs fonctions, et les lecteurs se consacrant surtout à chanter, les acolytes devinrent presque les seuls clercs inférieurs en service actif." The disappearance of the intermediate orders seems, therefore, to have been common throughout the Church.

7. *Idem,* pp. 229–30; also the article on holy orders, *The Catholic Encyclopedia* (New York, 1907–14, 16 vols.), XI, 279 ff.

terstices, as the terms were called, were generally abandoned by the fourteenth century.[8] Lyndwood duly notes the strictures of earlier canonists who inveigh against ordination *per saltum* for the minor orders but admits that he is unable to find anything in the pertinent statute of Archbishop Peckham that would prevent one person from receiving all the minor orders in one day.[9] He is firm, however, on the point that one candidate should not receive both the first tonsure and the other minor orders at one ceremony, although he carefully explains how the interstice can be reduced to a minimum of a few minutes.[1] Many bishops seem to have kept the ceremony of first tonsure altogether separate from that of acolyte, and so far as I can ascertain, many *tonsurati* advanced no farther in the ranks of the clergy.[2] A number of bishops leave no record of conferring the first tonsure,[3] but whether this is because they made all candidates acolytes without exception, omitting the stage of first tonsure or invariably performing the two offices together, or because they did not trouble to take the names of the *tonsurati,* I am unable to say.[4]

Langland's position may have been either that of acolyte or of *tonsuratus.* If the latter was really known in England as psalmist, and if he actually had the job of reading Psalms,[5] we might find a particular

8. Miss Lyle *op. cit.,* p. 121, observes that the names of the minor orders were retained in England, "and the clergy required to pass through them, but this was probably done at one ordination." Tixeront, *op. cit.,* p. 230, denies that clergy was required to pass through all the minor orders. But as Miss Lyle says, the Roman Pontifical provides that ostiaries shall be ordained after the first lesson, lectors after the second, and so forth, so that it is possible that a clerk being ordained acolyte acquired the other orders at the same time. Some weight is lent this theory by the account of the degradation of William Sawtre in 1400. The ceremony stripped him in turn of the badges of office of all the orders, major and minor, and even provided for the removal of the tonsure. See F. I. Cutts, *Scenes and Characters of the Middle Ages* (London, 1872), pp. 214–15. But when Bishop Martin records that of clerks ordained acolyte only certain ones were ordained exorcist, he suggests that the conferring of two orders at the same ceremony was unusual. See p. 203, n. 1, above. Probably the practice varied from place to place, and from bishop to bishop.

9. *Provinciale,* Bk. v, Tit. 11 (p. 310, n. *x* and *c*).

1. *Ibid,* (n. *x*): *Mihi videtur, quod opinio Hostiensis intellegi potest vera, ut scilicet in generali celebratione Ordinum prima Tonsura non detur cum aliis quatuor in aperto; potest tamen eodem die ante inchoationem Missae celebrationis Ordinum private conferri.*

2. Of a list of fifty-four *tonsurati* ordained in Simon Sudbury's first year as Bishop of London, forty-two are not mentioned again in the succeeding years of his incumbency. See *Registrum Simonis de Sudburia,* R. C. Fowler and others, eds. (London, 1927–38, 2 vols.), II, 1 ff.

3. Of the bishops listed on p. 204, n. 2, above, Trillek, Thomas Charlton, Halton, and Trefnant record only the names of acolytes ordained, while the others list both acolytes and *tonsurati.*

4. The second alternative seems the more probable. Thomas Brantyngham is careful to record the fact, as if it were irregular, that he gave a certain canon the first tonsure and then *incontinenti postmodum* ordained him acolyte. See *The Register of Thomas de Brantyngham, Bishop of Exeter,* F. C. Hingeston-Randolph, ed. (London, 1901–6, 2 vols.), II, 829.

5. The only evidence for the use of the term *psalmist* in connection with *tonsuratus* in England that I have found is DuCange's citation of Lyndwood: *Prima tonsura, quae apud nos vocatur Psalmistatus, non est ordo, sed tantum dispositio ad ordinem,* where

felicity in the idea of Langland's having been a psalmist : *psalmistatus* he certainly was, in heart if not in title. But there is some slight evidence for thinking that he was an acolyte. In the dialogue between Reason and the poet in the C-text, the former asks him whether he can serve or sing in a church.[6] This question is the first of a whole series, until the completion of which Langland has no chance to get a word in. When he does reply, he does so in a half-serious, half-jocular, and altogether ambiguous way. Furthermore, his speech is so cast that we cannot tell whether he is answering all Reason's questions, or only the last.[7] We may observe, however, that Reason bases his questions in the main on Langland's unfulfilled capabilities and that he postulates nothing that a man slightly acquainted with the poet would not consider him able to do. The dialogue thus suggests that Langland was an acolyte, who would be expected to serve at the altar of a church, but that for one reason or another he was not performing his office.

That a clerk in minor orders in the medieval Church could take a wife is now and always has been a commonplace, though a commonplace that has had some difficulty in getting itself firmly established in scholars' minds.[8] The canon law is perfectly clear on the subject, and Lyndwood repeats on several occasions the fact that matrimony was permitted to clerks in orders below that of subdeacon.[9] But the law did impose certain limitations upon married clerks. In the first place, no married clerk could, without the greatest irregularity, advance beyond the grade of acolyte.[1] That married clerks sometimes did advance beyond this grade, and that there were married priests, does not, I think, affect the present discussion : Langland may have been irregular in some respects but not in so important a point. In the second place, according to a strict interpretation of canon law, a married clerk was held to have separated himself from the clergy and to have identified himself with the laity, so far as participation in the celebration of the services of the Church was concerned. It is true that, outside the church, he was still considered a clerk in that he was still permitted to enjoy the *privilegium clericale* so long as he preserved the tonsure and wore clothing which distinguished him from the laity.[2] But in other respects he was no different from a layman

---

apud nos may mean "in England" or "in this book" (the *Provinciale*). I have been unable to find the sentence in Lyndwood. See *DuCange, psalmistatus.*

6. C, VI, 12.

7. C, VI, 22 ff. Langland's first words are : "Certes, . . . and so me god helpe, Ich am to waik to worche with sykel oþer with sythe, And to long, leyf me, lowe for to stoupe."

8. Even Skeat shows some uncertainty. See his note which suggests that he believed Langland's marriage to have been contrary to the spirit, if not the practice, of the Church in his day, *CP,* II, xxxvii and n. 2.

9. *Provinciale,* Bk. III, Tit. 3 (p. 128) : Statute *Si qui clerici;* also *idem,* Bk. I, Tit. 8 (p. 45, n. *c*).

1. *Idem,* Bk. III, Tit. 3 (p. 129) : Statute *Cum ex eo.*

2. *Idem,* Bk. III, Tit. 7 (p. 142, n. *q*) : *Si autem fuerit Conjugatus, non tamen Bigamus, dum tamen habitum & tonsuram gerat Clericales, habebitur ut Clericus in duobus; ut*

and inside the church he took his place with them and not with the celibate clergy.[3] Furthermore, he lost whatever *titulus* he might have possessed as a single man: that is, he could hold no regular sustaining ecclesiastical position, although he could, according to Lyndwood, receive a fee for performing various janitorial duties.[4] He could no longer serve at the altar, however, and hence he could not, theoretically, hold the position of parish clerk.[5]

Canon law, then, did not provide for the maintenance of married clerks on active service except as janitors: it merely permitted minor clerks to marry if they desired a wife more than they did service in the Church. Thus the minor orders held roughly the same position in regard to the secular clergy as the novitiate did in regard to the regular. Celibacy remained, however, the prerequisite for genuine ecclesiastical service and theoretically it was impossible for a married acolyte to fulfill the functions of his order. It would, of course, be a gross exaggeration to suggest that the law was strictly enforced. At a time when the Church was still having trouble with married priests, one would scarcely expect too scrupulous enforcement in respect to the minor clergy. Lyndwood himself, in speaking of parish clerks, whose duties must have required the rank of acolyte,[6] clearly echoes a liberal interpretation of the law when he says that a married man might continue to serve the parish priest *in defectu Clericorum non conjugatorum.*[7] Doubtless the shortage of unmarried clerks would always seem acute to a priest who had a good, though married, parish clerk and did not want to lose him. According to Ditchfield, a number of fourteenth-century parish clerks in good standing had wives.[8]

We should be careful, on the other hand, not to make the mistake of assuming that canon law was never enforced upon the minor clergy. Coulton states that occasionally a bishop recorded an objection to a

---

scilicet in Persona gaudeat Privilegio Clericali . . . & non trahatur coram Judice Saeculari. . . . In caeteris vero habebitur ut Laicus. . . . Clericus conjugatus non stabit, nec sedebit inter Clericos, sed inter Laicos. This is one of the several passages from Lyndwood to which Coulton refers, *op. cit.,* pp. 143 ff.

3. A clear discussion of the meaning of the word *titulus* is given by J. M. Moeder, *The Proper Bishop for Ordination and Dimissorial Letters* (Washington, D. C., 1935), pp. 1–18. *Titulus* originally signified the church "at which clerics were stationed," but it later became identified with *beneficium,* the portion of a church's temporal good reserved for the use of a single clerk. By Lyndwood's time, the word seems ordinarily to have become synonymous with *beneficium.*

4. *Provinciale,* Bk. III, Tit. 3 (p. 128, n. i).

5. *Idem,* Bk. III, Tit. 7 (p. 142, n. q): *Unde ex praemissis apparet, quod istud officium* [that of *aquaebaiulus,* or parish clerk] *non debet conferri Clerico conjugato. Quia Clericus iste habet deservire Presbytero in Altari; secum Cantare; & Epistolam legere.*

6. For the duties of a parish clerk, see last note and P. H. Ditchfield, *The Parish Clerk* (New York, 1907), pp. 31–62. Tixeront, *op. cit.,* p. 93, describes acolytes as "essentiellement des *suivants (sequentes)* qui accompagnaient l'évêque, et se trouvaient toujours à sa disposition"—parish clerks in essence.

7. *Provinciale,* Bk. III, Tit. 7 (p. 142, n. q).   8. Ditchfield, *op. cit.,* p. 35.

married parish clerk,[9] and it is probable that certain scrupulous clerks voluntarily withdrew themselves from ecclesiastical service upon marriage. I am disposed to believe that this is what Langland did. We know that he was intensely orthodox, if a little old-fashioned, in most of his religious opinions and that he never expresses any dissatisfaction with canon law itself, so that it hardly seems likely that he would flout it, even though to do so was not uncommon. In any case, whether he withdrew voluntarily from the Church's service upon his marriage, or whether he encountered a bishop who was a stickler for the letter of the law, or whether, indeed, he had other reasons for not wishing to associate himself closely with the Church, the position he describes himself to be in is that of a married clerk in minor orders—acolyte or *tonsuratus*—without *titulus* or other connection with a specific church. This is, indeed, the very position in which we should expect to find a married acolyte if canon law were strictly enforced. Certainly, the Church was no longer providing for him, even though in the Church lay his greatest interest.[1] Yet despite his severance from the Church he preserved, apparently, both the tonsure and those distinctive clothes which set him apart from the laity.

How did a married clerk without benefice make his living? He might, as many did, make use of his learning to perform secretarial or stenographic functions, and it has been several times suggested that Langland may have found occasional employment as a clerk—in the modern sense—inditing charters and wills.[2] Langland himself says nothing about working in this way. According to his account, he supported himself by praying for the souls of those who gave him food and he goes so far as to name six of the "tools" of his profession: Placebo, Dirige, the Psalter, the Seven Psalms, the Pater Noster, and the Primer.[3] On the basis of this statement, it has been generally agreed that he earned his living by saying prayers for the souls of the dead.

The evidence for this assumption is, of course, good, for all these tools were used in medieval England in the performance of intercessory services for souls in purgatory. All but one are included in the list given in the early fifteenth-century *Vision of William Staunton*, which Skeat quotes in his notes.[4] St. John of Bridlington tells William that souls may be helped out of purgatory "as to lernyd men as bi masses singyng, saing of sawters, *placebo,* and *dirige,* commendacions, .vij. psalmes, and the .xv. psalmes, with the letenye, bi almesdede and bi pilgrimage: and also bi lewidmen with the *pater noster,* the *ave Maria,* and the crede,

9. Coulton, *op. cit.,* p. 145.
1. Coulton suggests that Langland may have at one time served as a parish clerk, though he warns that there is no direct evidence for such a theory. See *idem,* p. 146. It is certainly more likely that Langland was a parish clerk than that he was a priest.
2. Skeat, *EETS,* IV, xxx; Jusserand, *Mysticism,* p. 96.
3. C, VI, 45–8. 4. *EETS,* IV, 89.

almesdede, fastyng, and pilgrimage, and bi many other good dedis."[5]
Testators of the fourteenth century—and, in greatly increasing numbers,
those of the fifteenth and sixteenth centuries—commonly devised that
some of these acts of devotion be performed for the sake of their souls.
By all odds the most popular—since it was also believed to be the most
efficacious—of the offices was the Mass. Of rather less popularity, but
still in great demand, were Placebo and Dirige.[6] The former of these,
Vespers of the Dead, is relatively short, consisting of six Psalms and the
Magnificat with antiphons, the short prayer *Inclina, domine, aurem tuam,*
and prayers for the departed soul.[7] Dirige is divided into two parts, for
Matins and Lauds, and is a longer office. The first part is subdivided
into three nocturnes, each with three psalms and three readings, with
antiphons. The second part consists of eight psalms with antiphons,
selections from Isaiah and Luke, the prayer *Inclina, domine,* and special
prayers as in Placebo.[8] Both Placebo and Dirige have, of course, appropriate versicles and responses.

The other items in the catalogue of intercessory offices seem to have
possessed a less uniform popularity.[9] The Seven Penitential Psalms—
favorite subject for commentary—are frequently requested in medieval

5. Thomas Wright, *St. Patrick's Purgatory* (London, 1844), p. 149. The *Vision of
William Staunton* appears in full in G. P. Krapp, *The Legend of St. Patrick's Purgatory: Its Later Literary History* (Baltimore, 1900).

6. For but a single one of a vast number of instances, see the will of Thomas More,
written in 1419: *Item volo quod tres capellani honesti celebrent ad minus per tres annos a
die obitus mei pro salute anime mee et aliorum quibus teneor . . . et quod quolibet die
dicant devote pro anima mea . . . Placebo et Dirige iuxta regulam usus Saresburiensis.*
See *The Register of Henry Chichele,* E. F. Jacob and H. C. Johnson, eds. (Oxford,
1937–45, 3 vols.), II, 231.

7. For the origin and nature of the devotions discussed here, see Edmund Bishop's
essay in *The Prymer or Lay Folks' Prayer Book,* Henry Littlehales, ed., EETS, 105
and 109 (London, 1895–97), pp. xi–xxxviii, reprinted with additions in Bishop's *Liturgica
Historica* (Oxford, 1918), pp. 211–37; also Littlehales' illustrative historical notes in the
EETS volume; Herbert Thurston's article on the Primer in the *Catholic Encyclopedia,*
and the introduction to his edition, *The Prymer* (London, 1923). Littlehales discusses the
variation in the forms of the offices among the several English uses. Such variation does
not seem to have extended to the Biblical excerpts contained in them. The Psalms
of Placebo, according to the Vulgate numbering are 114, 119, 120, 129, 137, and 145.
The Magnificat precedes the final Psalm, which is followed by miscellaneous prayers.

8. Dirige, Matins, has the following composition: First Nocturne, Psalms 5, 6, 7;
Job 7.16–21, 10.1–7, 10.8–12; Second Nocturne, Psalms 22, 24, 26; Job 13.23–8, 14.1–6,
14.13–16; Third Nocturne, Psalms 39, 40, 41; Job 17.1–3 and 11–15, 19.20–7, 10.18–22.
Dirige, Lauds: Psalms 50, 64, 62, 66; Isaiah 38.10–20; Psalms 148, 149, 150; Luke
1.68–79; Psalm 29; miscellaneous prayers.

9. John Apsley in 1507 wishes a priest to sing for him for five years, "and I will the
same preest to say every Friday in the weke vij psalmes and latany, dirige and comen-
dacions." *Transcripts of Sussex Wills,* W. H. Godfrey, ed. (Lewes, 1935–41, 4 vols.), IV,
225. Specific requests for minor offices are fairly rare in the fourteenth century, but become increasingly common thereafter. A catchall request like this is rare at any time.
It may be observed here that testators became more circumstantial in their bequests
during the fifteenth century. Earlier they tended to leave the details of their commemora-
tions to their executors.

wills : according to the Vulgate numbering, the Psalms are the sixth, the thirty-first, the thirty-seventh, the fiftieth, the one hundred and first, the one hundred and twenty-ninth, and the one hundred and forty-second. Requests for the Fifteen Gradual Psalms (Psalms 119 through 133 in the Vulgate) are rather less common, as are requests for the Litany of the Saints—an appeal to some sixty saints for mercy, accompanied by appropriate responses and versicles. Commendations, which consists of the very long Psalm 118 along with Psalm 138 and a prayer *Tibi, domine, commendamus,* shows a sporadic popularity. The three prayers that might be efficaciously said by the unlearned—the Pater Noster, the Ave Maria, and the Creed—are ordinarily asked of the poor of the parish in return for a dole.[1]

The Primer, the only one of Langland's tools that is omitted from the list in the *Vision of William Staunton,* is not, of course, a devotion but a book of devotions.[2] Many fourteenth- and fifteenth-century Primers, both in Latin and in English,[3] have been preserved. Three aspects of the Primer are of particular interest here. First, with the exception of the Hours of the Virgin, which ordinarily forms its first component, it is exclusively a repository for intercessory offices, containing all those discussed above. The one commonly requested devotional act that could not be accomplished with the aid of the Primer was the recitation of the complete Psalter :[4] for this a separate text would be necessary, since the Primer contained only about fifty of the one hundred and fifty Psalms and these not in sequence. Second, as the subtitle, *Lay Folks' Prayer Book,* which Littlehales appended to his edition of an English Primer would indicate, the Primer was a book of hours "intended especially for the laity"[5] and had, apparently, no official standing with the Church. Finally (and this point is closely connected with the preceding), the Primer seems to have been essentially a book of *private* devotions. Its contents had not originally been a part of the canonical hours but were extensions of, and accretions to, the regularly established hours. Although the use of Sarum had adopted certain of these accretions and brought them into more or less constant employment, the Primer could hardly have been of much value in assisting its reader to follow a public rehearsal of the canonical hours. It seems, indeed, to have been a collec-

1. In 1449 Walter Dolman arranges a dole for the poor, in return for which he expects "every of hem to sey v pater nosters v ave and j credo." *Sussex Wills,* III, 207.

2. For information on the Primer, see references cited on p. 209, n. 7, above.

3. Langland's Primer was undoubtedly in Latin. Thurston in his article on the Primer in the *Catholic Encyclopedia* observes that "it must be remembered that the Psalms, the Officium B.M.V., the Vigiliae Mortuorum, etc., were recited by the laity as well as by the clergy in Latin" (XII, 425).

4. Walter Metford in 1421 arranges that seven "innocent" women shall be paid a fee on condition that each *dicat pro salute anime mee adstatim audito de morte mea unum plenum psalterium.* See *Register of Chichele,* II, 252.

5. F. Cabrol, *The Books of the Latin Liturgy* (London, 1932), p. 136.

tion of offices that would ordinarily be said in the home rather than in the church.[6]

Taking up these points in reverse order, let us see what effect they have upon our understanding of Langland's account of his occupation. The fact that he used a Primer, a repository of private devotions including all those he mentions except the Psalter, suggests that we should be correct in interpreting literally the lines,

> [This] ich [segge] for hure soules of suche as me helpen,
> And þo þat fynden me my fode vouchen sat ich trowe,
> To be welcome whanne ich come, oþer-whyle in a monthe.[7]

That is, the poet did his praying at the houses of those whom he visited. The unofficial nature of the Primer corroborates this interpretation and lends support to the theory, already expressed, that Langland had no close connection with the Church and that, so far as the ecclesiastical organization was concerned, his position was more nearly that of a pious layman than of a practicing cleric. Certainly we should expect a beneficed clerk to be static rather than peripatetic and to employ the officially sanctioned service book of the altar to which he was attached, rather than a Primer. But if he actually worked in the manner he describes, then the Primer and a Psalter would logically be his tools.[8]

6. Thurston, in his article on the Primer in the *Catholic Encyclopedia*, says that the "sense that these things [the contents of the Primer] were accretions to the Divine Office itself was not lost. Hence there was a tendency to perform these devotions in private, and for this purpose they were probably often collected into a separate book." Bishop, on the other hand, tries to show that the Primer was a prayer book in the modern sense, but his tabulation of the Canonical Hours opposite the offices contained in the Primer seems to show that it was a very inefficient prayer book at best. It seems necessary to assume some other function for it. When Agnes Bedford in 1426 leaves her Primer, *quo cotidie utor*, to John Swan, it is easier to believe that she read the book in the privacy of her home than that she went daily to services at church. See *Testamenta Eboracensia*, J. Raine and J. W. Clay, eds. (London and Durham, 1836–1902, 6 vols.), II, 236. My guess is that the Primer enjoyed greater use in the operation of the parish guilds than in the regular services of the Church.

7. C, VI, 48–50. In the first line I give the XI-reading, which seems preferable to P's *Thus ich synge*.

8. One cannot suppress the fact, perhaps inimical to many of the conclusions drawn in this chapter, that in quoting from the Bible Langland shows no bias whatsoever in favor of the selections included in Placebo and Dirige, the Seven and Fifteen Psalms, and Commendations. These offices contain forty-one Psalms, of which only fourteen are quoted in *Piers Plowman*: four of the Seven Psalms, two of the Fifteen, nine of Dirige's seventeen, and one of Commendations' two (Psalms 6 and 50 are included both in the Seven Psalms and in Dirige). Langland quotes neither Psalm 119 nor 120, which appears in two of the offices, nor 129, which appears in three, nor any of the six Psalms in Placebo. He quotes none of the fifty-five verses in Dirige from Job, nor of the eleven from Isaiah, and only one of the twelve from Luke. These figures are derived from Skeat's table of quotations, *EETS*, IV, 503 ff. The table shows that Langland quotes fifty-four of the total number of a hundred and fifty Psalms, or about one in three, which is the same ratio that prevails in his quoting from the Psalms included in the offices under discussion. But as an artist he was not, of course, bound to repeat what he knew best, unless he considered that it was appropriate to the sense of his poem.

The first point mentioned about the Primer—its character as a repository of intercessory material—accords, as has already been suggested, with the generally accepted idea of Langland as a suppliant for the souls of the dead. There is, however, some doubt in my mind about this. In the first place, while such offices as Placebo and Dirige were almost by definition intended for the welfare of the soul in purgatory, it seems erroneous to assume that this was their exclusive purpose. The immortality of the soul was less a matter of speculation in the fourteenth century than it is today, and if one believes the soul to be immortal it is, in a sense, only procrastination to wait until the soul has quit the body before one becomes interested in having it prayed for—procrastination plus, possibly, a natural if hardly laudable desire to have one's heirs rather than oneself foot the bill. As we know from the example of Chaucer's Clerk of Oxford, in Langland's time intercession for the living was also practiced, even if, in England, it was overshadowed by intercession for the dead. In many parish guilds, as Canon Westlake's study makes clear, the priest whom the members supported, and the members themselves, were enjoined to offer prayers for both the quick and the dead.[9] And whereas in the formula employed by testators the Mass-priest was ordinarily bidden to pray *pro animabus omnium fidelium defunctorum*[1] (as well as for the testator and his family, friends, and benefactors), occasional deviation was made to favor the living as well.[2] In Brunswick, Germany, the formula seems almost invariably to have included the living: thus a typical will bids the priest pray for the testator and his wife *unde vor orer elderen unde frunde selen, de rede vorstorven sin unde noch vorsterven schullen unde vor alle cristenen sele.*[3] Perhaps the

9. See H. F. Westlake, *The Parish Gilds of Mediaeval England* (London, 1919), pp. 138–238, "Origin, Purpose, and Religious Provisions" (of the guilds); also p. 13: "The rule of the gild [St. Nicholas at Bury] contains the usual regulations with regard to the offering of masses and alms for the living and the dead on the festival day, with *Placebo* and *Dirige* on the eve, but lays down an obligation of daily prayer which is worth notice. The priests were to say every day on behalf of the living *Deus Misereatur, Pater Noster,* and *Ave Maria,* with other versicles and collects, and *De Profundis* with *Pater Noster* and Salutation of the Blessed Virgin, with other prayers on behalf of the departed. The duty of the lay brethren and sisters was the daily recitation of three paternosters and aves for the living and as many for the dead. . . . At all divine offices the priests must remember the brethren living and departed."

1. See the will of W. Waldern (1424) in *Register of Chichele,* II, 277.

2. For example, in 1485 John Wode requests that his chaplain pray for all the brothers of St. John the Baptist, *tam vivis quam defunctis.* See *Sussex Wills,* I, 282. In many wills the formula is so phrased that it is impossible to tell whether the souls to be prayed for are in this world or the next. Thus Eleanor, Countess of Arundel, in 1445 desires that the Master and Fellows of Holy Trinity College, Arundel, pray *pro dicti Comitis ac mea omniumque parentum et progenitorum nostrorum et Christi fidelium animabus.* See *idem,* I, 53.

3. Johannes Heepe, *Die Organisation der Altarpfründen an den Pfarrkirchen der Stadt Braunschweig im Mittelalter* (Göttingen, 1913), p. 60, n. 3. The will is dated 1407 and is, according to Heepe, typical of a large number. Heepe (p. 60) describes the formula: "In ihren Messen und sonstigen Gebeten mussten die Messpriester nach Vor-

custom was more prevalent in England than the records indicate: the great majority of these are of the fifteenth and sixteenth century, and it is possible that many of the less circumstantial fourteenth-century wills contained provisions like the German one. Certainly it seems to be some such formula that Langland is echoing in the lines

> Prestes and persons *placebo* and *dirige,*
> Here sauter and here seuene psalmis for alle synful preyen.[4]

Here there is no suggestion that the sinful have to be dead. Rather, the point seems to be that priests should pray for all members of the innumerable caravan, whether on this or the other side.[5]

It is pertinent to observe that Edmund Bishop in his study of the origin and use of the Primer nowhere mentions its employment in connection with intercessions for the dead in fourteenth-century England, although he traces the history of the Offices of the Dead it contains from their beginnings in the monasteries of Europe. He believes that the popularity of the Primer was due to the deeply devotional nature of its contents, which might have a strong appeal to the pious medieval layman.[6] Yet he ignores the fact that the pious layman was extraordinarily preoccupied with the expeditious passage of his soul through purgatory and that the contents of the Primer were peculiarly adapted to effecting this. Perhaps this was an oversight on Bishop's part and the illustrations that certain Primers contain, showing a coffin surrounded by praying clergy and laymen, suggest that it was.[7] On the other hand, perhaps the Primer was in fact used primarily by laymen in praying for their own souls and for the souls of their friends. In that case it is possible that Langland, like Chaucer's Clerk, earned his living by praying, not for the souls of the dead, but for the souls of the quick, and that we should understand with absolute literality the line,

> [This] ich [segge] for hure soules of suche as me helpen.

So far as I can ascertain, however, no accounts, beyond such simple statements as Chaucer's, exist which will give us a clear picture of a beadsman-for-the-living of this sort, although there is plentiful reason to believe that such a thing very commonly did exist. With Langland, as with

---

schrift der Stiftungsurkunden 'innichliken,' 'vlitliken' bitten für die Fundatoren, deren Verwandte und Freunde, lebendige wie tote, für alle Wohltäter der Stiftung und für aller Christen Seelen."   4. C, iv, 467–8.

5. It is necessary to remember that there was a certain risk of wasted effort in praying for the souls of the dead, since according to orthodox thought only souls in purgatory might be assisted thereby. Souls in hell were past praying for. See Auguste Molinier, *Les Obituaires français au moyen âge* (Paris, 1890), p. 1. But *Saint Gregory's Trental* seems to accord memorial offices complete efficacy. See Furnivall's remarks, *Political, Religious, and Love Poems*, pp. xv–xvi.

6. Littlehales, ed., *op. cit.*, p. xxxviii.

7. See *idem*, p. 1, and Littlehales' *English Fragments from Latin Medieval Service-Books*, EETS, xc (London, 1903), p. 8.

the Clerk of Oxford, we might readily assume the existence of patrons,[8] men of sufficient discernment to see in the tall russet-clad figure a rare spirit worth fostering for piety's sake, as well as for literature's. Indeed, some men—and women, too [9]—might well consider the support of such a man an act of compound piety, bringing benefit to themselves through the poet's prayers and to the world through the poet's works. Such persons exist today and doubtless existed then.

Langland might, then, have earned his living praying for the souls of the living rather than for those of the dead. There is sufficient evidence for the theory, as well as sufficient doubt in establishing the alternative, that it has seemed necessary to present the case. Now let us examine the more commonly accepted theory that Langland was a sort of professional suppliant for the dead. When one considers the enormous sums that were diverted into the establishment of prayer-foundations in medieval Europe, one has no difficulty in supposing the existence of a huge class of persons whom economics, if not piety, would attract into the business of praying for the dead. Part of this class—and because of the fact that their salaries had to be regulated in order to prevent a complete collapse of the parochial system[1]—the part that we know most about, was made up of chantry priests. These were, it should be observed, of two kinds: the first were those priests assigned to definite chantries in the physical sense—chapels or altars such as the chantries of St. Paul's; the second, a rather more numerous class, merely made use of the facilities of existing churches without having a chapel or altar set aside for their exclusive use.[2] In addition to the chantry priests, there was a group, probably very large in size, of chantry clerks—clerics in minor orders who served the chantry priests as choristers and acolytes. Almost nothing is known about these beyond the fact that they were cited, along with their masters, by Parliament for negligence in the performance of their duties, as Jusserand has pointed out.[3]

It is to this class that Langland, on the basis of Jusserand's researches,[4] is generally agreed to have belonged. Some modification of the theory

8. Chambers, Mind, p. 168, employs this suggestive word to describe Langland's benefactors but does not elaborate.

9. See the phrase "now with hym and now with hure" in C, VI, 51.

1. See B. H. Putnam, "Maximum Wage-Laws for Priests after the Black Death, 1348–1381," American Historical Review, XXI (1915–16), 12–32.

2. It is important to note that the word chantry means either a chapel or altar at which intercessory services are held, or an endowment for the maintenance of intercessory services. See OED and Webster's. The phrase chantry priest tends to suggest one attached to a specific chantry chapel, such as the chantries of St. Paul's. Probably the priests of this class formed a much smaller number than those who lived from various relatively small endowments that did not include the setting aside of a particular altar or chapel. For a good discussion of medieval chantries see the essay "Chantries" by K. L. Wood-Legh, Studies in Church Life in England under Edward III (Cambridge, England, 1934), pp. 89–126.

3. Mysticism, p. 89, n. 1; Rotuli Parliamentorum (London, 1767–77, 6 vols.), II, 184, 271.   4. Mysticism, pp. 88–94.

seems, however, necessary. From the wills of certain prominent men like William de Roos we know that in endowing perpetual or long-enduring chantries testators would provide not only for priests but also for clerks to serve the priests.[5] On the basis of his own description Langland could not have been one of these, for the point he most emphasizes is his vagrancy, whereas the essence of the permanent chantry was its stability. Furthermore, he says nothing that would suggest that he was attached to a church or chantry, but rather, as we have seen, seems specifically to deny any such connection. He might, however, still have been a chantry clerk, if one is willing to take the word *chantry* in its wider sense of "an endowment for prayer." That is, he might have lived by partaking of such endowments, though he could not have derived his sustenance from any one endowed physical chantry, as Jusserand, probably unintentionally, leads one to suppose.

For a living could certainly be made by any one who was willing to take heed when the passing bell sounded. Even the poorest and most ignorant layman, by attending the funeral of a well-to-do fellow parishioner, might, in return for a few Pater Nosters, a Creed, or an Ave or two, receive a penny, or at the least his portion of bread, cheese, and beer —the funeral baked meats of many a medieval Englishman.[6] Or, if he were a recognized pauper, he might be chosen as a torchbearer and receive a gown of russet, similar, probably, to the one Langland describes himself as wearing.[7] We do not have to suppose that Langland himself was ever in such a position, though we are at liberty to wonder whether his russet clothing may not, after all, have some special significance besides being a mark of the clergy. As a clerk, and a learned one at that, Langland might receive, in addition to a dole of food, a fairly sizable fee for the saying of the Psalter—as much, possibly, as two shillings.[8] Six-

5. Having arranged for ten chaplains to sing for his soul for eight years, William de Roos in 1412 leaves nearly twenty-seven pounds *ad inveniendum duos honestos clericos ad ministrandum dictis capellanis per dictos octo annos.* See *Register of Chichele,* II, 24.

6. Alicia Story in 1414 makes the following bequest: *Et auxi je divise et ordeigne qe xxv livres soient distributz as poverez veignantz le jour de mon enterment cest assavoir a chescun homme et femme iiij d., et a chescun effant alant ij d., et a chescun femme enseinte ou enfant en lez bras j d.* See *Register of Chichele,* II, 7. John Wotton (1417) leaves a penny to each pauper attending his funeral. *Idem,* II, 131. John de Maydenhith, Dean of Chichester, in 1407 bequeaths *cuilibet pauperi venienti die solempnis sepulture et exequearum mearum j d. et prandium pro illo die.* See *Sussex Wills,* I, 281. The distribution of food was evidently more common in later times—or at least provision for specific foods was. In 1548 Thomas Wyke devises: "I wyll there shalbe bestowed at my buryall, my monthes mynd and yeres mynd, I will there shalbe a barell of bere, iiij doosan of Breade, and chese yerto, sufficiently for to releffe poor peple." *Idem,* I, 203.

7. The Countess of Salisbury (1414) desires *qe xxiiij poveres homes soient vestuz chescun en un hopeland et un chaperoun de Russet portant chescun deux une torche de cere al mon dirige et al messe de requiem a ma terment.* See *Register of Chichele,* II, 15. See also the will of Thomas Burye (1413) in *Sussex Wills,* III, 74.

8. In 1479 William Jacob promises the "morowmasse preste and the scolemaster of the gramer scole" that each of them will receive "ij s. for seying of David Sauter, if it please them." *Idem,* I, 341. This was probably an unusually high fee. In 1346 Emma Paynot

pence was sometimes available to a clerk in minor orders who would say Placebo and Dirige for the departed spirit on the day of burial.[9] His presence at a funeral might in itself bring him a small fee, even though he was required to do nothing more specific than join in the general prayers for the dead man.[1]

Nor were the possibilities exhausted upon the day of the funeral, for the testator ordinarily made provision for the repetition of his obsequies on the first month-day of his death—the day of the month's mind—as well as upon the anniversary of his death. Once again the clerk in minor orders might receive a small fee for his presence or assistance at intercessory services, or for adding a Psalter or a Placebo to the number of devotions dedicated to the soul of the dead man.[2] In this connection it is perhaps well to note that the presence of a congregation at Placebo and Dirige seems to have been more highly valued than attendance at Requiem Mass, possibly because it was felt that only the priest contributed to the saying of a Mass, whereas with the other offices every one present who could follow them was in a sense saying them independently of the official conducting the service. In any case, Langland makes no mention of Masses in the account of his livelihood, but speaks only of those offices which could be repeated by any literate person.

It is true that the fees discussed above would normally accrue only to clerks present in the church or at the burying ground, while Langland describes himself as going from house to house, rather than from church to church. Furthermore, most of the legacies were evidently expected to fall to the clerks regularly assigned to a church, the *intitulati*, not to just any passing clerk—though this was not always true.[3] We must,

---

leaves a penny *clericis psalteria dicentibus cuilibet.* See *Testamenta Eboracensia,* I, 22. In 1390 John Okele leaves "to every poor clerk who says one psalter on the night and day of my burial one penny." *Liber Albus Civitatis Oxoniensis,* W. P. Ellis, ed. (Oxford, 1909), p. 68. The citizens of Oxford were particularly thoughtful of poor clerks, who formed, however, a cheap labor market.

9. William Neel of Chichester in 1418 provides as follows: *Lego cuilibet canonico Cicestrensi presentibus in obsequiis meis xij d.; item cuilibet vicario Sacerdoti eiusdem ecclesie presentibus in eisdem ij s. vj d. et cuilibet vicario ibidem non Sacerdoti ad dicendum Placebo et Dirige pro anima mea ij s. vj d.* See *Sussex Wills,* IV, 428. A *vicarius non sacerdos* was probably one of the vicars choral of the cathedral. See *OED, choral,* a.1, 1, b. Neel's interesting will is printed at length in *Register of Chichele,* II, 150–3.

1. Thomas Beek, Bishop of London, in 1346 leaves one shilling *cuilibet pauperi clerico presenti in exequiis meis.* See *Testamenta Eboracensia,* I, 24. In 1382 Canon Geoffrey le Scrope leaves two shillings for the same. See *Lincoln Wills,* C. W. Foster, ed. (Lincoln, 1914–30, 3 vols.), I, 13.

2. Thus the will of William Jacob (1479), cited in n. 8, above, provides that "every vicary aforseid, the morowmasse prest and scolemaster, beyng present at my dirige, at my moneth mynde and att my masse at morowe, have everych of tham viij d." See *Sussex Wills,* I, 341–2.

3. Some wills, like that of Beek cited in n. 1, above, employ the phrase *cuilibet pauperi clerico* in an apparently nonrestrictive manner.

therefore, somehow adjust our picture of a clerk who supported himself in the manner we have seen was possible with what Langland says about himself. The difficulty may be at least partly obviated if we remember that wills, like Lyndwood's canon law, do not invariably tell us what actually happened: they merely tell us what testators wanted to have happen. Provision for intercessory services was originally rather narrowly limited to the rich, but as time went on the practice became more and more widespread, until in the sixteenth century a farmer might leave a single cow as the endowment of his prayer-foundation.[4] Vast as was the body of medieval clergy, it could scarcely be vast enough to accede to all the requests it received for prayers for the dead. Some testators recognized that their desires might not be fulfilled in every detail and left wide discretionary powers to their executors. As early as 1372 John Borle, rector of West Tarring in Sussex, having set aside twenty-three marks for three chaplains to say Mass for him at specified times, was cautious enough to add *et si contingit quod sacerdotes ad divina celebranda minime inveniri poterunt . . . tunc volo quod pecunia illa in aliis* [MS *al'*] *piorum usorum convertantur executorum meorum arbitrio.* Moreover, he left the residue of his estate, after specific legacies had been paid, for the purpose of *missis celebrandis distribucionibuz pauperum et aliis operibuz caritatis secundem disposicionem executorum meorum.*[5]

"Other works of charity." We should be careful not to be misled by the fact that this phrase follows mention of a distribution to the poor into thinking that the other works were necessarily similar in nature. John Borle considered the saying of Masses for his own soul just as much a work of charity as taking care of West Tarring's hundred neediest cases.[6] Nor would he have had reason to complain in purgatory if his executors, unable to find three chaplains to say Mass for him, had parceled out his legacy to poor but worthy clerks who, while they could not say Mass, could at least recite the Psalter, the Seven Psalms, Placebo, and Dirige in his behalf. The Mass was, as we have seen, the most serviceable currency with which to buy one's soul quick passage through purgatory, and the common agent in the transaction was therefore the priest. But it would be an error to underrate the importance of the prayers of any pious man. The author of the *Vision of William Staunton* did not underrate them, and the same attitude is evident in the fourteenth-century parish guilds. Not all of these maintained a priest to pray for the mem-

4. In 1454 Hugh Perin of Crawley devises as follows: *Lego ecclesie parochiali de Ifeld unam vaccam precii viij s., ad orandum pro animabus dictorum Hugonis et Alicie.* See *Sussex Wills,* III, 40.

5. *Idem,* IV, 211. I have expanded the abbreviations.

6. Notice that the Countess of Salisbury also leaves the residue of her estate for the execution of four acts of piety: *cestassavoir come en messe ditez prisoners releves poverez susteignez et males voies amendes par bon avys de mez executeurs.* See *Register of Chichele,* II, 18. For similar bequests, see *idem,* pp. 220, 520, 521, 551.

bers, and the execution of pious offices was frequently left up to the lay brothers and sisters. Even where a priest was maintained by the guild, much of the labor of prayer fell upon the members, who, as in the Guild of St. Katherine in Norwich, might be required to say upon the death of a fellow guildsman Placebo and Dirige if they were lettered, or, if they were unlettered, twenty Pater Nosters and Aves.[7] A lettered clerk like Langland, though without *titulus,* could have been of service when the *intitulati* were too busy to undertake an additional prayer-foundation. Where the clergy were busy, their churches would also be busy, so that an executor of a will might be forced to have commemorative offices repeated at his own house, which would account for Langland's itineracy.

The most serious objection to the theory that Langland was a professional intercessor for the souls of the dead arises from the fact that he definitely tells us that he had a more or less regular itinerary which he could complete in a month : that is, he visited only certain houses where he was known and these once a month. If the celebration of the month's mind had been recurrent, we could picture him going every month on the appropriate day to a household which had lost a member. But the month's mind was not, except in rare instances, recurrent and after the thirtieth day following death, unless a longer period of daily services had been arranged, there was normally no further celebration until the obit, or anniversary.[8] Of course, individual executors who had been given discretionary powers might choose to make the month's mind recurrent, and there is no reason to suppose that they did not occasionally do so if that was the only way they could get in the proper number of services. After all, what was important was not so much the time of prayer, although time had a definite significance, but the prayers themselves.

In view of what has been said about the possibility of Langland's having supported himself by praying for the living rather than for the dead, and in view of the objection noted above in connection with the theory that he prayed only for the dead, it is probably reasonable to take a compromise position : that he did both, or either, as required. In Langland's description of his means of livelihood there seems to be an awareness on his part of its irregularity. He is not a practitioner of any of the clearly defined callings that Reason lists ; nor is he, apparently, a simple chantry clerk, as Jusserand would have him ; rather, he is conscious of a certain abnormality in his occupation. For this reason I am disposed to visualize him as a sort of itinerant handy man, like a modern neighbor-

7. See *English Gilds,* Toulmin Smith and L. T. Smith, eds., EETS, 40 (London, 1870), p. 20.

8. See *OED, month's mind:* "The notion that it meant a commemoration recurring every month is baseless." See also *Lincoln Diocese Documents, 1450–1544,* A. Clark, ed., EETS, 149 (London, 1914), pp. 9–10. Clark notes, however, one will where the testator, Ralph Wooton (1533), arranged a recurrent month's mind. *Idem,* p. 159.

hood gardener who performs odd jobs for a whole suburban block—
except, of course, that Langland's odd jobs were prayers. The figure
will be found shocking only by those who have become accustomed to
maintaining a strict separation between acts of worship and the other
everyday acts of life. In Langland's day, such a separation did not exist
among pious men.

> The lomes þat ich laboure with and lyflode deserue
> Ys *pater-noster* and my prymer, *placebo* and *dirige*,
> And my sauter som tyme, and my seuene psalmes.
> [This] ich [segge] for hure soules of suche as me helpen,
> And þo þat fynden me my fode vouchen saf, ich trowe,
> To be welcome whanne ich come, oþer-whyle in a monthe,
> Now with hym and now with hure, and þus-gate ich begge,
> With-oute bagge oþer botel, bote my wombe one.[9]

Probably we have to take the fourth line, which is a clear echo of B,
XII, 16–17,

> And þow medlest þe with makynges and myȝtest go sey þi sauter,
> And bidde for hem þat ȝiueth þe bred,

both in its literal sense and in a semi-quibbling sense as referring to the
souls of those who by their legacies have made it possible for him to live.
It is not necessary to assume that they were rich, so long as they were
fairly numerous, as Langland gives us to believe they were. Indeed, some
of them may have been of the clerical class, pious priests who might
particularly esteem Langland and welcome him when he came to visit.[1]
But whether clergy or laymen, these patrons—the term seems appropriate so long as we do not associate it with Chesterfield or Maecenas—in
their support of Langland were assuredly performing what contemporary testators would place among *alia opera caritatis* helpful for the
souls of all Christians.

Such, then, is my notion of Langland at the time he was writing the
C-text and probably the B-text as well: a married clerk, of an order
certainly no higher than acolyte, who made his living in an irregular
fashion by saying prayers for the dead or for the living who supported
him. As I said at the outset, there is nothing particularly original in this
picture. I have merely tried to add to it a certain depth.

The reason that added depth is necessary will be found in the cavalier
way in which Langland's account of himself has been treated. As early
as 1901—some years before Manly formulated the theory of multiple
authorship—Jack rejected as fictional the entire C-autobiography chiefly
on the grounds that the poet's manner of living as therein described is

9. C, VI, 45–52.
1. Miss Hort, *Piers Plowman and Contemporary Religious Thought*, pp. 156–7,
makes the reasonable suggestion that Langland's work would be of particular interest
to priests.

elsewhere said by the poet to lack virtue altogether.[2] This point of view, which finds the breach between Langland's preaching and his practice too wide for belief to span, was given strong affirmation by Manly, who, while adding little to the argument himself, asserted that Jack's presentation was conclusive.[3] Actually, Jack's argument was far from conclusive and it is doubtful whether he himself considered it so.[4] Without going into its details, we should observe that the rejection of the poet's account of himself entails one great responsibility that no one has ever attempted to meet: that is, to explain what purpose the autobiographical passage was meant to serve if it is fictional.[5] Detractors of C, like Manly, possibly feel that here as elsewhere C's motivation is so poor or obscure—an impression which I hope that this book will tend to correct—that no explanation is requisite. But until a satisfactory one is given, it seems best to assume that Langland was telling the truth about himself and not whimsically devising an elaborate fiction.

Perhaps the chief element in this distrust of Langland's account of himself is the conviction that he was a priest or a monk. I know of no misconception about the poet that is older or of wider currency than this. Whitaker, identifying the author as "Robert Langland, a secular priest of the County of Salop," was forced to the conclusion that "William, the dreamer of all these dreams, is a purely imaginary personage."[6] To the second part of this statement Wright would agree, since he believed that Langland was a monk.[7] Jack apparently thought that he was a priest and made the worse mistake of thinking that the poet described himself as a priest who made his living "singing masses for those who would give him food and drink."[8] This same error seems reflected in Wells's assertion that the Dreamer "is a scholar-priest, who makes a living by performing too irregular religious services in the houses of the well-to-do in London," though Wells does not say that the poet, as distinct from the Dreamer, was a priest.[9] Most recently Bloomfield has, with the ut-

2. A. S. Jack, *JGPh*, III, 406–11. Although I disagree with many of Jack's conclusions, at least one part of his attack on literal interpretation of the biographical references is wholly justified—namely, his remarks on the reliability of numbers for working out significant dates in the poet's life. See *idem*, pp. 398–404. Skeat, *CP*, II, 179, note to C, xv, 3, and Jusserand, *Mysticism*, p. 73, were too credulous in their interpretation of lines possibly containing dates, and Jusserand's refusal to give ground on this point, *MPh*, VI, 323–4, gave proponents of multiple authorship an advantage in common sense. The exhaustive study of Fritz Krog, "Autobiographische oder typische Zahlen in *Piers Plowman?*" *Anglia*, LVIII (1934), 318–32, makes it clear that numbers are to be treated with extreme circumspection.

3. Manly, *CHEL*, II, 39.

4. See *JGPh*, III, 413–14, where Jack somewhat mitigates the rigor of his theory.

5. Chambers, *Mind*, p. 109, observes that those who believe the autobiography to be fictional "have been challenged for nearly thirty years to produce a precedent, and have not yet done so."

6. Whitaker, *Visio Willi de Petro Plouhman*, title page and note to p. 75, line 1.

7. Wright, *op. cit.*, I, ix.   8. *JGPh*, III, 409.   9. Wells's translation, p. 290.

most diffidence, suggested an identification of Langland with a certain Benedictine monk.[1]

Now if Langland was a priest we should, I think, be justified in rejecting as fictional the autobiography he has left us. It would certainly be difficult to explain how he was able both to be a priest and to have a wife, and it would be impossible to harmonize his own austere conception of the responsibilities of priesthood with the essentially irresponsible life that he describes himself as leading. But he does not say that he was a priest and we can wring such a statement out of him only by grossly misunderstanding the nature of the offices which he tells us that he rehearsed—*Placebo, Dirige,* and the rest—not one of which but could be performed by any literate person whatsoever, whether clerk or layman. This point the present chapter has, I hope, made amply clear. There are only two other reasons, neither of them very sturdy, for our choosing to regard him as a priest. There is the tradition that is represented by Bale, who calls the author *sacerdos, ut apparet*—as it appeared, apparently, to Bale.[2] This tradition seems little better than its fellow, that he was a monk of Malvern[3] and the two traditions tend to weaken each other. Or, striking out boldly on our own, we may say that Langland's learning and ideas are such as to preclude his having been anything but a priest. But such a theory, even given full presentation, would remain dubious and since it has received no such treatment it hardly seems necessary to stop over it. For Langland's having been a monk there is, so far as I know, no good evidence—nothing, indeed, except the vague tradition mentioned above.

Some of Jack's suspicion of C's biographical passage was caused by the fact that the poet presents himself as taking money for performing intercessory offices, although he strenuously condemns priests for this practice.[4] The point is, of course, less troublesome if we recognize that Langland himself was not a priest. His condemnation, expressed on several occasions, seems caused primarily by his conviction that a priest's duty is mainly parochial—to take care of his flock and to guide it on the path to salvation—and not to insure the passage of rich men's souls through purgatory. Whether he considered chantry singing a form of simony is not absolutely certain. The lines in which he reproves parish priests for abandoning their cures and going up to London,

And syngen þere for symonye, for siluer is swete,[5]

have become so inextricably associated with Chaucer's similar, and possibly derivative lines about the good priest,

1. M. W. Bloomfield, "Was William Langland a Benedictine Monk?" *MLQ*, IV (1943), 57–61.
2. See p. 200, n. 2, above.
3. See *CP*, II, xxviii.
4. *JGPh*, III, 409–10.
5. B, Pro., 86 (C, I, 84, A, Pro., 83).

> He sette nat his benefice to hyre
> And leet his sheep encombred in the myre
> And ran to Londoun unto Seinte Poules
> To seken hym a chaunterie for soules,[6]

that it is frequently assumed that Langland's *symonye* has reference to
Chaucer's *chaunterie*. In reality, Langland's priests may have gone to
London because it was the chief source of ecclesiastical and political pre-
ferment, where benefices were most readily bought and sold—the orthodox sort of simony that is probably in the background of Chaucer's
mention of hiring out benefices.

Langland's attitude toward chantry singing is probably best expressed
in the following lines addressed to priests:

> The title þat ȝe takeþ ȝoure ordres by telleþ ȝe beþ auaunced,
> And needeþ nat to nyme seluer for masses þat ȝe syngen;
> For he þat tok ȝow title sholde take ȝow wages,
> Oþer þe bisshop þat blessed ȝow and enbaumede ȝoure fyngeres.[7]

These lines have reference to the canonical rule, frequently violated, that
no clerk should be ordained priest unless he had a *titulus*—a benefice—
which he would straightway assume and which would support him.[8]
According to Langland, this *titulus,* however poorly paying, should not
be eked out by chantry singing: apparently the Lord will provide that
the priest does not starve. Langland does not seem to have faced the
possibility that the *titulus* might in itself have been a chantry. Nevertheless, I cannot find that he ever condemned the practice of chantry singing for its own sake, as the Protestants did.[9] In any case, his remarks
seem to have application only to the *intitulati* and to priests, not to
clerks in minor orders without title. According to the ancient doctrine
of the Church, the priest has a right to live by the altar—from his
titulus.[1] By analogy, the untitled minor clerk might expect, if he devoted
his life to the service of God and man, to earn his living thereby. In
viewing what seems a discrepancy between practice and principle we
should remember the poet's insistence upon responsibility as the determining factor in spiritual success or failure.[2] A minor clerk, without
specific responsibility, may lead the life that Langland did and go to
heaven, but a priest leading the same life will go to hell. One will recall

---

6. *The Canterbury Tales,* Prologue, ll. 507-10. Skeat, *CP,* II, II, comments on
Chaucer's lines somewhat as if they were Langland's.

7. C, XIV, 104-07. B, XI, 281-4 varies slightly.   8. See Moeder, *op. cit.,* pp. 1-18.

9. Jusserand, however, finds it necessary to apologize for Langland: "He strongly
condemned the abuse [chantry-singing], and yet profited by it, not without pangs, it is
true, and without feelings of indignation against himself; but he soon found he had
no other means of living. . . ." See *Mysticism,* p. 94.

1. See *Catholic Encyclopedia,* XIV, 741 f., article on tithes. The principle is based on
I Corinthians 9.13.

2. See Chapter V above, pp. 126 f.

that a Pater Noster admits a plowman to paradise, but the admission fee for the higher clergy is greater.

Both Jack and Hall are deeply distressed by the fact that the poet—and in particular the C-poet—deplores all types of mendicancy and nevertheless describes himself as a kind of mendicant.[3] The perturbation of his readers does not, however, even approximate the perturbation of Langland in this matter. It seems to have been the ultimate irony of his life that he should come to resemble a member of a class of which he greatly disapproved. There is no doubt that we have here to deal with a genuine discrepancy between preaching and practice, and since the poet himself recognized this discrepancy it would be the merest sentimentality on our part to pretend that it did not exist. Rather more serious, we should then overlook a most striking psychological similarity between the B- and C-texts. We have already seen that in both versions the poet describes himself as a vagrant and a mendicant.[4] We have seen, too, the changing gravity of his condemnation of mendicancy, given in connection with Hunger's advice to Piers and with the clauses of Piers's pardon. But while Langland condemned the beggar's life he seems also to have sought some sanction for it, or for the particular sort of beggar's life that he himself practiced. Thus in C he specifically exempts from his harsh strictures practitioners of that peculiar development of the minstrel's craft, God's minstrelsy, while in both B and C he assimilates himself to one of God's minstrels.[5] In C, furthermore, he rather hopefully exclaims that he would gladly make his living begging at men's doors if he could find charity thereby—as if, indeed, his own sort of begging constituted a life of charity.[6] It is true that Liberum Arbitrium, to whom this remark is addressed, denies that charity can exist among beggars of any sort; it is true also that, in the last passus of the poem, a peculiarly cryptic passage spoken by Need seems to condemn the manner of the poet's life;[7] and, above all, it is true that in his own analysis of begging his honesty prevents him from formulating any coherent definition of allowable mendicancy. Yet each of these passages conceals within itself to a greater or less degree the same irony of effect that is brilliantly realized in the poet's dialogue with Reason in the C-text. Despite his deep desire that his way of life should be found respectable, the poet knows in his heart that all the most subtle distinctions in the world are never going to succeed in lending it respectability. This point is made clearly and unequivocally in his conversation with Reason, which all the other passages I have mentioned seem to foreshadow. But even if it had never been written I think that we might, without becoming oversubtle, have guessed from a reading of B and C

3. Jack, *JGPh*, III, 406–11; Hall, *MLR*, IV, 8.
4. See Chapter V above.   5. See above, pp. 135 f.
6. C, XVII, 334–5. Cf. C, VI, 29.   7. B, XX, 4–49, C, XXIII, 4–50.

those facts about the poet's life which the dialogue with Reason presents to us directly. They are implicit in much of what is said elsewhere.

Another recurrent theme having to do with the poet's manner of livelihood appears in his remarks about dishonest hermits, whom he belabors fairly frequently, particularly in the C-text.[8] These, whom he calls lollers, he also resembles, though perhaps in a more superficial and less damaging way than he does beggars. Nevertheless, the resemblance is sufficiently close so that in speaking of hermits he shows even less impersonality than is usual with him and uses terms such as suggest that he regarded them as unworthy rivals in his way of life. Hermits, like beggars, are supported by the charity of their neighbors and, like Langland, are presumably dedicated to a clerkly life of prayer. Reason, indeed, is unable to tell the difference between Langland and the other great loafers who under color of clergy profit by the piety of the London public, and the poet is hard put to make the distinction clear. Thus his life is bound up with two disreputable classes, beggars and hermits, from whom he is distinguished only by some inner conviction of sincerity and rectitude—qualities that are, perhaps, like B's charity, perceptible in the will alone. Certainly they are not readily noticeable to the unprejudiced observer, and Langland, as he makes his pious rounds from door to door, in London and upland both, praying for the souls of his benefactors, is constantly embarrassed by the consciousness that his is in each external the life of a beggar or of a dishonest hermit—in each external, and who knows in what internals? Naturally, he shows himself sensitive in speaking of these two types of parasite. But is not this acute sensitivity, evident in both B and C, a kind of proof of the truth of the autobiographical passage in which it receives its fullest expression?

Miss Day has shown that the passage itself has its roots in the Dreamer's dialogue with Imaginative in the twelfth passus of the B-text.[9] There he is rebuked by Imaginative for certain of the actions of his life, particularly for wasting his time writing,

> . . . for þere ar bokes ynowe
> To telle men what dowel is, dobet, and dobest bothe.[1]

The poet's excuse is lame. He says that he writes only for recreation and cites Cato's advice, *Interpone tuis interdum gaudia curis.* The whole passage is a delightful one. We see Langland, under some sort of spiritual duress, endeavoring to explain himself and failing to do so as inevitably as he fails to find sanction for a beggar's life.

Despite its charm, the full significance of the lengthy interlude between the Dreamer and Imaginative has only recently been rendered altogether intelligible. Chambers has shown that the poet, in the A-text,

8. See Chapter V above, pp. 127 f.
9. *MLR*, XXIII, 1–2, and p. 26, above.					1. B, XII, 17–18.

encountered certain problems that he was unable to solve through his reason and consequently abandoned his poem. After some years he found the solution and resumed his work in its B-form.[2] In B, xi he describes allegorically the failure that he had experienced as A—the failure to find Do-Well through the aid of reason, or, personified, Reason. "The seeker has signally failed to understand through Reason. Now [in B, xii] comes Imaginative, explaining where he is at fault, and reconciling him to Reason."[3] Imaginative is able to do this because, as Jones showed, he stands in scholastic psychology for *ars commemorativa*, the effective agent which enables the reason to function.[4] As a result of his conversation with Imaginative, the poet assumes a reasonable attitude. His doubts are answered and the Dreamer, heartened, is able to go on with his search. Thus in the encounter Chambers has enabled us to read the record of a spiritual experience of the poet's.

In C the passage dealing with Imaginative is much condensed and it contains no such record as may be read in B. We can only guess what went on in Langland's mind as he made the C-revision, but here, I think, we can guess with some probability of being correct. Since he had completed B, his failure to complete A was no longer significant and he could expunge the record of the failure from the already enormously complicated *Visio de Do-Well*. But it is probable that, as he revised the part played by Imaginative, his mind, under the sway of *ars commemorativa*, was induced to think of other failures in his life. It was no longer a single one that he had to apologize for, but an accumulation, topped, perhaps, by the beggar's life he was leading : an accumulation whose sum made up, indeed, the failure of his life itself. For earlier lapses he had made amends, but there was not now much time left. Before it was too late he wrote his ultimate explanation, which is both an apology and a prayer for grace, and placed it at the beginning of the sixth passus of his latest text.

The position is logical. In B Imaginative, the effective agent in enabling the reason to function, had been the intermediary in the poet's explanation of his failure to go on with his search. Now it is a larger failure that must be explained, and the intermediary is Reason himself. Previously, indeed, the failure had been caused by the poet's not being reconciled to Reason, and once Imaginative had effected the reconciliation, the failure was redeemed. Now, however, the failure transcends Reason's control and must be redeemed, not by him, but by the grace of God. But Reason remains a most important one of man's psychological attributes, and a proper recipient of the poet's explanation. Thus, "romynge in remembraunce," Langland substitutes Reason for Imaginative, *ars commemorativa*. The sixth passus of the C-text is altogether Reason's passus. There he preaches on the Field of Folk the sermon that brings the

2. *Mind*, pp. 138–42.   3. *Idem*, p. 139.
4. H. S. V. Jones, "Imaginatif in Piers Plowman," *JEGPh*, xiii (1914), 583–8.

Deadly Sins to their confession. Of the confessions the poet's is, in a sense, the first, and has a natural place in that part of the poem wherein Reason provides the incentive for the search for Truth which is the subject of the *Visio* and of the whole of *Piers Plowman*.

And what a splendid *apologia pro vita sua* Langland utters! Though it contains an ironical humor, we should not, like the Virginian, beguile ourselves into believing that we do not have to take seriously what is said with a smile. It is as serious as any of the poet's most unsmiling lines— perhaps the more serious because the humor implies a greater depth of understanding. And though it seems to emanate from a discussion of Langland's begging (which, incidentally, it fails altogether to explain), it goes far beyond this topic and becomes something more profound— a brilliant portrait of the personality of a man who knew himself well. The hit-or-miss way of life of the author of *Piers Plowman;* his independence of spirit, displayed both to his fellow mortals and to the august allegorical personages he is always meeting; his inability to justify himself either for writing or for begging, and his perfectly obvious intention to go right on doing both so long as they are necessary to his search for Truth; and finally his faith that, no matter how deceived by himself and tricked by the world, he can somewhere and sometime arrive at the end of his quest and justify the means by which it was carried on—what better apology, what better summary, could be made for such a man?

> . . . ich by-knowe
> That ich haue tynt tyme and tyme mysspended;
> And ʒut, ich hope, as he þat ofte haueþ chaffared,
> Þat ay hath lost and lost, and atte laste hym happed
> He bouhte suche a bargayn he was þe bet euere,
> And sette hus lost at a lef at þe laste ende,
> Suche a wynnynge hym warth þorw wordes of hus grace;
> > *Simile est regnum celorum thesauro abscondito in agro, & cetera:*
> > *Mulier que inuenit dragman vnam, et cetera;*
> So hope ich to haue of hym is al-myghty
> A gobet of hus grace, and bygynne a tyme,
> Þat alle tymes of my tyme to profit shal turne.[5]

If the discrepancies between the three texts of *Piers Plowman* were many times more grave than they are I should still find it difficult not to believe that the authors of all three were the one man who expresses himself in these lines—the man whose life we have examined in this chapter. Surely if C was another than A and B his theft of a personality is the most successful the world of literature has ever seen.

5. C, vɪ, 92–101. Quoted by Christopher Dawson, *Mediaeval Religion* (London, 1934), p. 166, with the observation: "The autobiographical passage of which this is the conclusion is of itself, to my mind, a sufficient refutation of Professor Manly's view that the author of the C text was an unimaginative pedant, and that the picture of the poet himself is merely a rhetorical device."

APPENDIX A

The MSS of Piers Plowman

FOR the reader's convenience I give below a list of the known MSS of *Piers Plowman,* along with a brief summary of the genealogy and classification of the C-MSS. For the list the chief sources are R. W. Chambers and J. H. G. Grattan, "The Text of 'Piers Plowman'," *MLR,* XXVI (1931), 50–1 (referred to here as Chambers and Grattan), and Carleton Brown and R. H. Robbins, *The Index of Middle English Verse* (New York, 1943), items 745 and 1458–9 (*Index*), with supplemental information from my own research. For the discussion of C-MSS the chief sources are the four volumes of Skeat's EETS edition (*EETS,* I etc.); F. A. R. Carnegy, *An Attempt to Approach the C-Text of Piers the Plowman* (London, 1934) (Carnegy); and Chambers, "The Manuscripts of *Piers Plowman* in the Huntington Library, and Their Value for Fixing the Text of the Poem," *HLB,* VIII (1935), 1–25 (Chambers). The pertinent part the last was reprinted, with additions, as an introduction to the reproduction of MS X: *Piers Plowman: the Huntington Library Manuscript (HM 143)* (San Marino, Calif., 1936), pp. 1–23. The study by B. F. Allen (Mrs. Tapping), "The Genealogy of the C-Text Manuscripts of Piers Plowman," has not been published, but its chief conclusions are summarized by Chambers and Carnegy.

No discussion of A- and B-MSS has been attempted. For information on B-MSS, see the articles by Elsie Blackman (referred to above, p. 5, n. 1) and George Kane (below, p. 235, n. 4), and Donaldson, "MSS R and F in the B-Tradition of Piers Plowman," *Transactions of the Connecticut Academy of Arts and Sciences,* XXXIX (1955), 177–212. For A-MSS, see Chambers and Grattan's article on the text (referred to above, p. 15, n. 7); their later study, "The Text of 'Piers Plowman': Critical Methods," *MLR,* XI (1916), 257–75; Thomas A. Knott, "An Essay toward the Critical Text of the A-Version of 'Piers the Plowman,'" *MPh,* XII (1914–15), 389–421; David C. Fowler, "Contamination in Manuscripts of the A-Text of 'Piers the Plowman'," *PMLA,* LXVI (1951), 495–504; Knott and Fowler, *Piers the Plowman: a Critical Edition of the A-Version* (Baltimore, 1952), pp. 20–8; and, definitively, George Kane, *Piers Plowman: the A Version* (London, 1960), pp. 1–172.

In the Table of MSS, the sigils and the order of citation are those of the editions of the three texts now being carried out under the general editorship of George Kane. In addition to Kane's already published A-text, the B-text is being prepared by Kane and Donaldson, and the C-text by G. H. Russell, who is completing work begun by A. G. Mitchell.

I. *Table of MSS*

(An asterisk denotes a mixed MS. Numbers in parentheses are those given in the *Index*.)

A-Class

*T	Trinity College, Cambridge, R. 3. 14 (594). Base for Knott-Fowler's and Kane's texts. C-text after A, XI
R	Bodleian, Rawlinson Poet. 137 (Bodl. 14631)
U	University College, Oxford, 45
D	Bodleian, Douce 323 (Bodl. 21897)
*Ch	Liverpool University Library F. 4. 8. C-text after A, XI†
*H2	British Museum, Harleian 6041. C-text after A, XI
V	Bodleian, Vernon (Bodl. 3938). Skeat's A-text
H	British Museum, Harleian 875
J	Pierpont Morgan Library M 818. Formerly Ingilby
L	Lincoln's Inn 150
E	Trinity College, Dublin, D. 4. 12 (213)
A	Bodleian, Ashmole 1468 (Bodl. 7004)
*K	Bodleian, Digby 145 (Bodl. 1746). C-text (D2) after A, XI
*W	The Duke of Westminster's MS, Eaton Hall. C-text after A, XI
*N	National Library of Wales, Addl. 733, B. C-text (N2) after A, VIII
M	Society of Antiquaries, London, 687. Formerly Bright
*H3	British Museum, Harleian 3954. B-text (H) to A, V, 1
*(Z)	Bodley 851 (Bodl. 3041). Apparently a memorial reconstruction of A. C-text after A, VIII
. .	Pembroke College, Cambridge. Fragment containing about 140 lines
*. .	MSS Bm, Bo, and Cot of the B-class (O, B, L of the C-class) are A-texts from A, II, 90 through 212

B-Class

W	Trinity College, Cambridge, B. 15. 17 (353). Wright's text
Hm	Huntington Library HM 128. Formerly Ashburnham 130
Hm2	Fragment in Hm of a MS copied from the same archetype‡
Cr1	Crowley's first edition of 1550, representing a lost MS
Cr2–3	Crowley's two later editions, corrected from another MS
G	Cambridge University Library Gg. 4. 31
Y	Newnham College, Cambridge. Formerly Yates-Thompson
O	Oriel College, Oxford, 79
C2	Cambridge University Library Ll. 4. 14
C	Cambridge University Library DD. 1. 17
*Bm	British Museum, Addl. 10574. C- and A-text through B, II
*Bo	Bodley 814 (Bodl. 2683). C- and A-text through B, II
*Cot	British Museum, Cotton Caligula A. XI. C- and A-text through B, II
L	Bodleian, Laud Misc. 581 (Bodl. 987). Skeat's B-text

† See J. H. G. Grattan, "The Text of 'Piers Plowman': a Newly Discovered Manuscript and Its Affinities," *MLR*, XLII (1947), 1–8.
‡ See R. B. Haselden, "The Fragment of *Piers Plowman* in Ashburnham No. CXXX," *MPh*, XXIX (1931–32), 391–4.

M   British Museum, Addl. 35287. Formerly Ashburnham 129
R   Bodleian, Rawlinson Poet. 38 (Bodl. 15563). Four folios of this MS are
         in British Museum, Lansdowne 398
F   Corpus Christi College, Oxford, 201
*H   H3 in A-class. A-text after B, V, 128
(Ht)   Huntington Library HM 114. Formerly Phillipps 8252. A conflation of
         all three texts, based on B†
. .   Caius College, Cambridge, 201. Transcript of Roger's printing
. .   Bodleian, James 2. Modern transcript of a few hundred lines

C-Class

X   Huntington Library HM 143
Y   Bodleian, Digby 102 (Bodl. 1703)
I   University of London Library, V. 88. Formerly Ilchester
P2   British Museum, Addl. 34779. Formerly Phillipps 9056
*D2   K in A-class. C-text from C, XII, 297
*O   Bm in B-class. C-text through C, III, 128
*L   Cot in B-class. C-text through C, III, 128
*B   Bo in B-class. C-text through C, III, 128
U   British Museum, Addl. 35157. Passus III–V printed by Carnegy
D   Bodleian, Douce 104 (Bodl. 21678)
*T   T in A-class. C-text from C, XII, 297
*H2   H2 in A-class. C-text from C, XII, 297
*Ch   Ch in A-class. C-text from C, XII, 297
P   Huntington Library HM 137. Formerly Phillipps 8231. Skeat's C-text.
         Whitaker's text.
E   Bodleian, Laud Misc. 656 (Bodl. 1059)
R   British Museum, Royal Library 18. B. XVII
M   British Museum, Cotton Vespasian B. XVI
V   Trinity College, Dublin, D. 4. 1 (212)
A   University of London Library V. 17. Formerly Sterling‡
Q   Cambridge University Library, Addl. 4325
S   Corpus Christi College, Cambridge, 293
*Z   (Z) in A-class. C-text from C, XI
*W   W in A-class. C-text from C, XIII
F   Cambridge University Library Ff. 5. 35
K   Bodleian, Digby 171 (Bodl. 1772)
G   Cambridge University Library Dd. 3. 13
N   British Museum, Harleian 2376
*N2   N in A-class. C-text from C, XI
. .   Caius College, Cambridge, 669, Transcript of 17 lines

There are fifty-two complete or almost complete MSS of the poem, plus the
three Crowley printings of B which are accorded MS status. Of these MSS,

† See G. H. Russell and Venetia Nathan, "A *Piers Plowman* Manuscript in the Hunting-
ton Library," *Huntington Library Quarterly,* XXVI (1963), 119–28.
‡ See A. G. Mitchell, "A Newly-Discovered MS of the C-Text of Piers Plowman," *MLR,*
XXXVI (1941), 243.

eleven are mixed, seven combining A- and C-texts, one combining the A- and B-text, and three combining B- and C-texts with a small portion of A. Two of the MSS, Ht and Caius College Cambridge 201 of the B-class, provide no help to an editor; nor does the A-portion of MS Z. Of the four fragments, only Hm2 of the B-class is of editorial interest.

II. *Genealogy and Classification of C-MSS*

A. Genealogy

The following is quoted from Carnegy, p. 9, and is Carnegy's summary of the conclusions reached by Miss Allen in her study of the C-MSS:

(1) The C-text MSS. fall into two groups, the *t*-group. . . , and the *y*-group. . . .

(2) The *y*-group falls into two sub-groups, the *i*-group and the *p*-group.

(3) Of these groups and sub-groups, *t* is nearest to the original C-text, and *i* is much nearer to *t*—and therefore to the C-text—than is *p*.

(4) *p*, which Skeat considered to be the author's "last word" on the C-text, is in reality a sophisticated recension.

B. Classification

1. The "i"-group

X   The best MS of the "i"-group and hence the best complete MS of the C-text. (Chambers, pp. 23–4; also introduction to Huntington Library reproduction, pp. 13–23.)

Y   A rival to U, but failing to III, 156. (*EETS*, III, xlv-xlvi; Chambers, p. 22; Carnegy, p. 19.)

I   An interesting MS with many good readings, but seriously imperfect and in part A-contaminated. (*EETS*, III, xxxiii-xxxviii; Chambers, pp. 19–20.)

P2   Confused. (EETS, III, xlix-l; Chambers, p. 22; Carnegy, pp. 19, 23.)

U   The second best MS of the "i"-group. (Chambers, p. 23; Carnegy, pp. 16–18.)

D   The third best MS of the "i"-group. (*EETS*, III, xlv-xlvi; Chambers, p. 23; Carnegy, pp. 18–19.)

Mixed MSS of the "i"-group

D2   A late MS, dated 1534. (*EETS*, I, xxiv; Chambers, p. 22.)

O   From the same original as B. (*EETS,* II, xxvi-xxvii; Chambers, p. 22.)

L   From the same original as B. (*EETS*, II, xxvii; Chambers, p. 22.)

B   Good readings, but a C-MS only to III, 128. (*EETS*, II, xxv-xxvi; 391–3; III, xxxviii-xxxix; Chambers, p. 22; Blackman, p. 506.)

2. The "t"-group: mixed MSS (no complete C-text)

T   The best MS of the "t"-group and the nearest of all C-MSS to the author's original, but only partially a C-MS. (*EETS*, I, xviii-xix; III, xxxviii; Chambers, pp. 18–19; Carnegy, p. 9.)

H2   A pale reflex of T. (*EETS*, I, xx-xxi; Chambers, pp. 18–19.)

Ch   Apparently from the same remote original as TH2. See Grattan, *MLR,* XLII, 2, and Kane's edition of A, p. 89.

3. The "p"-group

P   The best MS of the "p"-group. (*EETS*, III, xix-xxiv; Chambers, pp. 20–1.)
E   Almost a duplicate of P. (*EETS*, III, xxiv-xxx; Chambers, p. 21.)
R   Differs little from P. (*EETS*, III, xlviii-xlix; Chambers, p. 22.)
M   Inferior to P. (*EETS*, III, xxxix-xl; Chambers, pp. 19, 22; Carnegy, pp. 22–3.)
V   A serious rival to P. (*EETS*, III, xlviii; Chambers, p. 22.)
AQSFKGN   The remaining MSS of the "p"-group are, for one reason or another, inferior to those discussed above. (*EETS*, III, xxx-xxxiii, xl-xlv; Chambers, pp. 21–2; Carnegy, pp. 20–3; Mitchell, *MLR*, XXXVI, 243.)

Mixed MSS of the "p"-group

Z   A good representative of "p." (*EETS*, III, xxx-xxxii.)
W   Unsatisfactory. (*EETS*, IV, 853–6.)
N2   Very corrupt: perhaps unclassifiable. (Introduction to Huntington Library reproduction, p. 4; Chambers and Grattan, p. 51.)

In completing this study, I had access to the following C-MSS: P, as printed by Whitaker and Skeat; U, in the three passus printed by Carnegy; X, in the splendid Huntington Library reproduction; B, in the photostatic copy in the Yale University Library; and T, in the photostatic copy deposited in the Library of Congress by the Modern Language Association of America* and loaned to me through the courtesy of that organization. Of the B-MSS I had access to L, as printed by Skeat; to W, as printed by Wright; to Cr, as printed by Crowley (along with Crowley's later issues and the edition by Owen Rogers); and to Prologue through Passus VII of GYOC2CB, in the photostatic copies in the Yale University Library. Of the A-MSS I had access to V, as printed by Skeat, and to T, as explained above.

*Library of Congress, Modern Language Association Deposit No. 251.

APPENDIX B

The Authenticity of the C-Text

IT IS essential, in making a detailed study of a medieval poem, that one establish with some firmness the authenticity of the text one has under examination. Otherwise the suspicion might well arise that one is wasting time explaining in the name of the poet certain matters that are in reality attributable to his scribes. This is particularly true with *Piers Plowman,* concerning the text of which the scholarly world has developed a high degree of sensitivity, so that one sometimes hears it categorically stated that no further work should be done upon the poem until all textual problems have been fully resolved. Such an injunction seems far too drastic, and if it were carried out *Piers Plowman* would have to be relegated to Limbo for an indefinite period.[1] Nevertheless, it would be dangerous to write this book unless one were reasonably confident, as I am, that in the best MSS of the C-text we have an accurate reproduction of what the C-poet actually wrote. It is the purpose of this appendix to demonstrate the reasons for this confidence.

The materials we have to work with are none too copious. We have, of course, the positive statements by Chambers and Miss Blackman that the B-MS upon which C based his revision was far better in some respects than any B-MS we now possess, and that the C-text often gives readings which stood in the original MS of B but have since been lost through scribal deviation.[2] It follows that the C-text as a whole is probably more accurate than the B-text as a whole, but this relative statement gives us no idea of how accurate the C-text is. Furthermore, no critical text of C is in existence except a specimen of three passus not based upon the best MS now available.[3] Finally, while I have had access to several of the best C-MSS,[4] I have not had access to many and am in no position to speak with the authority of an editor of a critical text. But despite this shortage of tools there is, I think, a method whereby we may test the accuracy of C as represented by the best C-MSS.

1. See the note by G. R. Coffman, "The Present State of a Critical Edition of *Piers Plowman," Speculum,* xx (1945), 482–3, which contains a pessimistic statement by Grattan concerning the progress of the project.

2. "Whatever the cause may have been, there is one significant fact which cannot be overlooked by students of *Piers Plowman*—the extant evidence suggests that the writer of the C-text worked from a B-text MS. which, in certain respects, was better than the ancestor of the extant B-text MSS." Blackman, *JEGPh,* xvii, 530. See also Chambers and Grattan, *MLR,* xxvi, 2.

3. See F. A. R. Carnegy, *An Attempt to Approach the C-Text of Piers the Plowman,* which contains the version of MS U for Passus iii–v, along with variant readings from a large number of MSS. X, a better MS than U, was not available when Carnegy made his study.   4. See Appendix A, note at end.

Since this method involves a detailed comparison of two passus of B and C, it will be necessary to summarize certain information about the MSS of the two versions, in order that the reader may be assured that the comparison is proceeding under the best conditions possible at the moment. So far as B is concerned, Chambers and Miss Blackman tell us that MS L, Skeat's text, is probably the best of the B-MSS and that L, corrected by W (Wright's text), Y, and O, forms a good basis for a critical B-text.[5] Since Skeat collated W and O throughout, and portions of Y, his B-text represents a limited critical text, which we shall be fairly safe in using in our comparison.[6] An actual critical text must, of course, take into consideration all the B-MSS. But even this would not differ radically from Skeat's version, inasmuch as the MSS all resemble one another rather closely. Furthermore, it would furnish only a faulty reproduction of the author's autograph, inasmuch as all extant MSS stem from the same archetype, which was itself a faulty copy some distance removed from the autograph. Despite a large number of MSS, therefore, the editor of B is in somewhat the same position as if he had only one MS and that not the author's. With *Piers Plowman* he has, however, this advantage: in parts of the poem in which there is evidence that no revision took place he may compare the readings of the MSS of his version with readings of the other versions, and if there is sufficiently good reason to suppose that one or both of the other versions preserve the right reading and that his MSS are corrupt, he may amend against all MS authority. Working in accordance with this principle, Miss Blackman and Chambers have pointed out a number of passages in which all B-MSS have gone astray, but where the C-text has preserved the right reading for B.[7] It is this method that I intend to use in testing the authenticity of C—a method the propriety of which I believe to have been sufficiently established by the researches of the scholars named.

While it is safe to use Skeat's edition of B in making the comparison, the same cannot be said for C, the MSS of which show a greater divergence from the norm. It is apparently true that the C-MSS, like those of B, derive from a common archetype that was not the author's autograph[8] and that deviated from it to an extent which it is our hope to estimate. But according to Miss Allen,[9] unlike the B-MSS, the C-MSS are divided into two distinct families stemming from their common archetype. One of these families she calls "t," the designation for the remote ancestor of the extant "t"-group MSS. The other is "y," the designation for the remote ancestor of extant "i"-group

---

5. Chambers, *HLB*, viii, 13–14; Blackman, *JEGPh*, xvii, 529–30.

6. It is necessary for the time being to ignore the lines in Skeat's text introduced from MS R. See Chambers, *HLB*, viii, 12; Blackman, *JEGPh*, xvii, 501–03; and Appendix C, note on MS R.

7. See Blackman, *JEGPh*, xvii, especially 518–21, 530; Chambers, *MLR*, v, 26–7; Chambers and Grattan, *MLR*, xxvi, 1–11. Of particular clarity is the example from B, v, 336, where Robin the Roper "arose bi þe southe" according to virtually all MSS. C, vii, 387 reads "aryse þei bysouhte." See *MLR*, xxvi, 3–4.

8. The only statement that I recall having seen about this important point is that of Chambers and Grattan, *MLR*, xxvi, 19, who speak of readings "inherited from the archetype of all the A-, B- or C-MSS., which, at any rate in the case of B and C, was certainly not the author's autograph."

9. Miss Allen's conclusions are quoted above, Appendix A, p. 230.

and "p"-group MSS. The MSS of the "t"-group, which Miss Allen considers the nearest approach to the author's MS, are all fragmentary. As a result we are forced to work with "i," a subfamily which, while somewhat inferior to "t," is in many respects much closer to "t" than it is to its own related subfamily "p."

In editing the C-text, Skeat printed from MS P, the same MS that Whitaker had used before him. P is, unhappily, a representative of "p," the least reliable of the families and subfamilies of C. Indeed, the "p"-scribe was a tireless sophisticator and meddler and is, I think, responsible in part for the C-text's evil reputation: his alterations show that he was a pedant of the worst sort—a good deal worse sort, indeed, than C himself, whose work "p" tends to spoil by many minute revisions frequently attributed to his original.[1] It follows that Skeat's C-text is some distance removed from a critical text that could now be made on the basis of two "i"-group MSS that have come to light since his edition[2]—MSS X and U—plus, where it is available, the "t"-group as represented by MSS T and Ch. In making our comparison, then, it is necessary to purify Skeat's text by corrections from the better MSS. Those I have had access to are X, which Chambers considered the logical basis for the critical C-text,[3] and T. The question we must now try to answer is, To what extent does the C-text, as transmitted by the best MSS, deviate from the author's original? In order to accomplish this, let us turn our attention to the last two passus of the poem in B and C—the *Visio de Dobest*.

These passus, B, xix–xx, C, xxii–xxiii, are, even in Skeat's editions, much the same in B and C. If there was any revision of them by the C-poet, it was carried on according to an entirely different plan from that which prevailed in the rest of the poem—so different that scholars generally, I think, admit the truth of Chambers' statement that the passus "were not

1. Carnegy, *op. cit.*, pp. 10-11, lists several examples of P's sophistication of his text; see also Chambers, *MLR*, v, 27–8. I append here examples from the first five passus of C, along with readings from X and (where available) U, and from the B-text ("B"). C, I: 2, P *shrobbis*, "B"X *shroudes* (see Chambers, *ibid.*); 2, P *shepherde*, "B"X *shepe;* 49, P *vn-wyse*, "B"X *wise;* 72, P *blessede*, "B"X *bonched;* 195, P *trauail*, "B"X *studye;* 225, P omits "B"X *vous;* 229, P omits "B"X *wyn* (2). C, II: 33, P *wylne*, "B"X *ȝerne;* 92, P *trespassours*, "B"X *tran(s)gressores;* 199, P *cristine*, "B"X *careful.* C, III: 5, P *quath hue*, "B"XU omit; 63, PX *contreis*, "B"U *courtes;* 160, P *falsnesse*, "B"XU *false-witnes;* 228, P *houted out*, "B"XU *yhowted.* C, IV: 19, P *wende*, UX *wedde*, "B" *be wedded;* 67, P *see and seye*, UX *see*, "B" *seyn* (WCO *seye*); 227, P *hals*, "B"XU *half;* 285, P *at my knowynge*, U *as my þinkeþ*, "B"X *as me thynketh;* 498, P *Tristilich a teneful*, "B"XU *A ful teneful.* C, V: 61, P *quarters oþer twelue*, "B" *quarteres of otes*, U *quarter otes*, X *quarteres otes.* These examples bear out Miss Allen's statement, quoted by Carnegy, *op. cit.*, p. 15, that "when established, the C-text will be much nearer to the B-text than the printed edition shows." Perhaps even more damaging to the C-poet's reputation than these obvious alterations is the "p"-scribe's tendency toward a sort of minute verbosity, an itch to make tiny elaborations in infinitesimal matters which has a disastrous cumulative effect on style.

2. It is necessary to say that Skeat chose what was probably the best complete MS available to him, P being the best of the "p"-group: see Chambers, *HLB*, VIII, 20–2. He had originally planned to use MS I of the "i"-group, but was forced to abandon the project because of I's many gaps. See *EETS*, III, xxi.

3. See his statement in *HLB*, VIII, 24, and the results of his tabulation of errors in "i"-group MSS, *idem*, p. 23, where X appears the least faulty of the group.

revised at all for the C-text, either by the poet or by anyone else. Such differences as there are between B and C . . . are purely scribal."[4] If this is true—my own study of the discrepancies has convinced me that it is—we may make the following assertions:

(1) In these passus B and C should, ideally, agree exactly.
(2) If they did agree exactly, we could feel confident that we had before us the author's original version. Where they do agree exactly, we may be sure of this, inasmuch as
    (a) B- and C-MSS represent two entirely different MS traditions,
    (b) there is no suggestion of cross-contamination in the MSS on which we are basing our comparison;
    (c) agreement could not occur accidentally except in very rare instances.
(3) If in any instance we can perceive in what way the reading of one text was corrupted into the reading of the other, we may feel confident that the first text is correct and represents the author's original.
(4) If in a majority of such instances one text is at fault, the other text may be assumed to reproduce with fair accuracy the poet's own version.
(5) If either text proves to have accurately reproduced these passus, it is probable, though by no means inevitable, that that text reproduces its author's original accurately throughout the poem.

Since we have only Skeat's edition to make reference to, it is necessary first of all to strip his C-text of those deviations which we know to be the work of the scribe of "p." Collation of the two passus with MSS of "i" and "t" reveals a large number of variations between P and its fellows on the one hand and such MSS as T and X on the other, and in almost all these instances we are safe in condemning the P-reading. No list of variants is included here, since the reader may consult Skeat's base notes for the T-readings:[5] MS X has little to add to T in these passus.[6] The reader will observe also how often T-variants agree with the readings of the B-text— often enough so that one could without too much inaccuracy read "B" for T in the base notes.

But when we have eliminated in this way all the variations we can, we still find ourselves faced with a considerable number that cannot be so easily

4. *Mind*, p. 167; see also the preface to Bright's *New Light on "Piers Plowman,"* p. 15. I must note here that an examination similar to the one made in this Appendix, though with a different end in view and, inevitably, with some differences in findings has recently been performed by George Kane, " 'Piers Plowman': Problems and Methods of Editing the B-Text," *MLR*, XLIII (1948), 1–25. I regret that this excellent article by one of the editors of the proposed new *Piers Plowman* appeared too late for me to take it into consideration in this study.

5. In the first hundred and fifty lines of C, XXII note, for instance, the variant readings given for T in lines 39, 45, 87, 104–05, 110, 114, 116, 122, 127, 132, 137, etc. Variant readings of some of the B-MSS eliminate several more discrepancies between B and C (MS R, however, is C-contaminated): see, for instance, B, XX, 82, where W, like C, XXIII, 83, has *scabbes*.

6. But see C, XXII, 277, where X omits *seed*, like B, XIX, 272; C344, where X like B338 terminates the line with *þe sedes;* and C, XXIII, 227, where B, XX, 226 and X have *holynesse*. X frequently follows T-readings unrecorded by Skeat.

explained away and, in accordance with our original assumption, we must attribute these also to scribal deviation. A comparison of B, xix with C, xxii reveals eight lines in C that do not appear in B and three in B that are wanting in C. Moreover, verbal discrepancies of a readily perceptible nature appear in some forty-two lines.[7] In the final passus of the poem (B, xx, C, xxiii), which is a hundred lines shorter than the one before it, there are about thirty-seven discrepancies between the two texts, and C has two more lines than B. In a total of 867 lines (using C's total) there are, then, about eighty verbal discrepancies between the two texts, while C has ten lines lacking in B and B three lacking in C. This amounts roughly to one discrepancy, varying in magnitude from the omission or addition of a single word to the omission or addition of a single line, in every nine lines of the two passus. If we could show with certainty that the same text was correct in every instance, we could lay upon the remote scribes of the other a heavy charge of error, though not so heavy a one as we can lay upon the scribe of any given bad MS.[8] Let us see how accurately we can fix the blame.

Of the lines which appear in C but are lacking in B, one (C, xxii 236b–7a) has been definitely shown by Chambers and Grattan to have been a part of the original text, but to have been skipped by the archetypal B-scribe, who, while copying

> And somme he lerede to laboure a londe and a watere,
> And lyue by þat labour a leel lyf and a trewe,

let his eye slip from the first *laboure* to the second, omitting the intervening words.[9] Not much harm was done to the sense here, but in another omission (C, xxiii, 261) the B-scribe was rather less fortunate. The poet is telling us that kings, when they hire mercenaries, record them among the numbers of their host—presumably assign them serial numbers and make up pay-books. For

> Wol no treserour take hem wages, trauayle þei neuere so sore,
> Bote hij beon nempned in þe numbre of hem þat ben ywaged.

The original B-scribe omitted the second line, making it appear that pay-masters will not pay mercenaries, an absurdity which later B-scribes exercised their ingenuity in various ways in order to eliminate.[1]

No such sure explanation may be advanced for the other lines omitted in B. The four-line passage C, xxii, 56–9 is a part, and an integral part, of a summary of Christ's death and resurrection, in which the poet is picturing Christ as a valiant conqueror. The lines omitted from B describe His binding

7. These and the following discrepancies are listed below; the list is probably not exhaustive.

8. The errors of MS V of the A-text (Skeat's A-text) are much more numerous and of greater magnitude than those that might be charged to either text on the basis of the examination.   9. See *MLR*, xxvi, 6. Cf. B, xix, 231.

1. Cf. B, xx, 259. The most ingenious solution is that of Cr, which adds *Or* before the first line quoted. See Skeat's base note. MS C2 has a second line with much the same sense as C263. See Blackman, *JEGPh*, xvii, 497, n. 30. Miss Day argues that the reading was corrupt in the B-MS from which C was copying, but the assumption cannot be supported by evidence. See *MLR,* xxiii, p. 12.

of Satan, an action that has been treated at length in the preceding passus and which we should expect to find mentioned in a summary.[2] Perhaps the fact that the omitted passage, as well as the first line following it, begins with *And* is significant, for the B-scribe's eye may have fallen from the first use of the conjunction to the second. In any case, it seems more likely that the lines were accidentally omitted from B than that they were intentionally inserted in C. The same is true of C, xxii, 336. The poet has been describing Grace's gifts to Piers and how Grace

> . . . made preosthood haiwarde, the while hym self wente
> As wide as þe worlde is, with peers to tulye treuthe,
> And þe londe of by-leyue, þe lawe of holychurche.[3]

The last line, which, as Skeat might say, is exactly in our poet's manner, and which concludes the section on Grace's actions, does not appear in B-MSS. It seems more reasonable to assume that the line was present in the original and accidentally omitted than that a poetic scribe inserted it.

During the lewd vicar's discourse in C, xxii, Piers is praised because, like God, he toils both for the righteous and the wicked. Having described how God sent His Son to save the unjust, the vicar continues:

> Ryght so peers plouhman peyneþ hym to tulye
> As wel for a wastour oþer for a wenche atte stuwes,
> As for hym-self and his seruauns, saue he is furst yserued;
> So blessed beo peers plouhman þat peyneþ hym to tulie,
> And trauaileþ and tuleþ for a tretour al-so sore
> As for a trewe tydy man alle tymes ylyke.
> And worsheped be he þat wrouhte al, boþe good and wykke.[4]

B omits the fourth line of this passage and upon first glance the passage may seem better without it, since it contains a repetition of the phrase "þat peyneþ hym to tulie," and an over-working of the word *tulie*. Nevertheless, such repetition and overworking is typical of the poet, and indeed the repetition of the phrase will help to account for an accidental omission of the line. The scribe may have paused after writing the third line; upon resuming work he may have read the fourth line before writing and, finding that it sounded familiar, he may have assumed that he had copied it and gone on with the fifth line. That the fourth line is genuine seems indicated by the fact that its imperative "Blessed be Piers Plowman," is exactly balanced by the imperative of the final line, "Worshipped be he."

It is more difficult to make up one's mind about the lines in which the angelic visit to the Sepulchre is mentioned. According to C, the angels

> Comen kneolynge to þat corps, and songen,
> *'Christus resurgens,'* and hit aros after,
> Verrei man by-fore hem alle, and forþ with hem ʒeode.[5]

In B the first two lines are expressed by a single one,

2. The lines should appear between B, xix, 55 and 56.
3. C, xxii, 334–6. Cf. B, xix, 329–30.   4. C, xxii, 436–42. Cf. B, xix, 432–7.
5. C, xxii, 151–3. With MGX I omit *rex* before *resurgens*. Cf. B, xix, 147–8.

> Come knelynge to þe corps & songen, *christus resurgens,*

which may represent a scribe's effort to join two very short lines in the original. On the other hand, the C-version may result from a scribal attempt to break up a long line in the original. One might observe that the B-version seems to lack a verb for the phrase in the first half of the third line in C— a very awkward construction, though one which was not impossible to the poet. That C represents the original and that the B-scribe was trying to compensate for two short lines is, perhaps, indicated by the fact that certain of the C-scribes, including P, also tried to expand the second line in C by inserting *rex* after *Christus,* thereby improving the length and the alliteration, though misquoting the Easter hymn.[6] The poet may have intended the short lines to achieve a spondaic effect in keeping with the solemnity of the scene.

The last of the additional lines in C occurs in the passage in which Need explains his character—a passage that shows signs of disturbance in both texts and produces a number of scribal variations. According to P, Need says,

> *Homo proponit, deus disponit:* god gouerneþ alle
> Goode vertues. Next hym is neode, for a-non he meokeþ,
> And is as louh as a lomb, for lackynge of þat hym neodeþ;
> For neode makeþ neody for neode louh-herted.[7]

It is obvious that something has gone wrong in the first two lines, for MSS PEMFSGT all put *Goode vertues* as I have printed it, at the beginning of the second line. Skeat restored the phrase to the end of the first line, thereby achieving something like the B-text reading, which follows:

> *Homo proponit & deus disponit,* & gouerneth alle good vertues.
> Ac nede is next hym, for anon he meketh,
> And as low as a lombe, for lakkyng of þat hym nedeth.[8]

So far as sense is concerned, the C-version is preferable, inasmuch as the third line in B seems to be dangling in mid-air. But much of C's sense is probably attributable to the ingenuity of the "p"-scribe, who, if we can make up a composite text from the readings of X and T, probably was faced in his original by something like this:

> *Homo proponit & deus disponit* god gouerneþ alle goode vertues
> And nede is next hym for a-non he mekeþ
> And as louh as a lombe for lackynge þat hym nedeþ
> For nede makeþ nede fele nedes louȝ herte.

While the wording is closer to B's, the sense is more obscure than that of the P-version, and as in B the third line is left dangling.

It is my opinion that in this passage, as in certain others that will be

---

6. Miss Day, *MLR,* xxiii, 12, believes a line has been lost in B but considers C's line an attempt to restore the loss. Probably an original short line bothered scribes of both texts. T has the angels kneeling *on knes,* which is reasonable but hypermetrical.

7. C, xxiii, 34–7. For the line division in 34–5, see Skeat's base note.

8. B, xx, 34–6. In both B and C the Latin should be separated from the metrical line: see X.

mentioned below, neither B nor C gives us the original reading, and that the B-MSS represent the archetypal B-scribe's way out of a difficult passage, while the C-MSS represent a variety of ways out—based, however, on a firmer foundation. Since we are dealing with two entirely different MS-traditions, the difficult passage must have been in the poet's own MS, which, I conceive, originally read, for the lines following the first,

> And nede is next hym, for a-non he mekeþ;
> For nede makeþ nede fele nedes louȝ herte,
> And as louh as a lombe, for lackynge þat hym nedeþ.

"And Need is next to God, for Need straightway makes (men) humble; and Need makes the needy[9] experience Need's humble heart, and (makes them) as low as a lamb because of the need they suffer." The only difference between this version and the composite one I have given above is that the second line—the one omitted from the B-MSS, precedes instead of following the third. If my reconstruction is right, then the line was a part of the original. But it may have been accidentally omitted by the poet from his text and then added in the margin, its position being indicated by an arrow— which was, perhaps, incorrectly drawn, so that the C-scribe copied it in the wrong place, while the B-scribe, perplexed, omitted it entirely. Regardless of the accuracy of this explanation, it seems likely that C preserves the original better than B, at least quantitatively, since the line omitted by B is not the facilely composed sort that we expect and get from scribes. Rather, it is characteristic of the poet, who in this passage is making every possible play upon the word *need*. The blame for the omission, however, lies not so much with the archetypal B-scribe as with the original text, which seems to have been faulty while it was still in the author's hand.

While all the C-lines omitted from B seem to me to be genuine, I incline to the opposite point of view concerning the B-lines omitted from C. The first of these occurs in a speech by Grace (B, xix, 246–8),

> "Thowgh some be clenner þan somme, ȝe se wel," quod grace,
> "Þat he þat vseth þe fairest crafte to þe foulest I couth haue put hym,
> Þinketh alle," quod grace, "þat grace cometh of my ȝifte."

This idea is expressed less clumsily in C, xxii, 252–3,

> "Thauh somme be clannere þan some, ȝe seon wel," quaþ grace,
> "That alle craft and connynge cam of my ȝyfte."

The awkwardness of the second line in B is not such as to preclude its having been written by the poet, but it suggests the work of a paraphrasing (or gap-filling) scribe. It has a rhythm most unusual in *Piers Plowman,* while the repetition of *quod grace* in the third line, apparently in order to gain a semblance of alliteration, is the work of an amateur. And for Grace to announce that he is the source of grace seems tautological, to say the least. It is possible that in the MS that the B-scribe was copying from there was a blot covering the lines—the line preceding the passage also varies in B[1]—

9. *OED, needy,* a., gives the form *nede,* though I cannot recall having seen this form elsewhere in the MSS of the poem that I have consulted.   1. B, xix, 245.

and that the scribe was forced to improvise. The source of difficulty here seems, however, to have been cleared up before the archetypal C-scribe began his copy, unlike the last passage explained above.

The other two additional B-lines occur at close intervals. The poet is telling how all kinds of Christians repented, with the exception of prostitutes; B adds,

> And fals men, flatereres, vsureres and theues,
> Lyeres and questmongeres þat were forsworen ofte.[2]

A few lines later the poet says that

> Þere nas no crystene creature þat kynde witte hadde,[3]

who did not help in making holiness grow, a statement which in B is modified by the line

> Saue schrewes one suche as I spak of.[4]

In C, the unrepentant sinners are limited to prostitutes,

> And a sisour and a somenour þat weren for-swore ofte.[5]

C then neglects to exempt these sinners from his assertion that there was no Christian who did not help increase holiness. At first glance B's version seems more logical, and it appears that the C-scribe unwittingly omitted a necessary line. If, however, we read C carefully, we see that the second omitted line is not required. Let us repunctuate the passage in C:

> Thenne alle kynne crystyne saue comune wommen
> Repentede and refusede synne; saue thei one—
> And a sisour and a somenour þat weren for-swore ofte,
> Witynge and wilfulliche with þe false þei helden,
> And for seluere were for-swore (sothly þei wisten hit)—
> Ther ne was cristyne creature þat kynde wit hadde
> Þat he ne halp a quantyte holynesse to wexe.[6]

The grammar is complex but the sense is clear and the style is characteristic. We might observe that the B-lines describing the sinners are at best feebly alliterative, although this does not place them beyond the capability of the poet. More important is the fact that B's second additional line seems tied to the first—seems, indeed, to point back to it. It is easier to see how a writer who had just expanded a list of sinners would be careful to except them from any part in holiness (even though, strictly speaking, the grammar already excepted them) than it is to see how a scribe might accidentally omit within a short space two related lines.

Of the eighty other variations that have been mentioned, twenty-eight seem to me to be clearly the result of deviation from his original by the archetypal B-scribe, while in only one instance do the best of the C-MSS give an indisputably incorrect reading. In the remaining fifty-one variations I have been able to find no entirely satisfactory evidence that one text rather

2. B, xix, 366-7.
3. B, xix, 370 (C, xxii, 375).
4. B, xix, 371.
5. C, xxii, 372.
6. C, xxii, 370-6.

than the other gives the right reading, though C is often obviously preferable. Let us examine those examples where C seems to display the original reading.

In twelve of the twenty-eight instances the alliteration is better, and more natural, in C than in B, as I think the reader will agree. The lines are as follows:

B, xix, C, xxii

1. C73 *Reuerencede hym ryght faire with richesse of eorthe.* B69 omits *ryght.*
2. C97 *Was noþer kyng ne conquerour til he comsede wexe.* B93 reads *gan to for comsede.*
3. C101 *And so dude ihesus in hus dayes ho so dorste tellen hit.* B97 reads *had tyme to* for *dorste.*
4. C154 *The Iuwes preyede hem of pees and preyede [þe] knyghtes* (so T). B149 reads *bisouȝte* for *preyede* (2).
5. C180 *þat neuere shullen seo [me] in syht as þou seost nouthe* (so T). B175 reads *doste* for *seost.*
6. C243 *Bothe of wele and of wo and be war by-fore.* B237 reads *wo telle it or it felle* for *wo . . . by-fore.*

B, xx, C, xxiii

7. C27 *And bete men ouere bittere and som body to lyte.* B27 reads *of hem* for *body.*
8. C155 *And to for-ȝete ȝouthe and ȝyue nauht of synne.* B154 reads *sorwe* for *ȝouthe.*
9. C163 *This sleuthe was sleyh of werre and a slynge made.* B162 reads *war* for *sleyh.*
10. C218 *Proude preostes cam with hym passend an hundred.* B217 reads *moo þan a thousand* for *passend an hundred.*
11.–12. C375–6 (X) *Conscience criede eft cleregie come help [hym], And bad contricion to come to helpe kepe þe ȝate.* B373–4 *Conscience cryde eft and bad clergye help hym, And also contricioun forto kepe þe ȝate.*

In (2), (3), (4), (5), (7), (8), (9), and (10) B shows simple substitution of similars, for the most part probably caused by carelessness, although in (4) the scribe may have been trying to avoid a repetition of *preyede* and in (5) of *seo*—both examples of a sort of repetition characteristic of the poet. In (10) the alteration of the numeral may have resulted from an effort to attain eye-alliteration after accidental substitution of *moo þan* for *passend: þan* and *thousand.* In (1) it seems more likely that *ryght* was in the original than that it was added by a scribe, for the poet commonly alliterates on adverbs (particularly *well, full,* and *right*) modifying non-alliterating adjectives and adverbs. In (11–12) and in (6) the B-scribe is guilty of paraphrase. In (6) the original was perhaps difficult to make out, since the lines conclude a passage that shows a number of discrepancies between B and C. In (11–12) the scribe's eye jumped ahead and picked up *bad,* with sorry results. In both these last instances C is crisper and more pointed.

Of greater interest and weight are the eighteen lines wherein, on grounds of sense or style or because B's error is patent, we have reason to trust C's readings.

B, XIX, C, XXII

1. C94 says that the Magi offered *Eorthliche honeste pynges* to Christ. B90 *Thre yliche* for *Eorthliche*. C72–3, B68–9 say that angels and kings reverenced Christ with *richesse of erthe*. The C-text carries out this thought.

2. C118 describes Christ as a *fauntekyn ful of wytt*. B114 *faunt fyn* for *fauntekyn*. An obvious misreading, prompted by the *f*-alliteration.

3. C148, summarizing the prophecies of Christ's death and resurrection, says *thus me by-fore deuynede*. B144 *demed* for the verb. C's is the common word for prophecy and B's an easy and common misreading.

4. C253, B248. These lines have already been noticed in connection with the added B-line 247, p. 239, above. The B-line is clumsy and pointless.

5. C273 says that the four "stots," which harrowed all Holy Writ, did so with *to eythes*. B268 *two harwes,* copied from the verb *harwed* in the preceding line.

6. According to C274 Grace gave *peers* the cardinal virtues. B269 omits the indirect object, which is present in C262, 267, B257, 262, lines that describe in similar terms Grace's gifts to Piers.

7. C280 speaks of *keeling* a crock with a ladle, B275 of *keeping* it. As Chambers and Grattan have said, *MLR*, xxvi, 7, C is correct, B pointless.

8. C283 says that whoever eats of the seed of *spiritus temperantiae* shall not be made to swell by *mete ne myschief*. B278 *mochel drynke* for *myschief*. The B-line thus means that the temperate man will not fall ill from meat, which he does eat, or from much drink, which, being temperate, he does not take. The scribe manufactured the usual doublet *meat and drink* and then added the adjective for alliteration.

9. C316–17 read *And so dop vices vertues and for-thi quap peers, Harwep alle pat connep kynde wit by counsail of theose doctours.* B311–12 *worthy* for *and for-thi* and all the following words are squeezed into the second line. Chambers and Grattan, *MLR* xxvi, 7, have shown that B read *for-thi* as *worthi,* and became confused. Possibly the original had a West Midland spelling *vor pi.*

10. C366 says that Holy Church stood in *holiness,* as if it (holiness) were a pile—a foundation. B360 has the Church standing in *Unity.* But Unity and Holy Church are synonyms and the context shows that it is the fundament, holiness, that is under discussion. B picked up *vnite* from the preceding line.

11. C455 says that the community is only obedient to Conscience if *hit soune as by syght* to some material profit. B450 for the verb has variously *seize, seigh, seie, seen, sight, se,* and *sowe.* The B-archetype was illegible, the last reading alone reflecting the original.

B, XX, C, XXIII

12. C127 says that Avarice and Simony, having assailed Conscience, *pressede on pe pope and prelates thei maden.* B126 *preched to pe peple.* Simony is a perverter of the clergy and would go to the Pope for political appointments, not to the pulpit.

13. C130 says that Simony *knockede conscience In court.* B129 *kneled to* for the verb. There is a furious war going on between Simony and Conscience. B is pointless.

14. C256 says that God gave all things their names, B255 *new* names. The inserted adjective is pointless, and was probably added to give a fourth, unnecessary, rhyme-letter.

15. C260, B259. These lines have been discussed on p. 236 and n. 1, above.
16. C308 says that men's penitence brought it about that Piers's pardon was repaid, *redde quod debes*. B306 has Piers repaid, omitting the pardon. C, xxii, 392, B, xix, 388, upon which the present line depends, speak of *peers pardon þe plouhman, Redde quod debes.*

With the other fifty-one discrepancies between B and C that I have noted I have been able to find no very cogent reasons for preferring the readings of one text over the other.[7] In a number of instances, however, C seems distinctly better on purely impressionistic grounds, and there are few instances where it seems even slightly inferior. Substantial bases for argument are, however, lacking and I shall not reproduce the results of my examination. It might be observed that there are eight or nine readings which in both texts seem to be corrupt, pointing perhaps to a fault in the B-poet's autograph from which all B- and C-MSS ultimately derive—such as that mentioned above in connection with B, xx, 34–6, C, xxiii, 34–7— or else to a metrical irregularity which the scribes have tried to correct, such as the short line C, xxii, 152, also discussed above. Occasionally with these irregularities the best of the C-MSS may preserve a good reading, while the inferior C-MSS and the B-archetype may represent scribal "corrections." This is possibly the case with the line which in B (xx, 182) reads,

> And elde anone after me and ouer myne heed ȝede,

and in C (xxiii, 183) reads, in the P-form,

> And elde hastede after hym and ouer my hefde ȝeode.

We may reasonably suspect that the original reading was the unemphatic

> And elde after hym and ouer myn hefde ȝede,

which is transmitted by X and T. We should, however, wish to know more before becoming dogmatic.

It remains to discuss the one line in which B unquestionably preserves the original reading, while all the C-MSS deviate. At the opening of the next-to-last passus the Dreamer is bewildered by the resemblance between Christ and Piers and asks Conscience which of them is the man he sees before him. At B, xix, 12–14 Conscience replies,

7. Lines in which discrepancies occur are as follows. An asterisk denotes lines which, on admittedly unscientific grounds, I prefer in their C-form, and a dagger denotes lines in which the B-form seems better. B, xix, C, xxii: *BC15; †B105, C109; *B126, C130; *B136, C140; *B174, C179; *B177, C182; B180, C185; *B224, C229; B232, C238; *B233, C239; B235, C241; †B243, C249; *B245, C251; *B249, C254; B262, C267; †B290, C295; B300, C305; B305, C310; B327, C332; B339, C345; B384, C388; B385, C389; B460, C465; *B461, C466; B476, C481. B, xx, C, xxiii: BC7; *BC34; *B37, C38; *B38, C39; B61, C62; *B66, C67; B125, C126; B140, C141; *B166, C167; *B182, C183; B190, C191; †B193, C194; *B197, C198; B201, C202; *B209, C210; *B210, C211; B248, C249; *B261, C263; *B275, C277; *B290, C292; *B334, C336; B335, C337; B357, C359; B368, C370; *B377, C379; B379, C381. Possibly the variations connected with B, xix, 180, 327, and 330 should have been omitted, since it is possible to make a composite C-reading to agree with B. Many of the variants concern only phrasing and word order. Variants in B, xix, 180, 232, 235, 300, 476; xx, 140, 182, 197, 290, and their C-equivalents, point to a fault or irregularity in the BC-original. Many of the preferred C-readings above are from XT.

> . . . þise aren Pieres armes,
> His coloures & his cote-armure, ac he þat cometh so blody
> Is cryst with his crosse, conqueroure of crystene.

C12 reads *cristes* for *Pieres* in the phrase "Piers's arms," an alteration that works havoc with the allegory. It is, in a sense, the fulfillment of the poem that Christ and Piers—mankind—should become one, and we have already been prepared for this in the preceding passus, where Faith explains that

> . . . þis iesus of hus gentrise shal Iouste in peers Armes,
> In hus helme and in hus haberion, *humana natura*.[8]

The whole point is lost through the C-error. It is possible that in the C-archetype, or in the MS from which it was copied, the name of Piers had been erased in preparation for illumination, as, indeed, Piers's name has been erased throughout MS X. The C-scribe faced, in a context which also contains a distinction between the names of Christ and Jesus, with a line reading,

> Quod conscience, & kneled þo, þise aren   armes,

let himself be deluded by the alliteration and filled in the third rhyme-word *cristes*. That the change was an accidental one is proved by the fact that in the second line of the passage MSS XI read, along with the B-text, *ac,* while T reads *but,* for "p"-group *and* at the beginning of the second half-line. If Christ's arms replace Piers's arms, there is no need for the adversative to introduce the clause that explains who the man himself is. The sophisticated "p"-scribe replaced it, while the scribes of "i" and "t" left it in, even though it made poor sense. If the "p"-reading had been the original, *ac* and *but* could not have intruded themselves into the line.

Operating under the assumption that the C-poet made no revision of the last two passus of the poem,[9] we have examined the divergencies between the two texts in order to find out which one represents the unrevised original the more faithfully. In something less than half of the total number of lines examined there is good evidence that C, in the best MSS, is the more faithful. In the majority of the remainder C's readings seem to me at least as satisfactory as B's, and frequently superior, so that if we leaped to the conclusion that, since B shows itself on several occasions to be flagrantly in error, all divergencies are attributable to the B-scribe we should lose very little of the essential sense. So sweeping a conclusion is, however, not justified, and our confidence in C is undermined by our having caught it in one bad error, qualitatively if not quantitatively. Hence we must divide the blame. In doing this, I believe that there is sufficient evidence against the archetypal B-scribe so that it is fair to lay upon him the major responsibility for error. After

---

8. C, xxii, 21-2 (B, xix, 22-3).

9. I take it for granted that the assumption requires no proof. If it did it would be possible to cite the fact that C's esthetic superiority over B in these passus is of an utterly effortless sort, and that easy esthetic superiority to B is by no means an inevitable result of C's conscious revision. If it were, my task in writing this book would have been facilitated; but even such of C's genuine revisions as I find superior to B

all, we have nowhere found C guilty of so careless a slip as that reflected in the B-line.

> And some he lered to laboure a lele lyf & a trewe,

between the two halves of which an entire line has been dropped out. If the B-scribe was capable of such faulty transcription, he was probably capable of causing two-thirds of the ninety-odd deviations we have examined. This leaves the C-scribe with responsibility for one-third, though he has been caught in flagrant error only once. But even if we load him with so generous a charge of error, it appears that, under our initial assumption that the C-poet himself made no revisions in the two passus under discussion, the best MSS of C reproduce their original with a very high degree of accuracy—a maximum probability of one error in every twenty-nine or thirty lines.

There is, of course, no guarantee that this accuracy continues throughout the C-text. It would be possible to argue that in the creation of the common archetype from which all our C-MSS derive a number of scribes, some good and some bad, were involved, the last two passus having fallen to a good one. But while this is a possibility, it is not a probability. Miss Blackman and Chambers include, among their examples of readings lost in B but preserved correctly in C, some from all parts of the C-text, and the presumption is that the accuracy reflected in the last two passus exists throughout the poem.

One matter remains to be briefly considered. The possibility that the C-text is interpolated with passages composed by some one other than the C-poet has been raised by Chambers, who, indeed, believed it a probability rather than a possibility.[1] He did not, however, elaborate or develop his theory, which, if correct, would allow us to clear C of the responsibility for some of the C-text's duller spots—an exoneration, let me hasten to add, that I consider neither necessary nor desirable. But let us face the possibility of interpolation.

With the statement that the C-text is much interpolated I agree, although, of course, I believe that the interpolations were penned and put into position by the C-poet himself. A number of such interpolated passages have been described in Chapter II.[2] By all odds the most suspicious-looking one is that to which Skeat himself appended a note in which the question of authenticity was raised.[3] The passage appears in the first passus of the poem.[4] In the B-text, the poet concludes some observations on the clergy who are engaged in secular pursuits with the following lines:

> And some seruen as seruantz lordes and ladyes,
> And in stede of stuwardes sytten and demen.

---

have required explanation. In the last two passus, no apology for the C-readings is ordinarily required.

1. See *Mind*, p. 167, and preface to Bright, *op. cit.*, p. 23. I deal here only with the theory that visualizes two hands in the C-text: the C-poet and an interpolator. That the C-text represents a series of interpolations performed upon B is, of course, a common point of view among those who favor multiple authorship.

2. See pp. 25 ff., above.   3. See *EETS*, III, 450.   4. C, I, 95–124.

> Here messe and here matynes and many of here oures
> Arn don vndeuoutlych; drede is at þe laste
> Lest crist in consistorie acorse ful manye.[5]

Upon his first revision, C either accepted these lines as they stood, or at the most recast the first two. At a later time, however, when he was revising B's *Visio de Do-Well,* he had occasion to eliminate an *exemplum* concerning the false priests Hophni and Phineas[6] which he thought he might use in the discussion of priests in the first passus. Hence he elaborated, or started to elaborate, the story and marked it down for insertion between the second and third lines of the passage quoted above. The elaboration took the form of a sermon by Conscience, who addresses himself directly to the priests. The end of the interpolation fits into the sense of the last three lines quoted, except that in C Conscience is still speaking to the priests. Therefore it becomes necessary in C to alter the third-person pronouns of the last three lines to the second person. Thus Skeat's text, and the MSS of "p," read as follows:

> Ʒoure masse & ʒoure matynes and meny of ʒoure houres
> Aren don vndeuotlich; drede ys at þe laste
> Leste crist in hus constorie of ʒow a-corse menye.[7]

MSS X and B2, however, preserve what is undoubtedly an earlier and more original form of the first and third lines. The first reads in both MSS.

> Ʒoure masse and here matynes and many of here oures,[8]

although in X the two third-person possessives have been crossed out and *ʒour* written above them in a different ink.[9] For the third line both MSS read,

> Lest crist in his constorie a-corse of hem manye,

retaining the third person. What the C-poet did, obviously, was to cue his insertion into the text by correcting the first pronoun of the line which would follow it. The insertion itself was, as I have already suggested, probably written on a sheet of paper and its position in the text marked by an arrow.

The great peculiarity of the insertion itself is, of course, that a large portion of it—some fourteen lines—is not in any recognizable alliterative form in most MSS, making the only nonalliterative passage of any length in *Piers Plowman.*[1] MS I, it is true, gives a more or less regular version which Skeat believed to be the "true form" of the lines,[2] but in this case I receives no support from the more reliable "i"-MSS.

The obvious inference, that the passage is an interpolation by an editor, seems proved wrong by the very imperfection of the lines and of their welding into the text. The first twelve lines (1, 95–106) alliterate properly, so that whoever was the author of them could do correct work when he wanted to. And I am under the impression that an editor making an in-

5. B, Pro., 95–9. Cf. C, 1, 93–4, 125–7.   6. See B, x, 280–3.
7. C, 1, 125–7.   8. Readings of X.
9. See the Huntington Library reproduction of X, p. 1 of the notes, note to line 17, folio 2b.
1. Of lines 107–24 only 109, 113, and 124 alliterate regularly.
2. See *EETS,* III, 450.

terpolation would be careful that his lines did alliterate and that they were properly fitted into the text. So far as the latter is concerned, we have seen in Chapter II that on several occasions the C-poet failed to hide the seams of his insertions. It seems to me that the failure to do so, as well as the failure to get the whole of the present passage into alliterative form, may have been caused by the poet's death, as I have suggested earlier.[3] Death also may have prevented his revising the last two passus. Since the C-text as a whole shows a number of signs of being incompletely prepared for publication, it does not seem logical to charge up even this most suspicious passage to an interpolator.

The suggestion that the C-poet died before he completed his revision is Chambers', who adds a second conjecture that some friend took "great liberties" with the text in preparing it for publication.[4] But the only liberty for which I have been able to find evidence is a failure to tidy it up, even as regards those faulty points in the original of the last two passus—points whose existence is suggested by the independent confusion of the scribes of B and C. One likes to think that if C had lived he would have properly proofread his MS for publication.[5] Until some better evidence is adduced to show the hand of an editor in the C-text it is correct to say that a strong presumption exists in favor of the C-text's being altogether the work of the C-poet. The situation is the same with the C-text as with a prisoner at the bar: it must be considered innocent until it has been proved guilty. As yet the case has not come to trial.

The examination conducted in this appendix, while it incidentally confirms the conclusions of Miss Blackman and Chambers concerning the relative accuracy of the C- and B-texts, has the more important effect for present purposes of inspiring confidence in the C-text. Whereas C has long since been known to be superior in certain respects to B in authenticity, its superiority has, as I have said, generally been expressed (as with every other aspect of C) in relative terms. It now appears that the C-text based on the best MSS is not only more authentic than B, but that its superiority in this respect is absolute as well as relative—a critical C-text will probably reproduce fairly faithfully what the C-poet actually wrote. We are thus assured that in subjecting the C-text to close study we have chiefly to deal with the original work of a fourteenth-century poet and not, except very occasionally, with the whims of his scribes.

3. See p. 32, above.   4. *Mind*, p. 167.

5. To the list of lines already cited where the originals of both B and C seem to have been faulty should, perhaps, be added the following in which the poet's C-text or the archetype of our C-MSS was faulty: IV, 493 (see Skeat's base-note); XIII, 204-07 (see Skeat's critical note, *EETS*, III, 460); XVI, 285 (see Skeat's base-note). See also Carnegy, *op. cit.*, pp. 12-13, where it is argued that a gloss has intruded itself into C, IV, 140-2.

APPENDIX C

The Extent of C's Revisions, Passus I–XII

C-Passus	A	AB	B*	B	ABC	BC	C*	C
I	109	98	132	230	74	64	93	231
II	183	161	46	207	90	15	99	204
III	198	128	108	236	71	36	145	252
IV	273	221	128	349	136	40	325	501
V	158	119	77	196	75	14	107	196
VI	57	41	58	99	23	20	158	201
VII	201	155	198	353	95	57	203	355
VIII	143	117	122	239	89	58	111	258
IX	306	226	103	329	166	21	167	354
X	182	134	66	200	86	5	260	351
XI	330	137	196	333	94	23	192	309
XII	288	132	301	433	40	33	188	261
TOTAL	2,428	1,669	1,535	3,204	1,039	386	2,048	3,473

Explanation:

A	Total lines in A
AB	A-text lines taken intact by B
B*	B's revisions of and additions to the material of A
B	Total lines in B
ABC	A-text lines taken intact by B, and from B taken intact by C
BC	B-text lines, new to or assuming a new shape in B, taken intact by C
C*	C's revisions of and additions to the material of B
C	Total lines in C

Notes

The following lines appearing in Skeat's editions were not counted:

A (39) I, 176–7; II, 31, 34, 48, 96, 118, 136–9, 141–3, 182; III, 19–20, 66, 91–4, 98, 234; V, 182; VI, 1–2, 5; VII, 26; VIII, 46, 101, 125–6. All in MS H only. VIII, 46 is possibly genuine.
II, 79. In MSS HH2 only.
VII, 158, 286. Omitted in MSS TU.
V, 55–6; VIII, 110–11. Only one line in T and so counted.
X, 200–02. Only two lines in TU and so counted.

B (7) V, 273; VI, 49. In MSS CBC2Cr only.
V, 338. In MSS COBC2Cr only.
V, 569. In MSS COBC2 only.

v, 190–2. Counted as two lines: compare A, v, 109–10, C, vii, 198–9.

x, 190–1. Latin lines present but not numbered in A: see A, xi, 145 ff.

C (191) xi, 271. In MS F only.

xii, 80. In MS I only.

ii, 141; ix, 339. Latin lines present but not numbered in B: see B, i, 139 f. and vi, 316 f.

vii, 30–60, 69–85, 175–85, 260–85, 430; viii, 70–119. Source in B, xiii outside the scope of the examination.

xii, 163–203, 304–13. Source in B, xi outside the scope of the examination.

The following lines not appearing in Skeat's edition were counted:

B (5) Line after iv, 9. In MSS YOC2; see A, iv, 10, C, v, 10.

Lines after v, 334, 344, 370. In no MS but see A, v, 178, 189, 215; C, vii, 385, 395, 422.

viii, 108. Counted as two lines: see A, ix, 102–03, C, xi, 107–08.

Summary

Of A, B retains unchanged 68.7% (AB)
Of B, C retains unchanged 44.5% (ABC + BC)
  Of AB-material, C retains unchanged 62.3% (ABC)
  Of B*-material, C retains unchanged 25.1% (BC)

Of B, 52.1% is unchanged A-material (AB)
Of C, 41.0% is unchanged B-material (ABC + BC)
  Of C, 29.9% is unchanged AB-material (ABC)
  Of C, 11.1% is unchanged B*-material (BC)

Of B, 47.9% is new or altered (B*)
Of C, 59.0% is new or altered (C*)

Note on MS R

Skeat's edition of B contains a hundred and sixty lines from MS R, which, along with its cognate F, presents a fuller version of B than any of the other MSS. Many of the RF-lines are paralleled in C in the same or slightly different form, while a few are paralleled in A. According to Miss Blackman, *JEGPh*, xvii, 501–03, RF are of the same class as L, but have been corrected from both A- and C-MSS. Traces of such correction are easy to find. Despite this, many of the lines peculiar to RF are necessary to the sense of B and by no means slavishly follow A- and C-text readings, so that one is reluctant to reject them utterly. It seems possible that the common ancestor of R and F was also corrected from a better MS of the B-text than we now possess. The correction from A- and C-MSS indicates that some one had a strong, if misguided, bibliographical interest, and perhaps while in general destroying the value of his MS he also enhanced it by collation with a superior B-text. In my statistical study I have treated the lines from R (x, 291–303, 381, 411–13) as if they were genuine B-lines, and I feel sure that they at least take the place of, if they do not reproduce exactly, something that was in the B-poet's autograph. Elsewhere in this book I have duly noted the fact, and modified my reasoning, when dealing with B-lines found only in R. Despite general distrust of R, no one seems disposed to eject its lines from the B-text. Chambers, who, *HLB,* VIII, 12, repeats Miss Blackman's suspicions, nevertheless quotes one of the most famous of R's lines (B, x, 303) in good faith in *Mind,* p. 95. For an interesting discussion of the problem, see Miss Day, *MLR,* XXIII, 25–7. Miss Day concludes that "although R is sometimes contaminated from C, those passages which have gone through a process of paraphrasing were certainly in C's version of B, and very probably those which agree identically were there also." *Idem,* p. 27.

Bibliographical Index

This is chiefly an index to authors quoted, cited, or discussed in text and notes. Titles of books and subjects of articles are listed after the names of their authors or editors, and page references are given for the individual works. Full bibliographical data for each work appear on the first page referred to. Middle English poems discussed only on pp. 43–5 are not indexed, nor are the bishops mentioned only on p. 204, n. 2, and p. 205, n. 3.

Alcuin, 193–4
Alexander A, 43, 45 n., 82 n.
Allen, B. F. (Mrs. Tapping), dissertation on C-MSS, 227, 229–30, 233–4
Anonimalle Chronicle, 107, 116 n., 118 n.
Aquinas, St. Thomas, 160
Augustine, St., 123, 183 n., 197

Bale, John, 200, 221
Bateson, H., ed. *Patience,* 171 n.
Baum, P. F., article on fable of rat parliament, 116
Bennett, H. S., article on medieval authors, 154 n.
Bennett, J. A. W., article on date of A, 18 n., 112 n.; article on date of B, 18 n., 115–16
Bernard, St., 188–93, 196–7
Bishop, Edmund, *Liturgica Historica,* 209 n.; article on Primer, 209 n., 211 n., 213
Blackman, Elsie, article on B-MSS, 5 n., 21 n., 227, 230–1, 232–3, 236 n., 247, 249–50
Blake, William, 75
Bloomfield, M. W., article on PP studies, 2 n.; article on Langland, 221 n., 220–1
Boswell, James, 200
Bradley, Henry, note on *PP,* 19
Brandl, A., 9 n.
Brantyngham, Thomas, 205 n.
Brett, Cyril, note on *PP,* 100 n., 113 n., 114–15
Bright, A. H., *New Light on PP,* 16 n., 151 n., 199 n., 200 n.: *see also* Chambers, R. W.; article on Langland, 151 n.
Bronson, B. H., *Joseph Ritson: Scholar-at-Arms,* 5 n.
Brooke, Tucker, *Shakespeare of Stratford,* 42 n.
Brown, Carleton, and Robbins, R. H., *Index of Middle English Verse,* 194 n., 227
Buchberger, M., *Lexikon für Theologie und Kirche,* 204 n.

Burch, G. B., ed. St. Bernard's *Steps of Humility,* 193 n., 196 n.
Burdach, Konrad, *Der Dichter des Ackermann aus Böhmen und seine Zeit,* xi, 13–15, 25 n., 87 n., 146 n., 162 n., 164, 172, 175 n., 179–80, 182 n., 183 n., 185–7
But, John, 16, 35 n., 39, 200 n.

Cabrol, F., *Books of the Latin Liturgy,* 210 n.
Caedmon, 148
Cambridge History of English Literature, xi, 1, 10, 14; *see also* Manly, J. M.
Cambridge Medieval History, 100 n., 110 n.
Cargill, Oscar, article on date of A, 18 n.; article on Langland, 200 n.
Carnegy, F. A. R., *Attempt to Approach the C-Text of P the P,* 13 n., 29 n., 33, 105 n., 126 n., 200 n., 227–31, 232 n., 234 n., 247 n.; *Relations between the Social and Divine Order in . . . P the P,* 13, 165 n.
Catholic Encyclopedia, 204 n., 209 n., 210 n., 211 n., 222 n.
Cato (-Book), 132, 134, 139, 224
Chadwick, D., *Social Life in the Days of PP,* 85 n., 202 n.
Chambers, E. K., *Mediaeval Stage,* 144 n., 146 n., 148 n., 154, 155 n.
Chambers, R. W., *Man's Unconquerable Mind,* xi, 1–2, 16, 21 n., 32, 86 n., 141, 148, 157–8, 160 n., 161, 162 n., 164, 165 n., 169–70, 172–3, 174, 180 n., 199, 214 n., 220 n., 224–5, 234–5, 245, 247, 250; preface to A. H. Bright's *New Light on PP,* 16, 21 n., 200 n., 235 n., 245 n.; introduction to *PP: the Huntington Library MS (HM 143),* 227, 230–1, 246
Article on authorship of *PP,* 15, 25 n., 68 n., 165 n., 233, 234 n.; article on grammatical forms of *PP,* 45, 48 n.; article on incoherencies in A and B, 2, 11, 12, 17, 32, 81 n.; article on Langland and salvation of heathen, 2, 32, 35 n.; article on MSS of *PP* in Huntington Library, 21 n., 227, 230–1, 233–4, 250; article on text of A, 35 n.